LITTLE 'RED SCARES'

Little 'Red Scares'

Anti-Communism and Political Repression
in the United States, 1921–1946

Edited by
ROBERT JUSTIN GOLDSTEIN
University of Michigan at Ann Arbor, USA

LONDON AND NEW YORK

First published 2014 by Ashgate Publishing

Published 2016 by Taylor & Francis
2 Park Square, Milton Park, Abingdon, Oxon OX14 4RN
711 Third Avenue, New York, NY 10017, USA

Routledge is an imprint of the Taylor & Francis Group, an informa business

Copyright © Robert Justin Goldstein and the contributors 2014

All rights reserved. No part of this book may be reprinted or reproduced or utilised in any form or by any electronic, mechanical, or other means, now known or hereafter invented, including photocopying and recording, or in any information storage or retrieval system, without permission in writing from the publishers.

Notice:
Product or corporate names may be trademarks or registered trademarks, and are used only for identification and explanation without intent to infringe.

Robert Justin Goldstein has asserted his right under the Copyright, Designs and Patents Act, 1988, to be identified as the editor of this work.

British Library Cataloguing in Publication Data
A catalogue record for this book is available from the British Library

The Library of Congress has cataloged the printed edition as follows:
Little "red scares" : anti-communism and political repression in the United States, 1921-1946 / edited by Robert J. Goldstein.
     pages cm
Includes bibliographical references and index.
ISBN 978-1-4094-1091-1 (hardback : alk. paper)
1. Anti-communist movements—United States—History—20th
century. 2. Political persecution—United States—History—20th century. 3. Social conflict—United States—History—20th century. 4. United States—Politics and government—1921-1923.
5. United States—Politics and government—1923-1929. 6. United States—Politics and government—1929-1933. 7. United States—Politics and government—1933-1945. I. Goldstein, Robert Justin.
  E743.5.L56 2013
  973.91—dc23

2013005597

ISBN-13: 978-1-4094-1091-1 (hbk)

Contents

List of Figures	*vii*
Notes on Contributors	*ix*
Preface by Robert Justin Goldstein	*xiii*

1	After the Red Scare: Civil Liberties in the Era of Harding and Coolidge *Ernest Freeberg*	1
2	The FBI and the Politics of Anti-Communism, 1920–1945: A Prelude to Power *Athan Theoharis*	23
3	Citizens versus Outsiders: Anti-Communism at State and Local Levels, 1921–1946 *M.J. Heale*	45
4	Red Herrings? The Fish Committee and Anti-Communism in the Early Depression Years *Alex Goodall*	71
5	Little Red Schoolhouses? Anti-Communists and Education in an "Age of Conflicts" *Timothy Cain*	105
6	Fighting the "Red Danger": Employers and Anti-Communism *Chad Pearson*	135
7	Leftward Ramparts: Labor and Anticommunism between the World Wars *Markku Ruotsila*	165

8	Premature McCarthyism: Spanish Republican Aid and the Origins of Cold War Anti-Communism *Eric Smith*	195
9	Laying the Foundations for the Post-World War II Red Scare: Investigating the Left-Feminist Consumer Movement *Landon R.Y. Storrs*	213
10	The Dies Committee v. the New Deal: Real Americans and the Unending Search for Un-Americans *Kenneth O'Reilly*	237
11	The Long Black and Red Scare: Anti-Communism and the African American Freedom Struggle *Robbie Lieberman*	261
12	Shooting Rabid Dogs: New York's Rapp–Coudert Attack on Teachers Unions *Stephen Leberstein*	289
13	The History of the Smith Act and the Hatch Act: Anti-Communism and the Rise of the Conservative Coalition in Congress *Rebecca Hill*	315
Index		*347*

List of Figures

12.1	'Mr. Schoenchen, principal ...' poster. Courtesy of Tamiment Library and Robert F. Wagner Labor Archives	298
12.2	Local 537 members marching in the May Day Parade, Union Square, NYC, circa 1940. Courtesy of New York State Archives	301
12.3	"Good Morning Dear Teacher ... ," in the Philadelphia *Inquirer*, March 23, 1940. Courtesy of the Philadelphia *Inquirer*	304
12.4	James Egleson, in Committee for Defense of Public Education, *Winter Soldiers: The Story of a Conspiracy Against the Schools* (1941)	308
12.5	Schappes teaching a class at the School for Democracy, where many of those dismissed from City and Brooklyn. Colleges taught in the mid-1940s. Courtesy of Tamiment Library and Robert F. Wagner Labor Archives	310

Notes on Contributors

Robert Justin Goldstein is professor emeritus of political science at Oakland University, Rochester, Michigan, and research associate at the Center for Russian and East European Studies at the University of Michigan at Ann Arbor. He is the author/editor of over a dozen books dealing with the history of civil liberties struggles in modern American and nineteenth-century European history, including *Political Repression in Modern America* (2nd edn, Urbana, 2001), *American Blacklist: The Attorney General's List of Subversive Organizations* (Lawrence, 2008), *Burning the Flag: The Great 1989–90 American Flag Desecration Controversy* (Kent, 1995) and (ed.) *The Frightful Stage: Political Censorship of the Theater in Nineteenth-Century Europe* (New York, 2009, 2011).

Timothy Reese Cain is associate professor in the Institute of Higher Education at the University of Georgia. He serves as a Senior Scholar at the National Institute for Learning Outcomes Assessment and directs the Ethnography of the University Initiatives. His historical research examining academic freedom, faculty unionization, campus speech and related issues has recently appeared in *Labor History, History of Education, Perspectives on the History of Higher Education, American Journalism* and other journals. He is an associate editor and the book review editor of the *History of Education Quarterly* and the author of *Establishing Academic Freedom: Politics, Principles and the Development of Core Values* (New York, 2012).

Ernest Freeberg teaches history at the University of Tennessee. He is the author of *Democracy's Prisoner: Eugene V. Debs, The Great War, and the Right to Dissent* (Cambridge, MA, 2008), which explores the World War I trial and imprisonment of socialist leader Debs for making an anti-war speech, and the role this controversy played in promoting a civil liberties movement in post-WWI America. The book has been awarded the David J. Langum, Sr. Prize in American Legal History and the Eli Oboler Award from the American Library Association's Intellectual Freedom Roundtable. In 2013 he will publish *The Age of Edison: Electric Light and the Invention of Modern America* (New York).

Alex Goodall is a lecturer in Modern History at the University of York (England). He focuses on the modern history of the Americas, with a particular focus on revolutionary and counter-revolutionary politics in the Western hemisphere. His primary field of research is the history of United States counter-subversion, particularly in the period between the world wars. Recent publications on aspects of the cultural, political, and international history of interwar counter-subversion have appeared in the *Historical Journal* and *Journal of Contemporary History*, and a monograph *Loyalty and Liberty: American Counter-subversion from World War One to the McCarthy Era* (Urbana, 2013).

Michael Heale is emeritus professor of American History at Lancaster University and, on retirement, became senior associate fellow of the Rothermere American Institute, Oxford University. Following early studies of the Jadesonian era, he has focused on the growth and development of American anti-communism. He is former editor of the *Journal of American Studies* and the author of *American Anticommunism: Combating the Enemy Within, 1830–1970* (Athens, GA, 1990) and *McCarthy's Americans: Red Scare Politics in State and Nation, 1935–65* (University of Georgia Press, 1998). His latest book is *Contemporary America: Power, Dependency and Globalization since 1980* (Wiley-Blackwell, 2011).

Rebecca Hill is associate professor of American Studies and director of the M.A. program in American Studies at Kennesaw State University in Georgia, USA. She is the author of *Men, Mobs and Law: Anti-Lynching and Labor Defense in U.S. Radical History* (Durham, 2008) which studies the history of defense organizing on the left from abolitionism to the Black Panther Party. She is currently writing a history of anti-fascisms of the left and right from the 1930s to the present. Her articles have appeared in *Labor: Studies in Working Class History of the Americas, American Quarterly, New Left Review, Radical Teacher* and *American Communist History*.

Stephen Leberstein founded and served as long-time executive director of the Center for Worker Education at the City College of New York, where he also taught history. Now retired, he teaches part-time on race, labor, radicalism and abolitionism in Brooklyn College's Graduate Center for Worker Education and occasionally at Cornell University's School of Industrial and Labor Relations. His research on radicalism and academic labor in the 1930s and 1940s led him to organize an effort to have the City University Board of Trustees apologize to the victims of the Rapp–Coudert Committee, which it did in 1981. His current project is a larger and longer study of the emergence of a left leadership in the New York Teachers Union in the 1930s, along with an analysis of the mechanisms and personnel of repression that authored the Rapp–Coudert investigation in 1940 and persisted until the 1960s. He has published previously on the Rapp–Coudert investigation, although before new archival materials became available.

Robbie Lieberman is professor and chair of the Interdisciplinary Studies Department at Kennesaw State University Georgia. Her publications include *"My Song is My Weapon": People's Songs, American Communism and the Politics of Culture, 1930–50* (Urbana, 1989, 1995), which won the Deems Taylor Award; *The Strangest Dream: Communism, Anti-Communism and the U.S. Peace Movement, 1945–63* (Syracuse, 2000); *"Prairie Power: Voice of 1960s Midwestern Student Protest* (Columbia, 2004) and, co-edited with Clarence Lanae, *Anticommunism and the African-American Freedom Movement* (London, 2009, 2011). She served as editor of *Peace and Change* from 2006 to 2011.

Kenneth O'Reilly is professor emeritus at the University of Alaska Anchorage and now teaches at Milwaukee Area Technical College. His books include *Hoover and the Un-Americans: The FBI, HUAC and the Red Menace* (Temple University Press, 1983); *Racial Matters: The FBI's Secret File on Black America, 1960–72* (The Free Press, 1989); *Nixon's Piano* (New York, 1995); and *Holy Cow 2000: The Strange Election of George W. Bush* (e-book, 2011).

Chad Pearson teaches history at Collin College in Plano, Texas. He received his Ph.D. in history in 2008 from the State University of New York at Albany and is currently writing a book about the relationship between progressivism and the open-shop movement. Pearson is interested in historiographical trends including the decline of the new left and the rise of centrists and liberals in the academy.

Markku Ruotsila is adjunct professor of American and British History at the University of Tampere, Finland, and adjunct professor of American Church History at the University of Helsinki, Finland. He took his Ph.D. at Cambridge University in 1999 with a dissertation dealing with the origins of Anglo-American anti-communism in the First World War period. He has published extensively on the history of U.S. anti-communism and on other aspects of U.S. and British political and religious history. Ruotsila has been a visiting fellow at Oxford University and a visiting scholar at New York University, and he is the author of six books, including *British and American Anticommunism before the Cold War* (2001) and *John Spargo and American Socialism* (2006). He is currently working on two books, one on socialist anti-communism in the United States and another on fundamentalist Christian anti-communism and its role in the Cold War.

Landon Storrs is associate professor of history at the University of Iowa. Her publications include *Civilizing Capitalism: The National Consumers' League, Women's Activism, and Labor Standards in the New Deal Era* (University of North Carolina Press, 2000) and *The Second Red Scare and the Unmaking of the New Deal Left* (Princeton University Press, 2012). Her articles have appeared in the *Journal of American History, Feminist Studies, Journal of Women's History,* and *Journal of Policy History.*

Athan Theoharis, professor emeritus of political science at Marquette University in Wisconsin, has published over 20 books and more than 100 articles, primarily focused on FBI political surveillance and abuses of power, especially during the directorship of J. Edgar Hoover. He has also written and studied extensively about intelligence agencies in other Western democracies. Professor Theoharis has served as an adviser to the American Senate Select Committee on Intelligence Activities and has participated in conferences in Canada and France sponsored, respectively, by the Canadian Security Intelligence Security Review Committee and the French Interior Ministry. His books include *The Boss: J. Edgar Hoover and the Great American Inquisition* (Temple University Press, 1988), *Seeds of Repression: Harry S. Truman and the Origins of McCarthyism* (Quadrangle, 1971), *Spying on Americans: Political Surveillance from Hoover to the Huston Plan* (Temple University Press, 1978); and *Abuse of Power: How Cold War Surveillance and Secrecy Policy Shaped the Response to 9/11* Temple University Press, 2012).

Preface
Little "Red Scares": Anti-Communism and Political Repression in the United States, 1921–1946

Robert Justin Goldstein

All scholars and many lay persons interested in modern American history are at least generally familiar with the two great "red scares" of 1919–20 and 1946–54 (the latter of which is generally, if very incorrectly, termed "McCarthyism"— incorrectly because it was well advanced before Sen. Joseph McCarthy appeared on the national anti-communist political stage in 1950 and navigated with exceptional skill a wave set in motion by others that was already powerfully influencing American politics). The 1919–20 red scare emerged from foundations and "little" red scares laid over many previous decades (such as the Haymarket Riot of 1886, the 1894 Pullman Strike, anarchist scares during the 1900–10 period and the intense political repression of the World War I period). Similarly, the "great" 1946–54 scare left strong traces that have influenced American politics ever since (for example, an enormous weakening of militant labor and the lack of debate over American involvement in Vietnam, or over the advisability of adopting of system of national health insurance by politicians who have feared being labeled "soft on communism". The first "great" red scare also left many traces and thus the emergence of the second red scare reflected decades of developing American anti-communism which never disappeared. In fact, the period between the two great red scares were marked by frequent instances of political repression, often justified on anti-communist grounds, at local, state and federal levels, yet it has been curiously neglected in the history of American political repression and anti-communism. While the two "great" red scares and, often, their subcomponents, have become the subject of an enormous scholarly literature, the "little" red scares in between them have left behind a dearth of scholarly traces, perhaps because much of the material deals with events scattered in time and space which never reached the intensity of the two great red scares.[1] The purpose of this book is to remedy this situation by bringing together a series of studies, by a baker's dozen of leading specialists, on the subject of American political repression and anti-communism between the two great red scares. Collectively the contributors and the editor have authored over 50 books, many of them on themes related to this collection.

Before summarizing each chapter, this preface may prove helpful to the reader by highlighting some of the themes that run between the chapters. First, as has been already suggested above, this collection makes a conclusive case for the argument that the red scare never really ended during the entire period between the first and second great red scares, but rather that the 1921–46 period witnessed a whole series of "little red scares" which, as some of the chapters such as those by professors Cain and Heale make clear reached literally, in the "land of liberty," from "sea to shining sea." Wherever communists were active—and often even where they were not—frequently broad conservative coalitions were mobilized to damn their activities, and often to take physical and/or criminal steps against them.

A second broad theme which runs throughout the chapters is the breadth and depth of the conservative anti-communist coalitions that lay in wait or could be easily mobilized where allegedly seditious activity was afoot. As the various chapters and other sources make plain, this coalition included conservatives of all sorts and from various walks of life—federal, state and local officials of all three branches, business organizations, educators, the Catholic Church, Southerners' veterans organizations and many others. Thus, the chapters by professors Goodall, O'Reilly and Hill discuss the anti-communist activities of federal legislators, while professors Storrs and Theoharis discuss the activities of the federal bureaucracy. Professor Leberstein's contribution covers the antics of a New York state legislative committee, while Professor Heale discusses a wide range of anti-communist activities undertaken by state and local officials throughout the country. Educators are covered by Professor Cain, organized business by Professor Pearson, conservative labor by Professor Ruotsila and the

---

[1]   For standard accounts of the first "great" red scare, see Robert Murray, *Red Scare: A Study in National Hysteria, 1918–1920* (New York, 1964) and Regin Schmidt, *Red Scare: The FBI and the Origins of Anticommunism in the United States* (Copenhagen, 2000). For standard accounts of the second "great" scare, see David Caute, *The Great Fear: The Anti-Communist Purge under Truman and Eisenhower* (New York, 1978); Richard Fried, *Nightmare in Red: The McCarthy Era in* Perspective (New York, 1990) and Ellen Schrecker, *Many are the Crimes: McCarthyism in America (Boston, 1998)*. For a specialized study of the first "great'" scare, see Beverly Gage, *The Day Wall Street Exploded: A Story of America in its First Age of Terror* (New York, 2009). For an exception to the rule concerning lack of specialized studies about the "little" red scares in between the wars, see Shirley and Wayne Wiegand, *Books on Trial: Red Scare in the Heartland* (Norman, 2007).

Catholic Church by Eric Smith. Professor Lieberman's contribution discusses the role of anti-communism in the anti-civil rights movement.

A third broad theme which runs throughout the chapters is that the sources and intensity of the little red scares varied from time to time and place to place. As professors Freeberg and Theoharis make clear, the anti-communist role of the federal government, including the FBI, diminished considerably during the 1920s, partly as a backlash to the perceived abuses of the great 1919–20 Red Scare, only to pick up again after President Franklin Roosevelt directed the FBI to increase its monitoring of allegedly subversive groups during the mid-1930s. The mid-1930s had already witnessed an upward "bump" in red scares, as reflected in a major campaign to require teachers to sign loyalty oath and in reaction to a serious of major strikes such as the Minneapolis and San Francisco general strikes of 1934. But unquestionably the greatest of the "little red scares" broke out in 1938–41 and was led by the federal government, with the Congressional Dies Committee (discussed by Professor O'Reilly) engaged in widespread red-hunting, the FBI in full vigor (as discussed by Professor Theoharis) and Congress as a whole (as discussed by Professor Hill) enacting legislation (the 1939 Hatch Act) barring "subversives" from federal employment and, in the 1940 Smith Act, outlawing advocating the violent overthrow of the government. These Congressional actions were to lay the legal groundwork for World War II federal loyalty programs and a secret Attorney General's List of Subversive Organizations which were both subsequently widely publicized by President Truman in 1947, and which, along with the activities of House Committee on Un-American Activities (a continuation of the Dies Committee) actually made Sen. Joseph McCarthy a latecomer to the anti-communist scene when he began to make his wild charges in early 1950.

Chapter Summaries

The transition between the first "great" red scare and the "little" red scares is covered in Chapter 1 of this book, by University of Tennessee historian Ernest Freeberg. Although the Harding and Coolidge administrations of the 1920s are remembered for ushering in a decade of political conformity, epitomized by the rise of the Ku Klux Klan, new laws restricting immigration and the trial and execution of Sacco and Vanzetti, Freeberg seeks to demonstrate that this trend was moderated by the emergence of the modern civil liberties movement, one that pioneered new forms of free speech politics that have grown in importance down to our own time. When Warren Harding swept to victory in the 1920, he promised the country "normalcy" and declared that "too much" had been said about the subject of "Bolshevism in America." While promoting conservative pro-business policies, Harding's agenda in office, in fact, included a more moderate approach to the federal persecution of radicals and their organizations than had marked the Red Scare. Pressured by an emerging coalition of free speech advocates organized to defend dissenters jailed for their opposition to World War I and a public reaction against the Red Scare's excesses, the new Republican administration defused tensions by lifting censorship restrictions on the radical press, releasing those still jailed for anti-war dissent (including notably imprisoned Socialist Party leader Eugene Debs), and declaring a ban on federal surveillance of radicals. The use of federal power against dissent did not recede entirely, however, as officials continued a program of red-baiting and the labor movement felt the pressure of court injunctions. The new coalition of civil liberties advocates enjoyed some success in moderating federal policy, but they watched in frustration as state and local governments continued to stifle labor and left-wing movements through "criminal syndicalism" (i.e. sedition) laws which punished radical speech and vigilante groups threatened and sometimes used violence to silence left-wing voices.

In Chapter 2, Marquette University history emeritus Professor Athan Theoharis notes that the Federal Bureau of Investigation, originally created in 1908 as the Bureau of Investigation, became heavily involved in monitoring political dissent during World War I and increasingly focused on radical activists during the post-World War I red scare, playing a major role in the 1919–20 Palmer Raids. However, a public furor over Justice Department and Bureau abuses led to a scaling back of its political surveillance activities in 1924. Nonetheless, it continued to quietly monitor radical activities, with a focus on communist activities and labor union militants, based on secret executive directives and the use of special records procedures. The newly christened (1935) FBI was especially re-energized as a political surveillance operation due to secret directives in the mid-1930s by President Franklin Roosevelt to engage in a general monitoring of communist and fascist activities, with the result that its personnel and appropriations exploded. While conservatives during the 1930s feared that the FBI and its director, J. Edgar Hoover, would become a New Deal agency, they soon welcomed FBI expansion as the Bureau increasingly focused on communist activities, including party efforts in the labor and civil rights movements, surveillance efforts which would expand exponentially during the post-World War II red scare with the open and covert support of private anti-communist zealots. Thus, while the information about radicals gathered between the two great red scares proved to have limited use at the time, it was subsequently effectively exploited by FBI officials during the Cold War Era to promote a militantly anti-communist politics.

Preface   xvii

In Chapter 3, British historian Michael Heale argues that with the fading of the first "great" red scare, federal authorities abandoned attempts to suppress the communist movement, noting that the 1930s would become known as the "heyday of American Communism" and that American communists were largely spared harassment by federal officials. However, he argues, they were subject to the often unfriendly attention of state and local authorities and private groups and vigilantes. Heale's chapter examines the anti-communist activity mobilized initially mainly against labor and civil rights groups and the emergence in the late 1930s of populist red scare impulses that were directed "upwards" at reformist state governors and the New Deal, a heritage that would contribute to the second "great" red scare. Heale argues that after World War an informal understanding was reached between federal and state authorities on the strategy for combating the perceived communist menace. The federal government erected formidable barriers in the form of immigration laws and deportation procedures to exclude subversive aliens, and the state assumed responsibility for internal security, deploying such instruments as sedition laws, revitalized National Guard units and city red squads. Often urging the public authorities on, and sometimes acting on their own responsibility, were a host of businesses, patriotic societies, veterans organizations, civic bodies and racist groups. "Citizens groups" were frequently created to take the offensive against the un-American "outsiders" who were apparently bent on subverting their communities. Heale's chapter maps these various activities, including the anti-labor drives in the south and west, the emergence of a strong "little" red scare against popular front groups in the late 1930s and the experience of World War II, when the federal government seized the opportunity to advance its authority at the expense of state governments in the internal security arena.

In Chapter 4, British historian Alex Goodall discusses the 1930 House of Representatives Special Committee to Investigate Communist Activities in the United States, generally known as the Fish Committee after its chairman, Hamilton Fish. An important precursor to the House Committee on Un-American Activities (generally known as HUAC), the Fish Committee operated under starkly different conditions and enjoyed a less spectacular fate, rapidly fading into obscurity after its hearings ended. The tremendous social and political dislocations of the Depression had destroyed the legitimacy of an older tradition of anti-radical politics, Goodall maintains, while efforts to create a new anti-communist movement by blaming the economic crisis on revolutionary radicalism were unconvincing. Neutered by a series of embarrassing scandals, the Fish Committee struggled to manage their hearings effectively and to assemble a coherent concluding report, but it quickly was written off as the single least influential anti-communist investigation in American history. Goodall seeks to explain why, at a time of such severe social crisis, anti-communist politicians were unable to engineer popular anxiety over the "red menace." He argues that although the committee was in some ways more rigorous and substantive in its work that comparable anti-radical investigations, it failed to develop a coherent narrative capable of reconciling the diverse political agendas of its supporting constituencies or to overcome the deeper concerns the public had over unemployment and economic collapse. Key groups which would be vital in the resurgence of mid-century anti-communist politics, especially business, were divided among each other and unable to agree upon a single vision of Soviet Russia. And although the committee worked hard to steer clear off the more extreme end of radical right-wing politics, it failed to appeal to liberal anti-communism. The result was relative isolation, incoherence, public embarrassment and, ultimately, political failure.

In Chapter 5, American history of education professor Timothy Cain focuses on one of the main targets of the "little" red scares: American education, examining internal and external efforts to expunge alleged communists from American schools, colleges and universities. The chapter first details three categories of actors investigating and protesting the subversion that they believed threatened the nation's youth and its institutions: loosely and tightly formed non-government organizations; legislative and related governmental bodies; and individuals and groups within the schools and colleges themselves. These groups, working alone and in concert, campaigned for loyalty oaths for teachers, sought the removal of alleged communist students and teachers, and threatened both the livelihoods of heterodox educators and the education of their more vulnerable students. Cain's chapter then highlights the targets of these anti-communist efforts, including individuals and groups and groups of teachers, student demonstrations, curricular materials, alternative schools and teachers unions. In doing so it demonstrates that although the public efforts to unseat leftist educators were largely unsuccessful, until the end of the decade, the ongoing struggles over teachers', faculty members' and students' political rights and civil liberties were significant. They were, likewise, both specific to the decade and part of long-standing battles over American education.

In Chapter 6, American historian Chad Pearson focuses on employers and employers' organizations as one of the main organizers and sponsors of ant-communist movements during the interwar "little" red scares. Such employers fought on multiple fronts, challenging communists in their workplaces and communities, seeking to delegitimize Marxist ideology and portraying communists as a threat to American institutions and values. Employer anti-communism had deep roots, with some of its organizations such as the National Association of Manufacturers (NAM) dating from the Progressive Period, but

Preface xix

their efforts, which often included a general view of unions collectively seeking to impose socialism on the American people, peaked in the immediate aftermath of the Bolshevik Revolution, during which they eagerly joined hands with government officials during the first "great" red scare. For example, employer associations published essays about the evils of communism in theory and practice, typically written by ordinary people, which described in gruesome detail food shortages, poor-quality housing and political repression in revolutionary Russia. During the 1930 employers, deeply irritated by rising Marxist influence in American labor, continued to insist that socialism, in its various forms, was un-American. Organized in groups like the NAM, the U.S. Chamber of Commerce and the Southern States Industrial Council, employers continued to disseminate anti-communist pamphlets and fought communist-led unions at the point of production. Many gladly supported HUAC in addition. Organized employers' anti-communist softened during World War II, but spokespersons continued to maintain that socialism, like fascism was fundamentally a foreign "ism" which was unappealing to the American people.

In Chapter 7, Finnish historian Markku Rukotsila seeks to demonstrate that in the United States, as elsewhere, mainstream labor and socialist groups were not only among the first and most energetic opponents of Russian communism, yet were also among the most prominent victims of the anti-communist campaigns of others. Throughout the period between the two world wars, the labor movement had to negotiate between its own principled public witness and organizing against communism and its need to defend against the political repression practiced by those in government and private agencies who conflated socialism, labor unionism and communism. Because of their often intimate collaboration with congressional and federal investigations of domestic communism, and despite their widely publicized protests against "anti-subversion" excesses, key leaders of the American Federation of Labor, the Social Democratic League and the Social Democratic Federation played a complicit role in much anti-labor repression in the United States between the two world wars. Rukotsila's chapter investigates both the victimization of labor by others under the guise of anti-communism and the sometimes overt support given to political repression by labor and socialist groups during the 1917–41 period. It will argue that neither could have taken place to the degree which they did had the key leaders of the labor union movement not accepted the core assumptions about the communist threat that characterized the interwar period's anti-subversion movements.

In Chapter 8, American historian Eric Smith writes about the "little red scares" and their impact on those who supported, in body and/or mind, the Spanish loyaltist cause during the Spanish Civil War. His article underscores the importance of Spanish aid activities as a node of interwar anti-communism and identifies the American Legion and a particular cross-section of Roman Catholics as the purveyors of "premature McCarthyism." These anti-communist activists provided intelligence information to the FBI and other government agencies and testified against Spanish aid activists before the House Un-American Activities Committee. As was the case with other McCarthyite investigations, Spanish aid activities were unfairly characterized as communist in origin.

In Chapter 9, American historian Landon Storrs discusses the women's consumer as—like the pro-Spanish loyalist movement—an especial target of the "little red scares." She argues that right-wing hostility to female consumer advocates who held federal jobs or had the ear of federal officials was an important and hitherto overlooked source of the crusade against "Communists in government," which in turn was a primary engine of the post-World War II Red Scare. The hunt for communists in the federal government, which began in the 1930s and reached a fever pitch in the 1950s, reshaped the terrain of party politics and halted expansion of the American welfare state. Conservatives' attack on the New Deal—often seen as triggered by the rise of mass production unionism—also was a reaction to the emergence of a consumer movement that was feminist, anti-racist, and pro-labor. That movement was predominantly female and wielded more influence over federal policy than scholars have recognized. Focusing on the League of Women Shoppers, the Consumers' National Federation, and the fate of their members who obtained positions in such New Deal government agencies as the Office of Price Administration, this chapters argues that conservative anti-communists' gendered animosity to the consumer movement was critical to the prehistory of the federal employee loyalty program created in 1947, and that civil servants with ties to consumer groups were prominent among that program's casualties.

In Chapter 10, American historian Kenneth O'Reilly examines Republican and conservative Southern Democratic attempts to portray the Franklin D. Roosevelt administration as "un-American." The Dies House Un-American Activities Committee HUAC), a forerunner to the so-called McCarthy era congressional investigating committees which policed the Hollywood blacklists and searched for communists in government, was the principal vehicle for this strategy, which marked the emergence of the congressional investigation as part of a partisan and ideological electoral strategy that remains intact to some degree in the twenty-first century. Renamed in the House Internal Security Committee in 1969, HUAC was not finally abolished until 1975. The Dies Committee focus on "un-American" activities also remains somewhat intact. The Republican Party's 2008 vice presidential candidate, for example, referred repeatedly to Democratic Party presidential candidate Barack Obama as someone who was "not one of us,"

Preface   xxi

someone who did not inhabit "the real America." Many observers assumed that the Dies Committee would concentrate on the threat that the German American Bund and other homegrown fascist movements posed to American security. But was not usually the case, as the committee most often concentrated on communist activities and defined them broadly enough to encompass the New Deal's liberal reforms. In the course of its work, moreover, the Dies Committee emerged as a principal conduit for surveillance data gathered by the FBI and various media and business interests who objected to Roosevelt administration policies. In effect, the Dies Committee served as a highly partisan and ideological vehicle for exposing and punishing New Dealers and their allies for engaging in activities otherwise protected by the First Amendment.

In Chapter 11, American historian Robbie Lieberman discusses the African-American civil rights movement as a special target during the "little red scares." According to Lieberman, World War I and the Bolshevik Revolution gave supporters of the racial and economic status quo a new way to undermine black freedom struggles, which could be equated with subversion. Thus began a long "black and red scare" in which, in the name of opposing Bolshevism, anti-communist networks in and out of government meet black demands for equality with fierce opposition, including surveillance, harassment, intimidation and violence. To be sure communist opposition to colonialism and racism did inspire many black activists and the particular efforts of the Communist Party to defend black rights—most notably in the "Scottsboro boys" affair—brought it a measure of respect in African-American communities. But during the Depression era, a host of organizations that included labor advocates liberals, socialists and communists took for granted the ties between racial and economic and justice and by the latter half of the 1930s and into World War I many linked the struggle against fascism abroad to the battle against racism at home. By then, however, the practice of branding black people's struggles for racial and economic justice as "Communist" had become routine. Thus, whether led by key communists or not, efforts to organize unions and the unemployed, and to defend African Americans against injustice, inflamed the opposition, leading to terror in the south and to repression and violence in the north as well. During World War II, the "double V" campaign, the FBI's investigations into black disloyalty and the relative strength of the Communist Party contributed to perpetuating the notion that struggles for black equality were communist-inspired. This set the stage for the division of liberal organizations over the issue of communism, the marginalization of effective and committed radical activists, and the concomitant narrowing of the civil rights movement in the early years of the Cold War.

xxii

Little 'Red Scares'

Chapter 12, by American historian Stephen Leberstein consists of a detailed case study of the New York state legislature's Rapp–Coudert Committee's attack on academic freedom, the largest purge of professors in American history, from its origins in 1940 through the McCarthy era, based on newly available archival resources. A convergence of different factors in a turbulent political time rendered the Rapp–Coudert Committee an ardent foe of academic freedom in ways echoed in the historical moment that threatens colleges today. The investigation emerged in an atmosphere of perceived threats from foreign enemies and domestic dissidents in the period between the Nazi-Soviet Non-Aggression Pact and the German invasion of the Soviet Union. Among these factors was the growth of a militant labor left in the 1930s, the role of the Communist Party in it, the practice of the left in these unions and the emergence of a reactionary response to the perceived threat to loyal Americanism of indoctrination allegedly posed by left-wing teachers, who were seen as occupying as critical position in the struggle for ideological hegemony. When the Philosophy Department at City College offered noted British scholar Bertrand Russell a professorship in 1940, the Catholic Diocese's *Tablet* joined Hearst's *Journal American* and others to ignite a firestorm of protest against him as "the Godless advocate of free love and Communism." The anti-Russell rage reached the state legislature, which passed a resolution condemning his appointment and then immediately authorized the Rapp–Coudert Committee, which was charged with examining the administration and financing of public education throughout New York state, as well as investigating "subversion" in the schools. A New York City sub-committee chaired by State Senator Frederick Coudert focused entirely on uncovering communists in the municipal colleges, with devastating results. In 1941 over 50 faculty and staff members at the City College of New York, the storied "Harvard of the proletariat," were fired or denied reappointment as a result of the committee's efforts to stamp out "subversion." Through its work to purge the city's schools and colleges of teachers suspected of being communists, the Rapp–Coudert Committee developed the mechanisms and trained some of the personnel deployed on a national scale during the McCarthy period and later. Its chief investigator, Robert Morris, for example, went on to work for the McCarran Senate Sub-Committee on Internal Security after the war. Many of those named as suspects in the 1941 investigation were subsequently called to testify before federal, state or city investigating committees and often lost their jobs.

In Chapter 13, American historian Rebecca Hill recounts the history of the passage of the 1939 Hatch Act and 1940 Smith Act, which laid much of the legal foundation for the post-war "Great" red scare, including the federal loyalty program and the prosecution of the American Communist Party. The anti-communist and anti-New Deal coalition was the driving force behind both Acts, while the major opposition to these laws in Congress was voiced by left

Preface xxiii

New Dealers in the language of anti-fascism. Examining speeches of supporters of the Smith and Hatch bills as well as earlier attempt at anti-immigrant and anti-communist legislation from 1930 to 1940 reveals the degree to which conservative anti-fascism was built on older anti-communist and nativist ideologies and in opposition to what conservatives called the "regimentation" of the New Deal. Congressional conservatives opposed both ideologies using arguments that defined communism and fascism as similar. Their attacks on communism came primarily through the following five arguments defining communism and fascism as (1) atheist or pagan ideologies; (2) foreign conspiracies imported by immigrant "aliens" and sponsored by foreign governments; (3) bureaucratic and collectivist; (4) a new version of the "Tyranny of Reconstruction"; (5) hateful and revolutionary. These reasons for opposing both communism and fascism were different from the left's arguments against which fascism, which it defined as xenophobic, racist and authoritarian. Strong labor, civil liberties and left opposition defeated efforts to pass federal anti-subversive laws in the mid-1930, but the New Dealers' opposition crumbled with the 1939 Hitler-Stalin pact, which led to the denunciations of communism in a number of left-liberal groups. The communists' opposition to U.S. intervention in the European War between September 1939 and June 1941 made them an obstacle to the president's push for intervention. Thus, the Smith Act, which had languished in the Senate after passing the House in the summer of 1939, finally passed the Senate in 1940 when FDR pushed against the threat of subversion in military production.

Chapter 1

After the Red Scare: Civil Liberties in the Era of Harding and Coolidge

Ernest Freeberg

As Warren Harding took office in March 1921, the United States had just come through the worst self-inflicted assault on its tradition of civil liberties in the nation's history. In 1798 John Adams had jailed some of his Jeffersonian critics; later the rights of abolitionists had been trampled by mob violence and a Congressional gag rule; and during the Civil War Lincoln had claimed emergency powers to suspend habeas corpus and silence Copperhead Democrats. But none of these compared to the wide and systematic assault on pacifists, labor radicals and war dissenters during the Great War and its immediate aftermath. Young men with conscientious objections to the draft had been jailed, and often physically and mentally abused; thousands of men and women were arrested by state and federal authorities for making anti-war statements the government considered seditious; the Post Office punished anti-war newspapers and magazines; and where state action failed to silence war critics, mobs intimidated, beat and even lynched those suspected of insufficient patriotism.

The beleaguered advocates of free speech could only shake their heads over the contradiction—the Wilson administration leading the charge to silence dissent and impose uniformity of thought, all in the name of a supposedly progressive "People's War" that promised to "make the world safe for democracy." In order to fight German militarism, the United States had created what the American Civil Liberties Union's Roger Baldwin called "new machinery for the suppression of opinion [and] traditional rights." Surveying the American scene as Woodrow Wilson left office in 1921, he concluded that "the forces of reaction" enjoyed unprecedented power over the nation's political and economic life. "Never before were the civil rights guaranteed by constitutional provision so generally ignored and violated."[1]

Those who shared Baldwin's concern about these threats to constitutional liberty had little reason to expect much relief from president-elect Warren G.

---

[1] ACLU, *The Fight for Free Speech* (1921), 4.

Harding, an amiable but undistinguished Ohio politician who seemed unlikely to play a strong leadership role on any issue, much less one as controversial as the rights of radicals. During the war, in fact, the senator seemed to lose his usual composure in the face of the national emergency, declaring that the government should shoot all spies, and place its war effort in the hands of a single "supreme dictator." "We have a republic to save," as he explained. "We can't do it with the processes of a republic."[2]

Yet President Harding deserves some credit for reversing Wilson's course. As part of his program to roll back the federal government's wartime activism and restore the country to a pre-war "normalcy," he curtailed much of the federal government's legal campaign against radical dissenters. But the more important gains for civil liberties in the early 1920s came not from any political leader in Washington, but from citizens, organized in various social movements, who put civil liberties on the national agenda for the first time in the nation's history.

In the two years before Harding took office the country experienced a sharp recession and a series of violent labor conflicts, while across Europe governments struggled against the threat of communist revolution. In those anxious days, many Americans criticized the Wilson administration for not being sufficiently zealous in rooting out the Bolshevik threat. After his own house was bombed by a radical, Attorney General A. Mitchell Palmer vowed "unflinching, persistent and aggressive warfare" against America's enemies within. More than two years after the 1918 armistice, Palmer continued to invoke his wartime powers to detain and prosecute anarchists, communists and labor radicals, most notably in a series of January 1920 "raids" that rounded up hundreds of suspects in various cities. While Palmer succeeded in deporting a boatload of alien radicals, public opinion began to turn that spring when Americans learned that these dragnets had produced no significant arrests, and that Palmer's predictions of an imminent red revolution had been unfounded. The Senate investigated the Attorney General for his abuses of power, while a group of distinguished scholars and editors published a protest, charging that government agents had violated the basic rights of the accused, the vast majority of them innocent. Among Palmer's sharpest critics was Zechariah Chaffee, a conservative law professor at Harvard Law School, who was provoked by the Wilson administration's war on suspected revolutionaries into making a particularly energetic defense of civil liberties. "It is not the soap box orators," he wrote, "but Mr. Palmer with his hordes of spies and midnight housebreakers, that have brought our Government into hatred and contempt."[3]

---

[2]   Randolph Downes, *The Rise of Warren Gamaliel Harding* (Columbus, 1970), 269–75.

[3]   Palmer cited in *Boston Globe*, January 2, 1920; on the Senate hearings, Beverly Gage, *The Day Wall Street Exploded: A Story of America in its First Age of Terror* (New York, 2009),

Palmer was undeterred by the criticism, but warned Congress that his legal authority to prosecute dangerous radicals rested on shaky ground—the extraordinary powers granted to him by wartime legislation. Warning that he had compiled a list of over 60,000 "radically inclined" individuals who were still at large, he asked Congress in 1920 to draft a peacetime law that would provide the federal government with a permanent power to jail Americans, and deport aliens, for their "seditious" utterances, which he defined as any attempt to promote political and economic change through violence and other illegal acts.[4]

As anti-communist passions cooled in the spring of 1920, many thought better of providing the federal government with a permanent mandate to prosecute seditionists. Editors and journalists opposed giving the Postmaster General a permanent right to censor the press, while the mainstream labor movement, which once praised the crackdown on their left-wing rivals, now worried that the federal government might use any new power to silence dissent against them, in their attempts to organize and strike. Others felt sure that the state authorities, in some cases backed by vigilante justice, were quite capable of putting down any radical menace without federal help. Congress dropped any plans to pass a peacetime sedition bill.[5]

When Warren G. Harding assumed office that spring, he declared that it was time for the country to be rid of both the lingering animosities of the war, and the federal government's "wild experiment" in progressive reform, restoring national harmony through business-friendly policies. As Harding put it in his inaugural address, "Our supreme task is the resumption of our onward, normal way." Harding sounded the old note of anti-radical anxiety in his speech, warning his countrymen to beware of "dangers from within," threats that included "sedition," "slackerism" and revolutionary groups that encouraged change through the use of force. "If revolution insists upon overturning established order," he warned, "let other peoples make the tragic experiment. There is no place for it in America." But Harding spent more time in his speech denouncing war profiteers, and he vowed to protect the rule of law, a constitutional order in which "minorities are sacredly protected."

232–6; Robert J. Goldstein, *Political Repression in Modern America* (Cambridge, MA, 1978), 159–61.

[4] "Congress Grapples with the Question of Bolshevism and Anarchism," *Current Opinion*, January 1920.

[5] Key provisions of the Espionage Act remained on the books, allowing the government to punish speakers who attempted to undermine the draft—though these provisions remained dormant when the country was not at war. On the public debate over a peacetime sedition bill, see "The Dead-Line of Sedition," *Literary Digest*, March 6, 1920.

4 *Little 'Red Scares'*

In the aftermath of the war and Red Scare, a growing number of Americans considered the government's policies on free speech to be a pressing concern. Harding had campaigned on the slogan, "Let's Be Done with Wiggle and Wobble," but gave ambiguous and contradictory statements about how he might handle the nation's vexing questions about the proper balance between free speech and social order. By temperament and ideology, Harding was a moderate conservative who thought of himself as a friend of civil liberties, at least for those who used their rights in a "responsible" way. After a momentary bout of war fever, he had recovered his composure, and during the war showed signs of genuine support for civil liberties. Along with other former newspaper editors in the Senate, he stopped the Wilson administration from claiming even more drastic wartime censorship powers over the press. He had also supported the right to conscientious objection on religious grounds, and joined a chorus of protest in 1920 when the New York Assembly expelled five of its members because they were socialists. The threat of revolutionary radicalism was real but "greatly magnified," as he put it while campaigning. Recognizing that the tide of public fear about communism was fast fading, he declared that "Too much has been said about Bolshevism in America."[6]

And so the mood of the country had already begun to shift when Harding took office in the spring of 1921, supported by an electoral landslide that most understood as a sharp repudiation of Wilson's policies, foreign and domestic. Among his administration's earliest attempts to make good on his vow to return America to its pre-war "normalcy" was the restoration of mailing privileges to radical publications. During the war, Wilson's Postmaster General, the conservative Texan Albert Burleson, had used the Espionage Act to deny second-class mailing privileges to any publication that he deemed to be too critical of the government's war effort. Armed with this power to bankrupt the administration's critics, Burleson bludgeoned the country's then-lively radical press, driving many left-wing, pacifist, German-language and otherwise contrarian publications out of existence, and blackmailing many more into editorial compliance with the nation's war policy. Long after the armistice he continued to wield this power over the administration's critics, on the pretense that until a peace treaty was signed, the United States remained in a technical state of war.

Harding did not sign the final peace treaty with Germany until November, 1921, but his new Postmaster General, Will Hays, did not wait that long to end the wartime practice of denying mailing privileges to radical publications. "The war is over," Hays explained as he announced the change. "We must return to the ordered freedom. Our method of safeguarding the public welfare, while at

---

[6] "Senator Harding on Labor," *The Outlook*, August 18, 1920.

the same time maintaining freedom of the press, has been found through a long period of stable civil liberty better for the public welfare and personal security of citizens than to establish a bureaucratic censorship, which in its nature becomes a matter of individual opinion, prejudice or caprice."[7] Hays ordered the government to reimburse the radical *Liberator* for expenses it had been forced to pay because of its long legal battle with the Post Office. The pro-war liberals at *The New Republic*, who had once supported the Wilson administration's "conscription of thought," now cheered because "Mr. Hays very plainly does not want to be a censor."[8]

The Post Office did continue to exercise censorship power over "obscene" books that discussed birth control, and other sexual matters. In 1922, Hays left his federal job to establish the office in charge of drafting and promoting a motion picture code of decency that inhibited free expression in the cinema for years to come. Busy defending the right of war protestors and labor radicals, the leaders of the new post-war civil liberties movement spent little of their scarce resources challenging state and federal Comstock laws, and defending the rights of those artists and radical libertarians who were prosecuted for using speech that offended sexual and cultural norms. Those free speech fights would have to wait for another decade.[9]

The most visible controversy over civil liberties in Harding's term concerned the fate of the hundreds of war dissenters who remained in federal prison, and some whose trials for federal Espionage Act violations were still pending long after the armistice. During the war, 1,200 war dissenters had been convicted, some sentenced to as many as 20 years in prison. Most visible among these was Eugene V. Debs, leader of the Socialist Party of America, who ran his fifth campaign for the presidency in 1920 from the confines of his jail cell in the Atlanta penitentiary. That year Debs had received over 900,000 votes, about 3 percent of the total cast. Since the Socialist Party was in disarray, many observers concluded that most of his support came from Americans who cared little about socialism, but hoped to cast a protest against the government's persecution of dissenters. A vote for Debs was a vote for free speech, as the socialists often put it, while many sympathizers agreed that each ballot cast for Debs, a man branded

---

[7]   *Editor & Publisher*, May 1921.

[8]   *New York Times*, May 26, 1921; *New Republic*, June 8, 1921.

[9]   David M. Rabban, *Free Speech in its Forgotten Years* (New York, 1997) 304–16; Margaret Blanchard, *Revolutionary Sparks: Freedom of Expression in Modern America* (New York, 1992), 138–9.

by the Wilson administration as a dangerous traitor, was "a scathing indictment of those who hounded this great man to prison."[10]

During the 1920 campaign Harding tried to avoid a serious discussion about the fate of those whom the amnesty movement called "the political prisoners." On those rare occasions when amnesty advocates forced him to clarify whether he would offer them a presidential pardon, Harding evaded, suggesting only that he could make no decision until he was in office, and could review the details of each case. To some he seemed to express sympathy for the prisoners, a willingness to release them as part of a program of post-war national healing. At other times he declared them to be dangerous felons, reckless zealots tearing at the vitals of American civilization.[11]

Debs's 1920 campaign to go "from the jail house to the White House" provided energy to a movement for amnesty that began when he first entered prison in April 1919, and continued to gain momentum during Harding's first year in office. A wide coalition of Americans joined the amnesty crusade. In Congress, Senator France of Maryland held hearings to pressure the administration to release these prisoners, while labor, church and socialist groups sent amnesty petitions and delegations to Washington. On the other hand, Harding heard from a counter-movement that demanded the president to stand firm. War veterans in the newly founded American Legion told him that pardoning wartime critics would dishonor the sacrifice made by American soldiers and their families, a sentiment echoed by other patriot groups and in many letters from private citizens.

Though eager not to inherit this controversy left to him by the Wilson administration, Harding took no action in his first months in office, except to ask his Attorney General, Harry Daugherty, to conduct a fresh review of the cases. Daugherty promised quick action, but then dithered, and in his public statements took a much harder line than the president, dismissing all those Americans who called for amnesty as cynical radicals who cared nothing for free speech, or their well-meaning dupes. As he summed up his attitude in a speech to the American Bar Association, "Those who do not believe in our Government and the enforcement of our laws, should go to a country which gives them their peculiar liberty." Behind the scenes, Harding pressed his Attorney General to move ahead, and Daugherty responded by taking the unusual course of sneaking Debs out of his prison cell, and allowing him to travel, unescorted, for a clandestine interview at the Justice Department. Though impressed by

---

[10] George S. Viereck, "What We Expect from President Harding," *American Monthly*, January 1, 1921; on Debs and the amnesty campaign, see Ernest Freeberg, *Democracy's Prisoner: Eugene V. Debs, the Great War, and the Right to Dissent* (Cambridge, MA, 2008).

[11] Downes, 632–3.

Debs personally, Daugherty remained convinced that the president should deny clemency, on the grounds that releasing him before he served his full 10-year sentence would encourage "disloyalty, lawlessness, and defiance of authority of the government." Harding ignored this counsel.[12]

After the United States finally signed a peace treaty with Germany in November, 1921, three years after the armistice, Harding used this moment to move ahead on the amnesty issue, presenting it as part of his wider program to restore a pre-war "normalcy." The Justice Department dropped the prosecution of some wartime Espionage Act cases still on appeal, and on Christmas morning 1921, liberated two dozen of the remaining wartime dissenters, including Eugene Debs. Announcing his decision, Harding insisted that Debs and his fellow inmates had been justly convicted, but had served sufficient sentences in light of the "changed conditions" of peacetime. In his final report on the case, Daugherty declared that Debs was a "man of much personal charm and impressive personality, which qualifications make him a dangerous man, calculated to mislead the unthinking and affording excuse for those with criminal intent." In spite of this claim that Debs remained "dangerous," Harding invited him to visit the White House on the day of his release, where the president and the seditionist evidently enjoyed a pleasant exchange.[13]

By freeing Debs, the most visible and contentious of the wartime prisoners, Harding calmed but did not end the national movement for amnesty. More than 100 radicals and pacifists remained in prison, the bulk of them unrepentant members of the Industrial Workers of the World, a group subjected to particularly intense government and vigilante persecution during the war. While many in the mainstream press and the trades union movement lost interest in amnesty after the Debs release, other amnesty advocates maintained their pressure on the president. Assuming a lead role in the amnesty fight, the fledgling American Civil Liberties Union won the endorsement of 50 Congressmen, who signed a petition asking Harding for a "general amnesty" for all those "war prisoners" who had been convicted under the Espionage Act for "expressions of opinion and not overt acts." While the most principled civil libertarians, and many of the prisoners themselves, continued to insist on their innocence, many more supported clemency on the grounds that the government had been right to jail dissenters during a wartime emergency, but should release them once peace returned. Choosing this pragmatic approach rather than a more principled defense of the First Amendment, the AFL leader Samuel Gompers asked

---

[12] *Washington Post*, January 8, 1921; James Giglio, *H.M. Daugherty and the Politics of Expediency* (Kent, 1978), 125.

[13] *Atlanta Constitution*, October 5, 1922. For Harding's statement on clemency, see *Christian Science Monitor*, December 24, 1921; Robert Murray, *The Harding Era*, 166–9.

Harding to clear the jails as part of his strategy to ease post-war labor tensions, returning the country to "an era of good feelings."

Plenty of Americans continued to provide Harding with the opposing view, declaring that a presidential pardon would undermine the rule of law, release dangerous radicals into an already volatile post-war society, and encourage traitors in future wars, whose tongues would no longer be curbed by the threat of a long prison sentence. Harding's own wife wanted him to take a tougher line against the wartime prisoners, while his Attorney General advised the president to stand firm, especially against members of the IWW, a group he considered "revolutionary, uncivil and wicked." Each time news reports circulated that the president was about to reach a decision on these prisoners, the American Legion, the Ku Klux Klan and other patriotic organizations sent the president angry letters of warning.[14]

Faced with pressure from both sides, and motivated by the somewhat conflicting demands of political calculation and humanitarian concern, Harding allowed prisoners to dribble out of the penitentiary, a few at a time. Some non-citizens took advantage of his offer to commute their sentences if they agreed to leave the country "and never return."[15] Others won their freedom by promising to be "law abiding in the future." These compromises failed to satisfy the most persistent branches of the now dwindling amnesty movement. Most notably, the socialist leader Kate Richards O'Hare kept political pressure on the White House by organizing a Children's Crusade. After being released from prison for her own conviction under the Espionage Act, O'Hare gathered a couple dozen children of the remaining political prisoners, toured them across the country on a well-publicized train ride, and delivered them to the gates of the White House to petition the president in the summer of 1922. For a month Harding refused their daily appeal for a meeting, declaring that he would not yield to a publicity stunt that amounted to political blackmail. O'Hare parried by organizing the children into a picket line at the White House gates. For weeks that summer they marched each day, wielding signs that read, "We Are Innocent Victims" and "4 Years Since I Saw My Daddy." When Harding claimed to be too busy to meet with the delegation, O'Hare published a list of those whom the president had *not* been too busy to see, a group that included Mae West and Babe Ruth. At last Harding yielded, releasing some of the prisoners, and promising a speedy review of the remaining cases.[16]

---

[14] Giglio, 142.

[15] *Chicago Tribune*, December 31, 1922.

[16] The ACLU's role in the Children's Crusade is noted in *A Year's Fight for Free Speech* (1923), 12.

In addition to providing financial and logistical support for the Children's Crusade, the ACLU experimented with other ways to force the plight of the political prisoners onto the public agenda. They organized a picket line of women designed to embarrass Harding during one of his finest hours as president, the Washington Naval Conference of 1922. The ACLU also enjoyed an alliance with Senator William Borah of Idaho, who demanded Congressional hearings on the remaining prisoners, and headlined several major amnesty rallies. "If a man thinks the war is unjust," Borah insisted, "it is his absolute right to say so." On platforms and in the press, Borah used the amnesty cause to draw public attention to the way war had undermined civil liberties in America.

Public sympathy for the dissenters was fueled by a palpable desire, felt by many, to set the animosities and divisions of war aside; others worried that the prisoners were becoming martyrs, and thus an irritant that would stir up class resentment; but the prisoners also benefited from the public's growing disillusionment with the war during the Harding years. Under the Espionage Act, many had gone to jail for saying that the war was a contest between rival imperial powers for commercial advantage, and that the United States joined the carnage not for noble, selfless reasons, but to protect loans made by JP Morgan and other American bankers to the Allied cause. As Debs had put it during the speech that led to his arrest, the working class "who freely shed their blood and furnish the corpses, have never yet had a voice in either declaring war or making peace. It is the ruling class that invariably does both." In the early 1920s, many Americans were shocked by the punitive terms of the Versailles treaty and scandalous reports about war profiteering, and a growing number of them concluded that the war dissenters had been jailed not for being disloyal, but for telling uncomfortable economic truths.

Caught between the amnesty forces and his conservative supporters, Harding was eager to resolve the controversy, but could find no face-saving compromise that would resolve the fate of the remaining prisoners. More than 50 Wobblies, most held at Leavenworth, refused to make any concession to the government in order to win their freedom. The most defiant of them repudiated the state's authority entirely, refusing even to file a petition for clemency, a principled act that kept them in prison until after Harding's death.[17]

Amnesty forces expected the worst when Calvin Coolidge took over the presidency, after Harding's untimely death in the spring of 1923. While governor of Massachusetts, Coolidge had gained national fame, and a vice-presidential nomination, thanks to his tough anti-labor stand during the Boston policemen's

---

[17] William Preston, Jr., *Aliens and Dissenters: Federal Suppression of Radicals, 1903–1933* (New York, 1963), 259–67; NYT, 20 Feb 1923; *Chicago Tribune*, October 8, 1922; *Washington Post*, October 17, 1922.

strike. But like Harding, Coolidge felt no desire to inherit the controversy over the wartime prisoners. Shielding himself from the political fallout, he followed the recommendations of a three-person panel appointed to finally resolve the controversy, a committee stacked to provide political cover for the decision to liberate the remaining 31 "wartime offenders." In December 1923, five years after the armistice, the last of these men left their cells. "The president has performed a distinctive service to the most fundamental principle of free government," Senator Borah declared. "These men were not in prison for violence to either person or property. They were there because they expressed their political views upon matters of government ... Intolerance, bigotry, prejudice kept them there for many years."[18]

Those who worked for amnesty deserve credit for rescuing hundreds of Americans from excessive and unjust jail terms. Perhaps more importantly, they provoked a nationwide discussion about the First Amendment, and the impact of war on democratic ideals. As one Chicago reporter observed, "The movement seems growing as a subject of general interest and discussion, pro and con. The ordinary citizen on the street is wondering what it is all about." In this way, the amnesty cause not only forced Harding and Coolidge to act, but contributed to a sustained public discussion, spanning years, over the nature and limits of the American citizen's right to speak in wartime—an unprecedented, powerful, and largely forgotten grass-roots protest movement that cultivated a new public concern for civil liberties that has shaped free speech rights ever since.

If many Americans joined what one called "a new fight for old liberties" in the post-war period, Harding deserves credit not for leading this battle but for yielding gracefully to it, particularly for what one biographer calls his "moral courage" in releasing the political prisoners. But in other areas his administration's record on civil liberties was less positive, thanks in large part to Attorney General Harry Daugherty. By his own admission, Daugherty was the least qualified man ever to be appointed to run the Justice Department. A long-time player in Ohio's Republican political machine, and Harding's friend and campaign manager, Daugherty knew little and cared less about the fine points of constitutional law.[19]

Daugherty inherited a Justice Department that had, since the war, engaged in spying and sabotage against economic and political radicals. In 1917 Wilson's first Attorney General, Thomas Gregory, had called on loyal Americans to spy on their neighbors, and he deputized the members of various patriotic groups as quasi-official "sedition busters." His successor, A. Mitchell Palmer, continued this mission with his illegal raids and deportations, and when Daugherty assumed control of

---

[18] NYT, December 16, 1923; Freeberg, 317.

[19] Oswald Garrison Villard, "New Fight for Old Liberties," *Harper's* (September, 1925).

the Justice Department in 1921, he likewise maintained the government's program of surveillance and illegal interference with radical groups.[20]

This clandestine war on radicals was handled by the Justice Department's Bureau of Investigation, which Daugherty entrusted to his crony William J. Burns, a move that Daugherty's biographer describes as his "most unfortunate" appointment." Burns was a celebrated detective, a self-appointed guardian of the republic who was hated by radical and labor groups for his red-baiting and his unscrupulous methods. While Daugherty promised to reform the Bureau after the excesses of Palmer's illegal raids, Burns proceeded to hire some of his disreputable friends, and used the power of his office to harass not only suspected radicals and strike leaders, but Congressmen and other public officials who dared to criticize the Harding administration. Burns compiled a list of "enemies," illegally searched and ransacked their offices, and trailed and intimidated them.[21]

Burns also used these unsavory methods against the country's fledgling communist party, planting spies and raising private funds from patriotic organizations that he used to persecute radicals far beyond the limits of federal law. Since the Espionage Act no longer applied, and Congress had failed to pass a peacetime sedition law, the Bureau had no basis on which to prosecute the country's fledgling communist party, which had gone "underground" after the Palmer raids in a vain attempt to avoid further harassment. In a highly publicized raid on a communist meeting in the remote town of Bridgman, Michigan, Burns skirted the law by working with state officials, and their extremely broad criminal syndicalism law, in order to arrest more than a dozen party leaders.[22]

After the Bridgman raid, which also produced two barrels of incriminating documents that the communists had buried, the Justice Department crowed that they were about to "abolish ... dangerous radicalism" in the country. The ACLU countered by protesting the government's "lawless, repressive tactics," and the federal use of a flawed state law in order to "wipe out the Communist movement." The ACLU criticized the communists for their decision to go "underground," but insisted that America's Bolsheviks were more melodramatic than dangerous. "The essence of the charge against the men," as the ACLU put it, "is that, holding communist views, they dared to meet together for discussion."[23]

---

[20]   Paul L. Murphy, *World War One and the Origins of Civil Liberties in the United States* (New York, 1979) 89, 92–4.

[21]   Giglio, 126–8; Goldstein, 173–5.

[22]   Theodore Draper, *The Roots of American Communism*, 197–209, 371–2; Paul L. Murphy, *Meaning of Freedom of Speech* (Westport, 1972), 184–8.

[23]   NYT, August 25, 1922; NYT, March 13, 1923; Paul Murphy, *The Meaning of Freedom of Speech*, 186.

In the minds of Daugherty and Burns, the ACLU's willingness to defend the communists only confirmed what they had long suspected, that the organization served as the legal arm of revolutionary radicalism. Under Harding's Justice Department, anyone who supported the ACLU was marked as a character of suspicious loyalty. In the end, the Bridgman raid produced just one conviction, and thanks to ACLU publicity, stirred further doubts about the Justice Department's use of illegal tactics to fight the phantom of "red revolution."[24]

As Red Scare fears receded, radical speakers were less likely to be silenced by state prosecutors or angry mobs. But in the view of the Civil Liberties Union, Harding's Justice Department posed an even greater threat to the basic democratic rights of working people through its use of sweeping injunctions against organized labor. Tarring mainstream union organizers with the brush of "radicalism," Daugherty brought the full power of the federal government to bear against the AFL during a 1922 railroad strike. After Harding failed to mediate a resolution to the strike, Daugherty won a court order against the union that one historian calls "the most comprehensive injunction ever imposed on American labor." Convinced that the strike was actually the handiwork of the IWW and communists, his injunction prevented strikers from picketing, and stopped their leaders from using "letters, telegrams, telephones, [and] word of mouth" to rally their members. "Entreaties, arguments, [and] persuasion" were banned by court order, and authorities arrested the editors of several newspapers who expressed sympathy for the strikers. Though Harding supported Daugherty's aggressive policy, the ACLU was not the only one outraged by this unprecedented assault on the speech rights of workers. Herbert Hoover, then Harding's Commerce secretary, called Daugherty's injunctions an "obvious transgression of the most rudimentary rights of men."[25]

In similar fashion, the Justice Department won sweeping injunctions against striking coal miners, federal intervention that contributed to already grim prospects for organized labor in these years. Believing that the conflict between labor and capital was the key battleground in the fight for free speech rights, the ACLU offered legal support to defend unions' right to strike, picket and assemble. This included a courageous attempt to provoke a test case during a strike in the Pennsylvania coalfields in 1922, when the ACLU's Arthur Garfield Hays arrived in Vintondale, PA to challenge the coal company's attempt to shut down all public meetings. "Vintondale is an armed camp," Hays found. "The coal and iron police, mounted and heavily armed, acting under the directions of the coal company, permit no one to stand for a moment on the streets and

---

[24] Giglio, 130–31; Murphy, 186–8.

[25] Christopher Finan, *From the Palmer Raids to the Patriot Act: A History of the Fight for Free Speech in America* (Boston, 2007) 44; Giglio, 148–9.

After the Red Scare

greet arrivals with threats of arrest, obscene language and physical violence." After trying to hold a meeting, Hays found himself first assaulted by company guards, and then arrested for breaching the peace. Bruised but unbowed, he won a court order opening the town to meetings of the United Mine Workers, a small victory at a time when organized labor won few.[26]

After a sharp period of labor unrest in the years after the war, radical protest and even mainstream union organizing declined through the rest of the decade, thanks to state harassment of labor and radical organizations, capital's successful campaign for the "open shop" and welfare capitalism, and the self-destructive factionalism of left-wing radicals in the United States. As ACLU director Roger Baldwin summed up the situation, the main reason that civil liberties violations declined in the Harding years was because fewer radical voices remained. "Repression and fear have silenced thousands who see no point in bucking the tide."[27]

The federal government under Harding and Coolidge was also able to pull back from the active prosecution of radical speech because many state legislatures had eagerly taken on the job, passing laws designed to criminalize radical organizations and punish unpopular speakers. The ACLU counted 35 "criminal syndicalism" and sedition laws, most passed by state lawmakers in the Red Scare years of 1919 and 1920, that aimed to punish those advocating social change through violence or revolution, or even joining an organization that welcomed a pending clash between labor and capital. According to historian Paul Murphy, state action against radicals under these laws "far exceeded those at the federal (level) both in numbers seized and in callousness of treatment." In Montana, for example, the state outlawed "any language calculated to incite or inflame resistance to duly constituted State authority." In several states, prosecutors used such laws to arrest members of the IWW, not for acts of violence, but for belonging to an organization devoted to economic revolution, and willing to consider industrial sabotage a legitimate tool in that struggle.[28]

Many city governments also joined in this war on unpopular speech. New York passed a law threatening to punish building owners who provided meeting space for groups whose activities might "breed a disregard for law," while Boston banned any meetings deemed "sacrilegious" or which "tended to promote immorality." Even when they lacked legal sanction to suppress speech, many mayors and police chiefs denied parade permits and broke up meetings of any group suspected of "radical tendencies." These included harassment and violence

---

[26] *Washington Post*, June 18, 1922; for ACLU work in West Virginia, see NYT, March 4, 1923; Goldstein, 188–91.

[27] *A Year's Fight for Free Speech*, 1922, 6.

[28] A.B. Reading, "The California Syndicalist Law—Strong or Wobbly?" *Overland Monthly* (March 1925); Goldstein, 177–8; Murphy, *Meaning of Freedom of Speech*, 79–84.

against those participating in strikes, advocating birth control, or attending "defense meetings" organized in support of the anarchists Sacco and Vanzetti.[29] In the election of 1924, to take another example, some campaign workers for Robert La Follette, the Wisconsin progressive leading a third-party insurgency, were attacked by mobs, led by men in uniform and evidently condoned by local police forces. In other places, local authorities denied speaking permits to La Follette's campaigners, and arrested speakers who challenged their ban.[30]

Such assaults on free speech rights were nothing new in the 1920s, but reflected a common form of local political control that authorities had used in America since the nineteenth century. More unusual was the fact that people now noticed, in part because the American Civil Liberties Union began to collect and publicize these incidents, raising public consciousness about the sharp limits often imposed in local communities on the right to free speech.[31]

Harding died in August, 1923, in the midst of serious allegations of corruption in his administration. Daugherty had been under fire from liberals and labor leaders since his heavy-handed use of injunctions against organized labor, and faced wide public criticism for dragging his feet on the prosecution of war-fraud cases. But Coolidge kept Daugherty in office until evidence surfaced that the Attorney General had been involved in many of the scandals just coming to light in the last months of the president's life. In Daugherty's case, this included a role in illegal oil leases on government land at Teapot Dome, Wyoming, the sale of government favors and illegal liquor licenses, and the illicit interstate trade of prize fighting films.[32] Threatened with a Congressional investigation and impeachment, and unwilling to release his files to investigators, Daugherty was forced to resign at the end of March, 1924. Declaring his innocence to the end, he claimed he had been the victim of the "hellish designs" of a communist conspiracy.[33]

Eager to distance himself from these scandals, Calvin Coolidge appointed Harlan Fiske Stone, dean of Columbia's law school, to lead the Justice Department. Stone moved quickly to reform the Bureau of Investigation, which he described as "lawless ... and engaging in many practices which were brutal and tyrannical in the extreme." As the clandestine activities of Daugherty's Justice

---

[29] Murphy, 24.

[30] See American Civil Liberties Union Cases, No 263, 1924, 233–5. See The Progressive Movement of 1924 (New York, 1966), 171–2.

[31] On these forms of speech control, see Christopher Capozzola, *Uncle Sam Wants You: World War 1 and the Making of the Modern American Citizen* (New York, 2008). For a useful overview of the national discussion on civil liberties questions in the 1920s, see *Selected Articles on Censorship of Speech and the Press*, ed. Lamar T. Beman (New York, 1930).

[32] NYT, March 18, 1924.

[33] Giglio, 160, 168–74.

Department came to light, Stone announced an end to the federal government's surveillance of radical political organizations and other "abuses of power." The Justice Department, as he put it, would no longer concern itself with "political or other opinions of individuals." Stone fired William Burns, and replaced him with J. Edgar Hoover. Though Hoover had participated in some of the Bureau's worst wartime abuses, including the creation of a detailed inventory of suspected radicals, he carried out Stone's mandate for reform, ending the department's clandestine operations and improving the professional training and ethical standards of its agents.[34]

Beyond the actions of federal and state prosecutors, the Harding/Coolidge era offers many examples that support its reputation as a time when economic conservatism and cultural conformity eroded minority rights. The "second" Klan enjoyed a rapid rise to power in these years, and joined with the American Legion and many other patriotic organizations in promoting a stunted version of "Americanism." Both the Klan and the Legion tried to impose their brand of patriotism on the public school curriculum, and to ferret out suspected subversives in school and government through laws requiring teachers to take a loyalty oath. While their leaders publicly denounced the use of violence, members of these groups used vigilantism to threaten and silence many who offered alternative ideas about the meaning and goals of American democracy.

But as war passions cooled, the Bolshevik threat receded, and labor unions lost much power and influence, the ACLU continued to note a "sharp decline in interference with civil rights" across the country by 1924. Perhaps, as Roger Baldwin suggested, fewer radicals were persecuted because fewer dared to speak in this hostile environment. However, the Wilson administration's wartime excesses, the brutish actions of American mobs during the war and the Red Scare, and the rise of fascist movements in Europe, all led American liberals and some conservatives to take a new interest in civil liberties. The founding text of their movement was *Freedom of Speech*, a history of the origin and evolution of America's speech rights published in 1920 by Harvard law professor Zechariah Chaffee. Troubled by the federal government's unprecedented violation of free speech rights during the war and Red Scare, Chaffee's book challenged prevailing legal wisdom about the origin and intentions of the First Amendment. He began by forcing the nation to take a good look in the mirror, reviewing many of the violations of basic freedoms that had occurred during the war. After reading Chafee's book, editor William Allen White wrote that his "amazing account" of the government's wartime assault on civil liberties made it painfully clear "how

---

[34] Harlan Stone cited in Geoffrey Stone, *Perilous Times* (New York, 2004), 230–31; *Harlan Fiske Stone, Pillar of the Law*, 149–53 (New York, 1956); ACLU, *Nationwide Spy System* (New York, 1924).

precarious is the hold which this supposedly fundamental national ideal has secured in our courts and legislatures."[35]

Through a close re-reading of the intentions of America's first generation of revolutionaries, Chaffee created a conservative argument for a radically new and expansive view of free speech rights. "The real issue in every free speech controversy is this," he argued. "Whether the state can punish all words which have some tendency, however remote, to bring about acts in violation of the law, or only those words which directly incite to acts in violation of the law." In this, Chafee took aim at the prevailing legal test used by judges and juries in his day, which allowed that a speaker could be justly punished for any utterance that might have a "bad tendency" to produce some illegal activity at some point in the future. In Chafee's view, such a broad test allowed any jury to convict a speaker whose ideas offended the majority, and he argued that the government should instead limit itself to preventing and punishing the illegal use of *force*. He urged his fellow citizens to "protect ourselves against bad thinking and speaking by the strength of argument and confidence in American common sense and American institutions, including that most characteristic of all, which stands at the head of the Bill of Rights, freedom of thought."[36]

Some dismissed Chaffee's claim that the government should punish speech only when it threatened to produce harmful "overt acts," calling this "a passing phase of incorrigible sentimentality."[37] But his argument struck home with two influential members of the Supreme Court, Oliver Wendell Holmes, Jr. and Louis Brandeis. In spring 1919, Holmes had spoken for a unanimous court in upholding the Espionage Act, sending Debs and others to prison, and granting Congress enormous powers to silence dissent during a wartime emergency.

In the *Abrams* case that fall, however, Holmes reversed course, offering the first in a series of articulate dissents that carved out a broader and more tolerant interpretation of the rights afforded by the First Amendment. Like many other liberals and progressives, Holmes and Brandeis had been alarmed by the excesses of the Palmer raids, and seemed to tacitly acknowledge Chaffee's criticisms about the Supreme Court's reasoning in the Debs case. Chaffee had urged judges to develop a new legal standard, restricting speech only when it posed a "clear and present danger" of lawless behavior; this was a principle that Chafee had discovered in an unlikely place, Holmes's decision in an earlier case, *Schenck v. US*, that upheld the conviction of a socialist for distributing anti-draft leaflets. Over the course of the next decade, Holmes and Brandeis took Chaffee's

---

[35] ACLU survey of 1924 noted in NYT, May 2, 1925; "Freedom of Speech," *The New Republic*, March 13, 1921.

[36] Zechariah Chafee, *Freedom of Speech* (1920), 228.

[37] Archibald Stevenson, "The World War and Freedom of Speech," NYT, 13 Feb 1921.

lead, elaborating on this 'clear and present danger" test, using it as what one scholar has called "a doctrinal peg for the protective interpretation of the First Amendment." In his dissent in the *Abrams* case, for example, Holmes sounded his new concern for free speech rights when he wrote, "I think that we should be eternally vigilant against attempts to check the expression of opinions that we loathe and believe to be fraught with death, unless they so imminently threaten immediate interference with the lawful and pressing purposes of the law that an immediate check is required to save the country." Over time this more protective "clear and present danger" test won acceptance by a majority of the court, one of the most important free speech legacies of the immediate post-WWI years.[38]

Chaffee, Holmes and Brandeis provided the intellectual underpinning for a crucial change in free speech law that greatly expanded the right to dissent in the twentieth century. At the state level, others moved to roll back the worst excesses of their state governments' assault on free speech that had been inspired by the war and Red Scare. Most notably, New York governor Al Smith vetoed the "Lusk" laws designed to impose political orthodoxy on the state's teachers, and blocked the legislature's attempt to outlaw radical political parties. He also pardoned five prisoners convicted under the state's criminal anarchy law. In releasing the Irish labor agitator James Larkin, Smith claimed that this was "a political case where a man has been punished for a statement of his beliefs." The governors of Illinois and California also pardoned radical prisoners.[39]

The new respect for civil liberties also drew support from many chastened liberals and progressives who had once put their faith in the federal government to wage a responsible and high-minded "people's war" against enemies of democracy, at home and abroad. Now, no less than Harding and his fellow conservatives, they saw federal and state power as a potential threat to individual liberty. One judge who had played a role in the government's post-war attack on radicals now concluded, "There are Reds—probably dangerous Reds. But they are not half so dangerous as the prating pseudo-patriots who, under the guise of Americanism, are preaching murder, 'shooting-at-sunrise,' and to whom the church parlors and public forums have hitherto been open ... It is time we had freedom of speech for the just contempt that every wholesome-minded citizen has and should have for the pretentious, noisy, heresy hunter of these hysterical times."[40]

While it remained small, the ACLU built a network of civil liberties supporters, who formed chapters across the country. They won few victories in

---

[38]   Rabban, ch. 8.

[39]   Finan, 36–7; NYT, January 18, 1923; January 8, 1924. On the ACLU petition to Governor Smith, see "Wants Anarchists Freed," NYT January 8, 1923; Goldstein, 172.

[40]   Judge George W. Anderson, cited in Elwood Jones, "Free Speech and Laws in Derogation Thereof," *The Central Law Journal*, November 18, 1921.

these years, but fed the public's interest in free speech by provoking high-profile test cases that kept constitutional rights in the news, and on the court's docket. Publishing a handbook to help radical speakers to better defend themselves from state prosecution, the ACLU advised, "Where meetings have been interfered with by official lawlessness, stage a protest meeting for the earliest practicable date." Roger Baldwin and other ACLU leaders practiced what they preached, holding free speech protests in some of the most violent battle zones in the early 1920s war between labor and capital. Confronted by the power of well-organized publicity and lawyers eager to bring First Amendment cases to court, many mayors and police chiefs folded, allowing unpopular speakers to have their say.[41]

On safer ground, the ACLU fought a lengthy battle against the City of New York, which denied them the use of their school buildings to hold a meeting to discuss "old-fashioned free speech." The Superintendent of Schools declared that "men that belong to an organization that advocates 'Red,' un-American principles" should not be allowed to use classrooms that the public had created in order to teach "love of American institutions." While the ACLU lost its appeal all the way to the state Commissioner of Education and the state Supreme Court, it won support from the city's teachers' union and other civic groups. By keeping the case in the headlines for months in 1926, the ACLU gave wider publicity to their cause than anything they might have said at their ill-fated meeting.[42]

Through the 1920s, schools became a particularly important new battleground for free speech fights, one part of the decade's intense culture wars. Many state legislatures and local school boards instituted loyalty oaths for their teachers, others mandated Bible reading, while some signed on to William Jennings Bryan's anti-evolution crusade by banning the teaching of Darwinian biology. At the college level, professors who held left-wing economic views voiced them only at the risk of their jobs, leading the ACLU in 1925 to declare that "invasion of teaching by the forces of intolerance" posed the greatest challenge to civil liberty in these years. College professors organized to fight back, particularly through their disciplinary associations, and the American Association of University Professors. Scholars also began to turn their attention to free speech questions as an area for further study. Harold Lasswell and others founded a new field of communication studies that conducted a searching examination of mass psychology, and looked for new ways to understand a

---

[41] "Radicals Issue Etiquette Guide for Police Raids," *Atlanta Constitution*, March 16, 1924; "Baldwin Convicted for Strike Meeting," NYT, April 1, 1925.

[42] NYT, May 19, 1926; "Free Speech and the Schools," *The Independent*, June 5, 1926.

very modern problem—government and corporate sponsored propaganda that distorted the democratic marketplace of ideas.[43]

In the free speech fights that shaped this decade, the rights of the Ku Klux Klan proved a distinctive challenge for liberals. In many places where the Klan enjoyed power, its members eagerly stifled the dissent of its ideological enemies. An expose in the *New York World*, and the annual reports of the ACLU, cataloged many of these offenses, including lynchings, floggings and the intimidation and disruption of meetings. In Oregon, voters passed a Klan-sponsored initiative to require all residents to send their children to public schools, a blow aimed specifically at the religious freedom of Catholic families who supported parochial schools. The Supreme Court overturned the Oregon measure, but none doubted that the Klan continued to pose a serious threat to democratic freedoms wherever it could muster the political or physical power.

But in some parts of the country, particularly cities where Catholics enjoyed the majority, the Klan found itself the victim, rather than the perpetrator, of repression. State and city governments threatened to withhold charters, passed laws banning the wearing of masks and membership in "secret societies," denied the Klan parade permits, and in some cases supported police or vigilante violence against Klan meetings. Mayor James Curley of Boston banned the Klan from gathering in his city, declaring a zero tolerance policy for "this creature of the night, which shames Christianity, insults Americanism, assails liberty and fosters treason." When the ACLU protested, Curley lectured them: "Your conception of what constitutes freedom of public assembly is untenable and far-fetched, and ... would open the door to disorder, revolution and anarchy." To which the ACLU replied, "You are evidently a believer in free speech only for your friends." While discomforting some of their liberal allies, the American Civil Liberties Union threatened to take Boston to court, and likewise offered the Klan legal support in similar conflicts across the country.[44]

At the other end of the political spectrum, communists felt no remorse about disrupting the meetings of their political rivals on the left, showing a contempt for the value of free speech that frustrated Roger Baldwin and others at the ACLU who had worked so hard to defend the speech rights of these political sectarians. Widely denounced as the legal arm of America's Bolshevik revolutionaries, the free speech radicals found their faith in America's constitutional liberties mocked by the very communists whose rights they defended, who declared the ACLU's faith in constitutional rights to free speech both naïve and bourgeois.

---

[43] "Clash over Free Speech in Sociological [*sic*] Session," *Washington Post*, December 29, 1923; Harold Lasswell, *Propaganda Technique in the World War* (New York, 1927).

[44] ACLU, *Free Speech in 1925* (1925–26) 19; Finan, 53–8; *Boston Globe*, October 6, 1923; *Chicago Tribune*, July 12, 1926.

"While we thoroughly disagree with the Communist attitude toward free speech," Roger Baldwin concluded, "we shall defend their right to meet and speak as they choose."[45]

In the intense economic and culture wars of the 1920s, civil libertarians found their principles tested by the intolerance of warring partisans on the right and left. But advocates of free speech also complained about the general apathy of the public toward social justice. As Roger Baldwin put it, "Intolerance is entrenched because so few people care about public issues. The right to drink agitates a good many of them, but the right to think hasn't much interest to people who have nothing to say." As it worked to create a nationwide network of lawyers willing to take on civil liberties cases, the ACLU thought that many shied away for fear that it might hurt their business. "The old tradition of the American bar apparently died with the war," the ACLU complained, "like most of our libertarian traditions."[46]

Surveying the struggle for civil liberties in the Harding era, H.L. Mencken declared that Americans loved to think of themselves as champions of free speech, but that this was only one of the country's "master delusions." On the contrary, he argued after watching the Scopes trial, "they are actually almost unanimously against it. It would be difficult, indeed, to find any record of a free people who went to greater trouble and expense to put it down." Mencken offered plenty of evidence to back his troubling claim that, in the 1920s, "the liberties envisioned by the fathers are being rooted out of the bill of rights." He noted the government's wartime and Red Scare attempts to silence "political heresy," the democratic "mob's ... fear of ideas" that he saw in the Klan, the fundamentalist war on evolution, the spreading demand for teacher loyalty oaths, and even the communists' attempts to break up socialist meetings.[47]

And yet Mencken's acidic contempt for the foes of free speech reflected a new cultural interest, at least among those moderns who fancied themselves members of the "smart set" in a vigorous defense of free expression. Mencken idolized few heroes, but he praised the leaders of the ACLU for waging a "gallant fight" for first principles. While they deserve credit for their sometimes lonely struggle, pushing against the tide of conservative public opinion, in fact they were the vanguard of a growing civil liberties movement, and a wider cultural respect for tolerance and dissent—a shift in opinion among all those Americans who had been first alarmed, and then energized by the forces of reaction that swept the

---

[45] "Say Workers' Party Denies Free Speech," *Washington Post*, March 27, 1925; Baldwin cited in Samuel Walker, *In Defense of American Liberties: A History of the ACLU* (Carbondale, 1998) 65.

[46] ACLU, *A Year's Fight for Free Speech* (1923).

[47] H.L. Mencken, "On Free Speech," *Chicago Tribune*, August 9, 1925.

country after 1917. Thus the Harding and Coolidge years were marked by high-profile standoffs between the guardians of an older order, and those "moderns" who fashioned themselves to be the advocates of greater tolerance and new freedoms—the critics of fundamentalism and prohibition, advocates of birth control, sexual liberation and greater gender equality, labor radicals and the artistic avant-garde.

And so, when Roger Baldwin surveyed the landscape of the Coolidge years, he had to concede that free speech rights had expanded significantly for political radicals since Harding had taken office in 1921. Mob violence and lynching had decreased, the Klan seemed "on the road to oblivion," and new voices appeared in academia, the courts and the mainstream press to defend a more expansive view of the individual rights guaranteed by the Constitution.

Still, Baldwin never paused to savor this accomplishment. Burned by years of conflict behind him, and aware of many of the battles that loomed ahead, he concluded that more speech was tolerated by the middle of the decade only because there was "not much listening."[48]

---

[48] Annual report cited in NYT, August 8, 1926; *New York Amsterdam News*, August 8, 1928.

Chapter 2

The FBI and the Politics of Anti-Communism, 1920–1945: A Prelude to Power

Athan Theoharis

The years 1920–45 proved to be pivotal for the Federal Bureau of Investigation (FBI). During this period, the Bureau evolved from a minor agency having limited influence to a powerful agency that profoundly, if at times indirectly, affected national policy and the political culture. This shift can be graphically captured in statistics recording the growth in the FBI's personnel and appropriations. Created by executed order of Attorney General Charles Bonaparte in 1908 as the investigation division of the Department of Justice, the Bureau of Investigation (formally renamed the FBI in 1935) then had only 34 agents funded by the Department's contingency funds. Its personnel and appropriations increased at first steadily and then dramatically in subsequent years: from 161 and $455,698 in 1914, to 630 and $2,272,059 in 1919, declining to 501 and $2,184,168 in 1925, only to rebound to 821 and $298,520 in 1932, increasing further to 1,580 and $5,000,000 in 1936, to 2,441 and $8,775,000 in 1940 and finally exploding to 11,792 and $44,197,146 in 1945.[1]

The creation of the Bureau in 1908 was the product of the changes in national policy adopted during the so-called Progressive Era. During these years (1901–14, federal regulatory powers expanded with the passage in 1906, for example, of the Pure Food and Drug and Meat Inspection Acts, while the federal government assuming a policing role, formerly the exclusive responsibility of local and state police, with the enactment of the White Slave Traffic (or Mann) Act in 1910. Federal powers, nonetheless, remained limited, reflected in the Bureau's minimal growth and appropriations between 1908 and 1914. Most American and majorities in Congress continued to oppose a powerful central government, fearing that such a development would threaten states' rights and privacy rights.

---

[1]   Athan Theoharis, *The FBI & American Democracy: A Brief Critical History* (Lawrence, 2004), 173–4.

These concerns resurfaced in strengthened form during the early 1920s, triggered by a series of dramatic revelations about the Bureau's surveillance activities during World War I and the immediate post-war years. Following U.S. entry into World War I in 1917, Congress acted to ensure military victory and address a perceived internal security threat by enacting the Conscription, Espionage and Sedition Acts. These acts expanded the Bureau's investigative responsibilities. Nonetheless, Bureau agents overreacted when conducting mass dragnet raids in New York City, ostensibly to enforce the draft registration requirements of the Conscription Act, by indiscriminately apprehending hundreds of individuals (including prominent businessmen) who had simply failed to carry their draft registration cards. Less controversial, because not fully known at the time, Bureau agents monitored thousands of pacifist, ethnic (German- and Irish-American) and radical citizens whose sole crime involved their public opposition to U.S. involvement in World War I (including Socialist leader Eugene Debs, radical labor leader William Haywood, U.S. Senator Robert LaFollette, Irish nationalist Eamon de Valera and settlement house leader Jane Addams).

Bureau agents during the early post-war era, moreover, exceeded their law enforcement responsibilities and in so doing provoked widespread public criticism. Following the 1918 end of the war, in response to the 1917 Russian Revolution and the formation of American Communist parties in 1919, in January, 1920 Bureau agents apprehended thousands attending meetings of the Communist and Communist Labor parties. The purpose of these mass dragnet raids was to effect the deportation of alien radicals under the provisions of the 1918 Immigration Act. While initially welcomed, the so-called Palmer Raids soon became mired in controversy in part because the Bureau lacked any authority to enforce the Act, which was the responsibility of the Immigration Bureau of the Department of Labor. In the course of the raids, moreover, Bureau agents arrested American citizens (not simply alien radicals), held the detainees in inhumane conditions and contravened deportation hearing rules. Bureau agents also monitored the roles of radicals in the 1919 and 1922 coal, steel and railway strikes and shared information about the identities and plans of labor union activists with corporate executives. They similarly shared information about the political activities of Communist leaders with conservative activitists (Richard Whitney of the American Defense Society) and the Michigan State police, thus exceeding their limited authority to assist federal law enforcement. These publicized abuses reached a crescendo in 1923–24 with sensational revelations that Bureau agents had monitored prominent members of Congress (including breaking into and wiretapping their offices) who had played leadership roles in the Congressional investigation of the so-called Teapot Dome scandal, an investigation that uncovered the corrupt actions of the Harding administration's Secretary of the Interior and Attorney General.

Cumulatively, these disclosures, and particularly the Teapot Dome scandal, created a political crisis which President Calvin Coolidge sought to quell by firing Attorney General Harry Daugherty in March 1924, replacing him with the respected dean of the Columbia Law School Harlan Fiske Stone.[2] On assuming office, Stone quickly moved to address the publicized Bureau abuses of power, firing Bureau director William Burns and appointing as his replacement Burns's 29-year-old assistant J. Edgar Hoover (whose appointment was probationary and made permanent only in December, 1924).

More substantively, Stone acted to preclude future abuses by dissolving the General Intelligence Division (the Bureau unit which had compiled dossiers on radicals and liberals), banning wiretapping, and prohibiting the monitoring of political activities. Henceforth, Stone announced, Bureau investigation would be limited to uncovering violations of federal statutes and would be subject to the supervision of an assigned Assistant Attorney General. "A secret police," he warned, "may become a menace to free government ... because it carries with it the possibility of abuses of power which are not always quickly apprehended or understood." In the future, Stone ordered that the Bureau not concern itself with the "political or other opinions of individuals," but "only with their conduct and then only such as conduct as is forbidden by the laws of the United States. When a police system passes beyond these limits, it is dangerous to the proper administration of justice and to human liberty, which it should be our first concern to cherish. Within them, it should rightly be a terror to the wrongdoer."[3]

Stone's actions succeeded, foreclosing any Congressional response as members of Congress tacitly agreed that the disclosed abuses had been due to deficiencies in oversight by attorneys general and the personal character of the agents involved. The newly appointed Acting Director moved quickly to implement Stone's directives. Senior Bureau officials were advised that henceforth "the activities of the bureau are to be limited strictly to violations of the federal statutes." (Hoover reaffirmed this position in Congressional testimony and when questioned as to when he had instituted these restrictions

---

[2]   The history of the Bureau's creation and subsequent controversial action is more thoroughly explored in Athan Theoharis and John Cox, *The Boss: J. Edgar Hoover and the Great American Inquisition* (Philadelphia, 1988); Curt Gentry, *J. Edgar Hoover: The Man and the Secrets* (New York, 1991), 70–123; Richard Gid Powers, *The Life of J. Edgar Hoover* (New York, 1987); William Thomas, *Unsafe for Democracy: World War I and the U.S. Justice Department's Covert Campaign to Suppress Dissent* (Madison, 2008).

[3]   Sanford Unger, *FBI* (Boston, 1975), 41–9; Frank Donner, *The Age of Surveillance* (New York, 1980), 12–47; Memo; Stone to Hoover, March 13, 1924, FBI 62–8782.

replied "within the last month.") Hoover also instituted a system to evaluate the conduct of all Bureau employees (including their deportment and personal lives), gave preference to applicants holding law or accounting degrees and based on their "general character, personality and integrity," terminated a number of current agents "for the best interest of the service," required that all non-Bureau employees holding "any official property" to return same and then "cancelled any official designation or connection which they may have had with the Bureau."[4]

Despite the probationary nature of his appointment and Stone's intent to limit Bureau investigations to violations of federal law and further to subject them to review by senior Justice Department officials, Hoover nonetheless devised a way to ensure that Bureau agents would continue to monitor radical activities. An ardent anti-Communist who was convinced that Communists threatened the nation's security, Hoover wanted to ensure that the Bureau could learn about the plans an associates of Communist activists.

His intent to do so was indirectly highlighted by his qualified assurance of October 1924 to Assistant Attorney General William Donovan (the Department official responsible for supervising Bureau investigations) that the "actions of Communists and other ultra radicals have not up to the present time constituted a violation of the Federal statutes and consequently the Department of Justice, theoretically had no right to investigate such actions as there has been no violation of the Federal laws".[5]

Hoover did not then admit that Bureau agent sought to anticipate future law violations—implying only that they should be permitted to do so insofar as radicals might in the future violate federal laws. Indeed, the acting director resorted to two complementary measures to ensure the desired continued monitoring. First, whenever conservative citizens, local and state police and various federal agencies (Customs, Treasury and State) reported to the Bureau about the detailed activities of Communists, the information was filed by Hoover, who personally responded to senders that while the Bureau could not act absent a reported violation of federal law that he appreciated the information and welcomed future submissions. Moreover, Bureau agents were required to clip press reports on Communist meetings and activities and to personally attend meetings of Communist or radical organizations. In the latter case, agents did not in their reports admit to having conducted an investigation, claiming they had obtained the information from a "very reliable and confidential source" or similar wording. In addition, Hoover devised a special reporting system, "personal and confidential letters," which were to be employed by heads of FBI

---

[4] Theoharis and Cox, *The Boss*, 85–91.
[5] Donner, *Age of Surveillance*, 46–7.

field offices whenever reporting on a matter to be "brought to my [Hoover's] personal attention before communication is opened and indexed" in the FBI headquarters file room (thus ensuring such information would not be indexed in the FBI's central records system). Use of this special communication, Hoover stressed, should be confined to matters of a "highly confidential nature which are deemed of sufficient importance to be brought to the Director's personal attention," and specifically about "subversive activities."[6]

Hoover might have successfully circumvented Stone's prohibition of Bureau investigations of political activities. Nonetheless, collection of such information about radical activists served no useful purpose as no evidence was uncovered of violation of federal laws. In at least one instance in 1932, however, the acquired information was exploited in an unsuccessful attempt to advance the political interests of incumbent President Herbert Hoover. Elected in 1928, Hoover had then commanded a positive reputation as a brilliant administrator and innovative reformer. By 1932, his positive reputation was shattered, the consequence of the October 1929 stock market crash which ushered in the Great Depression. Hoover was then viewed as an uncaring President unwilling to address the dire economic situation of many Americans. The President's response to the so-called Bonus March of 1932 symbolized this critical assessment of his presidency.

That summer, World War I veterans converged on Washington, D.C. to pressure the Congress to enact legislation whereby bonuses, approved by Congress in 1924 for payment in 1945, would be paid immediately. Camping out in the Anacostia section of Washington, the embittered veterans were physically dispersed by federal troops commanded by General Douglas MacArthur. The image of federal troops using force to disperse economically disadvantaged veterans became a public disaster for the Hoover administration. In an attempt to rebut this image and as justification for the military, President Hoover turned to Bureau Director Hoover for evidence that a Communist-engineered riot bent on provoking revolution had been suppressed. Assistant Attorney General Nujent Dodds, on September 1, 1932, accordingly asked Director Hoover for a summary of "all information" about the Communists' role "now in the hands" of the Justice Department. Although Bureau agents had monitored Communist activities throughout the 1920s, and more specifically Communist participation in the march, Bureau officials were unable to provide the President with the desired confirmation of a Communist revolutionary plot or evidence that Communists had played a leadership role in the march.[7]

---

[6]   Theoharis and Cox, *The Boss*, 92–4, SAC Letters file FBI 66–3286; Athan Theoharis (ed.), *From the Secret Files of J. Edgar Hoover* (Chicago, 1991), 3–4.

[7]   Donald Lisio, *The President and Protest: Hoover, Conspiracy and the Bonus Riot* (Columbia, 1974), 241, 246–68, 250, 310.

The Bonus March, insofar as participants were traditionally conservative veterans, reflected how the Depression crisis had brought profound changes in the nation's politics. Not only did many Americans begin to question the traditional tenets of limited government, but a reinvigorated radical movement had emerged with American Communists playing a visible and substantial role in the emergence of more powerful labor union and civil rights movements.

The politics of the 1930s was also shaped by popular (and, more importantly, Administration) concerns about the perceived influence of Nazi Germany and the Soviet Union over the American Communist and fascist movements. Indeed, President Franklin Roosevelt's concerns about this suspected influence led him in August 1936 to invite FBI Director Hoover to meet with him at the White House. Hoover was invited, according to his memorandum on this meeting of August 24, 1936, to discuss the "question of subversive activities" in the country, "particularly Fascism and Communism." The timing and catalyst to Roosevelt's invitation was his receipt of a series of reports sent to him by the FBI and the military intelligence that alarmingly recounted the potential espionage and sabotage threat posed by such elements. Hoover began the meeting by emphasizing only the Communist threat, particularly as stemming from Communist influence in labor union organizing and strikes. Hoover cited the actions of International Longshoremen and Warehousemen union President Harry Bridges, United Mine Workers President John L. Lewis and Newspaper Guild President Haywood Broun. "The Communists," Hoover warned, "planned to get control of these three [unions] and by doing so they would be able at any time to paralyze the county by stopping all shipping in and out" through Bridges' union, stop the operation of industry through Lewis' miners and stop publication of any newspapers through the Newspaper Guild. In addition, Hoover, added Communists had "inspired" recent suspect activities in various federal departments and in the National Labor Relations Board, and the "Communist Internationale in Moscow" had instructed all American Communists to vote for Roosevelt in the 1936 election because the Republican nominee was "opposed to class warfare."

Worried about this alleged foreign-inspired threat, President Roosevelt thereupon expressed interest in obtaining a "broad picture of the general movement and its activities as may affect the economic and political life of the country as a whole." The FBI Director, after pointing out "there is at the present time no government organization which is getting any so-called 'general intelligence' upon the subject," referred to a 1916 statute which he contended authorized the FBI to "investigate any matter referred to it by the Department of State." Expressing his reluctance to seek a "formal' request from the State Department because of the prospect of "leaks therein," Roosevelt proposed that the two of them and Secretary of State Cordell Hull meet the next day. At this second meeting, Roosevelt demanded that this matter "be handled quite confidentially," rebuffing Hull's willingness to submit such a request in writing. The President then orally directed Hoover to "speak to" the Attorney General "about this matter" and for Hull to "talk over the tactics to be followed in this particular aspect, with the Attorney General."[8]

In effect, the FBI had been secretly authorized by the President to conduct non-criminal "intelligence" investigations, that is investigations not predicated on suspected federal statutory violations. Roosevelt's oral directive, however, merely expanded what was already an ongoing practice whereby FBI agents actively monitored the activities of Communists and other radicals, a practice confirmed by Hoover's references during the August 24 meeting to labor activists. Nonetheless, the President's interest in secrecy, and further his decision without having first discussed the matter with Attorney General Homer Cummings, ostensibly Hoover's boss, did have one unintended consequence enabling Hoover to move beyond the President's more limited objective.

Hoover first briefed Cummings about Roosevelt's decision on September 10, 1936 (although he misleadingly dated the meeting as having taken place on September 1). Roosevelt, Hoover informed Cummings, had requested the FBI to investigate "subversive activities in this country, including fascism and communism." Cummings did not even attempt to learn more about Roosevelt's narrower purpose (that is to ascertain foreign decision and control) and simply verbally directed Hoover "proceed with this investigation" but "of course' to handle it in a "most discreet and confidential manner."[9] Significantly, Cummings did not institute a formal oversight system whereby Department officials would evaluate the resultant investigations to ensure they were confined to ascertaining German and Soviet control over the American fascist and Communist movements.

Indeed, prior to Hoover's briefing of Cummings, FBI Assistant Director Edward Tamm spelled out the broader targets of planned FBI "intelligence" investigations: specifically "Maritime industry, Government affairs, steel industry, coal industry, newspaper field, clothing, garment and fur industry, general strike activities, Armed forces, educational institutions, general activities—Communist and affiliated organizations, Fascisti, Anti-Fascisti movements, and activities in Organized Labor organizations." FBI agents were

---

[8]   Confidential memos, Hoover, August 24 and August 25, 1936, Franklin D. Roosevelt folder, Official and Confidential File of FBI Director J. Edgar Hoover (hereafter Hoover O & C).

[9]   Strictly Confidential memo, Hoover to Tamm, September 10, 1936, Franklin D. Roosevelt folder, Hoover O & C.

30 *Little 'Red Scares'*

to obtain information "from all possible sources" (including reading radical publications) and recruiting informers.[10]

Both before and, more intensively after, 1936, FBI "intelligence" investigations centered on individuals and organizations which actively (and publicly) challenged current economic and social conditions. One such target, not surprisingly in view of Hoover's comments during the August, 1936 meeting, was International Longshoreman and Warehousemen union head Harry Bridges, whose political and labor activities had been and continued to be closely monitored, especially his willing collaboration with Communists in planning and executing strikes and his sympathetic comments about Soviet policies. FBI officials in 1938 and 1940 also unsuccessfully sought to prove that Bridges was a Communist Party member, evidence that could be used to help deport him during Immigration Bureau hearings on his alien status. The FBI's covert monitoring of Bridges activities and associations, had one embarrassing consequence, when Bridges inadvertently learned that FBI agent had bugged his hotel room during a visit to New York City in 1941—a discovery published by the liberal newspaper *PM*.[11]

Bridges activities were monitored because of his suspect associations with Communists as a militant labor union and political activist. For the same reason, from the early 1920s John L. Lewis was also closely monitored, first in his role as president of the United Mine Workers union and then given his central role during the mid-to-late 1930s in forming and then assuming the presidency of the Congress of Industrial Organizations (CIO). Lewis' sin was his willing acceptance of the assistance of Communists in these two unions' organizing and strike activities, although (unlike Bridges) he did not sympathize with or endorse Soviet policies. Significantly, FBI officials' interest in Lewis began well before Roosevelt's 1936 directive, dating from his role in the 1919–20 coal strike. This interest intensified when Lewis became CIO president. His relationship with Mexican leader Alejandro Carrillo and strident opposition to President Roosevelt's foreign policy in the late 1930s and early 1940s, moreover, led to the FBI's interception of, at minimum, two of his international telephone calls in 1938 and 1940 and the preparation of a 1940 blind memorandum (a special records procedure that disguised the FBI as the source) that detailed Lewis'

---

[10] U.S. Senate Select Committee to Study Government Operations with respect to Intelligence Activities, *Hearings on FBI*, vol. 6, 94th Cong., 1st Sess., 1975 562–3.

[11] Charles Larrowe, *Harry Bridges, The Rise and Fall of Radical Labor in the United States* (New York, 1972), 113, 140–41, 223–48; Stanley Kutler, *The American Inquisition: Justice and Injustice in the Cold War* (New York, 1982), 120–21, 135–6; Ann Fagan Ginger, *Carol Weiss King: Human Rights Lawyer, 1895–1952* (Niwit, CO, 1993), 240, 312–13, 343–4.

relations with Carillo and Communists. While it is unclear whether Hoover shared this information with the White House in 1940 (given Lewis' strident opposition to Roosevelt's re-election campaign), he did sent a flurry of reports to the White House in 1943 describing Lewis's contacts and relations with critics of the administration and role in that year's coal strike.[12]

Hoover's obsession over the activities of labor union activists at the very time when organized labor first became powerful during the mid-1930s not surprisingly extended to the recently organized United Automobile Workers (UAW) and one of its dynamic leaders, Walter Reuther. Reuther's activities were closely monitored as well as his expressed sympathy for the Soviet Union and his willingness to work with Communists actively involved in the UAW's organizing and strike activities. In 1940, in fact, FBI officials listed Reuther (and his brother Victor) on the FBI special Custodial Detention index (an index of those to be detained in event of war or national emergency as perceived threats to national security). In 1941, FBI officials sent a detailed report on Reuther's Communist associations to White House aide Edwin Watson, William Knudsen (then a member of the National Defense Advisory Board and a former General Motors executive) and the conservative Democratic Congressman Eugene Cox.[13]

FBI officials' concerns about Reuther's UAW leadership led them to also monitor Maurice Sugar, a left-wing (Socialist) activist and key UAW legal adviser. FBI agents also closely followed the activities of other radical attorneys, including Carol Weiss King (also listed for Custodial Detention), who was intensively monitored due to her prominent role in defending Bridges during his deportation hearings, as well as her other activities involving Communists and radical activists, such as organizing the radical International Juridical Association and editing its newsletter. Other attorneys who attracted FBI interest including King's associate Joseph Brodsky, CIO general counsel and future Supreme Court Justice Arthur Goldberg, Justice Department attorney and future Yale University law professor Thomas Emerson and Assistant Solicitor General and future Columbia University law professor Herbert Wechsler. FBI officials also launched an intensive investigation of the National Lawyers Guild dating

---

[12] Melvyn Dubofsky and Warren Van Tine, *John L. Lewis: A Biography* (Urbana, 1977), 39, 210, 256–309; Athan Theoharis, "Labor and Civil Liberties: Senator Laxalt's FBI Charter Bill," *First Principles*, 6 (1981), 3–4; Theoharis, "Introduction," in Theoharis (ed.), *Beyond the Hiss Case: The FBI, Congress and the Cold War* (Philadelphia, 1982), 18.

[13] Nelson Lichtenstein, *The Most Dangerous Man in Detroit: Walter Reuther and the Fate of American Labor* (New York, 1995), 45, 50–51, 53–4, 166–7, 479 n40.

32   *Little 'Red Scares'*

from its 1936 formation, in the course of which FBI agents wiretapped and burglarized the Guild's Washington, D.C. office.[14]

This focus on individuals promoting social change also extended to radical U.S. Congressman Vito Marcantonio (listed for Custodial Detention), whose associations with Communists and criticisms of President Roosevelt's foreign policy during 1939–41 were duly recorded. Other FBI targets included the New York-based American Labor Party, artist and illustrator Rockwell Kent, University of Michigan student activist Ann Fagan, and the left-liberal newspaper *The Nation*, whose monitoring dated from 1921 but intensified with the publication of articles between 1937 and 1943 criticizing the FBI and calling for an investigation of the Bureau's abuses.

Individuals and organizations which actively challenged racial segregation and called for racial equality were similarly the subject of FBI investigation. Beginning in 1919–20, FBI agents monitored the activities of black nationalist leader Marcus Garvey and his United Negro Improvement Association, the editors of the African-American newspaper *The Messenger* and the NAACP's periodical *Crisis*, the NAACP itself and its adherents and the African Global Brotherhood. Such investigations continued throughout the 1920s. Then, in 1942 the FBI launched a massive investigation, code-named RACON, with the stated aim of uncovering suspected "foreign inspired agitation among American Negroes." The militancy of African-Americans during the war years and the outbreak of race riots in Detroit and Los Angeles underpinned this intensive, nationwide FBI initiative to "keep currently abreast with such agitation and to be cognizant of the identities of groups and individuals responsible for the same." FBI officials were specifically ordered to ascertain the NAACP's "connection with the Communist Party and other Communist controlled organizations."[15]

The RACON investigation captures the underlying political definition of "subversive activities" of senior FBI officials, and their antipathy towards

---

[14]   Theoharis, "Labor and Civil Liberties," 3–4; Christopher Johnson, *Maurice Sugar: Law, Labor and the Left in Detroit, 1912–1950* (Detroit, 1988), 48–9; Ginger, *Carol Weiss King*, 74, 160, 234–5, 325–7, 344, 355, 368–69, 371, 374–6, 389–90, 401–404; Percival Bailey, "The Case of the National Lawyers Guild," in Theoharis (ed.), *Beyond*, 134, 165 n17; Theoharis and Cox, *The Boss*, p. 13.

[15]   Kutler, *American Inquisition*, 101–102; Theoharis, "In House Cover-up: Researching FBI Files," and Waltzer, "The FBI, Congressman Vito Marcantonio and the American Labor Party," both in Theoharis, *Beyond*, 26, 31, 183–8; Ginger, *Carol Weiss King*, 371, 401–404; Kenneth O'Reilly, *"Racial Matters": The FBI's Secret File on Black Americans, 1960–1972* (New York, 1989), 12–14, 17–20; Robert Hill (ed.), *The FBI's RACON: Racial Conditions in the United States during World War II* (Boston, 1995), xiii, 5, 12–13, 15–17, 19 22–3, 25–6, 75–6, 622–38, 675, 678, 679; Penn Kimball, "The History of the 'Nation' According to the FBI," *The Nation*, 242 (March 22, 1986), 399–411.

movements and individuals advocating social change or challenging the conservative principles that, until the New Deal years, had determined a national consensus (in this case on race relations). As ardent anti-Communists, senior FBI officials suspected that movements which challenged racial segregation or a corporate-dominated economy, and their adherents, were influenced by or subservient to the Soviet Union. Their efforts to establish such a link were boosted by a secret May, 1940 directive by President Roosevelt authorizing FBI wiretapping, a directive issued out of his narrower concerns over foreign based (Nazi and Soviet) threats to national security.

Although 1934 Congressional action and recent Supreme Court rulings had seemingly outlawed wiretapping, Roosevelt contended that the Court had never sought to ban such action in "grave matters involving the defense of the nation." Therefore, given the government's need to anticipate sabotage and "fifth column activities," he authorized the FBI, subject to the Attorney General's prior review and approval on a case by case basis, to wiretap the "conversations or other communications of persons suspected of subversive activities against the government of the United States, including suspected spies," with such installations to be held to a "minimum" and limited "insofar as possible to aliens."[16] Sensitive to the political and legal ramifications of the President's decision to circumvent the Supreme Court and yet required to review and approve each proposed FBI wiretap, Attorney General Robert Jackson advised Hoover (as recorded by the latter) that "he would have no detailed record kept concerning the cases in which wiretapping would be utilized," but rather Hoover alone "would maintain a memorandum book" in his office "listing the time, place and case in which this procedure is to be utilized."[17]

Jackson's decision not to maintain records of approved wiretaps, and his further failure either to limit the duration or require the re-authorization of approved taps, repeated the actions of Attorney General Cummings in September, 1936. In effect, his ideologically motivated subordinate was allowed to determine the duration as well as the purpose of FBI wiretapping. Subsequent attorneys general would learn about ongoing wiretaps only if briefed by Hoover. Furthermore, the lack of close oversight invited the ambitious Hoover to circumvent the President's prior review and approval requirement and on his own authorize especially sensitive wiretaps.

FBI wiretaps continued, some for decades, even when no information was obtained about foreign-directed sabotage or espionage plans, FBI officials

---

[16]   Confidential Memo, Roosevelt to Jackson, May 21, 1940, Wiretapping Uses Folder, Hoover O & C.

[17]   Confidential Memo, Hoover to Tolson, Tamm and Clegg, May 28, 1940, Wiretapping Uses Folder, Hoover O & C.

having found such taps useful because they provided insights into the political (and at times personal) activities of the approved target. Thus, the Soviet embassy, Communist Party headquarters and branch offices, and prominent Communists were wiretapped. Yet, the FBI's far more numerous targets included labor unions, civil rights organizations and radical activists. Among these were Harry Bridges, John L. Lewis, the NAACP, March on Washington Movement, Alabama People's Educational Association, Congress on Industrial Organization Council, CIO Maritime Committee, National Maritime Union, UAW, United Mine Workers and a host of German émigré writers (Bertolt Brecht, Thomas Mann, Heinrich Mann, Helene Weigel, Berthold Viertel, Anna Seghers, and Bodo and Alma Uhse).[18]

Although decidedly incomplete, the known targets of FBI wiretaps and bugs does further confirm the ideological definition of "subversive activities" of the militantly anti-Communist senior FBI officials. And while these known wiretaps had been conducted pursuant to the Attorney General's approval, FBI officials on their own authorized other particularly sensitive wiretaps (sensitive because of their subjects—the administration's respectable critics and former White House aide Thomas Corcoran). Significantly, Hoover's insubordination in this instance is confirmed by preserved records originally maintained by FBI Assistant Director D. Milton Ladd (who headed the FBI's internal security division during World War II). These records document that senior FBI officials alone had authorized at least 15 wiretaps. These records are extant only because at his 1954 retirement Ladd transferred them to the secret office file maintained by FBI Assistant Director Louis Nichols and, for unknown reasons, Nichol's office file was not destroyed, unlike the office files of other assistant directors, which, pursuant to Hoover's March, 1953 order, were purged every six months.[19]

Hoover's insubordination when circumventing the intent of President Roosevelt's wiretapping directive was not exceptional. Emboldened by his

---

[18] The FBI's National Security Electronic Surveillance card file contains cards identifying the organizations tapped by the FBI during the 1940s. It also identified the individuals who had been wiretapped, but, when processing my Freedom of Information Act request, the FBI withheld all these cards on claimed "personal privacy" grounds. The FBI's wiretapping of German émigré writers was not exceptional but is confirmed by records released to Alexander Stephan. See his *"Communazis" FBI Surveillance of German Émigré Writers* (New Haven, 2000), 2, 20, 44, 467, 76, 117, 119–22, 125–7 195–6, 254–71. Other known FBI wiretap targets include Inga Arvad, Lillian Morehead and John O'Brien; see Athan Theoharis, "FBI Wiretapping; A Case Study of Bureaucratic Autonomy," *Political Science Quarterly*, 107 (1992), 107–11.

[19] Theoharis, "FBI Wiretapping," 106. On Hoover's office file destruction order, see Memo, Hoover to Tolson and 11 other FBI Assistant Directors, March 19, 1953, FBI 66-2095-100.

superiors (the President and Attorney General) interest in secrecy to preclude the discovery of their decision to expand the FBI's authority, Hoover in 1942 ordered FBI agents to conduct break-ins whether to install microphones or photograph the records of targeted individuals and organizations. This technique, senior FBI officials concluded, was "invaluable" because it advanced efforts to combat "subversive activities of a clandestine nature aimed at undermining and destroying our country" by enabling agents to obtain "otherwise unobtainable information" (obtainable, that is, through physical surveillance, wiretaps or recruiting informers). Privately conceding that break-ins were "clearly illegal," FBI officials accordingly concluded that "therefore it would be impossible to obtain legal sanction" (i.e. the approval of the Attorney General). This independent action, for this reason, was potentially suicidal. To foreclose this possibility, the wily FBI Director devised a special records procedure to ensure that this practice could not be discovered if the FBI was required to respond to a Congressional subpoena or court-ordered discovery motion. Before an agent could conduct a break-in, the heads of the FBI field offices had to obtain advance approval from Hoover or a designated FBI Assistant Director. Their written request had to "completely justify the need for the use of the technique [i.e. describe the value of conducting this operation] and at the same time assure that it can be safely used without any danger or embarrassment to the Bureau." Normally any written field office request to FBI headquarters would be serialized and indexed in the FBI's central records system, thereby create a record of its existence, but break-in requests and headquarters' approval were to bear the notation "do not file" to circumvent this general procedure. Instead they would be routed directly to the FBI Director's (or designate Assistant Director's) office and were subsequently to be destroyed. Field office directors, moreover, were to retain "informal" records of all such requests and FBI headquarters' approval in their office safe, which, because maintained separately and not "official" records, could be and in fact were destroyed after the regular semi-annual inspection of their field office's operations.[20] This sophisticated records destruction procedure enabled FBI agents to engage in recognizably illegal activities without discovery, and further ensured that these actions would not become known even by the Attorney General or the President.

Only carefully selected and specially trained agents could conduct break-ins. Furthermore, the preparation for and execution of break-ins were tightly planned operations. Members of a break-in squad (ranging from 8 to 10 agents depending upon the specific challenges posed by the target) would first case the

---

[20] Do Not File Memo, Sullivan to Deloach, July 19, 1966, Black Bag Jobs Folder, Hoover O & C.

premise of the targeted individual or organization to ascertain when it would normally be vacant and, in cases, to secure the support of a friendly janitor. Then, on the day of the break-in, one agent would act as supervisor maintaining contact by walkie-talkie with the other members of the squad. Two agents would conduct the actual break-in, with one responsible for retrieving the documents to be photographed and then returning them to their original place, and the second photographing them. The other agents would either safeguard the entrance to the building or would follow the resident to provide advance warning in case of an unexpected return.[21]

As with wiretaps, FBI break-ins extended beyond legitimate security threats. FBI agents did break into the offices of the Soviet Government Purchasing Commission (the Soviet agency stationed in the U.S. to expedite Lend-Lease deliveries), branch Communist Party offices, and the residences of prominent Communist Party activists. At minimum, however, other targets included the American Youth Congress, Washington Committee for Democratic Action, American Peace Mobilization, Independent Citizens of the Arts, Sciences and Professions, Veterans of the Abraham Lincoln Brigade, Negro Labor Victory Committee, Joint Anti-Fascist Refugee Committee, League of American Writers, American Slav Congress, Nationalist Party of Puerto Rico, International Workers Orders, Russian War Relief, American Association for a Democratic Germany, law offices of Carol Weiss King and the residences of a number of people, including Bertolt Brecht, Gerhart Eisler and Erwin Picator.[22]

The known targets of FBI wiretapping and break-ins confirm that senior FBI officials were motivated to exploit legitimate national security concerns to advance their own political agenda—namely, to contain efforts of individuals and organizations seeking to effect fundamental social, economic and political change. This essentially political objective differed from that of President Roosevelt, whose authorization (whether of intelligence operations or wiretapping) reflected a narrower purpose of anticipating and preventing foreign-directed espionage and sabotage operations.

The politically astute FBI Director accordingly purposefully conveyed to the President that the Bureau was acting to address a perceived international threat. Thus, in detailed reports to the White House in 1940 and 1941 Hoover assured Roosevelt that the FBI was fully informed about Soviet, German, French and Italian "espionage and counter-espionage operations" through "constant

---

[21]   Memo, name redacted agent to SAC New York, August 26, 1954, FBI 62-117166–131.

[22]   American Youth Congress and Department of Justice folders, Official and Confidential File of FBI Assistant Director Louis Nichols; Inga Arva folder, Hoover O & C; Surreptitious Entries file FBI 62-117166; Stephan, "*Communazis*", 20, 50, 199, 163, 254, 257.

observation and surveillance ... of known and suspected Agents" of their secret services and that FBI agents maintained a "careful check upon their "channels of communication, the sources of information, the methods of finance and other data." The "identification of all major representations" of these hostile governments, he added, "are known and their activities are under constant scrutiny."[23]

Hoover's follow-up reports to the White House, however, described only the interest of Soviet officials and American Communists in political or labor union activities. The FBI Director, for example, reported that Soviet officials were interested in the anti-Soviet activities of Americans of Baltic descent, Lend-Lease shipment allocations, the deportation hearings of labor union leader Bridges, the U.S. government's development of high octane gasoline, and Soviet funding of the American Communist Party. Hoover's reports on American Communists similarly disclosed that a secret Communist branch had been established in a CIO union in a Butte, Montana plant involved in military production and that Communist leaders Earl Browder and Steve Nelson were monitoring Bridges' deportation hearings, sought to recruit new Communist Party members, endorsed Soviet foreign policy objectives and actively supported civil rights and labor union organizing activities. More revealingly, Hoover's surveys on the FBI's espionage and counter-espionage operations, sent on a quarterly basis to the White House during World War II, contained a section on Communist activities. This section reported only that American Communists sought to recruit new members, distributed pro-Communist propaganda, were active in local and national politics, promoted Soviet foreign policy interests and were extensively involved in civil rights and labor organizing.[24]

The one exception to these essentially political reports was a May, 1943 Hoover memorandum to Roosevelt which informed the latter of the FBI's uncovering of a planned Soviet sabotage operation involving American Communist functionary Steve Nelson and Vassili Zubilin, the third secretary of the Soviet embassy in Washington. FBI agents in late 1942 had intercepted,

---

[23] Strictly Confidential Letter, Hoover to Watson, October 25 1940 and accompanying report, "Present Status of Espionage and Counter espionage operations of the FBI;" Personal and Confidential Letter, Hoover to Watson, May 23,141, both in OF 10-b, Roosevelt presidential library.

[24] See, for example, Personal and Confidential letters, Hoover to Hopkins, October 24, 1942, May 7, 1943, August 7, 1943, December 22, 1944 (and accompanying Quarterly Report on Espionage and Counterespionage Activities), December 24, 1944; Personal and Confidential letters, Hoover to Watson, November 16, 1939, August 3, 1943, September 30, 1943, October 27, 1943, March 21, 1944; General Intelligence Survey in the United States, September 1944 and January 1945, all in Of 10-B, Roosevelt presidential library. Letter, Hoover to Morgenthau, April 16, 1940 and Letter, Hoover to Morgenthau, April 14, 1940, Morgenthau Diaries, vol. 294, 231–2, Roosevelt presidential library.

through a wiretap of the Communist Party's New York headquarters, Browder's conversation alerting Nelson to a "sensitive" (but unspecified) future operation. Based on this discovery, FBI agents bugged Nelson's Oakland, California residence. The bug recorded that on April 10, 1943 Zubilin gave Nelson a large sum of money for the express purpose (as Hoover advised the White House) of placing Communists and "Comintern agents in industries engaged in secret war production" for the American government so that "information could be obtained for transmittal to the Soviet Union."[25]

Four months after the FBI's interception of this meeting, Hoover received an anonymous letter, written in Russian and postmarked Washington, D.C., in which the writer identified Zubilin, eight other Soviet officials stationed in the U.S. and American Communist Party officials Earl Browder and Boris Morros as spies.[26] Hoover responded to this advance intelligence about a planned Soviet espionage operation by authorizing a massive FBI investigation, code-named COMRAP (Comintern Apparatus). When conducting this investigation, FBI agents followed Nelson and the identified Soviet agents to learn about their actions and contacts. Nelson, the Soviet officials and their discovered contacts, moreover, were not only physically monitored by, in most cases, were the targets of wiretaps, bugs, break-ins and mail opening.

Despite the advantages of advance intelligence and the employment of intrusive, if illegal, investigative techniques, FBI agents uncovered no Soviet espionage operation. This is confirmed both by a February 6, 1948 CIA report based on a review of the FBI's COMRAP file and by an FBI agent's report of December 1944 summarizing the results of the FBI's by-then 17-month investigation. No example of a discovered espionage activity was cited in this report. Instead, the agent merely recounted that the targeted subjects (by then numbering 46) had sought to "influence" the American public to accept Soviet foreign policy objectives, had distributed "pro-Russian propaganda," had recruited American seaman for an "illegal courier system," had promoted "Soviet Russia's goal of world communism," had collected "political information of value" to the Soviet Union and had sought to ensure Communist infiltration of the federal bureaucracy in order to "secure information of value" for the American Communist Party.[27]

---

[25] Personal and Confidential Letter, Hoover to Hopkins, May 7, 1943, OF 10-B, Roosevelt presidential library.

[26] Robert Benson and Michael Warner (eds), *Venona: Soviet Espionage and the American Response* (Washington, 1966), 51–4.

[27] Benson and Warner, *Verona*, 104–15; Report, San Francisco, December 15, 1944; FBI 100-203581-3702. The Comrap investigation is covered in greater detail in Athan

This failure did not mean that the proposed espionage operation had been aborted. To the contrary, between 1943 and 1945 (as well as earlier during the 1930s) Soviet agents did recruit American Communists either to engage in atomic espionage or to steal other classified information (economic, diplomatic and military technology). This Soviet success during the World War II years was due in part to the fact that their highly trained agents had anticipated that they would be monitored and were fully aware that they were being monitored by FBI agents. Soviet telegraphic messages, sent from New York and Washington to Moscow were, dating from 1940, intercepted by U.S. military intelligence; these coded messages were eventually decrypted (partly in 1946 and more fully in succeeding years). These messages reveal that the Soviet agents were unconcerned that they were being followed by FBI agents and further describe the methods they adopted to preclude discovery. These included ensuring that their American recruits were trustworthy, were well trained in "conspiracy" (i.e., how to avoid discovery) and were "reliable undercover contacts" of the American Communist Party who "are not suspected" of espionage. The Soviet agents, moreover, used code names and not the "real surnames" of their recruits to safeguard their identities and further did not share these identities with other Soviet consular and embassy officials, avoided using consular or embassy telephones (suspecting they were tapped), used automobiles when arranging secret meetings (to counter FBI physical surveillance) and suspended a meeting when suspecting that they were being followed.[28]

These precautionary measures succeeded—partly because Soviet agents clearly had an interest in avoiding discovery. An additional factor for this FBI failure stemmed from the specific Communists whom FBI agents targeted: prominent Communists, thereby missing the low level Party activists (some of whom had completely severed any connection with the Party) who were actually recruited. This failure was in a sense predictable given the criteria shaping FBI surveillance decisions: namely, to focus on individuals who would be in a position to influence public policy, or who promoted economic and social equality or were publicly involved in organizing unions and strikes. This misplaced obsession over the Communist threat in fact underpinned two of the FBI's more important intensive investigations of the World War II era, one that focused on employees in the film industry, and the second on prominent German émigré writers who had fled Nazi Germany to settle in New York City and Los Angeles.

Theoharis, *The Quest for Absolute Security: The Failed Relations among U.S. Intelligence Agencies* (Chicago, 2007), 66–7.

[28] Athan Theoharis, *Chasing Spies: How the FBI Failed in Counterintelligence but Promoted the Politics of McCarthyism in the Cold War Years* (Chicago, 2002), 47–9.

FBI officials during the 1930s had become keenly interested in suspected Communist influence in Hollywood. Their concern (as with Bridges, Lewis and Reuther) centered on the militancy of the Hollywood employees who played key roles in the formation of the Screen Actors Guild and the strikes that swept across the industry that decade. FBI agents also closely monitored the involvement of these activists (in Hollywood as well as more generally nationally) in the so-called Popular Front politics of the late 1930s (collaborating with other radicals and liberals to promote, for example, a neutral, anti-interventionist foreign policy). By 1942, however, the concerns of senior FBI officials expanded as they had become troubled by what they concluded to be Communist influence in the production of movies. Indeed, Hoover that year ordered the FBI's field office to conduct what evolved into a massive 14-year duration investigation, code-named COMPIC (Communist Infiltration of the Motion Picture Industry).

In response, the Los Angeles field office predictably reported in February 1943 that American Communists had played a leadership role in Hollywood's labor unions and had further established "many Communist controlled front organizations." The Los Angeles office now identified a new threat, that of a "cultural group" of actors, writers and directors, who "appear to be under the control and direction" of the Party and followed the Party "line in all details." Agents were unable, the Los Angeles office nonetheless lamented, to "compile information showing the Communist connection of many" of those involved in the production of films or in the "large number of books, pamphlets, scenarios, plays, newsreels, speeches, letters, and other material—which indicate the enormous" Party effort to "get complete control of the motion picture industry and use it for propaganda purposes." As justification for this failure to establish the extent of Communist influence, the Los Angeles office claimed that local Communist leaders had purposefully created "closed units" for actors, writers and directors to disguise their connections with the Party and had also destroyed membership records and dues payment receipts."[29]

Four months later Hoover conveyed his dissatisfaction with this tentative report in light of the public and imminent release of 16 movies that year which he contended "demonstrated the extent to which the influence of the Communist Party has been felt in Hollywood" (specifically citing movies such as *Mission to Moscow*, based on the memoir of former American ambassador to the Soviet Union Joseph Davies, and *For Whom the Bell Tolls*, based on the Ernest Hemingway novel of that name). Accordingly, he demanded an "up to date" report on "significant developments" leading to the production of these films.

---

[29] Letter, Hoover to SAC Los Angeles, November 21, 1942, FBI 100-138754-2; Report, name redacted agent, February 18 1943, FBI 100-138754-4.

To meet this demand, on July 23, 1943 FBI agents broke into the office of the Los Angeles section of the Communist Party and photographed Party membership records. Identified Hollywood Communists were then correlated with films in which they had been involved and this list was reported to Hoover as a "complete memo of influence of Communists in motion pictures." Communists, the Los Angeles office now contended, had been able to exploit the "present apparent patriotic position of the party to recruit new members and control fellow travelers and sympathizers," had bored within the industry's unions, had "spread propaganda within and without unions to create sympathy for the Soviet Union and their system of government," had "force[d] the making" films depicting blacks in "most favorable terms as part of the general line of the Communist Party" and had been able to propagate un-American themes.[30]

Pleased by the Los Angeles office's more detailed reports, Hoover demanded the regular submission of future reports that would detail "all developments indicating Communist infiltration" of the movies and thereupon Los Angeles agents regularly broke into the Party's local office to update its records of known Hollywood Communists and to link them with films in which they played a role (as actors, writers, producers or stage hands).[31] Since Hollywood employees had no access to classified information and were not employed in an industry producing classified military technology, the acquired information advanced no legitimate security interest, especially as even pro-Soviet films could be viewed as war-time propaganda during the U.S–Soviet anti-Nazi alliance. Nor had the FBI uncovered evidence that the suspected Communists violated any federal statute. But, then, this intensive investigation had been launched out of concern over Communists in the production of films which could influence the political culture. In what proved an unsuccessful initiative to contain their perceived threat, in October 1944 Hoover briefed Attorney General Francis Biddle about the FBI's findings. Hoover falsely assured Biddle that FBI agents had conducted "no direct investigation," but added that the thought Biddle might be interested

---

[30] Letter, Hoover to SAC Los Angeles, June 21, 1943, FBI 100-138754-5; Teletypes, Hoover to SAC Los Angeles, July 3 and 9, 1943, FBI 100-137754-7 and 100-138754-10; Report, name redacted agent July 10, 1943, FBI 100-138754-9; Letters, Hood to FBI Director, May 14 and 27, 1943, July 10, 1943, August 9 1943, FBI 100-138754-9, 100-138754-13, 100-138754-14, 100-138754-19; Report, name redacted agent, February 16, 1944, FBI 100-138754-32; Report, name redacted agent, August 25, 1943, FBI 100-138754-21; Report, name redacted agent, October 11, 1943, FBI 100-138754-22.

[31] Letters, Hoover to SAC Los Angele, April 30 and May 4, 1944, FBI 100-158754-27 and 100-13875420; Letters, Hood to FBI Director June 28, 1947 and June 3, 1944, FBI 100-138754-173 and 100-138754-35; Memo, Coyne to Ladd, July 9 1947, FBI 100-138-754-unclear; Memo, Ladd to FBI Director FBI 100-138754-251x1; Report, name redacted agent, April 20, 1933, FBI 100-138754-26.

in the "attached data relating to the growing Communist influence" in the film industry, which "is recognized not only as a great medium for propaganda but also is one of the most influential agencies of education." Because Biddle did not share Hoover's anti-Communist obsession, absent any confirmation of illegal conduct, he did not respond to or even acknowledge Hoover's report. Yet Biddle's failure to at least inquire how the FBI had acquired the information, particularly in light of more pressing war-time priorities, underscores the latitude that Hoover by then commanded due to the Bureau's secretly assigned foreign intelligence and counterintelligence responsibilities.[32]

This obsession over Communist influence in Hollwod also informed another FBI target: radical German émigré artists and writers who had fled Nazi Germany and been granted refugee status during World War II. The political, professional and personal activities of these refugees were intensively monitored owing to their work in Hollywood and the Broadway theater and their efforts to include post-war policy toward Germany. Those targeted included Bertolt Brecht, Thomas Mann, Klaus Mann, Heinrich Mann, Helene Weigel, Billy Wilder, Ervin Picator and many others. The report of FBI agents particularly recounted the suspect cultural influence of these refugees (whether in writing poetry, books, or theater and film scripts) as well as their involvement in the political activities of the Free Germany Committee and the Council for a Democratic Germany. Not surprisingly, given their Marxist backgrounds, these refugees endorsed fundamental changes in the economic and political system that the victorious allies would be able to institute following the defeat of Nazi Germany.[33]

The FBI's monitoring of German émigré writers, Hollywood writers and directors, labor union leaders, radical attorneys—and even the vast majority of Communist Party members—served no legitimate law enforcement or security purpose. The exception was the concurrent discovery in 1943 (through bugging Steve Nelson's residence) of suspected espionage activities of Communists employed in the Radiation Laboratory at the University of California, Berkeley and the FBI's success in subsequently preventing the employment of these physicists at the Los Alamos bomb project. Far more significantly, however, FBI agents failed to uncover the espionage activities of Communists employed at Los Alamos and Oak Ridge in 1944–45 and their Communist couriers and the 1943–45 espionage activities of two Washington-based spy rights headed by Nathan Silvermaster and Victor Perlo. Otherwise, the FBI developed no evidence confirming that their targets violated any federal law or were spies or

---

[32] Personal and Confidential Memo, Hoover to Attorney General, October 31, 1944 and accompanying report Re: Communist Infiltration of Motion Picture Industry, FBI 100-138754-59.

[33] Stephan, "*Communazis*," *passim*.

saboteurs. As such, the massive amounts of information collected by FBI agents during the years 1920–45 were at the time unusable.

These records, however, proved to be an invaluable resource for senior FBI officials with the onset of the Cold War. The policy decisions of the Truman administration and Congress after 1945 were intended to counter the international political and military threat of an expansionist Soviet Union as well as an internal security threat seemingly posed by American Communists and Communist sympathizers. While acting to contain the Soviet international threat through increased military appropriations and initiatives such as the Truman Doctrine, Marshall Plan and NATO alliance, Truman administration officials were unable to counter the powerful domestic challenge of American conservatives who claimed that the Truman (and Roosevelt) administrations had been indifferent to a serious Soviet espionage threat. Senators Joseph McCarthy and Pat McCarran, Congressmen J. Parnell Thomas and Richard Nixon, the House Committee on Un-American Activities, the Senate Internal Security Subcommittee, and conservative newspapers such as the *Chicago Tribune* and the Scripps-Howard chain popularized this theme of an internal threat that stemmed from Communist infiltration of the federal bureaucracy. Their charges commanded widespread acceptance and were seemingly confirmed by the highly publicized revelations of Soviet espionage activities with the arrest and conviction of Julius Rosenberg in 1950–51, the indictment and conviction of Alger Hiss in 1948–50 and through the dramatic Congressional and trial testimony of Elizabeth Bentley in 1948–50. This obsession over the Communist threat further intensified with the indictment and conviction of key U.S. CP leaders in 1948–51.

Significantly, Soviet espionage successes had occurred years earlier whether in 1944–45 (Bentley and Rosenberg) or in 1938 (Hiss), while the CP leaders were convicted of violating the Smith Act (involvement in a conspiracy to overthrow the government) but not of having engaged in espionage. These trials and revelations precipitated rather pointed criticisms that the Roosevelt and Truman administrations' "softness toward communism" was responsible for Soviet advances in Eastern Europe and China and development of an atomic bomb. The FBI's failures (given its expanded powers) to have uncovered Soviet espionage at the time it was conducted, in contrast, escaped scrutiny.

This skewered perception of responsibility, however, was not mere happenstance and, ironically, was a byproduct of earlier FBI initiatives of the pre-Cold War era that led to the creation of massive files on suspect Communist activities. The collected information might have no or limited values for prosecution purposes. Increasingly after 1947, however, FBI officials surreptitiously leaked information suggesting the questionable loyalty of CP activists to favored members of Congress (Richard Nixon, Joseph McCarthy, Pat

McCarran), Congressional committees (House Committee on Un-American Activities, Senate Internal Security Subcommittee) and reporters and columnists (Walter Trohan, Don Whitehead, Frederick Woltman). These purposeful leaks proved to be crucial to the creation of a militantly anti-Communist political climate. The FBI's covert assistance remained unknown at the time, FBI officials having conditioned their aid on the recipients' agreement not to divulge the FBI as their source. In an ironic way, then the anti-Communist surveillance initiatives of the FBI during the 1920–45 period proved to be a prelude to power—diverting attention away from the agency's counterintelligence failures and legitimating the further expansion of its surveillance powers.

Chapter 3

Citizens versus Outsiders: Anti-Communism at State and Local Levels, 1921–1946

M.J. Heale

In the generation after 1921 there was little in the way of federal governmental repression of the Communist movement, at least compared to the attempts made during the Red Scare itself and in the later McCarthy era. The 1930s in particular are sometimes characterized as "the heyday of American communism," and one reason for that heyday was the relative tolerance of the federal authorities. But American Communists were not safe from everyone. State and city governments often turned a malign eye on the Communist presence, as did businesses, patriotic societies, veterans' organizations, civic bodies, and racist groups, while trade unions, churches and educational institutions were often keen to dissociate themselves from a perceived red menace. It was less government as such and more the American tradition of an active citizenry that sustained the anti-Communist cause during these decades. This was the associational activity that Alexis de Tocqueville had identified as a distinctive feature of American democracy, though it was a voluntarism closely associated with business imperatives and racial fears. Communities regularly mobilized "citizens committees" to repel un-American "outsiders."

Whether business and patriotic groups can count as "grassroots" is seriously open to question, but anti-Communist drives did not emanate from the very top of the American polity, at least after the Red Scare had faded. Anti-Communist sentiments were extensively mobilized against labor and civil rights groups, though by the 1930s populist attacks were being directed also at reformist state governors and Franklin D. Roosevelt. This upwards thrust of one strand of anti-Communist activism was to resume after the Second World War at state and national levels, though with the coming of the Cold War political elites would no longer try to resist it but attempt to accommodate and control it. Populist pressures would instead be redirected downwards again towards the powerless and the marginal with governmental endorsement, and political surveillance would become institutionalized. The inheritance from the interwar era, explosively interacting with new forces, was part of this powerful dynamic.[1]

***

By the early 1920s American authorities had arrived at a de facto strategy for guarding against the menace of red Communism. Communism, it was accepted, was an imported phenomenon, brought in particularly by the aliens of eastern and southern Europe who had been surging through American ports in such large numbers since the 1880s. The federal government accepted responsibility for choking off the supply of potential subversives, the new immigration laws erecting formidable barriers against unwanted newcomers. Those who somehow gained illicit entry could be deported. It fell to the state and local governments to protect their communities from any subversives in their midst. Attorney General A. Mitchell Palmer had attempted to secure a federal sedition law, but this had been frustrated, and its failure confirmed that the states would be the primary defenders of the republic in this respect. The federal government would patrol the nation's borders; the states would guard against the enemy within. When the U.S. Supreme Court upheld a Minnesota sedition law in 1920, Justice Joseph McKenna characterized it as part of a cooperative undertaking with the federal system.[2]

There was another legacy of the war years and the Red Scare. The sketchy nature of government machinery had led the federal authorities to rely on a private body, the American Protective League, for surveillance of the home front during the war, augmented by state and local "councils of defense", as well as other private groups. The APL boasted some 250,000 volunteers by 1918, and together with the councils allowed patriots to serve as citizen soldiers. Many acted responsibly, but others did not, often breaking up Socialist meetings or beating those deemed to be disloyal. Vigilante activity was not new, but in these years had been accorded a degree of legitimacy, and with the return of peace there was no shortage of citizens ready to hunt down subversives in the name of patriotism.

The 1910s had witnessed an upsurge of direct action by workers, prompting some states to employ criminal syndicalism laws, which were often turned against the Wobblies. With the Red Scare, states added to their protective

---

[1]   For a fuller explication of this argument, see M.J. Heale, *McCarthy's Americans: Red Scare Politics in State and Nation, 1935–1965* (Athens, GA, 1998), and "Beyond the 'Age of McCarthy': Anticommunism and the Historians," ch. 6 in Melvyn Stokes (ed.), *The State of U.S. History* (Oxford, 2002), 131–54.

[2]   Carol E. Jenson, *The Network of Control: State Supreme Courts and State Security Statutes, 1920–1970* (Westport, CT, 1982), 19.

legislation. By 1921 there were criminal syndicalism or sedition laws (or both) in 35 states, and for the most part they were upheld by the state courts. Prosecutions were often attempted. In New York Communist leaders, including Benjamin Gitlow, were charged under a criminal anarchy law. In California, which was exceptional, there were some 500 arrests made in the years 1919–24, and many were sentenced to long prison terms. The National Guard was also being re-established, and by October 1922 all but one state had its own unit. Police "red" or anti-radical squads had begun to appear in industrial cities in the late nineteenth century, but they were greatly boosted by the world war and especially the subsequent Red Scare, when they were often closely associated with local corporate interests. Along with the revived National Guard units, the urban red squads served as tools in the hands of authority that could be used against subversion. Philadelphia police in 1921 promised not to interfere in any meeting of strikers, "so long as the meeting is orderly and not of radical character, but all meetings of a radical character will be prohibited or broken up." In Los Angeles the celebrated red squad (or Radical Bureau), subsequently captained by William Hynes, owed something to the prompting of the Better America Federation, formed in 1920 by businessmen, bankers and others to warn of the "menace" of Communism; it helped fund the informers who were used in the criminal syndicalism trials.[3]

Local and state authorities were not acting entirely on their own, at least in the early 1920s. The failure to secure a federal sedition law disposed the Justice Department to encourage the states to enact their own sedition legislation; it also passed intelligence secured by its anti-radical investigators to the states and to industry. The federal Bureau of Investigation and the War Department's Military Intelligence Division often shared information with local officials and on occasion helped plan arrests. During the national railroad shopmen's strike of 1922, federal officers cooperated with local in combating it, the local authorities usually providing the men who were sworn in as deputy marshals. The federal agencies ended their anti-radical operations in 1924, though this did not render radicals much safer. The U.S. Supreme Court usually upheld the constitutionality of the state laws, most notably in the case of *Gitlow v. New York*

---

[3]   Patrick Renshaw, "The IWW and the Red Scare, 1917–24," *Journal of Contemporary History*, 3 (Oct. 1968), 70; David L. Sterling, "The 'Naive Liberal,' the 'Devious Communist' and the Johnson Case," *Ohio History*, 78, ii (Spring 1969), 95; William Preston, *Aliens and Dissenters: Federal Suppression of Radicals, 1903–1933* (Cambridge, MA, 1963), 244; Frank Donner, *Protectors of Privilege: Red Squads and Police Repression in Urban America* (Berkeley, 1990), 39, 41; Ingrid Winther Scobie, "Jack B. Tenney: Molder of Anti-Communist Legislation in California, 1940–49," (Ph.D. diss., University of Wisconsin, 1970), 29.

48 *Little 'Red Scares'*

in 1925, and two years later in the conviction of Charlotte Anita Whitney, a leader of the Communist Labor party in California.[4]

The states were not content with beefing up their sedition laws and their police and militia capabilities. Their obligation to protect the republic from Communist subversion also took them into the schools, a traditional area of state responsibility. In 1921 the New York legislature enacted the infamous Lusk Laws, which subjected schools to greater surveillance and required a loyalty oath from teachers. If this is reactionary, rejoiced the *New York Times*, "Give us reactionaries!" As the Lusk Report put it, "the success of the school system depends in the last analysis upon the character and viewpoint of the teachers," and it thus behoved the state to put measures in place to guarantee their character and loyalty. (With the Red Scare easing, Al Smith secured the laws' repeal in 1923.) A few states already had loyalty oaths for teachers, and several others adopted them during the 1920s. Between 1917 and 1923 charges of disloyalty were heard by departments of education in about 20 states. Veterans groups, their members no longer expected to take up arms on behalf of their country, considered it their duty now to promote patriotism at home, not least in the schools. "We are going to survey every school teacher and every school in the United States, and we will get the teacher reds," announced National Commander of the American Legion Frederic Galbraith in 1921: "If we find them disloyal, we will tell you and you can kick them out." School texts also drew their attention. The American Legion and the Veterans of Foreign Wars lobbied for the elimination of "un-American textbooks," a cause that won some support from bar associations and business corporations. The Ku Klux Klan also muscled in. "It is notorious," it said, "that our public school system, which is the strongest bulwark of Americanism, is being attacked from within and without by papists and antichristian Jews of the Bolshevik Socialist stripe." Some school boards dropped books that were held to be insufficiently patriotic, and the VFW claimed towards the end of the decade that it had "eliminated all of the objectionable features" in American history texts.[5]

---

[4]   Rhodri Jeffreys-Jones, *The FBI: A History* (New Haven, 2007), 75; Preston, *Aliens and Dissenters*, 242; Charles H. McCormick, *Seeing Reds: Federal Surveillance of Radicals in the Pittsburgh Mill District, 1917–1921* (Pittsburgh, 1997); Joan M. Jensen, *Army Surveillance in America, 1775–1980* (New Haven, 1991), 197–200; Colin J. Davis, *Power at Odds: The 1922 National Railroad Shopmen's Strike* (Urbana, 1997), 91–2.

[5]   Todd J. Pfannestiel, *Rethinking the Red Scare: The Lusk Committee and New York's Crusade against Radicalism, 1919–1923* (New York, 2003), 108; *Revolutionary Radicalism* ... being the Report of the Joint Legislative Committee Investigating Seditious Activities, Files April *24, 1920, in the Senate of the State of New York* (Albany 1920), Pt. I, vol. 1, p. 16; E. Edmund Reutter, *The School Administrator and Subversive Activities* (New

The harassment of radicals by state and local authorities and the campaign to promote patriotism in the nation's schools in the 1920s could be seen as parts of the larger ideological drive towards One Hundred Percent Americanism. The American Legion, other veterans groups and an array of patriotic societies tirelessly upheld such values. The Florida Department of the Legion endowed a chair of "Americanism" at the state university in 1925. In industry employers combated trade unions and defended the open shop with the American Plan, with its assumption that collective action by workers was unpatriotic. Anti-Communists of different kinds pressed their sentiments on the public. Catholic anti-Communism permeated many working and lower middle class communities, not least in areas of Irish ethnicity; Patrick Scanlon promoted a pugnacious variety in the *Brooklyn Tablet*. Protestant fundamentalists, a noisy battalion in the 1920s, agreed on little apart from resistance to evolution and Communism; after the anti-evolution campaign waned in mid-decade their anti-Communism became more pronounced. Anti-Communism was not infrequently joined with racism. The Ku Klux Klan was stridently hostile to foreigners and radicals, and was buoyant in several northern industrial cities. In Pennsylvania alone 423 "klaverns" were established in the dozen years from 1923. The values of One Hundred Percent Americanism also gave pause to many who did not identify with right-wing politics. In the labor movement, particularly as represented by the American Federation of Labor, and in the reformist sectors of public life, such as in the settlement houses, leaders distanced themselves from the suspect Communist movement, and some were not above demonstrating their political soundness by a little discreet red-baiting.[6]

These conditions were not those in which the Communist movement could easily thrive. By the mid-1920s the federal government had raised high the barriers against suspect immigrants, the states had equipped themselves with sedition laws, and some of the larger cities had created police red squads. The economy was also booming, serving to dissipate fears of red revolution. If tens of thousands of American residents had been attracted by the radical excitements of 1917–19, the Red Scare had devastated the left-wing groups, and the Communist Party itself

---

York, 1951), 7; Robert J. Goldstein, *Political Repression in Modern America from 1870 to the Present* (Cambridge, MA, 1978), 180; William Pencak, *For God & Country: The American Legion, 1919–1941* (Boston, 1989), 265–6; Jack Nelson and Gene Roberts, *The Censors and the Schools* (Boston, 1963), 28, 30.

6   Robert W. Iversen, *The Communists and the Schools* (New York, 1959), 176; Richard Gid Powers, "American Catholics and Catholic Americans," *U.S. Catholic Historian*, 22 (Fall 2004), 19; Clyde Wilcox, "The Christian Right in Twentieth-Century America," *Review of Politics*, 50 (Autumn 1988), 663; Philip Jenkins, "'It Can't Happen Here': Fascism and Right-Wing Extremism in Pennsylvania, 1933–1942," *Pennsylvania History*, 62, i (Jan. 1995), 34.

was subject to severe factional struggles. In 1929 it claimed only 9,300 dues-paying members. But Communists and other radicals were hardly safe from unwelcome attention, particularly those engaged in labor activity. Three Communists attempting to speak and distribute handbills in Martins Ferry, Ohio, were arrested in the summer of 1929 under a criminal syndicalism law; their prosecution was presented as an attempt to clean out "the damnable rat hole" of the Cleveland CP's headquarters. Among the most vulnerable were poor textile workers subjected to new management techniques and wage cuts as employers desperately tried to reduce costs. In company-dominated mill towns strikers faced formidable odds. A CP-led strike in the textile mills of Passaic, NJ, in 1926, was beaten through the deployment of police, deputy sheriffs, raids and arrests, and a textile strike in New Bedford, Massachusetts, in 1928 met a similar fate.[7]

The most fearful textile confrontation erupted in Gastonia, North Carolina, and would display some of the recurring features of local red scares, including the targeting of radical "outsiders" and the mobilization of a "citizens committee." Beginning in April 1929 business, civic, and law enforcement figures deployed the rhetoric of anti-Communism against a strike at the Loray Mill. "Red Russianism Lifts Its Gory Hands Right Here in Gastonia," ran a local headline. Giving an element of substance to the charge was the presence of Fred Beal of the National Textile Workers Union, both a Communist and an outsider to the community. The mayor called in the National Guard and the *Gastonia Daily Gazette* printed a full-page ad said to be paid for by local citizens anxious to alert others to the menace. This identified Beal as a "Red" who "stood against all American traditions and American government." The Communist organizers had also hoped to enroll white and black workers together, allowing the *Gazette* to denounce their belief in "racial equality, intermarriage of whites and blacks, abolition of all laws discriminating between whites and blacks, etc., etc." Some white workers went back to work but not all, and when the strike persisted, a mob of masked men destroyed its headquarters. Strikers suspected the instigation of the Committee of One Hundred, a citizens' committee sponsored by local employers and characterized by one striker as the mill's "strong arm squad," recruited from its "superintendents, foremen, specially privileged employees, professional thugs and special police deputies." The strikers then set up camp on the town's outskirts, protected by their own armed guards. Sporadic violence continued, and in June, when police and deputies arrived at the "tent city," a shoot-out occurred in which the police chief was killed and other officers and strikers wounded. Over 70 people were

---

[7]   David L. Sterling, "The 'Naive Liberal,' the 'Devious Communist' and the Johnson Case," *Ohio History*, 78, ii (Spring 1969), 96; Goldstein, *Political Repression*, 187.

arrested and 16 strikers or organizers charged with murder. The collapse of one trial precipitated a new round of violence in the county, which, according to one account, became "a howling wilderness of hysteria." A female strike leader was killed, but local courts exonerated those charged with her murder. Beal and other strike leaders skipped bail and took refuge in the Soviet Union, reinforcing public perceptions of alien manipulation. The strike failed and the incipient union was driven out of the area. Anti-Communism had done it work, reinforcing what Tim Minchin has characterized as "the anti-union hostility and corporate dominance of the South's small textile communities" by promoting a sense of powerlessness among the workers. Although there was a Communist presence in the South from this date, labor organization was set back for a generation. Gastonia also served as something of a model for anti-Communist and anti-labor forces, for similar scenes were to be played out in parts of the West and the South in the dark days of the 1930s.[8]

Commanding greater public attention in the 1920s was the infamous Sacco-Vanzetti case. The death sentences on the two Italian immigrants were confirmed in April 1927, triggering protests across the country and the world. That summer a handful of bombs exploded in American cities. Sacco and Vanzetti, of course, were anarchists who disdained Communism, but this distinction was often missed. The vocal upsurge of support for the two, itself in part a reflection of a greater willingness by progressives to speak out as the Red Scare faded, precipitated an outraged reaction in Boston and other New England towns. Armed members of the American Legion marched in Milton, Massachusetts, and the Ku Klux Klan staged a demonstration "in full regalia" demanding their execution. The Sons of the American Revolution warned the Massachusetts governor that the two were "part of a definite, well-organized program by Communists and Anarchists to weaken fundamental institutions of our form of government and pave the way for world revolution." One state official linked Sacco and Vanzetti to a nationwide conspiracy by "Reds, Socialists, Pacifists, and their college professor allies" to tear down everything "Americans hold dear." He added that the closer a place to the original crime imputed to the

---

[8] Harvey Klehr, *The Heyday of American Communism: The Depression Decade* (New York, 1984), 29; John A. Salmond, *Gastonia 1929: The Story of the Loray Mill Strike* (Chapel Hill, 1995), 26, 41–4; Glenda E. Gilmore, *Defying Dixie: The Radical Roots of Civil Rights, 1919–1950* (New York, 2008), 82, 96; Rebecca N. Hill, *Men, Mobs, and Law: Anti-Lynching and Labor Defense in U.S. Radical History* (Durham, 2008), 223–34; Gregory S. Taylor, *The History of the North Carolina Communist Party* (Columbia SC, 2009), 40–47; Timothy J. Minchin, "Coming into the Real World: Southern Textile Workers and the TWUA, 1945–1951," in Bruce Clayton and John Salmond (eds), *Varieties of Southern History: New Essays on a Region and Its People* (Westport, CT, 1996), 177.

two, the more people were convinced of their guilt, while "in those domains where foreign and un-American principles are in vogue, such as Russia, Harvard, Argentine, Wellesley, China, and Smith College, they are sure these men are innocent." This would not be the last time populist Massachusetts conservatives associated the state's distinguished Ivory Towers with subversion. In the heyday of One Hundred Percent Americanism, Sacco and Vanzetti's offence was to be Italian as well as radical.[9]

If employers could smash Communist-led strikes in local communities in the 1920s, the onset of the Great Depression brought Communism new recruits. Although there was an immediate fall in paid CP membership, the reported figure jumped to 26,000 in 1934. (It would continue to rise to 75,000 in January 1938.) Other movements on the left received a boost too. Norman Thomas, the Socialist party's perennial candidate for president, had secured 267,000 popular votes in 1928; in 1932 he more than trebled his vote to 882,000, though with the coming of the New Deal his appeal faded. Americans disposed to be apprehensive about political radicalism had some reason for their unease during the Depression years. Anti-Communist rhetoric might exaggerate the threat, but it could sometimes be employed with success because there were indeed Communists and other left-wingers at large.

Communists did sense opportunities as joblessness spiraled, and were active in organizing hunger marches and unemployed councils. Conditions, of course, varied greatly from community to community, and in some progressive and labor groups, respect for the law and civil liberties, and sympathy for the distressed were strong enough to prevail. In others business fears of the potential of labor organization and white fears of threats to the racial status quo precipitated anti-Communist convulsions. Some communities were effectively controlled by a formidable cluster of business, civic, police, and press interests, often flanked by conservative clerics and military veterans, disposed to see a subversive intent in every protest against the established order.

CP-led demonstrations in large cities risked harassment and arrests by the police; urban red squads once more expanded. The appearance of unemployed councils in Portland, Oregon, in 1930, prompted the city authorities to infiltrate the local CP with a police spy and then to raid its offices; leaders were charged under a criminal syndicalism law. New York's Radical Bureau vent its fury in a brutal confrontation with 50,000 protesters in March 1930. In the first five years of the Depression, Chicago's Communist Party "led, organized, or participated" in over 2000 demonstrations, braving the attention of the red squad. One such

---

[9] Moshik Temkin, *The Sacco-Vanzetti Affair: America on Trial* (New Haven, 2009), 25–6, 81; Hill, *Men, Mobs, and Law*, 192; Bruce Watson, *Sacco and Vanzetti: The Men, the Murders, and the Judgment of Mankind* (London, 2008), 299, 307.

protest in 1932 deteriorated into a vicious melee as rocks were thrown, and four demonstrators died after the police resorted to machine guns. In March 1932 a hunger march on Ford's River Rouge plant at Dearborn, Michigan, designed to point up Ford's responsibility for joblessness and its own harsh factory conditions, climaxed with the police or Ford security officers opening fire and four demonstrators, three of them Communists, being killed. The Wayne County Prosecuting Attorney, the Employers Association of Detroit, the American Legion and the local grand jury blamed Communists and "outside agitators" for what others called the "Ford Massacre." Anti-Communist sentiments could erupt almost anywhere. Local churchmen and other citizens fiercely protested at the murals painted by the radical Mexican artist Diego Rivera in the Detroit Institute of the Arts in 1932–33; those murals survived, though an unforgiving anti-Communism ensured the destruction in 1934 of a Rivera mural at New York's Rockefeller Center, with its depiction of Lenin.[10]

Red scare tactics tended to be most brutally applied in the areas of weak labor organization in the South and the West, where racial prejudice often accompanied class fears. Birmingham, Alabama, was both southern and a center of heavy industry. The CP in 1929 decided to make the city its headquarters for its operations in the Deep South. A hunger march organized by the Communists in May 1930 prompted the city commission to adopt a criminal anarchy ordinance to "curb communism," which was used against demonstrators during the summer. Later in the year anti-Communist apprehensions in the city were exacerbated by the hearings of a congressional committee chaired by Hamilton Fish into "communist propaganda" in Birmingham. Reinforcing suspicions was the celebrated case in northern Alabama of the Scottsboro boys which began to command headlines in 1931, and the prominent part played by the Communist Party. While this enhanced the popularity of the CP in the state's black communities, for whites it served to reinforce a fateful identification of Communism with black protest. Communists in Birmingham continued to be subject to police and Klan harassment, as were labor organizers in Tallapoosa County to the city's southeast. An attempt to organize a share croppers union in this rural area in 1931 led to brutal confrontations with police and white

---

[10]   Jenson, *Network of Control*, 30; Donner, *Protectors of Privilege*, 48; Randi Storch, *Red Chicago: American Communism at its Grassroots, 1928–35* (Urbana, 2007), 74, 260, n.62; Klehr, *Heyday of American Communism*, 58; Christopher H. Johnson, *Maurice Sugar: Law, Labor, and the Left in Detroit, 1912–1950* (Detroit, 1988), 120–23; Robert Conot, *American Odyssey* (New York, 1976), 284–6; Walter T. Howard, *Forgotten Radicals: Communists in the Pennsylvania Anthracite, 1919–1950* (Lanham, MD, 2005), 128; Alex Goodall, "The Battle of Detroit and Anti-Communism in the Depression Era," *Historical Journal*, 51, ii (2008), 457–80.

54   *Little 'Red Scares'*

vigilantes, the local police chief expressing a wish to "kill every member of the 'Reds' there and throw them into the creek." An NAACP official believed the vigilantes were "trying to get even for Scottsboro."[11]

In Atlanta, Georgia, two Communist organizers appeared in 1930, and, following hunger marches and an attempt to hold an integrated meeting, they were arrested and charged with insurrection under statutes inherited from Reconstruction. The publicity surrounding the affair precipitated the appearance of the Black Shirts, "to combat the Communist Party and to discourage the teachings of Communism and foster white supremacy," which held some appeal for Klansmen and unemployed white youths. Unlike the Communists they found that they could hold meetings without police harassment, although within months, with their leader accused of passing fraudulent checks (and misspelling "Fascisti"!), they had dissolved. There was a sustained controversy focused on Angelo Herndon, who was arrested in 1932 after organizing a hunger march and the discovery of Communist literature in his hotel room. Charged under the ancient insurrection law, he was found guilty in 1933 and sentenced to 18 to 20 years imprisonment, a ferocious sentence that together with the state's tenacious pursuit of the case following his appeal both amplified its notoriety and served to discourage unemployed demonstrations and radical activity in the state. A white liberal rendered judgment: "It is not the economics of Communism that frightens the white Southerner; it is the racialism of Communism that frightens him."[12]

Agricultural workers in California met similar experiences, in this case usually Mexicans rather than blacks. California's Imperial Valley, the so-called "cradle of vigilantism," was a major site of conflict. When Communist organizers prepared for a melon-workers strike in the spring of 1930, employers, local authorities, American Legion officials and many white citizens quickly reacted to this move to organize Mexican and Filipino laborers. The specter of "communistic activities" appeared in the local press. As elsewhere, a state criminal syndicalism law was used to crush the CP-led Agricultural Workers Industrial League (AWIL), which was infiltrated by spies sent by Captain William Hynes of Los Angeles's red squad. The Imperial County district attorney pressed charges against the AWIL agents, arguing that as admitted Communists their ultimate aim was the overthrow of government, and secured nine convictions. He claimed that what

---

[11]   Robin D.G. Kelley, *Hammer and Hoe: Alabama Communists during the Great Depression* (Chapel Hill, 1990), 14–17, 23, 41.

[12]   John Hammond Moore, "Communists and Fascists in a Southern City: Atlanta, 1930," *South Atlantic Quarterly*, 67 (1968), 437–54; Gilmore, *Defying Dixie*, 114–16, 164; James J. Lorence, *The Unemployed People's Movement: Leftists, Liberals, and Labor in Georgia, 1939–1941* (Athens, GA, 2009), 58–9. The U.S. Supreme Court eventually overturned Herndon's conviction.

local citizens really objected to about the defendants was that they were not local residents: "not a single one of them ever had a job in Imperial Valley, ever worked there, never did a day's work—not a single one of them ever did a day's work in Imperial Valley." Outsiders could always be demonized. Subsequently all those convicted won appeals or were paroled, as was often the case where such laws were used, but the strike had been crushed and the agricultural labor movement throttled in the name of averting red revolution. Further north in Solano County, where tree pruners struck in 1932, farm owners and American Legion members mobilized a large anti-Communist demonstration, which was told by a churchman that "a real menace confronts this community which must be met in the good old American way." The strike collapsed in the wake of police arrests and vigilante beatings.[13]

But Communists renewed their attempts to organize agricultural workers in the valley. "Red" Hynes in 1933 warned of a "campaign of agitation" planned by organizers of the Cannery and Agricultural Workers Industrial Union (CAWIU). In other parts of the state too farm workers who attempted to strike were subjected to the unfriendly attention of local lawmen, Legionnaires, growers and businessmen. Such elements formed a "Committee of 1500" in Lodi, Central Valley, where grape pickers were on strike, and many were clubbed and arrested. "These men are nothing but a bunch of rats, Russian anarchists, cutthroats, and sweepings of creation," stormed Judge J.K. Solkmore of those arraigned before him. A Farmers' Protective Association of Tulane County was formed to combat a major cotton strike in San Joaquin Valley in October 1933, and it instructed local citizens that these "Communist Agitators MUST be driven from town by you." The escalation of violence in the valley that fall brought the deaths of three Mexican workers. The Better America Federation of California called for legislation to close down Communist groups. The labor unrest of 1933 precipitated the formation (and formal incorporation in 1934) of the Associated Farmers of California, with the financial help of utility companies and the explanation that "the labor controversies in the farming areas had been fomented by communists as a definite part of Moscow's program to change the form of government in California."[14]

---

[13] Carey McWilliams, *Factories in the Field* (Boston, 1939), 231; Cletus E. Daniel, *Bitter Harvest: A History of California Farmworkers, 1870–1941* (Berkeley, 1981), 114–26, 136–8.

[14] Daniel, *Bitter Harvest*, 143–4, 150–51, 163–4, 186, 196, 201; *Better America Federation of California Bulletin* (Los Angeles), Feb. 19, 1932; Richard L. Neuberger, "Who Are the Associated Farmers?," *Survey Graphic*, 28 (Sept. 1939): http://newdeal.feri.org/survey/39b12.htm.

By 1933, of course, Franklin Roosevelt had been elected President and the New Deal offered some hope to the nation's distressed. A new political landscape was in the making, but by 1934 significant elements in the labor movement were becoming disillusioned with Roosevelt's promises while some on the right were distressed at the course the New Deal was taking. That year witnessed the greatest labor unrest in years, providing further evidence for those disposed to look for it of Communist machinations.

The eruption of labor unrest had complex causes, and Communists had little to do with many of the strikes that year, but their involvement in the early protests of the Depression meant that they were often blamed. An early confrontation, the Toledo Auto-Lite strike beginning in April, did involve the American Workers party, led by the Marxist A.J. Muste. The state governor called out the Ohio National Guard, and the "Battle of Toledo" left two strikers dead and 200 or more injured. In May the Teamsters union struck against the major trucking companies in Minneapolis. Among their leaders were members of the Trostskyite Communist League of America, and Communists were blamed for the violence that followed. Two people died and at one point the Minnesota governor declared martial law. Early in the century a Citizens Alliance (CA) had been formed to fight for the open shop in Minneapolis, and the disturbances prompted business leaders to propose a Special Emergency Citizens' Committee to coordinate the activities of the CA and other civic and law-and-order bodies. During the fighting the police were augmented by several hundred newly deputized CA members. A CA pamphlet spoke of "a deliberate attempt of the Communist League of America to stir up class warfare in this community." Ultimately the strikers prevailed, and their success transformed the city, for thousands of workers in other industries were emboldened to organize.[15]

In July, following a strike of longshoremen and seamen, a general strike was called in San Francisco, described by Mayor Angelo Rossi as "a Communist attempt to start a revolution and overturn the government." This was a view promoted by waterfront employers, ship-owners, uptown businessmen, and city and state officials; much of the city press inveighed against the "Communists and radicals" who apparently led the strike. The Communists indeed won some respect in the broader labor movement in California for their role. Always ready to resist any sign of labor organization was the open-shop Industrial Association, with its expertise in strikebreaking. Mayor Rossi encouraged prominent citizens to organize a Committee of Five Hundred, soon suspected by strikers of

---

[15]   Richard W. Steele, *Free Speech in the Good War* (Basingstoke, UK, 1999), 130; William Millikan, *A Union Against Unions: The Minneapolis Citizens Alliance and Its Fight against Organized Labor, 1903–1947* (St. Paul, 2001), 324, 334; Bud Schultz and Ruth Schultz, *The Price of Dissent: Testimonies to Political Repression in America* (Berkeley, 2001), 34–41.

instigating vigilante activity. The California Legion formed "safety committees ready to assist the constituted authorities when necessary," and characterized the labor action as "not a strike but an usurpation by force by self-constituted groups of the authority duly delegated by the ballots." The central role of the Australian Harry Bridges, the "alien Communist", allowed ample scope for depicting the strike as the product of outside and un-American influences. The CP headquarters was destroyed by vigilantes and the police arrested hundreds of strikers. Two men died in the confrontations, and a moving mass funeral brought the city to a halt. In the course of the conflict over 900 people were arrested; most were released without charge, but some 150 drew prison sentences and others were held for deportation. With the collapse of the strike Rossi assured the Committee of Five Hundred: "I will, to the full extent of my authority, run out of San Francisco every communistic agitator."[16]

In the fall a great national textile strike caught many local authorities off-guard; although called by an AFL union, it was quickly demonized. A number of New England states mobilized the National Guard. In Georgia Governor Eugene Talmadge declared martial law and interned strikers in a World War I prison camp. In Atlanta a red scare was under way by October, with arrests under the insurrection law. Liberals as well as radicals found their meetings raided, employers and patriotic groups used the Communist threat to assail what remained of unionism, and a grand jury probed "Red activities." In South Carolina the Commander of the state Legion called on local posts to support the governor's request that it "maintain law and order", blaming the local strike on "outsiders", notably Communists from North Carolina; in the ensuing confrontations between strikers and special deputies, 10 strikers died. Other parts of the South also experienced unrest. Birmingham's red squad increased its activities during the summer, often using a criminal anarchy ordinance, though when the courts proved uncooperative the city adopted a new ordinance making it illegal to possess "radical" literature, which could mean labor publications or even liberal periodicals like the *New Republic*. Arrests duly soared, but convictions remained elusive. Groups like the White Legion and the Klan helped to mobilize opinion against radicals and black activists, the subjects of vigilante attacks. Repeated attempts were made to assassinate the white CP leader, Clyde Johnson.[17]

---

[16] David S. Selvin, *A Terrible Anger: The 1934 Waterfront and General Strikes in San Francisco* (Detroit, 1996), 192–3, 197, 199, 202, 227, 233; Steve Murdock, "California Communists—Their Years of Power," *Science and Society*, 34 (Winter 1970), 480–81; Pencak, *For God & Country*, 222–3.

[17] Lorence, *Unemployed People's Movement*, 117–21; Pencak, *For God & Country*, 224; Kelley, *Hammer and Hoe*, 73–4.

In the agricultural valleys of California too labor unrest was still rife in 1934, particularly in the lawless Imperial Valley. An ACLU attorney, A.L. Wirin, was grabbed by vigilantes, who beat him and abandoned him barefoot in the desert, an outrage he blamed on American Legion members. "These outside labor agitators believe in overthrowing the government by violence," a reporter was told: "We can't wait for legal processes to handle people like that." Despite a National Labor Board investigation into conditions in the valley, vigilantes continued to take the law into their own hands. Employers established the Imperial Valley Growers and Shippers Protective Association; also created was the Imperial Valley Anti-Communist Association, casting itself as a "citizens" group to promote "Americanism" and resist Communism. In March the two associations met "to coordinate their plans in opposing the Reds." In San Joaquin Valley an Anti-Communist League was established "to cooperate with county officers in case of emergencies." Such groups were backed by the Associated Farmers of California, which succeeded in having private investigators infiltrate the CP and befriend CAWIU leaders. In the summer 17 CAWIU leaders and other radicals were charged under the criminal syndicalism law. The Associated Farmers, which by 1935 had developed "confidential" files on about a thousand "dangerous radicals," campaigned for their vigorous prosecution, and convictions were secured against eight defendants, after a trial in which the prosecution argued that Communism was incompatible with the criminal syndicalism law. The convictions were to be reversed on appeal.[18]

Paralleling the labor unrest of 1934 was Upton Sinclair's End Poverty in California campaign, with its objective of turning idle factories and farms into cooperatives. Sinclair captured the Democratic nomination for governor, a portent of the party's united front potential, though on this occasion the Communists remained aloof; nonetheless the EPIC movement was denounced as Communistic by conservatives and the Hearst press.

Despite—or because of—the brutality directed towards strikers, the great labor convulsions of 1934 helped to further the growth of industrial unionism, as did the overtures of the Roosevelt administration towards organized labor. A deepening polarization of American political culture was under way, characterized by heightened anti-Communist rhetoric by right-wing elements. In 1935 the ACLU's Roger Baldwin discerned a red-hunting drive more serious than any since the Red Scare. In that time, he had never "witnessed so powerful an alliance as today is in full cry for the complete annihilation by federal and state law of the Communist movement," with its unhappy implications for other

---

[18]   Pencak, *For God & Country*, 222; Daniel, *Bitter Harvest*, 238, 252–4; McWilliams, *Factories in the Field*, 233, 238.

Citizens versus Outsiders   59

left-wing politics. It was the simultaneous assault by all the elements at once that disturbed him, the Hearst press, the Legion, and the patriotic coalitions. The San Francisco general strike, he believed, had struck terror into the ruling class and had inspired the Hearst drive. In 1934 Homer Chaillaux, who as a Californian had played roles in defeating an Imperial Valley strike and the San Francisco general strike, had become head of the Legion's Americanism Division, which he led with considerable vigor. He required state departments to supply him with information on suspect radicals in each community and advised them to secure state laws to curb Communism.[19]

The American Legion had laid down that "the work pertaining to Americanism was the most important of the various departments for the year 1934–35," a stance endorsed by the Hearst press, other press barons, and patriotic groups such as the Daughters of the American Revolution. The Legion encouraged laws denying the ballot to any parties advocating sedition or the forcible overthrow of government, which were adopted by four states in 1935. "It is a shot at Reds, Pinks and Communists and radical doctrines and 'isms'," said the Georgia House Speaker of a bill requiring a loyalty oath of all state employees, including teachers. In Baltimore representatives from the local Legion branch and the Summerfield Methodist Episcopal Church assembled with a plan to combat "subversive efforts" through creating an American Loyalty League. In 1936 the ACLU reported that in the previous year the greatest single attack on civil liberties had been "the resort to force and violence by employers, vigilantes, mobs, troops, private gunmen and compliant sheriffs and police."[20]

Much of this heightened anti-Communist animus was directed at higher education, in part occasioned by the publicity accorded to student anti-war strikes in 1934 and 1935, though also by unease about the influence of prominent left-wing academics. If the New Deal was tainted red, some responsibility could be attributed to those intellectuals who enthusiastically supported the President, like those in his celebrated "brain trust." Some academics made no secret of their left-wing inclinations, such as New York University's Sidney Hook, who in 1933 had organized a new American Workers party, holding that "only communism

---

[19]   Roger N. Baldwin, "Red Scare: 1935," article in ACLU Archive, 1935, vol. 782, p. 271, Seeley G. Mudd Manuscript Library, Princeton University; Pencak, *For God & Country*, 237–8, 241.

[20]   American Legion, *Department of Massachusetts, Annual Proceedings, 1935, Seventeenth Annual Convention* [Boston 1936], 174; Roger N. Baldwin to Louis L. Redding, Dec. 24, 1936, ACLU Archive 1937, vol. 983, p. 353; "Oath of Allegiance Sought for Teachers and State Employees," *Atlanta Journal*, March 5, 1935, 1; "American Loyalty League Is Planned," *Sun* (Baltimore), June 2, 1935; ACLU, *How Goes the Bill of Rights? The Story of the Fight for Civil Liberties, 1935–36* (New York, 1936), 5.

60 *Little 'Red Scares'*

can save the world from its social evils." The Hearst press sent undercover reporters posing as students into colleges to expose red professors, and, when NYU declined to sack Hook and his colleague James Burnham, denounced the university as "an active center of treasonable plotting for the overthrow of the American government." In 1935 Chaillaux distributed 2000 copies of a speech on "Communism" by Congressman Hamilton Fish to American Legion leaders, in which several universities, including Columbia, Wisconsin and Chicago, were said to be "honeycombed with Socialists, near Communists and Communists." "Will the Communists Get Our Girls in College?" asked an article in *Liberty* magazine in September 1935. The Michigan legislature extended the existing teacher loyalty oath to college professors; by 1936 professors had to take loyalty oaths in 14 states. Some legislatures succumbed to pressures to investigate their colleges. In 1936 Democratic State Senator John J. McNaboe charged Cornell with being a "center of revolutionary communistic propaganda." The Wisconsin legislature concluded that the University of Wisconsin was "an ultra liberal institution in which Communistic teachings were encouraged." The Arkansas general assembly investigated Commonwealth College, a small labor school, and a bill was introduced to shut down any institution advocating the overthrow of government, against which a number of students testified, including a young Orval Faubus, who thought the bill un-American. At a time when FDR's New Deal was in the ascendant, such probes were generally shaken off, but some professors did lose their jobs in the mid-1930s.[21]

Suspicions spilled over into the high schools. Professional patriot Walter S. Steele's *National Republic* campaigned to expose "the contributing factors in the poisonous drive of the Marxian and atheistic elements within our country to convert the American educators and youth to foreign brands of nationalism." In 1934 the American Legion endorsed loyalty oaths for teachers at its national convention, though it left it to each state department whether to pursue that objective. New York, in which the prominence of Communists in the New York City local of the American Federation of Teachers had long been a cause for concern, adopted a teacher loyalty oath that year, which, it was thought, was the answer to "too much teaching of various "isms" in the schools." In 1935 another seven states adopted such oath bills, the greatest number recorded in any single year. There was a prolonged furor in Massachusetts, arraying Irish constituencies,

---

[21]   M.J. Heale, *American Anticommunism: Combating the Enemy Within, 1830–1970* (Baltimore, 1990), 111; Iversen, *Communists and the Schools*, 140, 186; Pencak, *For God & Country*, 241–2; Heale, *McCarthy's Americans*, 9, 30–31, 88; Jenson, *Network of Control*, 7; Lawrence H. Chamberlain, *Loyalty and Legislative Action: A Survey of Activity by the New York Legislature, 1919–1949* (Ithaca, 1951), 56–7; Roy Reed, *Faubus: The Life and Times of an American* Prodigal (Fayetteville, 1997), 103–104.

Citizens versus Outsiders 61

Democrats, Roman Catholics, and veteran and patriotic groups on the loyalty oath side and on the other patrician Yankees, Protestants, Jews, Republicans, Harvard professors and other educators, configurations that would recur in future confrontations over Communism. An oath law was passed in 1935, and some teachers resigned rather than take it.[22]

During Franklin Roosevelt's second term the anti-radical impulse hardened. This was partly the product of a conservative reaction to the New Deal. Roosevelt's re-election owed something to the growing association of the Democratic Party with labor, particularly the militant unions in the mass production industries of the CIO, whose largely successful sit-down strikes of 1937 powerfully dramatized the phenomenal surge of industrial unionism. The strike against General Motors in Flint, Michigan, precipitated the creation of the Flint Alliance and a Protestant Action Association to drive out the suspect Communist agitators; local citizens, albeit often nativist and anti-union workers, were again being mobilized against outsiders. U.S. Steel signed a union contract, but the refusal of smaller steel firms to follow suit led to the "little steel strike" and a confrontation with police in Chicago that left 10 demonstrators dead on Memorial Day. In California the Associated Farmers, which had been promoting meetings by such anti-Communist bodies as the Christian American Crusade, the California Crusaders and the California Cavaliers, were now disturbed by the CIO's activities among agricultural workers. Their president blamed Harry Bridges, warning Secretary of Labor Frances Perkins: "Farmers in California will never surrender to the organization of their workers under the dictation of this communistic alien." Pennsylvanian Legionnaires helped to break a strike led by elements "foreign to our community" at the Hershey chocolate company. The Trotskyists in Minneapolis also remained a target. In 1937 the National Association of Manufacturers sent an agent to the city to form a company union to try to supplant Teamsters' Local 544; it would be "an American movement first, last and all the time, there will be no place in it for the gangster, racketeer, thug or Communist." Also aiming to expose Communism in Local 544 were the revived Silver Shirts, with their slogan "Down With the Reds and Out With the Jews."[23]

---

[22] Walter S. Steele, "Communism in Schools," *National Republic*, 29 (May 1941), 21; Pencak, *For God & Country*, 268; Iversen, *Communists and the Schools*, ch. 2; Chamberlain, *Loyalty and Legislative Action*, 54; Lucille B. Milner to Mary R. Heard, July 18, 1936, ACLU Archives, 1936, vol. 872, pp. 214–15; Heale, *McCarthy's Americans*, Pt III (on Massachusetts); Lucille B. Milner to Robert A. McBane, Aug. 7, 1936, ACLU Archives, 1936, vol. 872, p. 217.

[23] Heale, *McCarthy's Americans*, 90; Donner, *Protectors of Privilege*, 51; Robert H. Zieger, *American Workers, American Unions*, 2nd edn (Baltimore, 1994), 56; McWilliams,

62   *Little 'Red Scares'*

The conservative reaction on the right was paralleled by the emergence of popular front politics on the left. With international calls for a united front against fascism, some American Communists won influence in a number of CIO unions, and others joined farmer-labor groups or relief organizations. Where socialism was not achievable, conceded the CP's Earl Browder in 1938, "it is a thousand times better to have a liberal and progressive New Deal ... than to have a new Hoover." In some states Communists sought to work with New Deal or other liberal political groups. In Minnesota the Farmer-Labor party admitted Communists, and in New York Communists came to play a significant role in the American Labor party. In Washington several were elected to the state legislature courtesy of the Washington Commonwealth Federation, castigated by opponents as a "Trojan Horse for the Communist Party." During Roosevelt's first term, the charge that he was subject to Communist influence held little credibility because the CP had made clear its opposition to him; now he seemed to have Communist allies, and the label of a "Red New Deal" was more readily applied. Anti-Communism could range from the eminently moderate stance of the Association of Catholic Trade Unionists (ACTU), formed in 1937 to combat Communist influence in the CIO, to the fascist groups which drew inspiration from the Nazi triumph in Germany, such as the German-American Bund, said by its founder to be a "militant group of patriotic Americans." Something of the new temper was revealed in 1938 when the House of Representatives created the House Committee on Un-American Activities (HUAC).[24]

The federal government was a relatively late recruit to the anti-Communist cause. In fact, one state had created a "little HUAC" even before Congress acted, and other anti-Communist measures too were under way. Several states sought to outlaw Communists from American politics before the Second World War.

Early in 1937 a "Special Commission" to investigate the activities of "Communistic, Fascist, Nazi and Other Subversive Organizations" was founded in Massachusetts, and developed as an anti-Communist and anti-popular front vehicle. It was soon publicly summoning popular front radicals. In May 1938 it published a report of 599 pages, almost all of which, apart from brief sections on "Fascistic Activity" and "Nazi Activity", were devoted to the menace of Communism, and implicated the ACLU and local progressive labor and church campaigners in a conspiracy directed by Moscow. In the event, two members of the commission, including its chair, lost their bids for re-election to the legislature in 1938, and in 1939 its proposals for a new sedition law and

---

Factories in the Field, 235, 240; Daniel, *Bitter Harvest*, 278; Jenkins, "It Can't Happen Here", 39; Millikan, *Union against Unions*, 335–7.

[24] Heale, *American Anticommunism*, 109, 114; Klehr, *Heyday of American Communism*, 256.

a permanent little HUAC were defeated. The latter was likened to OGPU or the Gestapo, "a permanent inquisition to smell out political heresy, independent of the ordinary police." The days of the Sacco-Vanzetti case were in the past, and apart from the opposition of labor groups and liberal Democrats, there was now a resilient civil liberties community in Massachusetts strongly rooted in the state's academic institutions. By this date too clear victory in the Spanish Civil War had been secured by General Franco, and the outbreak of war in Europe in the autumn suggested that it was fascism rather than Communism that was the greater threat to democracy. An attempt to bar the CP from the ballot was defeated in 1940.[25]

Michigan, the scene of major union drives, was also seared by intensive anti-Communist activity. The state's industrial cities, with their large immigrant populations, had been augmented by white migration from the rural South as well as by poor blacks. Thousands of southern whites in the mid-1930s joined the Black Legion, a hooded order similar to the Ku Klux Klan. It wanted to "stamp out Communism", and stamp on Communists and other labor activists it did. Its exposure in vivid newspaper headlines in 1936 suggested anti-labor collusion between big business, city councils and police departments, particularly in Detroit and Pontiac. The resentments of some southern white workers were articulated by the popular Baptist pastor, Dr. J. Frank Norris, who denounced the 1937 sit-down strike as "the Moscow plan imported to America." The urban ethnic populations were mostly Catholic, and their best-known priest, Father Charles Coughlin, also characterized the sit-downs as an attempt of "union labor to Sovietise industry", while Detroit's bishop described them as "illegal and Communistic." The Catholic hierarchy encouraged Catholic workers into the "sound unionism" of ACTU, but some elements were susceptible to red scare appeals.

Michigan Governor Frank Murphy, a prominent New Dealer, antagonized many by the apparent sympathy he accorded to the strikers, and during his 1938 re-election campaign his critics exploited the Democrats' association with the

---

[25]   American Civil Liberties Union, *Let Freedom Ring!* (New York, June 1937), 56; "Report of the Special Commission to Investigate the Activities within this Commonwealth of Communistic, Fascist, Nazi and Other Subversive Organizations," *Massachusetts Legislative Documents, House, 1938*, No. 2100, pp. 56, 318, 460; Robert Morss Lovett, "Witch-Hunting in Massachusetts," *New Republic*, Dec. 1, 1937, pp. 96–7; *Boston Sunday Post*, June 26, 1938; Civil Liberties Union of Massachusetts (CLUM), Minutes, June 1, 1938, and Otis Hood and Phil Frankfeld to Dear Friend, June 3, 1938, CLUM Papers, Massachusetts Historical Society, Boston; Joan Hopkinson to Howard Y. Williams, Oct. 26, 1938, Mather Papers, Mass. Hist. Soc.; Civil Liberties Committee of Mass., *To Members and Friends ...* , March 18, 1939, pp. 1–2; *Civil Liberties Bulletin*, April–May 1939, p. 11; *Daily Worker*, Sept. 14, 1940; "Attacks On The Communist Party," vol. 2203, 1940, ACLU Records, Seeley G. Mudd Library, Princeton University.

suspect popular front groups. HUAC itself became involved, visiting Detroit and enabling local officials to link the governor to the infamous strikes and their Communist supporters. The Republican gubernatorial candidate condemned the Murphy administration for harboring Communists, righteously adding "I don't want their support" and promising an administration that was "against invasion of our state by red 'isms.'" The Republicans were victorious in both the gubernatorial and legislative elections, and promptly introduced a bill for a "little HUAC", though there was sufficient opposition from liberal, labor, civil rights, and some church and farm groups to see it off. Nonetheless, the anti-Communist ranks in Detroit were augmented in 1939 by the celebrated preacher Gerald L.K. Smith, who took over Coughlin's radio network and led the Committee of 1 million, which, he said, was seeking "to educate the people to combat such menaces as Communism, Nazism, fascism, new dealism, Murphyism and the C.I.O."[26]

Reaction against popular front politics peaked a little later in California. There popular front groups, notably the Democratic Federation for Political Unity, a coalition of liberals, labor activists and Communists, helped to elect Culbert Olson as governor in 1938, the first Democrat to hold that office in the twentieth century. "In California," recorded Communist Steve Nelson, "the Democratic Party seemed more of a people's movement than the arm of the other branch of the capitalist class," and with Olson's election "we envisioned a move leftward." Eager to further New Deal reform, Olson appointed radicals to the State Relief Administration, which became the object of intense suspicion not only by Republicans but also by conservative Democrats (many sorely vexed by the distribution of executive patronage). In August 1939 the shocking news of the Nazi-Soviet Pact devastated popular front formations across the country, and by January 1940 some Democrats were repudiating Olson and joining with Republicans to take control of the assembly. One outcome was the establishment of a "little HUAC" to investigate the SRA, under the chairmanship of Sam Yorty, a former liberal who brusquely explained his change of course: "The

---

[26] "Red-Baiting," typescript in Civil Rights Congress of Michigan (CRCM) Papers, Reuther Library, Detroit; Michael C. Clinansmith, "The Black Legion," *Michigan History*, 55 (Fall 1971), 243–62; David J. Maurer, "The Black Legion," in Frank Annunziata et al., *For the General Welfare: Essays in Honor of Robert H. Bremner* (New York, 1989), 255–69; *Detroit Times*, Jan. 18, 1937; *Detroit News*, Jan. 11, 1937, Nov. 6, 1938, April 26, 1939; *Detroit Free Press*, 20 Aug., 14, 20, 21, 22, 26 Oct. 1938; Roger Keeran, *The Communist Party and the Auto Workers' Unions* (New York, 1980), 161–2; J. Woodford Howard, Jr., "Frank Murphy and the Sit-Down Strikes of 1937," *Labor History* (Spring 1960), 103–40; "Investigation of Un-American Activities in the United States," typescript of HUAC hearing, Oct. 1938, in CRCM Papers; *Who Defeated the "Little Dies" Bill?*, undated leaflet in CRCM Papers; Glen Jeansonne, *Gerald L.K. Smith: Minister of Hate* (New Haven, 1988), 66–72; B.J. Widick, *Detroit: City of Race and Class Violence* (Chicago, 1972), 89–90.

time has come for a cleanup in the Democratic party before the Communists wreck it." The committee descended on the SRA office in Los Angeles, held stormy sessions with popular front and labor activists, and issued a report that held Olson responsible for the Communist penetration of a major state agency. Attorney General Earl Warren also distanced himself from Olson, and would subsequently charge him with pardoning "communist radicals" when challenging him for the governorship. In 1941 the little HUAC was reconstituted under the chairmanship of the Los Angeles Democrat Jack B. Tenney, another former liberal who had swung to the right. The Tenney Committee was destined to become the most notorious of the little HUACs of the post-war period.[27]

The Nazi-Soviet Pact of August 1939 and the outbreak of war in Europe in September greatly intensified the "little red scare." American Communists were rendered highly vulnerable. They were now largely isolated as the popular front groupings collapsed and their sometime liberal allies scrambled away. Right-wing authorities seized the opportunity to strike at local radicals. In Iowa in September 1939 state CP officers were charged under the state's criminal syndicalism laws. California Communist Sam Darcy was arrested on a charge of falsifying a voter registration. The little red scare deepened in 1940. In North Carolina, the *Charlotte Observer* called for local Communists to be put in "concentration camps" as "foreign agents." In April Philadelphia police, in cooperation with HUAC officials, raided the CP headquarters of the International Workers' Order. By the middle of the year the recorded membership of the Ku Klux Klan, now headlining its anti-Communist credentials, had increased by nearly a third in 10 months. By this time many CP activists were going underground. In February the country's leading civil liberties group, the ACLU, declared it "inappropriate" for its governing bodies to contain members of political organizations supporting "totalitarian dictatorship" and CP member Elizabeth Gurley Flynn was expelled from the board of directors. In November 1940 the CIO national convention proscribed "Nazism, Communism, and Fascism" as "foreign ideologies" with "no place in this great modern labor movement."[28]

---

[27]   Steve Nelson et al., *Steve Nelson, American Radical* (Pittsburgh, 1981), 254, 271; *San Francisco Chronicle*, Feb. 1, 2, 4, 6, 14, March 8, 1940; California Legislature, *Report of the Assembly Relief Investigating Committee on Subversive Activities* (Sacramento, 1940); Edward R. Long, "Earl Warren and the Politics of Anti-Communism," *Pacific Historical Review*, 51, ii (Feb. 1982), 55.

[28]   Maurice Isserman, *What Side Were You On? The American Communist Party during the Second World War* (Middletown, CT, 1982), 50–51; Donner, *Protectors of Privilege*, 53; Gilmore, *Defying Dixie*, 349; Jenkins, "It Can't Happen Here," 36; Cletus E. Daniel, *The ACLU and the Wagner Act* (Ithaca, 1980), 134; Fraser M. Ottanelli, *The Communist Party of the United States: From the Depression to World War II* (New Brunswick NJ, 1991), 202.

But 1940 was an election year, and across the country there were determined attempts to bar the Communist Party, which was collecting signatures to put its candidates on the ballot. In a dozen states the American Legion reportedly circulated petition signers urging them to repudiate their signatures. In Ohio, West Virginia, New York and at least five other states newspapers published the signers' names, exposing them to possible harassment and job losses. A petitions scandal escalated in Pittsburgh, resulting in the state indicting 43 CP members and securing convictions against 27. The *Pittsburgh Post-Gazette* celebrated the "smashing attack against leftist activists in this important national defense area." In West Virginia the CP candidate for governor was charged with soliciting signatures to put the CP on the ballot under false pretenses and sentenced to 15 years imprisonment. Communist campaign meetings were often disrupted. The Alabama legislature outlawed any "flag, insignia, emblem or device" of any group or country "antagonistic to the constitution and laws of the United States, or to those of the State of Alabama." In Tennessee, according to the *Daily Worker*, Boss Crump instructed public officials to keep Communists off the ballot. "We must not handle Communists with gloves," he explained. "... We say most positively they will not speak, spread their propaganda or become active in any way in this community." In Michigan an unsuccessful motion to deny the ballot to the CP was filed by the ferocious red-hunter Blanche Winters, who explained that the word democracy was not in the Constitution and that "99 percent of the Congressmen are Communists." By November 1940, despite often formally satisfying registration requirements, the CP was barred in 15 states, the Socialist party in 11, and the Socialist Labor party in 14.[29]

In Oklahoma a celebrated cause célèbre flared after a police raid on the Progressive Bookstore in Oklahoma City in August 1940. Thousands of books and pamphlets were seized and 20 customers and proprietors arrested under the state's criminal syndicalism law; four were eventually convicted and sentenced to prison terms of 10 years. The charges rested on the premise that possessing and promoting "Communist" literature was itself subversive, and since the seized items were presumably to be destroyed, civil liberties champions across the country inveighed against such "bookburning", which could be compared to the behavior of German Nazis. Anti-radical nerves continued to flicker in the

---

[29] "Press Red Hunt Agitates Ohio." *Christian Century*, Sept. 25, 1940; "Barring of Minority Parties Set Record In 1940 Election," *St. Cloud News*, Nov. 7, 1940; Isserman, *What Side Were You On?*, 70, 71; Philip Jenkins, *The Cold War at Home: The Red Scare in Pennsylvania, 1945–1960* (Chapel Hill, 1999), 22; Ottanelli, *Communist Party*, 204; "Attacks on the Communist Party," ACLU Archives, 1940, vol. 2203, pp. 133–7; Kelley, *Hammer and Hoe*, 216; "Tenn. Political Boss Wants C.P. Driven Off Ballot," *Daily Worker*, Aug. 24, 1940; "Michigan Red-Baiters Try to Scare Voters," *Daily Worker*, June 24, 1940.

state. In 1941 the Oklahoma State Senate authorized an investigation into the CP and other suspect groups; the probe confirmed to its own satisfaction that there was a Communist Party in the state, and recommended a law outlawing it, but little came of this episode.[30]

Although the principal objective in 1940 was to keep the CP off the ballot, during the little red scare there was a modest wave of state sedition or criminal syndicalism laws. Congress enacted its own sedition law—the Smith Act—in that fearful summer, and some of the new state laws were imitations of it. Yet more loyalty oaths also appeared. In New York teachers became the subjects of a particularly wide-reaching inquisition. As discussed elsewhere in this volume, the legislature set up the Rapp–Coudert Committee to investigate subversive activities in colleges and schools. Fears about the vulnerability of young minds also renewed attention to teaching materials. A new attack on textbooks was launched in 1939, focused specifically on the texts published by education professor Harold Rugg, and was greatly intensified in 1940 with a campaign by the *American Legion Magazine* against "Treason in the Textbooks." Some localities responded with their own actions. At a hearing by the Georgia Board of Education, for example, a state police captain pointed at Rugg and shouted: "There sits the ringmaster of the fifth columnists in America, financed by the Russian government." School districts across the country dropped the texts, whose sales plummeted. So did membership of the Communist Party as its unpopularity increased; a Gallup Poll reported in May 1941 that 71 percent wanted the party outlawed.[31]

Yet there were limits to the "little red scare", and the excesses hardly compared with those associated with the First World War and its subsequent Red Scare. That scare had left sedition in the hands of the states while the federal government guarded the nation's borders. During the little red scare and the Second World War the balance changed as the states began to yield ground to federal authorities in the maintenance of internal security. Aware of the notorious vigilante activities a generation earlier, the Roosevelt administration did what it could to discourage such behavior, and discounted ideas of deploying quasi-official groups after the manner of the earlier war's American Protective League. Nonetheless "defense organizations" and rifle clubs did appear. In 1939

---

[30] Shirley A. Wiegand and Wayne A. Wiegand, *Books on Trial: Red Scare in the Heartland* (Norman, OK, 2007); "Attacks on the Communist Party," typescript in vol. 2203, 1940, ACLU Records; James A. Robinson, *Anti-Sedition Legislation and Loyalty Investigations in Oklahoma* (Norman, OK, 1956), 23–31.

[31] ACLU, *The States and Subversion* (New York, 1953), 8–9; Robinson, *Anti-Sedition Legislation*, 37; Nelson and Roberts, *Censors and the Schools*, 35–9; Heale, *American Anticommunism*, 129.

Roosevelt insisted that investigations into espionage and disloyalty should be the responsibility of the FBI; any information on such matters, he instructed local police authorities, should be "promptly" referred to the nearest FBI official. Over the next two years discussions to implement this objective were held with state officials, who accepted that state sedition laws should not be used. J. Edgar Hoover was happy to promote the message "Leave it to the FBI"; he was "diametrically opposed to anything suggesting vigilante activities." The FBI did use Legionnaires as a source of information, though this was largely a pre-emptive device to deter veterans from carrying out their own investigations. U.S. Attorney General Robert Jackson instructed his officers to discourage private citizens from acting on their own initiative, insisting that American liberties were endangered more by "our own excitement" than any enemy conspiracies. Major newspapers generally sustained this message, and in June 1940 the American Legion formally renounced vigilantism. A Justice Department report in May 1941 observed that while many repressive bills had been introduced into the state legislatures in 1940, few had made it into law.[32]

***

The celebrated Red Scare may have rapidly deflated in 1920–21 but anti-Communist activity had remained a disruptive motif of American life throughout the interwar era. In the aftermath of the First World War an informal understanding had been reached between the federal and state authorities on their strategy for combating the perceived menace of Communism. The federal government erected formidable barriers in the form of immigration laws and deportation procedures to exclude subversive aliens, and the states assumed responsibility for internal security, deploying such instruments as sedition laws, revitalized National Guard units and city red squads. Frequently urging the public authorities on, and often acting on their own responsibility, were a host of businesses, patriotic societies, veterans' organizations, civic bodies, and racist groups. "Citizens committees" were regularly created in particular communities to take the offensive against the un-American 'outsiders' who were bent on advancing Moscow's fell design (or so it was said of those who seemed to be threatening the established economic and social order of such communities). These various patriotic endeavors did not constitute a coherent movement, but their recurrence and resilience ensured that when the federal authorities again had reason to turn on the nation's Communists they would have vital allies

---

[32] Steele, *Free Speech in the Good War*, 78–80, 83; Donner, *Protectors of Privilege*, 46; Heale, *American Anticommunism*, 126; Pencak, *For God & Country*, 314.

scattered across the body politic. The interaction of such influences from below with the anti-Communist imperatives of Washington would give what became known as McCarthyism its potency.

But that was in the future. As active anti-Communism effectively disappeared during the Second World War it seemed possible that little more would be heard from it. Many on the left looked forward with confidence to advancing progressive causes in the post-war years. "For liberals," recalled Carey McWilliams, "... 1946 began as a year of bright promise and keen anticipations."[33]

---

[33] ACLU, *Liberty on the Home Front: In the Fourth Year of the War* (New York, July 1945), 5, 32; ACLU, *From War to Peace: American Liberties 1945–46* (New York, July 1946), 7; Carey McWilliams, *The Education of Carey McWilliams* (New York, 1979), 121.

Chapter 4

Red Herrings? The Fish Committee and Anti-Communism in the Early Depression Years[1]

Alex Goodall

I

What can be said of the Fish Committee beyond the damning indictment provided by the journalist Walter Goodman half a century ago? For years after it completed its work, Goodman noted, "critics were still pointing out that it took testimony from 225 witnesses in fourteen cities, produced a voluminous report, and passed at once into obscurity."[2] Even while the committee was conducting its investigations, between June and December 1930, newspapers and the general public showed little interest in its findings, distracted by the more pressing problems of rising unemployment and recession. When after a month in Washington the committee traveled to New York, then further afield, the *New York Times* commented that it had passed through the city "almost unnoticed." Even *Pravda* reportedly mocked the committee as a sideshow.[3] The committee's calls for a strengthened Federal Bureau of Investigation were widely rejected as excessive and unnecessary, the *New York Times* noting that "watchfulness without panic is plainly the method which the great majority of Americans would wish to see applied."[4] No legislation followed the submission of concluding recommendations to Congress, and no lucrative speaking tours followed for its members, who more or less vanished from the Congressional record after the

---

[1] For providing comments and suggestions during the drafting of this work, I wish to express my gratitude to Robert Justin Goldstein, George Lewis and Markku Ruotsila.

[2] Walter Goodman, *The Committee: The Extraordinary Career of the House Committee on Un-American Activities* (London, 1964), p. 12.

[3] "Moscow Pokes Fun at 'Sideshow' Here," *New York Times*, July 28, 1930.

[4] "Neither Indifference nor Panic," *New York Times*, August 2, 1930.

72   *Little 'Red Scares'*

hearings ended.[5] Only the chairman and leading light, the aristocratic, charming and somewhat feckless Republican from upstate New York, Hamilton Fish III, continued his restless search for political celebrity, leading him later in the decade to the anti-interventionist movement and an outspoken policy of Nazi appeasement that would ruin his reputation and see him gerrymandered out of office by his own party in the later years of World War Two.

For good or ill, the Fish Committee merits the singular qualification of being the only anti-Communist investigative committee in American history to have failed entirely to have a substantial political impact, either in terms of legislation or influence over public debate, begging the question why this particular dog did not bark when so many others did. After all, many of the features that historians have identified as underlying causes of anti-Communist fearfulness were clearly present in 1930, including a widespread sense of alienation from the processes of modernization, urbanization and industrial mass production; continuing tensions between deskilled industrial laborers, poor rural workers and employers over pay, conditions and the right to organize; anxieties among ruling elites over their potential displacement by rising social and ethnic groups; and large numbers of non-assimilated immigrants living in the nation's cities, borderlands and industrial regions. Nor were the committee's complaints entirely without substance: Fish and his colleagues publicized specific and damning evidence about the Gulag, three decades before Solzhenitsyn's works were published in the West, and uncovered suggestive material relating to covert Soviet activities in the United States, an issue that would be central to resurgent anti-Communist politics in the years after World War Two. If the party, as always, remained a miniscule presence in American life, the changes in the Soviet line that stemmed from Stalin's consolidation of power in Russia, most importantly the declaration of the "Third Period" in 1928, had given orthodox Communism a millenarian thrust that had been absent for much of the mid-1920s. Communists seemed to be riding the crest of a wave of political polarization, something that had the potential to open the party to a wider audience and open bloody wounds in American society. This was a cause of great disquiet to their foes.

Local level repression of political activism had surged in response to depression-related discontent, especially in terms of labor-employer disputes, yet this was not paralleled by anti-Communist action at the national level.[6] Despite the clear preconditions for Red Scare politics, Representative Fish's

---

[5]   R.N. Current, "Hamilton Fish: Crusading Isolationist," in J.T. Salter (ed.), *Public Men In and Out of Office* (New York, 1972), p. 215.

[6]   Robert Justin Goldstein, *Political Repression in Modern America: From 1870 to the Present* (Cambridge, MA, 1978), pp. 195–6; M.J. Heale, *American Anticommunism: Combating the Enemy Within, 1830–1970* (Baltimore, 1990), p. 101.

committee was unable to provide the spark to produce a national public outcry or to pass legislation to control radical activities. Indeed, inasmuch as it offered an unconvincing critique of Communism, the committee's exertions ended up strengthening claims that antiradical fears were simply a bugbear promoted by elites to preserve their privileges and resist reform.

Undoubtedly, part of the blame for this failure can be laid at the feet of the organizers, especially the chairman, who consistently overpromised and under-delivered. Even Fish's personal assets turned out to be political liabilities. His polite, meandering approach in the chair was a major departure from the hectoring tones one normally associates with anti-Communist committees, yet rarely produced the kinds of clashes likely to generate journalistic interest. Anticipating attacks from the left, Fish claimed to be developing a rigorous case against Communism on the basis of "facts" and "evidence", not accusations and opinion. Yet he and his peers were unable to avoid giving in to their own conservative prejudices when conducting the hearings. He attempted to marshal public anger over the economic crisis by blaming it on Communist machinations, but this failed to appeal either to business leaders or the suffering masses. Rather than strengthening his credibility, Fish's failed attempts at rigor saw him satisfy neither rationalists nor ideologues, while a series of blunders undermined key opportunities for the kinds of spectacular revelations that generally led to front-page coverage. Fish ended up expressing neither the force of deep expertise nor the explosiveness of McCarthyite histrionics. Rather than praising him for his restraint or fearing his excess, Fish was mocked for his flimsiness.

Nevertheless, one cannot entirely separate these individual failings from the more systemic weaknesses of anti-Communist politics in the depression years. The line adopted by the committee, a mistaken attempt to link anger over the depression to a more traditional anti-Communist agenda and to pre-empt liberal attacks by focusing heavily on Communist institutions rather than the left as a whole, was due to circumstance as well as philosophy. Many of the key groups that normally propelled the right wing into anti-Communist politics – patriotic organizations, federal investigators, bureaucrats and big businessmen – were divided among themselves, had been exposed as incompetent or were disengaged from the debate. Meanwhile, many of those who made the most effective case against revolutionary radicalism – especially anti-Communists in the union movement – used fears of Communism to lobby for reform rather than repression. The outcome was a discordant political message with contradictory conclusions that satisfied neither right nor left and failed to persuade the public that Communist activities were a pressing issue of national security. Only once a new set of anti-Communist alliances began to develop later in the 1930s, when anti-Communist politics was driven primarily by a new coalition of business groups, anti-federal populists and Southern segregationists, would anti-Communists again be able to substantively impact the direction of national politics.

II

Hamilton Fish was a fascinating and in many ways characteristic exemplar of the patrician order that still retained influence in East Coast politics in the interwar years. The Fish family traced their origins to Peter Stuyvesant, the Dutch colonial governor of New York, and Thomas Hooker, the founder of Connecticut colony. Later scions boasted histories of proud public engagement in both state and national politics; Fish's grandfather had been Secretary of State under Ulysses S. Grant. Fish was named after a cousin who had died in the Spanish-American War fighting with the "Rough Riders", and there can be little doubt that TR's image shone brightly in Fish's mind. While he demonstrated less of the roving intellect so characteristic of the twenty-sixth President, he shared many of Roosevelt's personal values, including an enthusiasm for energetic outdoor activity and spirited gamesmanship, and for the army as a workshop of a republican, democratic order. Fish had led the 369th Infantry in World War One, was inducted into the *Légion d'honneur* for his service in France, acted as a founding member of the American Legion in 1919 alongside Theodore Roosevelt Jr., and authored the bill providing for the return of the Unknown Soldier to Arlington National Cemetery. Despite his aristocratic heritage, he prided himself on affecting no airs and graces, and – like Roosevelt before him – believed that elite status came with an obligation to further progressive reform for the benefit of the less fortunate: even to the point of supporting social security, minimum wage and anti-lynching laws in the New Deal years.[7]

After his election to Congress in 1920, though, Fish had struggled to find an appropriate outlet for his patriotic energies, and the later years of the decade saw him engaged in what seemed like a scatter-gun search for an issue of public concern he might focus upon. In July, August and September of 1929 alone, Fish was quoted in the press denouncing Jim Crow laws in the South and praising the African American war record, defending the Kellogg–Briand pact as a glorious bloodless revolution for peace, attacking Franklin Roosevelt and Tammany Hall, calling for a US military intervention to defend Jewish settlers against Arab violence in Palestine and involving himself in a complicated debate with various political opponents, the State Banking Department, a judge and J.P. Morgan over

---

[7]   Current, "Hamilton Fish: Crusading Isolationist," pp. 210–24.

the proposed construction of a canal connecting the Great Lakes to St. Lawrence. Indeed, later in the year, he launched another ball into the air, correcting several misstatements in an ongoing debate over who was the tallest President.[8]

While anti-Communism was undoubtedly a deeply held commitment, then, there can be no doubt that it also offered a chance for an aspiring politician to attach his name to an issue in a way that would have offered clear advantages in any future bid for power within the Republican Party apparatus. As the effects of the depression had become increasingly visible, society had polarized over the issue of political radicalism. Many of the antiradical groups that had emerged during and after World War One remained active and energetic, but were confronted by a growing civil liberties-based opposition. Pressure was building for the recognition of Soviet Russia: the United States was the last great power not to have established formal ties with the Communist regime. However, opponents of recognition were given a fillip after reports of the persecution of Russian Jews and orchestrated attacks on Christianity were circulated in late 1929 and early 1930.[9] Indeed, opposition to the Soviet Union on religious grounds was as strong if not stronger than hostility to the "socialist" economics the nation also embodied. At home, unemployment protests in which radical activists loomed large descended into violence as demonstrators and police fought for control of the streets, but opinions starkly divided over who was culpable. A number of senior Communists – including the party leader, William Z. Foster – were tried and briefly imprisoned for allegedly provoking violence; however, liberals and socialists warned against a resurgence of "the lawless activities of Attorney General Palmer in 1919" and called for public hearings into police brutality.[10] Tensions continued to build in 1930 after three Communists, Alfred Luro, Steve Katovis and Gonzalo Gonzales, were killed during separate altercations with the police.

If resurgent anti-Communist feeling explained the appeal of the issue to the Republican representative, then growing resistance to the same politics of anti-Communism may explain why Fish sought to distinguish his case against the Reds from the more sweeping and uncritical forms of antiradicalism that had done so much damage to the credibility of the movement in previous years.

---

[8]   "Blames Politics for De Priest Case," *New York Times*, July 1, 1929; "New Citizens Urged to Obey Our Laws," *New York Times*, July 5, 1929; "Two Add $50,000 to Palestine Fund," *New York Times*, August 29, 1929; "Fish and Celler Urge Action in Palestine," *New York Times,* September 5, 1929; "Christians Appeal for Palestine Fund," *New York Times*, September 16, 1929; "St. Lawrence Canal Ridiculed by Fish," September 19, 1929; "City Trust Enquiry Demanded by Fish," September 29, 1929; "Topics of the Times," *New York Times*, November 1, 1929.

[9]   "Fish Urges Congress Protest Soviet Drive," *New York Times*, February 20, 1930.

[10]   "Whalen Tells Employers of 300 Reds They Hired," *New York Times*, March 11, 1930.

In a statement issued to the press at the opening of the hearings, Fish declared that "this committee does not propose to investigate socialism, radicalism or pacifism as such, nor does it seek to interfere with the political beliefs of any one in this country, nor with the rights of American citizens to freedom of speech, as guaranteed by the Constitution."[11] Instead, his indictment centered on three key assertions: that the Soviet Union was single-mindedly focused on the destruction of the American system of government; that the Communist Party in America was entirely a tool of Soviet foreign policy; and that to achieve their revolutionary goals Communists sought to exploit vulnerabilities in American society and undermine the social contract: orchestrating riots and strikes among unemployed or suffering workers, using the Soviet Union's economic muscle to destabilize American businesses and markets, provoking hostility among ethnic and racial minorities, causing people to question their faith in religion, and inciting America's young people to rebel against existing structures of social, pedagogical and familial authority.[12] Fish also argued that the current economic crisis could in large part be blamed on subversive efforts by Communists to destabilize the economy.

This line substantially differed from figures further to the right who expressed little or no interest in the difference between pro-Stalinist Communists and other actors on the left and center of American political life. Taken together, it was an almost exact inversion of the orthodox Communist view of the committee, which depicted Fish and his fellow Congressmen as part of a general effort among the capitalist classes to prepare the public for an imperialist war against Russia, as the stooge of Wall Street and corporate interests, and unable to recognize that it was the contradictions of capitalism, not the agitation of Communists, that made social harmony impossible.[13] The committee declared that Communism was not a legitimate political movement because it sought the overthrow of the American government through force and violence; Communists insisted that while any revolution would naturally end in violence this would stem from the actions of capitalists attempting to hold onto power.[14]

---

[11]   "Congress Red Quest Shifts Here Today," *New York Times* July 15, 1930.

[12]   United States Congress, *Hearing Before the Committee on Rules House of Representatives, Seventy-First Congress, 2nd Sess., on H. Res. 180* (Washington, 1930).

[13]   United States Congress, *Hearings before a Special Committee to Investigate Communist Activities in the United States of the House of Representatives, Seventy-First Congress, 2nd Sess., Pursuant to H. Res. 220, providing for an investigation of Communist propaganda in the United States* (Washington, 1930), Part 1, vol. 4, pp. 352, 358–9. Hereafter referred to as "Fish Committee."

[14]   Fish Committee, Part 1, vol. 4, p. 387.

In short, the committee focused on the Soviet Union, the relationship between the Communist International and the Communist Party of America, and the role played by Communists in the various Communist-dominated organizations through which the party worked. The only significant exception to this rule was the American Civil Liberties Union (ACLU): which was non-partisan but had a small number of Communists in senior positions and a reputation as the most outspoken defender of dissenters' rights, for which Fish and several witnesses pounded them incessantly.[15]

To emphasize their analytical credentials in the face of widespread criticism, the Congressmen repeatedly stated that their job was to gather "facts" about Communist activities, not to offer "opinions", and encouraged witnesses to read thousands of pages of documentary proof into the record to substantiate their claims (presumably in the belief that the quantity of documentary evidence somehow spoke to its quality). This tendency could be seen in previous antiradical campaigns, many of which sought to distinguish their "education" and "investigation" campaigns from radical "propaganda" activities; however, the depression crisis and poor record anti-Communists had earned for smearing and misdirection in previous years gave this language a new importance. To demonstrate its rigor, the committee studied Marxist-Leninist tracts, records of Communist Party proceedings and translations of the Soviet constitution.[16] Witnesses straying too far from the topic or speculating too wildly were warned to refocus their testimony on party organs and activities, and to avoid personal attacks and hearsay, while on several occasions Fish opened sessions by repeating his initial declaration that the committee had no interest in investigating socialists, pacifists or liberals.[17] "The only bad thing [Fish] could say about Socialist Norman Thomas," the historian Richard Gid Powers notes, "was that he had gone to Princeton."[18] Meanwhile, the most common lawyerly tactic deployed by the Congressmen was not bullying and defamation insulated by Congressional privilege, but damning through excessive civility.[19] Tactically, at least, the committeemen were more Joseph Welch than Joseph McCarthy.

---

[15] Ibid., Part 5, vol. 3, p. 11. In the case of professional patriot Francis Ralston Welsh, the committee offered the witness broad latitude to denounce the ACLU as an ally of Communists, but after his comments showed signs of obsession they tried repeatedly to get him to move on. Ibid., Part 1, vol. 4, pp. 128–32.

[16] For instance, see ibid., Part 1, vol. 1, pp. 11–17.

[17] Ibid., Part 1, vol. 1, p. 43; Part 1, vol. 2, pp. 5–10; Part 1, vol. 3, p. 12; Part 5, vol. 3, p. 287.

[18] Richard Gid Powers, *Not Without Honor: The History of American Anticommunism* (New York, 1995), p. 88.

[19] Fish Committee, Part 1, vol. 4, p. 377.

One of Fish's key early witnesses was the Jesuit priest and founder of Georgetown's School of Foreign Service, Father Edmund A. Walsh: a man whose attitude toward Communism had been fixed by his experiences during a Vatican-sponsored famine relief mission to Russia in 1922–23.[20] As with many Christian anti-Communists, the foundation of Walsh's personal opposition to the Soviet Union lay in a vision of Communism as the paramount force of organized atheism in the modern world. However, while he discussed this before the committee Walsh stressed that the geopolitical antagonism between the United States and the Soviet Union was at root a clash of political philosophies.[21] To him, Marxism-Leninism fundamentally conflicted with liberal republicanism because it declared all areas of society to be parts of a unified political whole, unlike the Anglo-Saxon tradition which designated certain key realms – the individual, the home, the community, the church – as 'non-political' spheres off-limits to state action. In this sense, Walsh's arguments grew from traditions of popular democratic anti-Europeanism that had infused American identity with a profound hostility to the centralized political systems of the Old World; although the Protestant underpinnings of this were downplayed by Walsh in his generalized assertion of the importance of non-sectarian Christian anti-Communism. Walsh also claimed that the Soviets were using trade policy to conduct "economic warfare" against the United States. He argued that the Soviets were using predatory pricing strategies to destroy American businesses by swamping them with cheap Russian imports. Over time, this would induce a state of dependency, weakening America's capacity in any future war between the two nations.[22] Fish followed up by arguing that Communists in America had been instigators of the current depression crisis, not least by creating tensions between employees and employers that ground down American business, and later in the hearings claimed that radicals had been promoting "whispering campaigns" in order to precipitate runs on banks.[23]

Clearly, this "economic warfare" theory represented an opportunistic attempt to link pressing public concerns over the economy to the presence of Communists in America (and the world). However, as well as suiting the autarchic temper of the times, it anticipated broader tendencies among conservatives in later years to present their hostility to Communism in terms of

---

[20] Warren I. Cohen, *Empire without Tears: America's Foreign Relations, 1921–1933* (New York, 1987), p. 88.

[21] For Walsh's anti-Communism, see Patrick McNamara, *A Catholic Cold War: Edmund A. Walsh, S.J., and the Politics of American Anticommunism* (New York, 2005).

[22] For a more extended development of these arguments, see Edmund A. Walsh, *The Last Stand: An Interpretation of the Soviet Five-Year Plan* (Boston, 1931).

[23] "Bank Run Laid to Reds," *New York Times*, December 25, 1930.

free market economics; as with the enthusiasm for Friedrich Hayek's *The Road to Serfdom* or the writings of Ayn Rand.[24]

In 1930, this was a novel approach to explaining US–Soviet relations; and in the months following the Wall Street crash was certainly brave, if not foolhardy. The basic premise that politics and ideology were interfering with a "natural" pattern of free commerce was leveled at many nations in the aftermath of the near total collapse of international comity following the crash: as, for example, with claims that French "golden bullets" had caused the collapse of the central European banking sector and subsequent global depression.[25] But authors and political actors who specifically thought about "economic warfare" in the interwar years tended to use the term to refer to strategies for targeting an enemy's productive capacity *during* military conflict.[26] Arguably, the closest echoes of Walsh's arguments about a hidden economic war being waged against America could be found in the Marxist tradition to which he was responding: especially the Leninist attack on empire as a search for markets, or arguments that the American government had used trade and fiscal policies to achieve dominance in the Caribbean, Latin America and Asia.

Later in the decade, the financial journalist Paul Einzig's *Bloodless Invasion* (1938) suggested that Nazi ambitions had been promoted prior to open warfare through the economic penetration of the Danube Basin and the Balkans by a secret "Nazi International."[27] By the time of the Cold War, the language of military struggle would be regularly used in reference to not only the economic but also the social and cultural spheres when describing the confrontation between East and West. In this sense, Edmund Walsh and the Fish Committee were ahead of their time. However, in another way this was a very traditional American argument. By linking moral outrage with economic self-interest, the effort to articulate an idea of Soviet economic warfare resembled the kind of free labor arguments that were so effective in mobilizing the North against the "slave power conspiracy" before the Civil War. It also picked up on anti-trust traditions

---

[24] Alan Brinkley, "The Problem of American Conservatism," *American Historical Review* 99, no. 2 (April 1964), pp. 416–7; Jennifer Burns, *Goddess of the Market: Ayn Rand and the American Right* (Oxford, 2009).

[25] Paul Einzig, *Behind the Scenes of International Finance* (London, 1931), pp. 10, 121–2.

[26] For instance, D.T. Jack, *Studies in Economic Warfare* (London, 1940). Cf. Jacob Viner, "The Prevalence of Dumping in International Trade," *The Journal of Political Economy* 30, no. 5 (October 1922), pp. 655–80; Robert J. Young, "Spokesmen for Economic Warfare: The Industrial Intelligence Centre in the 1930s," *European History Quarterly* 6 (1976), pp. 473–89.

[27] Paul Einzig, *Bloodless Invasion: German Economic Penetration into the Danubian States and the Balkans* (London, 1938). See also Thomas P. Brockway, *Battles Without Bullets: The Story of Economic Warfare* (New York, 1939); Paul Einzig, *Economic Warfare* (London, 1940).

in American political discourse. Walsh took ideas about the dangers of anti-competitive business practices in the commercial sphere and applied them to geopolitics, following a broader early twentieth century tendency to shift the language and ideals of American business into the conduct of foreign affairs.[28] He argued that since the Soviet Union exercised total control over its productive base through state-owned industrial and commercial enterprises, export cartels and foreign trade bodies, it was able to use monopoly influence in international commerce to promote a revolutionary agenda around the world.

Walsh's stress on clashing political philosophies and use of economistic arguments to structure his approach to international relations was useful to the committee, not least because it allowed Fish to distance himself from several strands of anti-Semitic, ultra-conspiratorial or racially derived anti-Communism that were in circulation in the interwar years. Unlike the earlier anti-Communist investigations at a state and national level headed by Lee Slater Overman and Clayton Lusk, none of the Fish Committee members and only a few of their witnesses claimed that Soviet Communism was part of a deep rationalist-collectivist conspiracy dating back to Adam Weishaupt and the Order of the Illuminati: a trope common among ahistorical right-wing conspiracy theorists who had been influenced by extremist writers such as the British anti-Semite and fascist, Nesta Webster, as well as many religious radicals who saw the Soviet Union as just another front in the eternal battle against Satan.[29] *The Protocols of the Elders of Zion*, which had fuelled theories of the Bolshevik state as the manifestation of a hidden conspiracy to engineer a Jewish world government, made no appearance; despite the fact that Fish would be accused later in the decade of using his Congressional office to circulate the *Protocols* to isolationist supporters.[30] When witnesses made casually racist remarks about Jews, Italians and Greeks as temperamentally more inclined to adopt radical ideologies, the chairman intervened to stress the patriotic loyalty of minority groups.[31] At one point, Fish repeated a claim that had been suggested to him by a Russian

---

[28] For instance, Emily Rosenberg, *Financial Missionaries to the World: The Politics and Culture of Dollar Diplomacy* (Cambridge, MA, 1999).

[29] Richard M. Gilman, *Behind "World revolution": The Strange Career of Nesta H. Webster* (Ann Arbor, 1982); Markku Ruotsila, "Mrs. Webster's Religion: Conspiracist Extremism on the Christian Far Right," *Patterns of Prejudice* 38 (June 2004), pp. 109–26; Martha F. Lee, "Nesta Webster: The Voice of Conspiracy," in *Journal of Women's History*, 17, no. 3 (Fall 2005), pp. 81–104. At one point, Representative Nelson asked William Z. Foster to clarify whether Marx's ideas were "based more or less on the belief and teachings of the Order of the Illuminati." Foster replied: "Of whom?" Fish Committee, Part 1, vol. 4, p. 347.

[30] Ernest Volkman, *A Legacy of Hate: Anti-Semitism in America* (New York, 1982), p. 42.

[31] Fish Committee, Part 1, vol. 1, pp. 77–8, 119.

immigrant and former member of the Industrial Workers of the World: that the correlation between non-citizenship and revolutionary radicalism was the result of social conditioning rather than racial or national character; the experience of repression in Europe had accustomed immigrants to be hostile to all forms of government, a view they had "received with their mother's milk" and had left them unable to see that the United States was qualitatively different to the undemocratic countries they had left.[32] Fish continued to associate radicalism with immigrants, but emphasized this was a political and cultural, not a racial, phenomenon. Though he supplied no evidence to support the claim, Fish even implausibly suggested that Communism in the black community was linked solely to West Indian immigrants, not natural born citizens.[33] Fish had been regimental commander of the 369th Regiment in World War One – the "Harlem Hellfighters" were the first African American regiment to serve during the war – was a fervent opponent of lynching and was outraged by suggestions of black disloyalty. When one black ex-Communist claimed that there were 100,000 African American Communists in the Southern states ready to revolt, Fish vigorously dissented, pointing out that "by and large, the colored people in this country, men and women, are Christians who attend church and believe in God and ... the Communists teach hatred of God."[34] To support his view, he called upon black liberal leaders such as Illinois Congressman Oscar de Priest and the union leader A. Philip Randolph, who were eager to distance black people from any taint of Communism for understandable reasons of their own, and conservative churchmen such as the Baptist preacher Dr. William A. Venerable, who when quizzed by the chair about the influence of Communism in his church wryly remarked that he had generally found "more among the Methodists," much to the amusement of the audience.[35]

Clearly, then, the chairman was more of a conservative than a right-wing radical in his anti-Communist politics, at least at a point in his career when he still aspired to a position of national leadership within the Republican Party. Nor were his fellow Congressmen especially extreme in their analysis, although the presence of Carl Bachmann of West Virginia, Edward E. Eslick of Tennessee, and Robert Hall of Mississippi – with Bachmann playing a particularly vocal role – did give the committee a distinctly Southern feel. The hearings thus presented a less extreme indictment of Communism than that offered by more radical counter-subversives, who were either excluded from the witness rosters

---

[32] The same point was repeated by Ellis Searles of the United Mine Workers' Association. Ibid., Part 3, vol. 4, p. 4; Part 4, vol. 1, p. 125; Part 5, vol. 3, p. 245.

[33] Ibid., Part 4, vol. 2, p. 337.

[34] Ibid., Part 6, vol. 1, pp. 222–3.

[35] Ibid., Part 3, vol. 1, pp. 243, 252; Part 4, vol. 2, p. 336–7; Part 5, vol. 3, p. 284.

82   Little 'Red Scares'

or carefully managed when giving evidence. It offered a critique shaped by anti-authoritarian and free market capitalist political assumptions, a whole-hearted endorsement of American political institutions, a rejection of simple ethnic determinism, and a focus upon Communist institutions rather than on the left as a whole. Indeed, their detailed analyses of Communist activity were founded on substantive evidence and were sometimes plausible and convincing.

Among other things, the committee uncovered some of the first evidence of Soviet covert operations in the United States: an issue that would become a central part of the anti-Communist debate after World War Two. The most revealing discoveries came from some of the earliest Soviet defectors, who shed light on the role of secret agents working within Amtorg: the Soviet trading bureau in New York that, in the absence of formal diplomatic infrastructure, had come to resemble something close to a Soviet embassy in the public mind.[36] Edmund Walsh presented information that had come from the published memoirs of a senior defector from the Parisian Embassy, Grigori Bessedovsky, who had been scheduled to take up post as president of Amtorg but was diverted at the last minute. Bessedovsky had abandoned Communism after he came under suspicion of disloyalty and subsequently released a slew of self-justifying accounts of the secret side of Soviet diplomacy.[37] Much of this material had so far only been published in French. The most important witness to appear in person before the committee was Basil Delgass, who until recently had been the Vice President of Amtorg. Delgass had been summoned back to Moscow a few months prior to the hearings' commencement and, fearing for his safety, resigned once the Fish Committee began and offered to testify against his former colleagues. Delgass declared that Amtorg was systematically lying about the presence of Soviet secret police (OGPU) operatives on American shores. He claimed that the current president, Peter A. Bogdanov, and his office manager Feodor Mikhailovich Ziavkin were political appointees and in all likelihood members of the Soviet secret service themselves; a claim substantiated by another émigré witness.[38] Delgass also stated that there was a hidden party cell within the bureau whose members passed themselves off as trade delegates while they conducted covert operations. He ridiculed the idea that it was possible to have such an important bureau in the United States without close supervision from the secret

---

[36]   See testimony in ibid., Part 3, vol. 3.

[37]   Grigory Bessedovsky, *Revelations of a Soviet Diplomat* (London, 1931), pp. 90–91, 109–18; Gordon Brook-Shepherd, *The Storm Petrels: The First Soviet Defectors, 1928–1938* (London, 1977), pp. 85–106. Bessedovsky also implicated Boris Skvirsky, the Director of the Soviet Union Information Bureau, in covert activities; something that was strongly denied by Skvirsky on the stand. Fish Committee, Part 1, vol. 5, p. 39.

[38]   Fish Committee, Part 3, vol. 3, p. 301–2; Part 3, vol. 4, p. 28.

apparatus.[39] Witnesses from Amtorg claimed that their employees were either not Communists or had left the party before coming to the United States; this was shown to be largely an administrative fiction designed to overcome visa and immigration issues in the wake of the 1918 Immigration Act, which made it a deportable offense to belong to an organization committed to the overthrow of the United States government by force or violence.

In uncovering this material, the committee did not concern itself with the distinction between espionage conducted against the American government and crucial industries, of which there was relatively little evidence uncovered, and Soviet efforts to monitor their own people while they worked in foreign lands, which was clearly endemic. Nevertheless, the testimony suggested much about how deeply the habits of a surveillance state had come to shape the Communist world.[40]

While Soviet espionage activities in the United States spoke most directly to the committee's claims about a national security threat at home, arguably the committee's most important efforts were in publicizing the testimony of journalists, Russian exiles and former Communists about the conditions of millions of Soviet prisoners held in the labor camps known as the Gulag.[41] This stretched far beyond the committee's mandate, which was only to investigate Communist activities in the United States. Nevertheless, the Congressmen effectively ignored their brief by claiming – in line with the "economic warfare" hypothesis – that the Soviet Union was exporting goods to the United States that had been effectively produced by slave labor. This, they argued, was not only a moral outrage but also a violation of anti-dumping laws. It was also, in their terms, a domestic issue since it threatened to push American businesses into bankruptcy. The theme of "Soviet slave labor" had been developed sporadically in the past by anti-Communist politicians, but now was given full rein through a detailed study of Russian labor practices.[42]

Despite the best Soviet efforts to keep foreigners away from and unaware of the Gulag, after several years of large-scale operation it had become increasingly

---

[39] Ibid., Part 1, vol. 4, pp. 211–3; Part 3, vol. 4, pp. 173–6.

[40] For the development of Soviet espionage during the 1930s, see Katherine A.S. Sibley, *Red Spies in America: Stolen Secrets and the Dawn of the Cold War* (Lawrence, 2004).

[41] Fish Committee, Part 1, vol. 4, pp. 27–8, 95–109, 158–62, 202–206; Part 3, vol. 4, pp. 28–9; Part 4, vol. 2, pp. 437–44.

[42] See, for precursors, the attacks upon the Russian Information Bureau in United States Senate, *Russian Propaganda. Hearings before a subcommittee of the Committee on Foreign Relations pursuant to S. Res. 263, directing the Committee on Foreign Relations to investigate the status and activities of Ludwig C.A.K. Martens, who claimed to be a representative of the Russian Socialist Soviet Republic* (Washington, 1920).

84 *Little 'Red Scares'*

possible to construct a surprisingly detailed picture of life in the camps.[43] Although mention was made of forced labor in the Doretz Basin mines, Karelia, the forests around Kirov Oblast, and regions of collectivized farming in the Ukraine, the committee principally focused on the lumber camps on the mainland close to Solovetski Island, where several hundred thousand people were being worked to death to produce material for commercial exportation. This was on the grounds that such activities could be directly traced to trade with the United States. Witnesses provided information on conditions, working hours, rates of pay and nutrition, as well as estimates of export volumes. The most powerful testimony was of course the anecdotal experiences of escapees and their families. Alexander Lukovitz, who had fled to the United States after a harrowing escape from the camps through Finland in 1929, told the committee he had endured 16 to 18 hour days cutting wood in freezing weather, fed only on salted fish heads, black bread and thin barley soup, and sleeping at night in damp, overfilled barracks. In an environment that resembled something akin to a Darwinian nightmare, those who couldn't keep up with the vicious work routine were stripped naked and made to stand on freezing tree stumps, cudgeled to death, or simply shot by guards. Meanwhile, typhus, scurvy, gangrene and a variety of other diseases were common and lethal.[44] Another witness, an indigent Latvian merchant sailor named Alexander Grube, told how he had been arrested after going ashore illegally in Russia and had been imprisoned by the OGPU for four months before being sent to the labor camps for two and a half years. Because of his rough and rambling manner, several of the representatives doubted the wisdom of hearing Grube's testimony, but Fish insisted on it. As a result, the committee heard how Grube had been sent on lumber details in which literally thousands of prisoners had died from malnourishment and overwork.[45]

Communist witnesses explicitly denied the existence or the scale of the camps, or that the Soviet system would ever make use of forced labor.[46] These denials formed part of a broader set of implausible arguments about the character of international Communism put forward by its American defenders: that the Soviet leadership had no responsibility for the activities of the Comintern; that Russians working for the Soviet government in the United States were non-political appointees; that workers' conditions in proletarian Russia were sublime; and that Stalin did not really run the Soviet government since he was only the head of the

---

[43] Despite the criticism he would later receive for his later articles on the hunger and starvation in the *kolkozy*, Edmund Walsh recommended consulting the writings of Walter Duranty for information on forced labor in Russia. Fish Committee, Part 1, vol. 4, p. 26.

[44] Ibid., Part 1, vol. 4, pp. 430–35.

[45] Ibid., Part 1, vol. 4, pp. 84–94.

[46] Ibid., Part 1, vol. 4, p. 357; Part 3, vol. 4, p. 230.

Communist Party.[47] These were joined by self-justifying circumlocutions, as when, confronted with the apparent contradiction between Communist demands for constitutional protection in the United States and their refusal to accord similar rights to protestors in Russia, William Z. Foster explained: "The worker in America who fights for the program of the Communist Party is a fighter for the progress of society in general. The capitalist who proposes the overthrow of the Soviet Government is an enemy of the human society."[48]

Others on the non-Communist left – unaware or unwilling to listen to evidence of Soviet repression and hopeful that socialist politics more generally offered a way out of the crisis of capitalism in which the nation found itself – also rejected, and even mocked, the evidence raised by the committee on these issues. One writer for *The Nation* described Fish's decision to question Amtorg's president Bogdanov about the origins of Soviet exports as "play[ing] medicine ball with a man who is in charge of trade worth at least $100,000,000 a year to the United States," and dismissed debates over the patterns of control within the international Communist movement as "tedious metaphysical discussions."[49] In a particularly extreme *ad hominem* attack in *The New Republic*, Edmund Wilson denounced one escapee from the Gulag as "one of the most untrustworthy characters who has surely ever been called upon to testify to anything, a pale-eyed, shifty-eyed, shaved-headed man, represented as an honest Russian farmer sent to prison for criticizing the Soviets." Several decades later, when republishing the piece in a collection of essays, Wilson apologized for his comments, noting they were the "kind of thing that is to be sedulously avoided by honest reporters. On the strength of a physical impression and solely out of sympathy toward the Soviet Union about which at firsthand I knew nothing, I assumed that this man was lying. His experience may well have intimidated him and turned his face grey, and he may well have been made uneasy by the presence of the American Communists. I leave my report of the incident as an example of the capacity of partisanship to fabricate favorable evidence."[50]

---

[47] Ibid., Part 1, vol. 4, pp. 382–3; Part 1, vol. 5, pp. 55, 58, 60–61, 86–8; Part 3, vol. 3, pp. 61, 69, 116, 216; Part 5, vol. 1, p. 83.

[48] Ibid., Part 1, vol. 4, p. 376.

[49] Emanuel Blum, "A Fish out of Congress," *The Nation*, 131, no. 3398, pp. 202–3.

[50] Edmund Wilson, "Foster and Fish," *The New Republic*, December 24, 1930, p. 162; Daniel Aaron, "The Life and Thought of Edmund Wilson," *Bulletin of the American Academy of Arts and Sciences* 28, no. 5 (February 1975), p. 27.

III

Despite their comparatively moderate conservatism and important achievements in publicizing issues of global humanitarian significance, though, the committee and its carefully chosen witnesses ultimately failed to live up to their high aspirations of objectivity or to deflect accusations of systematic bias sufficiently to gain a wide hearing for their ideas. Defining the conflict between Russia and America in terms of a clash of competing political philosophies may have been an advance on social Darwinist visions of anti-Communism as *volkskreig*, but it still permitted fundamentalist readings that left little space for a more open examination of the historical evidence or an ironic and nuanced understanding of the complex, often conflicted behavior of Communists. In Walsh's words, the Bolshevik revolution had been "entirely different ... from every other revolution that the world has ever known" because it had been founded with the intention to "block out, lock, stock and barrel, every form of civilization whatever, whether they knew anything about it or not." As such, it represented a "frank and open declaration of war against all humanity."[51] None of this rhetoric helped explain why Americans joined or aligned with the party. The committee also often took Communists' statements of their large and growing influence at face value rather than recognizing such statements might be conditioned by Communists' own delusions of grandeur.[52] By contrast, it almost completely ignored evidence of the compromises that Bolshevik ideologues had made when putting their ideas into practice, the ways the aspirations of the Communist movement had been shaped by Russian power politics, and the manner in which American Communists struggled to reconcile their global, revolutionary ideology with tendencies toward localism and nationalism: all of which would have substantial implications for devising policies to undermine the appeal of revolutionary politics in America and the world. Not only was this a dogmatic vision, it offered little appeal to a public that conceived of America's exceptionalism as lying in its commitment to liberty. Were Fish's arguments about the scale and unity of the Communist conspiracy to have been accepted, they would have required a vast array of new police powers, something that held as little appeal for traditional conservatives, states' rights advocates and populists as it did for civil liberties activists. Whether it was party organizers helping strikers in repressive company

---

[51]   Fish Committee, Part 1, vol. 1, pp. 2, 6.

[52]   This point was put by Rep. Nelson to William Green of the AFL, and accepted. However, in practice it was entirely ignored. On only one occasion, Representative Bachmann's prickly exchange with Walter S. Steele, was there any sustained engagement with the idea that propaganda and action were not indistinguishable, and that there was a large distinction between a riot and revolution. Ibid., Part 1, vol. 1, p. 73; Part 1, vol. 2, pp. 6–15.

towns, radical lawyers defending imprisoned revolutionaries or angry young teenagers picking fights with rivals in school, according to Fish all Communist actions should be seen as part of a singular master plan directed from Moscow and focused upon the destruction of American civilization.

Moreover, as inventive as it may have been, Walsh's concept of Soviet economic warfare offered a simplistic account of Soviet. The more straightforward explanation for Russian trade policies – that Stalin was using primary exports to build up currency reserves in order to fund breakneck industrialization – could certainly accommodate an eventual goal of worldwide revolution, but it suggested that the US could not only influence Soviet economic policy but also that the American economy stood to benefit from the sale of industrial goods and services to a rapidly industrializing Russia, rather than being driven into the ground by accepting cheap primary imports. It obscured the tension between the Soviet need for foreign technical expertise and the Stalinist desire for isolation, as manifested through the contrast between the amelioristic policies of the Commissariat of Foreign Affairs (Narkomindel) and Amtorg, and the more radical agenda of the Third International (Comintern). Perhaps most importantly, it entirely ignored the fact that France, Britain and the United States held the overwhelming majority of the world's gold reserves and were thus the only states with genuinely monopolistic potential in international commerce. If the Soviets had subsumed their economic policy to political goals, which they undoubtedly had, it was more accurate to see this as part of a desperate effort to catch up with the capitalist world than the actions of an all-powerful monopoly threatening the security of a weak and febrile America. Stalin's policies were driven by a near-paranoid fear of capitalist "encirclement" rather than an ambitious agenda to remodel the world. The substantive components of anti-Communist thought were therefore undermined by a sense of American victimhood and national fragility that simply did not hold up to the United States' position as one of the most powerful nations in the world.

While stepping back from the worst and most overt extremes of racism, the veneer of objectivity laid over the committee's work did little to obscure the underlying prejudices which shaped the Congressmen's worldviews. Even while the chairman made great effort to stress the patriotic loyalty of immigrant groups, the premises underpinning the committee's work equated ethnic groups at a basic level with children and youths on the grounds that a shared irrationality left them more vulnerable to subversive propaganda than mature Anglo-Saxon Americans; a position that was used to justify immigration restriction as a quick and easy solution to America's problems with radicalism. Even Fish's avowals of African American loyalty were so repetitive that it is hard not to see in them the peculiar cognitive patterns that originally emerged

88   *Little 'Red Scares'*

from American "Sambo" stereotypes: whites determined to stress that African Americans were among the most loyal social groups and content with their lot, yet anxious to the point of obsession that secretly they might not be.[53] A whistle-stop tour through Chattanooga, Memphis, New Orleans, Birmingham and Atlanta was designed to meet his Southern colleagues' desire to assess the danger Communism posed to the Southern racial order, and the influence of Communists among black people was one of the most common questions raised by the committee elsewhere as well. In response to accusations of racism leveled by William Z. Foster, the Southern Congressmen vigorously denied there was a problem with lynching in the South except in the rare occasions when it was necessary to preserve Southern women's honor, while even the token liberal on the committee, Representative John E. Nelson of Maine, engaged in exchanges with witnesses on the stand about the susceptibility of "darkies" to radical utopian promises.[54]

While they were fodder for the committee's critics, such prejudices conversely did little to strengthen the anti-Communist agenda among its supporters. Efforts to envision Communists as a new form of carpetbagger lacked salience as long as white supremacy remained firmly entrenched in the South and it was still assumed, in Hall's words, that "the Southern Negro is too wise to listen to this social equality propaganda that they put out."[55] Father Edmund Walsh informed the committee that "the large mass of negroes, especially in the South, as I know rather well, are considered a conservative element, rather than an inflammatory element."[56] Until the New Deal years, when government action raised the real possibility that the state, in combination with an emerging civil rights movement, might genuinely upset the racial order in the South, the equation of Communism with African American protest remained a minority pursuit and white supremacists contented themselves with self-justifying beliefs that black people were generally satisfied with their lot.

An equally strong set of gendered prejudices running through the committee's descriptions of Communism offered greater potential for winning supporters to the anti-Communist cause by presenting the radical project as an inversion of gender norms and a threat to the sanctity of the home. The Congressmen repeatedly enquired into rumors that Communists had a policy of cynically placing women and children at the front of violent demonstrations in the hope

---

[53]   Ibid., Part 1, vol. 1, pp. 24–5, 35, 63; Part 3, vol. 1, p. 110; Part 6, vol. 1, p. 62.

[54]   Ibid., Part 1, vol. 4, p. 352, 359–60, 387–9; Part 6, vol. 1, p. 239.

[55]   Ibid., Part 6, vol. 1, p. 281; "Tennessee Smiles at Fish Statement," *New York Times*, November 23, 1930.

[56]   Fish Committee Hearings, Part 1, vol. 4, p. 8.

Red Herrings?

of generating effective propaganda of police brutality.[57] Inspector John Lyons of the New York Police Department's Anti-Radical Bureau said that he had seen women and children pushed up during strikes, "while the men skulk behind the women and children and throw bricks and other missiles at the police."[58] Despite being denied by other witnesses, these claims served to reinforce the idea that revolutionary radicals were set upon destroying traditional male and female roles – in this case, the male's responsibility to protect women from harm – which in turn spoke to anxieties about masculinity in the context of a climate of widespread unemployment and social instability.[59] Other witnesses expressed disgust at the un-feminine behavior of female Communists. One union activist explained, "The women Communists were equally as bad as the men. They were mad fanatics. They all carried Gillette safety razor blades, and in this mass of people trying to get to work these women would walk behind our women, behind our men and slash them down the back with these razors."[60] The editor of *Labor World*, Louis McGrew, declared that under a Communist state women were turned into prostitutes and their families were declared property of the state; echoing claims heard before earlier Congressional committees that Communists practiced "free love" and the "nationalization of women."[61] Meanwhile, conservative women in the Daughters of the American Revolution used their gendered status to privilege their attacks on Communism, as when Mrs. Ruben Ross Holloway explained that, as "a mother, and the grandmother of six children" she was particularly concerned that educators were not required to take the pledge of allegiance.[62]

Given this tendency to trade on group identity to justify anti-Communist views, it was perhaps unsurprising that the most salacious interest expressed by the committee was when race and gender intermingled, as with claims that Communists were using white women at interracial dances to seduce black men

---

[57] Ibid., Part 1, vol. 4, p. 55; Part 3, vol. 2, p. 47; Part 4, vol. 2, p. 475.

[58] Ibid., Part 3, vol. 1, p. 178.

[59] Ibid., Part 4, vol. 1, p. 123. On the effect of the depression and unemployment on masculinity and gender relations, see Alice Kessler-Harris, *In Pursuit of Equity: Women, Men, and the Quest for Economic Citizenship in 20th-Century America* (Oxford, 2001), ch. 2; Alice Kessler-Harris, "Measures for Masculinity: The American Labor Movement and Welfare-State Policy during the Great Depression, in *Gendering Labor History: The Working Class in American History* (Urbana, 2007).

[60] Fish Committee, Part 1, vol. 1, p. 118.

[61] Ibid., Part 1, vol. 4, p. 172–3; United States Senate, *Brewing and Liquor Interests and German Propaganda: Hearings Before a Subcommittee of the Committee on the Judiciary, United States Senate, Sixty-Fifth Congress, second and third sessions, pursuant to S. Res. 307* (Washington, 1919), vol. 2, 2777; vol. 3, 147.

[62] Fish Committee, Part 1, vol. 4, p. 166.

into joining the party.[63] A representative of the ultra-patriotic American Vigilant Intelligence Federation declared that there had been at least three dances in recent months in Chicago, "in which Japanese, Filipinos, Chinese, Negroes, and whites all intermingled and danced together." To the concern of the Congressmen, he reported that a member of the AFL news service who attended one such event had told him that the "white girls at that dance would not dance with the white men and the negro girls would not dance with the negro men; in other words, the theory was that they should not dance with their own races, but should dance with those of the opposite races."[64] The sexual implications of such forms of interracial Congress were left unsaid, but clear to all.

Despite professions of open-mindedness and investigative rigor, then, the committee repeatedly showed itself to be subject to prejudicial assumptions that clouded their understanding of Communism, weakened their diagnoses for dealing with revolutionary politics and aided critics in presenting the committee as more interested in defending conservative values than in challenging Communism. The committee's depiction of the relationship between non-citizenship and political radicalism as a cultural inheritance stemming from the experience of growing up in repressive regimes abroad encouraged them to emphasize education, especially the teaching of American history, alongside more straightforwardly repressive policing activities and restrictions on immigration as ways of dealing with Bolshevism.[65] But it also shifted attention away from poverty, social exclusion and political repression in America as causes of Communist growth. Meanwhile, debate was often closed off at the point when liberal ideas were put forward. The committee generally responded favorably to suggestions from conservative union leaders that improving the conditions of labor would reduce Communism's appeal, but witnesses who suggested that police violence was acting as a tool for radical recruitment were told that this was not relevant to an investigative committee solely focused on Communist activities.[66] When African American leaders argued that, as Alderman Fred R. Moore put it, "if Congress could adopt or enforce the thirteenth, fourteenth, and fifteenth amendments, protecting the negroes from the South who are lynched, I think that would help [reduce support for Communism]", the committee declared that civil rights and anti-lynching bills

---

[63] Ibid., Part 1, vol. 4, p. 168; Part 3, vol. 1, pp. 188–9. The point was put to A. Philip Randolph during his testimony, but he carefully avoided responding. Ibid., Part 3, vol. 1, p. 249.

[64] Ibid., Part 4, vol. 2, p. 33.

[65] At one point Representative Fish complained, "There are many people who know the names of the kings of France and the kings of Great Britain, and yet know nothing of American history ... [we should] give them less geometry and medieval history than we do, and increase the necessary knowledge of American history." Ibid., Part 3, vol. 3, p. 35.

[66] Ibid., Part 3, vol. 1, p. 260.

Red Herrings? 91

were, whatever their merits, a diversion from the committee's object of study and therefore not to be discussed.[67]

The tendency of the committee to interweave focused attacks on the institutions of international Communism with gendered, racial and class-based agenda items shows how hard it was to separate "anti-Communism" – opposition to the Soviet Union and its institutional manifestations around the world – from "anti-Communism": opposing the broader values and goals that were correctly or incorrectly ascribed to Communists.[68] In this sense, it should not be surprising that, like most anti-Communists, Fish revealed complex intermixtures of both accurate analysis and prejudice in his attacks on the "Red menace."

However, it is hard to see these as conscious attempts to smear by association so much as manifestations of the latent prejudices of the time. Indeed, when testimony conformed to the Congressmen's assumptions, it proved difficult for the committee to separate real risks from peripheral matters best addressed through studied neglect. In one particularly extensive wild-goose chase, the committee obsessed about Communist efforts to recruit children into their ranks, trading on perennial fears over the safety of young people in educational environments in which teachers were assumed to be politically to the left of parents. The Boy Scouts movement in Great Britain was created at the turn of the century in response to fears that modern mass education had failed to instill discipline in future generations. For anti-Communists in the United States in the interwar years, these same fears were newly refracted through claims that Communism sought to destroy parental authority, bring about the collapse of the family and encourage the "utter debauchery of youth."[69] This line of

---

[67] This was not an unbreakable rule. Despite being told not to, Secretary Walter White of the NAACP was able to make the same point. Randolph raised these issues when asked why some black people had turned to Communism and was listened to without interruption. Ibid., Part 3, vol. 1, pp. 246, 254; Part 3, vol. 4, p. 203.

[68] Joel Kovel, *Red-Hunting in the Promised Land: Anticommunism and the Making of America* (London, 1997; 1st edn 1994), p. x. Related dichotomies are highlighted in Michael Paul Rogin, *Ronald Reagan, the Movie: And Other Episodes in Political Demonology* (Berkeley, 1987), p. 272; and Alan Wald, *The New York Intellectuals: The Rise and Decline of the Anti-Stalinist Left from the 1930s to the 1980s* (Chapel Hill, 1987), p. xv.

[69] Allen Warren, "Sir Robert Baden-Powell, the Scout Movement, and Citizen Training in Great Britain, 1900–1920," *English Historical Review* 101, no. 399 (1986), pp. 376–98; Allen Warren, "Popular Manliness: Baden-Powell, Scouting, and the Development of Manly Character," in J.A. Mangan and James Walvin (eds), *Manliness and Morality: Middle-Class Masculinity in Britain and America, 1800–1940* (1987), pp. 199–219; Robert H. MacDonald, *Sons of the Empire: The Frontier and the Boy Scout Movement, 1890–1918* (1993); Tammy Proctor, "(Uni)forming Youth: Girl Guides and Boy Scouts in Britain, 1908–39," *History Workshop Journal* 45 (1998), pp. 103–34; Sam Pryke, "The Popularity of Nationalism in

argument combined latent anxieties over young people's sexuality with a more overt political hostility toward left-wing thought. As Holloway of the Daughters of the American Revolution put it, "All over the country, they will tell you in the schools they have not the same wonderful respect from children that they had. Look into the homes and you will see they are taught, 'Your bodies are your own to do with as you please,' every place you go."[70] The response was to call for greater supervision over students, the curriculum and teaching profession, including teacher loyalty oaths and measures to oblige educators to "teach patriotism" to their students. According to New York's recently retired Police Commissioner, Grover Whalen, these measures would "offset ... seditious propaganda" by selling "our national ideals to the younger generation." Whalen argued, "We must recreate in our children the thrill of devotion that characterizes a silver-thatched veteran of the Civil War", promoting activities "that aim at the building up of body and mental health through recreation." This would ensure "sound thinking, hearty enjoyment of life, and, inevitably, a spirit of devotion to our flag and the national life which that flag so beautifully symbolizes."[71]

Despite this, the committee actually uncovered no evidence of teachers' involvement in promoting radical ideas and strong evidence that the tiny number of young Communists identified by school officials were influenced by their radical parents.[72] If anything, the reams of testimony from principals, superintendents and members of school boards showed that teachers were extraordinarily severe with young people who had become involved in radical politics. A 14-year-old child from the Bronx was suspended for refusing to give the pledge, despite later pleading that she didn't even know what she was doing wrong.[73] Another student, Harry Iseman, who persistently refused to accept his school's orders banning him from handing out leaflets, was suspended. After getting involved in an altercation with some Boy Scouts, he was sent to reform school for six months. Following his release, he attended a demonstration against the Scouts at Union Square and was promptly returned to the reformatory until he was 21 – spending a total of six years behind bars.[74]

---

the Early British Boy Scout Movement," *Social History* 23, no. 3 (1998), pp. 309–24; Fish Committee, Part 1, vol. 1, p. 40; Part 1, vol. 4, pp. 59–60, 96, 121–2, 135, 176, 219.

[70] Fish Committee, Part 1, vol. 4, p. 167.
[71] Ibid., Part 3, vol. 3, p. 34.
[72] Ibid., Part 3, vol. 1, pp. 1–2, 5, 30, 59.
[73] Ibid., Part 3, vol. 1, p. 2.
[74] Ibid., Part 3, vol. 1, pp. 15–16.

IV

The limits to the committee's objectivity were not just a matter of individual failings and personal prejudices. From the beginning, the committee's efforts were shaped by a fragmented anti-Communist community that struggled to substantiate the conservative vision of Communism laid out by Fish and his peers at a time when conservatism itself seemed to be in crisis.

While Fish may have been acting pragmatically in his effort to link anti-Communism to a broader selection of contemporary social anxieties, Congressional support for the committee had been based on a narrower definition of national security than the one articulated by Representative Fish: namely, that Soviet agents were working in the United States to overthrow the American government. The defense of the state against subversive conspiracy was the foundational objective that underpinned the first wave of national security legislation passed during World War One and it persisted as virtually the only basis for consensus over national security restrictions to civil liberties in the interwar years. The resolution creating the Fish Committee had initially been killed by the Rules Committee in March 1930. It was only approved after a set of documents were released to the press by Police Commissioner Whalen that seemed to offer conclusive evidence of an organized conspiracy of secret agents in Amtorg plotting against American institutions and working with the American Communist Party; a claim that was strengthened by the fact that some years earlier the equivalent organization in Britain, Arcos, had been caught engaging in similar activities.[75]

The problem was that even before the committee began its hearings, rumors had begun to circulate that the crucial Whalen Documents were not genuine. In fact, they turned out to be not only forged, but forged so badly that they called into question either Commissioner Whalen's integrity or his competence.[76] (Whalen had been attacked for his police force's aggressive response to a Communist protest in Union Square in March, and was desperate to uncover evidence that would heighten the threat of Communism and justify his heavy-

---

[75] Goodman, *The Committee*, p. 6; Harriette Flory, "The Arcos Raid and the Rupture of Anglo-Soviet Relations, 1927," *Journal of Contemporary History* 12, no. 4 (October 1977), pp. 707–23.

[76] Scholars originally raised the possibility that the documents may have been a product of a Bolshevik disinformation campaign; however, more recent evidence suggests that this was almost certainly not the case, making the most likely source a disgruntled émigré. Harvey Klehr, John Earl Haynes and Fridrikh Igorevich Firsov, *The Secret World of American Communism* (New Haven, 1995), p. 126; John Earl Haynes, Harvey Klehr and Alexander Vassiliev, *Spies: The Rise and Fall of the KGB in America* (New Haven, 2009), pp. 161–3.

handedness.) In hearings in late July, John Spivak, a left-wing fellow traveler and occasional writer for the *New York Graphic* and Communist *Daily Worker*, showed how rudimentary detective work had led him to the printer who produced the letterheads on which the forged documents had been typed; the printer had no link to Amtorg.[77] Whalen admitted he had done nothing to verify the documents' accuracy beyond accepting assurances from his subordinates.[78] Furthermore, an employee of Amtorg identified several dozen basic errors of fact and language in the documents.[79]

The revelations forced Fish to distance himself from the material on which the committee had been founded.[80] Despite the attendant embarrassment, Fish repeated almost exactly the same mistake several months later, when he followed another set of false leads supplied by the patriotic organization, the National Civic Federation, in the hope of uncovering a cache of Soviet espionage documents that did not exist.[81] Coming at the tail-end of a decade which had seen repeated exposure of forged documents relating to Soviet activity in the Western hemisphere, these debacles consolidated an image of anti-Communists as so viscerally hostile to Bolshevism that they were unable or unwilling to give the evidence before them even the most cursory analysis; an ironic turn for a committee that had staked so much on its single-minded focus on facts.

Whalen's embarrassment turned out to be only the first example of a broader pattern of unprofessional conduct that revealed the limits of using police forces in sensitive political investigations. Some of the larger forces with anti-radical bureaus or bomb squads were able to supply officers who had detailed knowledge of the history and development of American Communism. However, many policemen who testified before the hearings revealed varying degrees of ignorance, incompetence, aggression, casual racism and anti-Semitism, not to mention brazen disregard for constitutional rights. Officers openly, often proudly, explained how they routinely arrested radicals using petty local ordinances that banned "speeling" on sidewalks or parading without a permit.[82] The Pittsburgh-based editor Louis McGrew assured the committee that the police knew how to control radicals in his city: "They just knock their blocks off."[83] Other witnesses explained how policemen worked closely with conservative groups to undermine protests, as when unemployed members of the Ku Klux Klan in

---

[77] Fish Committee, Part 3, vol. 3, pp. 278–83.

[78] Ibid., Part 3, vol. 3, p. 22.

[79] Ibid., Part 3, vol. 3, pp. 315–20.

[80] Ibid., Part 3, vol. 3, p. 21.

[81] "Fish in Anti-Red Drive," *New York Times*, November 19, 1930.

[82] Fish Committee, Part 3, vol. 5, p. 39; Part 6, vol. 1, pp. 203–4.

[83] Ibid., Part 1, vol. 4, p. 179.

Red Herrings? 95

Birmingham cooperated with the police and local business leaders in efforts to identify, monitor and harass Communist organizers in their city. As the historian Robert P. Ingalls noted, this kind of local antiradical violence in Alabama was "purposeful and economically motivated", directed against union workers and African Americans and ceasing as soon as labor disputes were settled.[84] It also suggested that the disturbed conditions the committee was investigating were less a product of Communism and more down to police impunity and collusion.

Although the South ran a close second, perhaps the most open admissions of police misconduct came in the committee's hearings in the industrial Midwest. The region had some of the highest concentrations of Communist membership as well as, not coincidentally, the most divisive industrial environments. After the Chief of Police in Flint, Michigan, Caesar J. Scavarda, told the committee that he routinely arrested radicals without charge, Congressman Bachmann suggested that he try arresting them for "disorderly conduct" instead. Scavarda replied, "Well, possibly that would be a good excuse."[85] Even more egregiously, the Chief of Police in Pontiac, Floyd R. Alspaugh, explained his method of dealing with radicals: "We just hide them, that is all – bury them within the jails so that they cannot get a writ out and get released."[86]

While it seemingly raised little concern for the committee, the routine admission of illegality provided opportunities for opponents to condemn Fish by association. Representatives of the ACLU and the Socialist Party attacked the committee for giving too much credence to patriotic groups and for failing to identify police corruption as a major recruiting tool for the Communist Party.[87] "Your committee's work is based on the proposition that revolutionary propaganda produces revolution," the ACLU president Roger Baldwin said when he took the stand. "All history refutes that notion. Revolutions are produced by unbearable conditions, not talk."[88] When the Congressmen reached California, a hastily assembled band of civil liberties activists managed to hijack the last day of the hearings by recounting routine constitutional violations by the LAPD. The writer and socialist Upton Sinclair told how he had been arrested and held incommunicado for more than 18 hours after participating in a non-partisan free-speech protest earlier in the 1920s, during which time his wife was driven frantic by rumors that he had been handed over to the Klan for extra-judicial punishment.[89]

---

[84]   Ibid., Part 6, vol. 1, p. 194; Robert P. Ingalls, "Antiradical Violence in Birmingham During the 1930s," *Journal of Southern History*, 47, no. 4 (November 1981), 521–2.

[85]   Fish Committee, Part 4, vol. 1, p. 3.

[86]   Ibid., Part 4, vol. 1, p. 111.

[87]   Ibid., Part 3, vol. 5, p. 82; Part 5, vol. 3, pp. 299–321; Part 6, vol. 1, pp. 69–70.

[88]   Ibid., Part 1, vol. 4, p. 407.

[89]   Ibid., Part 5, vol. 3, pp. 325–8.

Not that Fish would have admitted it, flawed police testimony offered an ironic testament to the truth of one of the central claims promoted by the committee: that existing forces were ill-equipped to deal with the complexities of counter-espionage investigations, especially when unsupported by a professional Federal Bureau of Investigation. The Bureau had rarely been staffed with professionals, and after the excesses of the post-World War One Red Scare had been banned from investigating political extremism altogether, which is why Bureau chief J. Edgar Hoover did not appear before the committee.[90] Neither did the committee benefit from liaisons provided by Military and Naval Intelligence which had been available to the World War One Overman Committee but had been discontinued in 1919 in response to constitutional concerns over spying on citizens in peacetime.[91]

Nevertheless, instead of admitting the limits of their competence, most police witnesses were determined to show that they were in command of the streets and described Communist activities as well "in hand."[92] This further undermined the claim that there was an urgent problem to be fixed. Inspector Lyons of the NYPD's Anti-Radical Bureau claimed that a month's worth of wholesale deportations would see "the bottom ... drop out of the Communistic movement in this country."[93] When pressed on the wisdom of federal assistance for local policing, Detroit's Police Commissioner agreed it would be "a nice thing if we had a Federal law to stand back of us." But this hardly amounted to a clarion call for action.[94] Other executive branch officers also revealed strong professional incentives to show that Communism was under control or to resist Congressional oversight over their activities. Achmed H. Mundo, from the Alabama governor's office, declared in exaggerated terms that there were 8,000 Communist sympathizers in the state who had been shipping in tear gas bombs to use against the police, but swiftly added that state authorities were entirely on top of things.[95] Indeed, A. Dana Hodson, the Chief of the State Department's visa office, not only refused to testify in public session under instructions of the Secretary of State (who believed that

---

[90]   Fish had stated during the Rules Committee hearings of his desire to call the Bureau chief to the stand, but apparently Hoover had claimed he felt he did not have the right to testify, even under invitation. United States Congress, *Hearing Before the Committee on Rules House of Representatives, Seventy-First Congress, 2nd Sess., on H. Res. 180* (Washington, 1930), pp. 6–7.

[91]   Roy Talbert, *Negative Intelligence: The Army and the American Left* (Jackson MS, 1991), pp. 148–9.

[92]   Fish Committee, Part 3, vol. 1, pp. 206, 233; Part 3, vol. 5, p. 72.

[93]   Ibid., Part 3, vol. 1, p. 204.

[94]   Ibid., Part 4, vol. 1, p. 122.

[95]   Ibid., Part 6, vol. 1, p. 190.

Red Herrings? 97

undue public attention could only draw unwanted attention to the department), but also refused to say why he was refusing.[96]

Without effective support from the police or the executive branch, Fish turned to the loose network of patriotic and veterans' groups to promote the anti-Communist message. However, many of these also performed badly. Walter S. Steele, editor of *National Republic* magazine, was unprepared for the hearings, having only been called at the last minute, and was taken to task by Representative Bachmann for making excessive, unsubstantiated claims about Communist activity. On the same day, Bachmann also attacked the General Counsel of the Daughters of the American Revolution, H. Ralph Burton, for exaggerating America's vulnerability to internal subversion, and mocked suggestions that the Communist propaganda might manage to demoralize the armed forces.[97]

Undoubtedly the strongest testimony against the Communist Party in America came from the leadership of the American Federation of Labor, whose accounts of Communist activities were based on experiences fighting them for control of the union movement for more than a decade. In the context of a badly weakened anti-Communist community, the AFL came to form much of the motive force behind the committee. Matthew Woll, the current vice president of the organization, stated that unemployment riots were solely caused by the Comintern, while John Lewis of the United Mine Workers complained that radicals were seeking "to impose their boiler plate, oriental [*sic*] philosophy upon the western world."[98] AFL agent Edward McGrady told how, during efforts to resist Communist influence in the fur workers unions, "Men who were more courageous than the average were beaten into insensibility" while people who refused to collaborate with radicals found "gangs of men were sent into their homes, their furniture was destroyed, their women folk insulted and in some cases assaulted."[99]

Even here, though, the committee's agenda was undermined by the distinctive priorities of their witnesses. AFL representatives honed the argument first popularized by Samuel Gompers earlier in the century, that the first and last line of defense against Communism was a powerful union movement. William Green, president of the AFL, framed this in apocalyptic terms. In his view the British and German trade union movements had saved their nations from Communism, while the absence of trade unionism in Russia was the reason why

---

[96]   Ibid., Part 1, vol. 5, pp. 121–2.

[97]   Ibid., Part 1, vol. 2, pp. 9–12; Part 1, vol. 3, pp. 6–9.

[98]   Ibid., Part 3, vol. 2, pp. 1–49; Part 4, vol. 3, p. 72.

[99]   Ibid., Part 1, vol. 1, p. 115.

it fell to Bolshevism.[100] If such testimony strengthened claims that Communism was an unhealthy presence in American life, it weakened the case for government action to fight it. Some union officials supported calls for a federal secret police force, but generally the desire to legitimize the union movement caused them to stress that the non-Communist trade unionists "will handle it."[101]

Perhaps the only force that could have countered these contradictory messages and consolidated the support of influential groups behind Fish's anti-Communist campaign was business, which would become the lynchpin of resurgent conservative anti-Communist politics in mid-century.[102] However, in 1930 business groups revealed themselves to be deeply divided over Communism. Companies that had been directly targeted by Communist-led strikes were eager to send representatives to testify against the party.[103] But a surprising number of corporations and professional bodies showed no real interest in the issue. Indeed, representatives of the Atlanta Chamber of Commerce, Georgia Manufacturers' Association and the Citizens' Committee of Detroit all explained that they generally left such issues to the police.[104]

Viewed with hindsight, this appears surprising. However, much of this indifference was driven by straightforward commercial factors as business groups divided according to their positions along the supply chain rather than on simple fault lines between employers and employees. Primary producers who were threatened by cheap Russian imports – especially the lumber and pulpwood companies of the Pacific Northwest, the Association of Manganese Producers of America, and iron ore miners – were quick to buy into the idea that the Soviet government was employing unfair dumping tactics for political ends. Hearings in Seattle and Portland were almost overwhelmed by representatives from lumber companies and logging unions who were suffering under the pressure of the depression and keen to make the case for protection.[105] By contrast, secondary industries – such as steel producers who benefited from cheap manganese supplies and some of the larger paper companies who relied upon wood imports for production – had no interest in cutting off cheap imports, and manufacturers who had developed export relations with Soviet Russia at a time when domestic demand was collapsing sought to minimize fears of Communism

---

[100] Ibid., Part 1, vol. 1, pp. 44, 70.

[101] Ibid., Part 1, vol. 1, p. 125.

[102] See Kim Philips-Fein, *Invisible Hands: The Businessmen's Crusade against the New Deal* (New York, 2010).

[103] Fish Committee, Part 1, vol. 4, p. 46; Part 6, vol. 1, pp. 65–7, 181–2.

[104] Ibid., Part 4, vol. 1, pp. 107; Part 6, vol. 1, p. 230–1.

[105] Ibid., Part 5, vol. 1. See also http://depts.washington.edu/depress/fish_committee. shtml [accessed: 2 August 2011].

altogether. Indeed, the General Manager at Ford, Charles E. Sorenson, not only challenged the suppositions of the committee directly but also gave interviews to the press criticizing the idea of a federal police force, saying "If the Reds are as explosive and can do what they boast in America, then there is something wrong with our system."[106] In a tense and somewhat hostile session with the Congressmen, Sorenson was forced to backtrack. Nevertheless, he insisted that Ford had dozens of Russian engineers working with them in Michigan and that their relations with Amtorg had been of only the highest order.[107]

As a result, more often than not the attempt to deploy anti-Communist arguments in favor of protectionism ended up turning one set of American businessmen against another. Looking at their corporate customers with unconcealed anger, one iron ore producer declared that "the political stomach turns at the sight of American steel and Soviet Russia in the same bed."[108] Union leaders opportunistically joined these patriotic attacks on multinational manufacturing industries; John Lewis declared that any businessman who traded with the Russians might as well be a Soviet agent.[109]

Perhaps the most intriguing case in which the arguments of the committee were frustrated by divisions within the business world came in an extended debate over a series of financial operations by Soviet traders on the Chicago Stock Exchange, the original home of the derivative. Soviet representatives had made a series of large purchases of grain futures through Chicago trading houses, hoping to hedge their sales in a declining European market. Since these trades related to several million tons of wheat, and since the Soviets were involved in short trading, wheat producers claimed that the deals were part of a scheme to depress the American grain market and exacerbate the already intense sense of crisis among American wheat farmers who were witnessing the collapse of their livelihoods. After the story became public, farmers' associations, aided by Secretary of Agriculture Hyde, accused the Russians of "Communistic activities ... threatening the welfare of the American farmer" and forced through a temporary embargo on certain Soviet goods.[110] In early 1931, this was followed up by bills put to Congress to

---

[106] "Ford Chief Back; Doubts Red Menace," *New York Times*, July 15, 1930.

[107] Fish Committee, Part 4, vol. 1, p. 304; "Ford Chief Alters Statement on Reds," *New York Times*, July 27, 1903. This was a notable contrast to Ford's attitude during the Dies Committee hearings, when the company offered to supply HUAC and its staff with cars. Ellen Schrecker, *Many Are the Crimes: McCarthyism in America* (Boston, 1998), p. 91.

[108] Fish Committee, Part 1, vol. 4, p. 78.

[109] Ibid., Part 4, vol. 3, p. 78.

[110] "Embargo List Against Soviet May Increase," *Washington Post*, July 27, 1930; "Soviet Grain Deals Put Up to Chicago by Secretary Hyde," *New York Times*, September 21, 1930; "Legge Backs Hyde in Grain Price Quiz," *New York Times*, September 23, 1930.

embargo the importation of all Soviet products and strengthen restrictions on the importation of goods produced by forced labor.[111]

The problem was that the committee's argument made no sense to anyone with a basic understanding of the stock market. As a series of traders insistently and repeatedly pointed out to the confused Congressmen, short selling was a perfectly normal operation designed to *stabilize* the price of commercial exports not collapse the market. If the Soviets had wanted to engineer a panic, they would not have bought quietly and in the largest grain market in the world, they would have signaled their intent very publicly and targeted a smaller market, such as Liverpool, England, in order to maximize the psychological and material impact of their purchases. Indeed, one did not need to understand the function of derivatives trading to realize that the idea of generating a panic in secret was a contradiction in terms. As it was, the supposedly enormous volumes of trading turned out, to America's financial wizards, to be not much more than that taking place on a normal day and certainly not enough to have substantially affected prices. This was especially true when compared to the carnage wrought in the markets by the global glut in supply of key commodities such as wheat – against which the Soviets had been trying to hedge in the first place.[112]

Certain that there was a nefarious conspiracy at work, the Congressmen nevertheless continued to insist that short trading was not about price insurance but "gambling", subterfuge and economic warfare. Since Soviet "economic warfare" as articulated by Fish and Walsh was precisely supposed to follow from the Soviet's unfair, anti-competitive, anti-capitalist instincts, it could hardly have been more ironic that the behavior for which the committee was attacking the Soviet Union was in fact an instance of the Soviets operating in a particularly capitalistic manner. Among other things, it showed that, like many Americans at the time, the committee members did not properly understand the mechanics of the free market system that they were so vigorously defending. As Edmund Wilson pointed out, "one of the most striking features of this Committee which has been investigating the Communists for six months is its apparent ignorance of everything connected with Communism ... And they not only ask Foster what he understands by Communism, a question perhaps defensible – but want

---

[111] United States Congress, *Embargo on Soviet Products, Hearings Before the Committee on Ways and Means, House of Representatives, Seventy-First Congress, 3rd Sess., on H.R. 16035, A Bill to Prohibit the Importation of Any Article or Merchandise from the Union of Soviet Socialist Republics* (Washington, 1931).

[112] Fish Committee, Part 3, vol. 4, pp. 77–86, 115–24; Part 4, vol. 3, pp. 1–10, 53–6.

Red Herrings? 101

to know, also, what he means by capitalism, a word which seems honestly to puzzle them."[113]

V

Not all of the committee's claims were red herrings. If he lacked the faculties to answer his own questions, Congressman Fish's endeavors revealed a genuine attempt to highlight the challenge Communism posed to a liberal, republican political order. For this, the committee deserves to be removed from the blanket "McCarthyite" designation commonly applied to right-wing anti-Communists. While he and his fellow Congressmen tended to respond to difficult issues with closed and prejudicial assumptions, at certain moments their efforts, however inarticulately, raised serious questions about a world system in which Communism and capitalism competed on entirely conflicting terms. Historians often argue that their job is to give voice to the voiceless and make sense of the apparently contradictory expressions of the inarticulate, to interpret the views of individuals lacking the ability to clearly express themselves in order to separate kernels of truth from apparently discordant utterances. Perhaps this instruction should be as true for Republican politicians educated at fine public schools and among the elites at Harvard as for the oppressed, the weak and the excluded.

However, even while he steered clear of more extremist visions of Communism, Fish was never fully able to make the leap toward a purely evidential and institutional analysis of the movement he opposed. Unable to escape its members' prejudices or avoid the perennial politician's temptation to link the anti-Communist crusade to the pressing concerns of the day, the committee found itself falling into an intellectual double bind. Efforts to demonstrate rigor and fidelity to the American liberal tradition and anticipate attacks from left-wingers encouraged the committee to define Communism through reference to its authoritarian and illiberal features. However, logic dictated that, if this were true, the best way of responding to Communist totalitarianism would be through the expansion of liberty to those who as yet did not feel its benefits, sweeping the rug from under revolutionaries who claimed that the American system was incapable of reform. This challenged the conservative inclinations of Hamilton Fish and his peers, whose preferred prescriptions were immigration restriction, policing, and ritualistic patriotic education. Even the committee's efforts to stress the basic loyalty of ethnic and racial minority groups ended

---

[113] Edmund Wilson, "Foster and Fish," *The New Republic*, December 24, 1930. Later reprinted in Edmund Wilson, *The American Jitters: A Year of the Slump* (New York, 1980; 1st edn 1932), pp. 19–20.

up undermining the case for action, since doing so challenged the vision of a powerful, united and dangerous Communist movement.

As a result, the committee's final report, issued in January 1931, presented a set of conclusions that were in stark dissonance to the messages that had emerged during the hearings. While witnesses' testimony in 1930 had revealed forged evidence, conflicting testimony, lackadaisical police officers and self-reliant trade unionists, the Fish Committee assembled from these fragments a vision of a disciplined Communist movement with more than half a million members and "active sympathizers", on the verge of driving the United States into the ground.

The Whalen Documents, the sources on which the committee had been founded, were dismissed in less than a paragraph. This marked a fitting epitaph for the committee, and a demonstration of how far the fear of imminent revolution had diminished in the months the Fish Committee had been operating. Once the initial shock of the crash had receded (and before politics began to polarize once again in the New Deal years), many Americans seemed to have been surprised not by the fragility of their compatriots' republican faith but by its resilience. "The Chairman seems honestly to believe that there is imminent danger of a Communist revolution here, and that our Government and our institutions may be overthrown unless we adopt radical measures," a *New York Times* editorial averred. "This is not the judgment of our police authorities, or of the keenest and most impartial observers ... Indeed, the wonder is that, given the favorable conditions for violent agitation during the past fourteen months, there have been so few demonstrations by Communists."[114]

It was little surprise, then, that the committee's recommendations, which included outlawing the Communist Party, cancelling the citizenship of all party members who had previously been naturalized, barring Communist propaganda from the mails, prosecuting people caught spreading rumors about banks and a complete embargo on all Soviet trade, were ignored. The only liberal member of the committee, John E. Nelson, refused to sign the report. Denouncing anti-Communist "hysteria", he said that "our best defense against the red shirt of the Communist and the black shirt of the Fascists is the blue shirt of the American working man."[115]

In this sense, and not for the last time, right-wing anti-Communists' lax approach to evidence and argument made them their own worst enemies. As Boris Skvirsky, the Director of the Soviet Union's Information Bureau in New York, pointed out in his statement to the committee, allegations about the

---

[114] "Communists and Criminals," *New York Times*, January 19, 1931.

[115] "Fish Report Asks Outlawing of Reds As National Menace," *New York Times*, January 18, 1931.

Red Herrings? 103

Bolshevik destruction of civilization were part of a "fine harvest of stories" that dated back to the absurd post-war claims about the Soviet nationalization of women, while the forged Whalen Documents were "quite similar to previous forgeries" designed to build up a "war psychology against the Soviet Union."[116] This consistent pattern of failure was more than enough to pull a curtain over the legitimate points being made by the committee about the international Communist movement, which were effectively ignored by many Americans for a generation to come.

Still, the failure of the Fish Committee was not solely a product of the intellectual limitations or analytical errors of the Congressmen who sat on its benches. It was both shaped by and reflected in the composition of the witnesses who were called to testify before it, which in turn spoke to the systemic weakness of anti-Communism in the early depression years. Critics were wrong to argue that the committee was little more than the mouthpiece of capitalism. The most consistently conservative anti-Communist groups, whose vision would have most strongly supported the committee's dogmatic interpretation of Communism, presented weak or compromised evidence. Meanwhile, the most powerful indictments of Soviet politics came from moderate union leaders, who focused upon reform as the best response to revolutionary radicalism.

In this sense, the more moderate the investigations became, the more incoherent the narrative they presented. Fish's efforts were uniquely hampered by bad timing. However, they also highlight many of the difficulties experienced by conservative anti-Communists hoping to work with liberals who may notionally agree with their basic hostility toward revolutionary radicalism but disagree profoundly with the implications they drew from it. As a result, many figures – including Fish himself – preferred to drift rightwards, rather than to the center, in search of allies who shared not only their antipathy to Communism but their prescriptions for defeating it. In Fish's case, this led to a shift during the rest of the decade towards an implicit defense of Nazism as the only force on the global stage capable of restraining Soviet Russia. While by the onset of World War Two his committee was already disappearing from memory, this new course would ultimately leave his name entirely blackened in history.

---

[116] Fish Committee, Part 1, vol. 5, p. 40. The point was also made by Bogdanov. Ibid., Part 3, vol. 3, p. 231.

Chapter 5

Little Red Schoolhouses?
Anti-Communists and Education
in an "Age of Conflicts"[1]

Timothy Reese Cain

In their 1929 tract *The Red Fog*, Bonnie Busch and Lucia Ramsey Maxwell warned that "The teachings of Lenin—Communism and World Revolution through Civil War—are now being instilled into the minds and hearts of the children of our U.S.A., through systematic education by paid propagandists who use not only the schools, but also the children's camps, sports, plays, the press and forum, to foster and encourage hatred and distrust of God and Government and REVOLT against all authority."[2] Dedicated "To the Patriotic Women of the United States of America," the book told of the Communist campaign to "Grab 'em young and keep 'em red" and claimed that institutions of higher education were "pipelines of propaganda" intent on destroying the nation and plunging it into atheism.[3] Just more than a decade later, one of those patriotic women, Elizabeth Dilling, interrupted and disbanded a student peace rally sponsored by the American Student Union (ASU) at the University of Chicago. Dilling, by then a well-known crusader against Communism, declared to the assembled students: "You are all guinea pigs of Stalin. The University of Chicago is a red school."[4] In the intervening period, the nation experienced its second significant Red Scare, one that again focused criticism on American schools and colleges, as well as those who ran, taught, and attended them. At times vitriolic, at others absurd, the rhetoric around Communism was inflammatory, and the related attacks could be damaging to Communist and allied educators and students. Though it has

---

[1]   Charles A. Beard, "The Scholar in an Age of Conflicts," *School and Society* 43, no. 1105 (February 19, 1936): 278–83.

[2]   Bonnie Busch and Lucia Ramsey Maxwell, *The Red Fog*, 2nd edn (Washington, DC, 1929), 7.

[3]   Ibid., 9, 45.

[4]   "Mrs. Dilling Storms Rally at U. of C. and Routs 'Reds,'" *Chicago Daily News*, May 24, 1940.

since been conceived of as the "Red Decade," in the moment historian Charles A. Beard considered it "an age of conflicts," threatened by "Individuals and cliques [who] wrap the American flag around their shoulders; they vociferously proclaim themselves to be the only wise, true and honest patriots; and then they demand that the schools accept their versions and commands."[5]

Although specific to the time, these anti-Communist attacks on education were also rooted in long-standing contentions around schooling and intellectuals. They were, as well, evolving amid domestic economic struggles and broader international challenges. They implicated fears over indoctrination of youths, concerns over an active student movement, and challenges to pedagogical strategies and textbooks. Though no perfect classification of the pressures or their sources is possible, they might best be understood as emanating from three categories of actors: loosely and tightly formed non-governmental organizations, legislative bodies, and individuals and groups from within the schools and colleges themselves. Of course, there was great diversity within these groups and overlap among the categories. Moreover, they drew on and contributed to broader anxieties and excitements. William Randolph Hearst's newspapers stoked fears, for example, but willing members of the larger public purchased and acted upon the frequent articles alleging subversion. As Beard noted in his 1936 address to the Department of Superintendence of the National Education Association (NEA), "All over the country, schools are attacked by highly organized and well-financed minorities that seek to browbeat legislatures, the Congress of the United States, school boards and teachers."[6]

Controlling Education and Educators in American History

Concerns over heterodox political, economic, and religious perspectives in schools are long-standing, as are broader efforts to control and influence teachers. From colonial educational settings—which were at times staffed by indentured servants—through the nineteenth-century common schools, teachers operated under strict societal control and were required to adhere to local behavioral and religious norms. Controversy was to be avoided, and students were to be protected from unsettled and politically divisive ideas. Efforts to both professionalize and organize teachers in the early twentieth century were, in part, in response to the pervasive restrictions placed on both teachers' work lives and their home lives. As Howard K. Beale noted in his classic 1941

---

[5] Beard, "Scholar in an Age," 282.
[6] Ibid.

book *A History of Freedom of Teaching in American Schools*, restrictions were widespread, if varied, with teachers at small rural schools frequently laboring under the harshest constraints.[7] In higher education, modern understandings of professors' freedoms to teach, research, and fully partake in the political debates and activities date, in part, to the battles over economic philosophies and controversial speech in the late nineteenth century. A series of cases centering on unionization and socialism helped to galvanize both the field of economics and the professoriate around academic freedom and due process rights.[8] Yet the solutions to the controversies were hard to reach: as long as public support was needed for higher education, faculty espousal of heterodox views was inherently limited. Cases, both publicized and hidden, continued in the early twentieth century, highlighting the ongoing restrictions on educators, especially those who held minority opinions on economic and political issues.[9]

Of course, in both K-12 and higher education, these fears over educators' speech and beliefs took on a new and more pernicious nature during World War I, when attacks on those associated with Germany were rampant in education and more broadly. With the end of the war and the beginning of the First Red Scare, notions of "un-American" spread, and leftist educators came under fire. Where a socialist faculty member might have been endangered in earlier years for offending wealthy donors, in the post-World War I era, teachers and faculty who harbored similar views were deemed to be disloyal and unfit for their positions.[10] Perhaps most famously, three leftist teachers were removed from their positions in New York City, generating substantial and lengthy protests by the New York Teachers Union and the National Civil Liberties Bureau (soon to become the American Civil Liberties Union [ACLU]).[11] In California, the Better America

---

[7]   Howard K. Beale, *A History of Freedom of Teaching in American Schools* (New York, 1941).

[8]   Mary O. Furner, *Advocacy and Objectivity: A Crisis in the Professionalization of American Social Science, 1865–1905* (Lexington, 1975); Walter P. Metzger, *Academic Freedom in the Age of the University* (New York, 1961), 39–193.

[9]   Timothy Reese Cain, "Academic Freedom in an Age of Organization" (Ph.D. diss., University of Michigan, 2005), 337–9; Leon Whipple, *The Story of Civil Liberty in the United States* (New York, 1927; Westport, CT, 1970), 320; Daniel H. Pollitt and Jordan E. Kurland, "Entering the Academic Freedom Arena Running: The AAUP's First Year," *Academe* no. 84 (July–August 1998): 45–52.

[10]   Carol S. Gruber, *Mars and Minerva: World War I and the Higher Learning in America* (Baton Rouge, 1975), 163–212; Timothy Reese Cain, "'Silence and Cowardice' at the University of Michigan: World War I and the Pursuit of Un-American Faculty," *History of Education Quarterly* 51, no. 3 (2011): 297–329.

[11]   Timothy Reese Cain, "'Only Organized Effort Will Find the Way Out!': Faculty Unionization at Howard University, 1918–1950," *Perspectives on the History of Higher*

Foundation tried to counter Communism in schools and colleges by sending students into classrooms as spies, forcing the removal of publications such as the *Nation* and the *New Republic*, and publishing anti-radical tracts including Woodworth Clum's *Making Socialists out of College Students: A Story of Professors and Other Collegians Who Hobnob with Radicals*. More broadly, more than a half dozen states enacted loyalty oaths, requiring that educators pledge to uphold the state or federal constitution; some extended further and specified the explicit teaching of patriotism. As the ACLU declared in 1931, "The laws requiring special oaths of loyalty from teachers force on them the uncritical acceptance of our political and economic institutions. They have resulted in intimidation, and a fear to express any but majority beliefs."[12]

Even though the worst of the First Red Scare soon subsided and some specific restrictions were eased, pressures on real and alleged socialist and Communist educators—two groups that, despite differences within and between them, were often conjoined in the minds of their attackers—remained amid the intolerance of the 1920s. Most of the loyalty oaths stayed in effect, and both the Fundamentalist and nativist attacks of the 1920s threatened teachers. National Education Week, begun in 1921 by the American Legion and the NEA, emphasized patriotism with substantial militaristic overtones; it was among activities causing the ACLU to warn that the American Legion had superseded even the Ku Klux Klan (KKK) in its intolerance and active repression.[13] Women's organizations such as the American Legion Auxiliary and the Daughters of the American Revolution (DAR) similarly emphasized patriotism in schooling and among children, thereby focusing their efforts on issues traditionally associated with and entrusted to women. Both individually and collectively through events including the Women's Patriotic Conference on National Defense in 1927, they called for expanded teacher loyalty oaths, urged the use of specific anti-radical textbooks, and supported the Reserve Officer Training Corps (ROTC)

Education 29 (forthcoming); Edwin Layton, "The Better America Foundation: A Case of Superpatriotism," *Pacific Historical Review* 30, no. 2 (May 1961): 137–47; Norman Hapgood (ed.), *Professional Patriots* (New York, 1927); Woodworth Clum, *Making Socialists out of College Students: A Story of Professors and Other Collegians Who Hobnob with Radicals* (Los Angeles, 1920); Henry R. Linville and Thomas Mufson, "American Scholarship in Bondage: A Study of the Control of Education in the Nation," Sinclair Mss., Manuscripts Department, Lilly Library, Indiana University, Bloomington, IN.

12 American Civil Liberties Union, *The Gag on Teaching* (New York, 1931), 18.

13 William Gellermann, *American Legion as Educator*, Teachers College, Columbia University Contributions to Education, no. 734 (New York, 1938); American Civil Liberties Union, *Free Speech in 1924: The Work of the American Civil Liberties Union, January to December 1924* (New York, 1925), 11, 27–8, 38; American Civil Liberties Union, *Free Speech 1926: The Work of the American Civil Liberties Union* (New York, 1927), 3–5.

Anti-Communists and Education in an "Age of Conflicts" 109

and other school-based patriotic and military programs.[14] In specific instances, patriotic organizations were able to cancel events on college campuses that they viewed as inimical to the American way, including in 1926, when the DAR and American Legion forestalled pacifist Lucia Aims Mead's planned talk at Agnes Scott College amid unfounded claims that she was a radical Bolshevik.[15] Other groups, including those beholden to conservative business interests, pursued similar ends, if from slightly different angles.

With the onset of the Great Depression and the shifting political dynamics in Europe, educational institutions and systems experienced dramatic difficulties, though at times in different ways than other sectors of society. At first schools remained somewhat protected and maintained their allegiance to businesses, but soon budgets were slashed for K-12 and higher education at the same time that schools were called on to house students and keep them from entering the devastated labor market. Some educators began to question the influence of business leaders in education and their larger roles in American society.[16] The shift toward child-centered progressive education, which had troubled conservatives, continued and expanded in the era, taking on new import and meaning amid the disrupted society. In February 1932, Columbia University Teachers College professor George S. Counts stunned and challenged the profession with several talks that would later be printed together as *Dare the School Build a New Social Order?* Counts advocated the use of schools as a mechanism for radical societal change, argued that capitalism "no longer works," and called on educators to "make certain that every Progressive school will use whatever power it may possess in opposing and checking the forces of social conservatism and reaction."[17] Counts's efforts energized progressive educators around the idea of social reconstruction through schooling, and groups such as the Progressive Education Association (PEA) took on new urgency. Along with colleagues at Columbia, in 1934 Counts founded *Social Frontier*, which provided an outlet for reconstructionist educators to argue for fundamental economic, educational, and social change. Their rhetoric worried many in the schools and beyond, and, amid continuing economic

---

[14]   Kirsten Marie Delegard, "Women Patriots: Female Activism and the Politics of American Anti-Radicalism, 1919–1935" (Ph.D. diss., Duke University, 1999), 159–65.

[15]   John M. Craig, "Redbaiting, Pacifism, and Free Speech: Lucia Ames Mead and Her 1926 Lecture Tour in Atlanta and the Southeast," *Georgia Historical Quarterly* 71, no. 4 (Winter 1987): 601–22.

[16]   David Tyack, Robert Lowe, and Elisabeth Hansot, *Public Schools in Hard Times: The Great Depression and Recent Years* (Cambridge, MA, 1984), 22.

[17]   George S. Counts, *Dare the Schools Build a New Social Order?* (New York, 1932), 47, 24.

struggles, a growing conservative backlash unleashed attacks on educators and education across the nation.[18]

These controversies over schooling entangled higher education as well, including because colleges were seen as the sources of troubling educational ideology and were accused of indoctrinating students in atheism, free love, and Communism. Small-scale student involvement in May Day events and other leftist political activities early in the decade was soon replaced by a mass nationwide student movement with proportionally greater participation than even during the 1960s heydays of student protests.[19] Epitomized by hundreds of thousands of students taking the Oxford Oath and pledging not to support the government in any war, the movement attracted an array of participants, some of whom had links to the Communist Party and the Young Communist League. As James Wechsler, a leader of the movement both as a student at Columbia University and afterwards, later recollected, "Many of those disposed to think much about the chaos were captivated by the view that the Soviet 'experiment' showed us how to resolve the grotesquerie of poverty in a country so richly endowed as ours."[20] By the Popular Front years of the late 1930s, campus-based efforts to aid the Loyalist cause in Spain—along with presidential straw polls indicating campus support for Communist Party candidate Earl Browder—stoked fears of Communist infiltration in American institutions. When the Popular Front broke down following the Nazi-Soviet Non-Aggression Pact in 1939, campus leftist groups likewise suffered disaffection and difficulties. For those both inside and outside of academe who were already concerned with Communism on campuses, these events provided further evidence of the corrupting influences of faculty, professional agitators, and ethnic minority students on campus.

Sources of Anti-Communism in the 1930s

J. Flint Waller began his 1932 *Outside Demands and Pressures on the Public Schools* with the blunt statement: "It is well known that public school officials are subject to demands and pressure by individuals and groups outside of the school. Literally hundreds of useful and well-meaning persons and groups attempt to

---

[18]   Tyack, Lowe and Hansot, *Public Schools*, 58–67.

[19]   Philip G. Altbach, *Student Politics in America* (New York, 1974), 57–108; Robert Cohen, *When the Old Left Was Young: Student Radicals and America's First Mass Student Movement, 1929–1941* (New York, 1993).

[20]   James Wechsler, *Revolt on the Campus* (Seattle, 1973), viii.

use the school's organization to accomplish their aims."[21] Though Waller was speaking broadly, those on both sides of the debates over Communism in the schools and colleges in the decade in which Waller was writing would surely have agreed with the assessment. And yet, the pressures were not just extra-educational and non-governmental: elected officials, educators, and students themselves were also intimately connected with the effort control schools and colleges due to their presumed influence over young and impressionable students. Indeed, on all sides of political debates, concerns over propaganda in schools and colleges were expressed, with those about Communism growing to be especially malicious at the end of the decade. Those working against Communism in education interacted in networks, building off of one another, sharing sources, and trumpeting shared claims. Despite some overlap, they might still be best understood in three loose categories, each with their own avenues of pressure and foci: non-governmental organizations, governmental bodies, and individuals and groups from within the educational system itself. Considering each of these individually, along with particularly important or representative efforts, offers insights into the scope and scale of anti-Communist efforts in education during the 1930s.

Non-Governmental Organizations and Networks

Professional patriots and the reactionary press were active progenitors of vociferous attacks on schools and colleges as bastions of Communism, propaganda, and indoctrination. Working independently and collaboratively, these individuals and groups were able to place pressure on schools and colleges, raise alarm among the general public, and encourage governments to act against alleged Communists. The aforementioned DAR and American Legion are among the best known of the patriotic organizations and two that continued their efforts to influence American education in the 1930s. Through its National Defense through Patriotic Education Committee, the former proclaimed the importance of education and launched multiple initiatives to search for and monitor perceived subversive influences. At the national, state, and local levels, members campaigned for ROTC and loyalty oaths, provided patriotic educational materials to schools and libraries, and formed school and college chapters specifically intended to counter Communism and pacifism in the schools. As committee chair Florence Hague Becker proclaimed to applause at the 1935 conference, the DAR wanted "no communism or any other 'ism'

---

[21]   J. Flint Waller, *Outside Demands and Pressures on the Public Schools*, Teachers College, Columbia University Contributions to Education, no. 542 (New York, 1932), 1.

but Americanism."[22] The following year, at the American Federation of Teachers convention, the then-Marxist historian Louis Morton Hacker offered a competing assessment, calling DAR members "the most dangerous enemies of free schools in America," and arguing "It is time these busybodies were told what their ancestors fought for."[23]

The American Legion boasted over a million members when the decade began and, under the auspices of its National Americanism Commission (NAC), was already engaged in efforts to rid the schools of radicals. In 1927, it was a key player in the removal of two instructors from Pennsylvania's West Chester Normal School for their sponsorship of the Liberal Club and, in ensuing years, was instrumental in dismissals in Bangor, Maine, and at Tulane University in New Orleans, Louisiana. The Legion was particularly concerned that the growing protests against mandatory ROTC programs evinced radical attacks on American society and revealed "communistic sympathies." In the middle of the decade, the organization increased its efforts for loyalty oaths, called on its members to work with school boards to identify and remove disloyal teachers, and used its influence to prohibit allegedly Communist and subversive speakers from using school buildings as venues.[24] Noting "the web of un-American propaganda which is being woven in by radical agitators," in 1934 National Commander Edward A. Hayes announced that the NAC "centered its counter attack upon the schools."[25] The following year, the NAC ominously reported that its survey of colleges revealed that "a number of professors in such institutions are cooperating with young Communists in the colleges," and that it had uncovered their names.[26] At the 1936 convention, the Legion resolved against the "Communistic Youth Movement"; claimed that the fight against Communism was a primary organizational purpose; and paved the way for the production of *Isms: A Review of Alien Isms, Revolutionary Communism and*

---

[22] Florence Hague Becker, "Report of the National Defense through Patriotic Education Committee," *Proceedings of the Forty-Fourth Continental Congress of the National Society of the Daughters of the American Revolution* (Washington, DC, 1935), 128–34, 132.

[23] "Education: A.F. of T.'s 20th," *Time* (August 31, 1936). On Hacker, including his conversion to anti-Communism, see Scott C. Zeman, "Historian Louis M. Hacker's 'Coincidental Conversion' to the Truth," *Historian* 61, no. 1 (1998): 85–99.

[24] William Penack, *For God and Country: The American Legion, 1919–1941* (Boston, 1989), 267–8; Gellermann, *American Legion as Educator*, 91; Dorothy Culp, "The American Legion: A Study in Pressure Politics" (Ph.D. diss., University of Chicago, 1939), 180.

[25] "Report of Edward A. Hayes, National Commander of the American Legion," *Proceedings of the 16th National Convention of the American Legion* (Washington, DC, 1935), 51–2.

[26] "National Americanism Commission," *Proceedings of the 17th National Convention of the American Legion* (Indianapolis, 1936), 111–20, 116.

Their Active Sympathizers in the United States. A compilation of articles, reports, and artifacts alleging widespread Communist sympathizing, *Isms* was intended to be distributed to schools and libraries, in the hope that it would help to rid the country of Communism, radicalism, and subversion.[27] Throughout, the Legion declaimed any interest in stifling academic freedom but simultaneously remained a strong proponent of loyalty oath legislation and insisted that only those whose loyalty was beyond question were fit to teach.[28]

These and other large and well-funded national organizations influenced education—Beale found that 75 percent of teachers were afraid to criticize the American Legion or DAR[29]—but they were just one component of the professional patriots who sought to strip educational institutions of anything they deemed un-American. They were joined by smaller organizations and crusading individuals, such as Edwin Marshall Hadley, a former military officer who dedicated his 1929 novel *Sinister Shadows* "To the Worthy Professors of My Youth ... with the hope that, in a humble way, it may aid them and their worthy successors in purging their ranks of those who are bringing discredit upon on of the noblest of professions."[30] In 1930, he claimed before the Chicago chapter of the DAR that the recent interracial marriage of Dolores Ford and Eugene Newton resulted from a Soviet plot to turn wealthy American children into amoral atheists. According to Hadley, Ford's professors at Smith College were part of the larger national effort.[31] The following year, he extended his attacks in *T.N.T.*, which blamed Communistic faculty for the American educational system's ruin, warned of "the unholy alliance of the parlor pink and the gutter red," and claimed that colleges and universities might need to be closed to end the corruption of American youth.[32] In November 1932, with Elizabeth Dilling as a co-founder and secretary, Hadley organized the Society of Paul Reveres, a Chicago-based patriotic society dedicated to educating the nation about the reality of Communist infiltration which eventually had 200 chapters across the nation.[33]

---

[27] *Isms: A Review of Alien Isms, Revolutionary Communism and Their Active Sympathizers in the United States*, 2nd edn (Indianapolis, 1937).

[28] Gellermann, *American Legion as Educator*, 122–34.

[29] Beale, *History of Freedom*, 240–41.

[30] Edwin Marshall Hadley, *Sinister Shadows* (Chicago, 1929).

[31] See, for example, "Reds Are Blamed for Marriage of White Heiress," *Baltimore African-American*, November 29, 1930; "Her Marriage Subtle Red Plot," *Milwaukee Sentinel*, November 26, 1930.

[32] Edwin Marshall Hadley, *T.N.T.* (Chicago, 1931), 10.

[33] "Forms 'Paul Reveres' to Fight School Reds," *New York Times*, April 9, 1933; Glen Jeansonne, *Women of the Far Right: The Mothers' Movement and World War II* (Chicago, 1996), 16; Mildred Diane Gleason, "In Defense of God and Country: Elizabeth Dilling, A Link between the Red Scares" (Ph.D. diss., University of Arkansas, 1997), 58–60.

114   *Little 'Red Scares'*

Dilling and Hadley split in 1934 and the Paul Reveres soon folded, but Dilling achieved new prominence with her self-published *The Red Network: A "Who's Who" and Handbook of Radicalism for Patriots*. *The Red Network* alleged widespread infiltration of Communist agents throughout American society, including its educational system. Specific educators, such as University of Wisconsin president Glenn Frank and Columbia University's Counts, and organizations—including the Student Congress Against War at the University of Chicago, the National Student League (NSL), the American Federation of Teachers (AFT), the PEA, and even the NEA—were among the more than 450 organizations and 1,300 individuals condemned for a variety of allegedly dangerous and disloyal activities. Copies of *The Red Network* sold quickly to organizations and to individuals, despite the dubiousness of many of its claims. Dilling wrote and published more than 20 pamphlets and two additional books, and remained an active speaker at DAR and American Legion events, women's colleges, churches, and meetings of voluntary associations. In 1938, she launched her Patriotic Research Bureau and widely circulated her anti-Communist and anti-Semitic claims through subscription newsletters and similar means.[34] Though leftist educators were frequently among a larger group that Dilling antagonized, they occasionally took a more central role, including in 1935, when she testified at legislative hearings into subversion at the University of Chicago. In 1939, Henry Ford paid Dilling $5,000 to investigate Communism at the University of Michigan. The resulting 96-page report detailed the various speakers, organizations, and professorial activities that demonstrated that the institution was "typical of those American colleges which have permitted Marxist-bitten, professional theorist to inoculate wholesome American youths with their collectivist propaganda." She noted that over one thousand library books evidenced Communist influence—including 81 by the "filthy Sigmund Freud"— and that the institution received the *Communist Internationale* but did not have a copy of the recent Massachusetts legislative report on Communist subversion in the schools.[35] She offered similar conclusions after considering Communism at UCLA, with funding from the Los Angeles Chamber of Commerce, and at Cornell and Northwestern Universities, where her children attended.[36]

---

[34]   Dilling, *Red Network*; Christine K. Erickson, "'I Have Not Had One Fact Disproven': Elizabeth Dilling's Crusade against Communism in the 1930s," *Journal of American Studies* 36, no. 3 (2002): 473–89; Jeansonne, *Women of the Far Right*, 16–21; Gleason, "In Defense," 60–138.

[35]   [Elizabeth Dilling], "Radicalism in the University of Michigan," 2, 79, Joseph A. Labadie Collection Subject Vertical Files, Communism–U.S.–Anti-Communism–Dilling, Elizabeth, University of Michigan, Ann Arbor, MI.

[36]   Elizabeth Dilling, *Reds at Cornell University* (Chicago, [1940]); Jeansonne, *Women of the Far Right*, 20–21.

Dilling might be the best remembered of the professional patriots but she was certainly not alone. Her work drew on that of like-minded reactionaries, including Harry A. Jung, the founder of the Chicago-based American Vigilante Intelligence Federation, who claimed subversion in the labor movement. In 1935, Nelson E. Hewitt, whom Dilling praised as a "super-expert-patriot," asked *How "Red" Is the University of Chicago?* His 100-plus-page answer consisted of a compilation of quotes and articles purported to prove that it was overwhelmingly Communistic and in need of cleansing.[37] William Wallace Cowan's 1933 *Red Hand in the Professor's Glove* took broader view. It warned: "When the red flag of anarchy and communism is hoisted above the American flag, when the Stars and Stripes are burned on a college campus by college students—whose minds have been perverted with a seditious and destructive philosophy under the aegis of socialistic and communistic college professors—it is time to purify the insidious atmosphere that is contaminating the patriotic citizenship of thousands of students in a large number of our institutions of higher learning."[38]

Through their various books and pamphlets, as well as magazines such as the *National Republic*, these professional patriots spread their fear of Communism in the schools and colleges. In the middle of the decade, they were joined and abetted by William Randolph Hearst's newspapers, which launched their own campaigns against subversion in education. In late 1934 amid attacks on Columbia, New York, and Syracuse Universities, Teachers College faculty decried Hearst's "campaign of terrorism against American teachers," and the *New York Evening Post* called for a Congressional investigation into his activities.[39] The following February, almost the entire issue of *Social Frontier* was dedicated to a critique of Hearst's "peculiarly unprincipled" attacks on educators and their institutions, which by then had spread to include Harvard University and the University of Chicago.[40] Columbia University philosopher John Dewey believed that educators' response to Hearst was promising, but Malcolm Wiley, in his report on higher education during the Depression written for the American Association of University Professors, saw it otherwise. Calling Hearst's tactics "especially vicious," he warned, "It is difficult to meet these attacks, since any

---

[37]   Dilling, *Red Network*, 5; Nelson E. Hewitt, *How "Red" Is the University of Chicago?* (Chicago: Advisory Associates, 1935).

[38]   William Wallace Cowan, *The Red Hand in the Professor's Glove* (Manchester, NH: Author, 1933), [iii].

[39]   Howard K. Beale, *Are American Teachers Free? An Analysis of Restraints upon the Freedom of Teaching in American Schools*, Report on the Commission on the Social Studies 12 (New York: C. Scribner's Sons, 1936), 537; "W.R. Hearst Baits College 'Reds,'" *Social Frontier* 1, no. 4 (January 1935): 3.

[40]   "W.R. Hearst and the Press," *Social Frontier* 1, no. 5 (February 1935): 3.

counterreaction at once leads to charges of disloyalty."[41] Although extreme, Hearst's efforts were part of a larger pattern, and Beale identified the press as among the greatest impediments to teacher freedom in the country.[42]

Beale's concern over business influences was, however, even greater. Calling them "most dangerous and most subtle," Beale argued that "Business's chief interest in the schools is the indoctrination of pupils and teachers with concepts that will silence criticism of business and its methods to insure large profits for the future."[43] At times, this control was used to limit the perspectives that could be aired in classrooms or in public forums on school property. At others, it was used to remove specific offending educators, such as James M. Shields, a Winston-Salem principal who published a novel critical of a fictional tobacco company's control over schools to its own ends.[44] More often, it shaped the larger tenor and tone of the educational system, including by affecting hiring decisions and what would be included in textbooks. As historian Carleton J. H. Hayes noted, this influence could trickle down to individual teachers: "If the local school authorities, pressed by the Chamber of Commerce or banking members of the Board of Education, ordain that in a world so menaced by the specter of Communism, sound principles of economics and capitalism shall be inculcated in special classes, the teacher of history is likely to assent, however perfunctorily."[45] This influence could either be direct in the role of a board member or indirect through larger organized pressure tactics, somewhat similar to those of professional patriots. The National Association of Manufacturers (NAM), for example, turned explicitly to propaganda as a way of portraying the free enterprise system as integral to the American way of life—in 1937, it spent almost $750,000 on propaganda efforts— and used schools as a primary venue for delivering its message. Amid substantial budget distress, schools proved open to materials that the NAM provided through its Public Information Program, materials which both implicitly and explicitly argued against socialism and Communism.[46]

---

[41] John Dewey, "The Crucial Role of Intelligence," *Social Frontier* 1, no. 5 (February 1935): 9–10, 9; Malcolm M. Wiley, *Depression, Recovery and Higher Education: A Report by Committee Y of the American Association of University Professors* (New York: McGraw-Hill, 1937), 445.

[42] Beale, *Are American Teachers Free?*, 536–40.

[43] Ibid., 545–6.

[44] James M. Shields, *Just Plain Larnin'* (New York: Coward-McCann, 1934); "Professional Security," *Social Frontier* 1, no. 1 (October 1934): 10–11.

[45] "History Teaching Curbs Deplored," *New York World*, May 11, 1930 (as cited by Beale, *Are American Teachers Free?*, 571).

[46] Colleen Ann Moore, "The National Association of Manufacturers: The Voice of Industry and the Free Enterprise Campaign in the Schools, 1929–1949" (Ph.D. diss., University of Akron, 1985), 351–421.

The extensive anti-Communist efforts of business organizations, the reactionary press, and professional patriots should not obscure the efforts undertaken by a wider range of individuals and organizations. The NAM and United States Chamber of Commerce were violently opposed to unionization but were joined in their anti-Communist efforts by the American Federation of Labor (AFL), which sought to purge its union of Communist influence and distance itself from labor activities thought to be aligned with Communists. AFL leaders such as William Green and Matthew Woll were known for the depths of their anti-Communism; Woll frequently aligned with superpatriots in his attacks and, in late 1934, joined with Representative Hamilton Fish to urge a Congressional inquiry into radical subversion in American colleges.[47] Woll's activities threatened academic freedom, and *Social Frontier* specifically called on Green to distance the AFL from Woll and defend academic freedom in the face of "red herrings like 'Communism', 'alien ideas', [and] 'subversive activities.'"[48] Woll's anti-Communism both was reflective of and contributed to the long-standing struggles between the AFL and the AFT. The AFL threatened the AFT with charter revocation, although Woll's rhetoric actually briefly helped the left wing of the union maintain power in the late 1930s. Of course, the anti-Communists reasserted control at the end of the decade with the backing of the AFL and the Committee on Cultural Freedom—an organization of liberal educators and intellectuals formed in 1939 by Dewey, Counts, and New York University's Sidney Hook in opposition to Communists and to Franz Boas's recently formed American Committee for Democracy and Intellectual Freedom.[49]

Fearful of godlessness in education and society, religious organizations and churches also contributed to the efforts to eliminate Communism from the schools, frequently working with professional patriots who conflated religious belief with anti-Communism.[50] In 1932 in North Carolina, church leaders joined with businessmen to urge the governor to purge schools of Communism. They were unsuccessful, but Fundamentalists' efforts in Texas the same year forced the removal of 18 faculty from Texas Technical College for their "atheism and

---

[47] "Probe of College Reds Demanded by Woll," *Detroit Times*, December 28, 1934; "Dr. Butler Derides Communist Charge," *New York Times*, January 5, 1935.

[48] "An Open Letter to William Green," *Social Frontier* 1, no. 5 (February 1935): 8.

[49] Marjorie Murphy, *Blackboard Unions: The AFT and the NEA, 1900–1980* (Ithaca, NY: Cornell University Press, 1990), 150–74; Cain, "Academic Freedom," 310–12; Andrew Hartman, *Education and the Cold War: The Battle for the American School* (New York: Palgrave Macmillan, 2008), 39–40.

[50] "Church-Labor Tie for Red War Urged," *New York Times*, April 14, 1937.

sovietism."[51] Moreover, the ACLU argued that the Catholic Church was second only to the American Legion in its attempted suppression of civil liberties, and historians have since noted the extremity of American Catholic anti-Communism.[52] Bishop John Francis Noll warned of the "folly" of not countering the Communism in American schools and colleges, and Catholic educational leaders such as Georgetown University vice president Father Edmund A. Walsh actively participated in attacks on it.[53] Indeed, Walsh, who has been called "the country's most ardent, and best-known, Catholic anti-Communist,"[54] celebrated Jung's work; testified before legislative investigating committees; and sought to rid schools, colleges, and the country of Communism. In 1936 Fordham president Father Robert Gannon saw Communism in New Deal reforms and warned: "What they want is not so much our money as our children. They want our schools and colleges ... Later they hope, when they have the youth of the nation in their power, to eliminate all religion and all morality that does not conform to their peculiar ideology."[55]

Taken together, then, a wide range of non-governmental and extra-educational individuals and organizations attacked Communism in public schools, colleges, and universities. They campaigned against subversion, called for legislative investigations, and provided "evidence" of infiltration. Through popular publications and materials targeted at specific schools, they helped to coalesce concern across the nation and in individual communities. Ultimately, they fostered both governmental and institutional action, threatened the livelihoods of educators, and endangered the educations of leftist students.

Governmental Anti-Communism

Building on and responding to these external pressures were governmental efforts, including investigations into teachers and textbooks at local, state, and

---

[51] Robert W. Iversen, *The Communists and the Schools* (New York: Harcourt, Brace, 1959), 180.

[52] Robert L. Frank, "Prelude to Cold War: American Catholics and Communism," *Journal of Church and State* 34, no. 1 (1992): 39–56; Richard Gid Powers, "American Catholics and Catholic Americans: The Rise and Fall of Catholic Anticommunism," *U.S. Catholic Historian* 22, no. 4 (Fall 2004): 17–35.

[53] "Catholics Plan Organization to Stop Communism," *Chicago Tribune*, September 12, 1936.

[54] Alfred S. Regnery, *Upstream: The Ascendance of American Conservatism* (New York: Threshold, 2008), 332.

[55] Bruce Nelson, *Divided We Stand: American Workers and the Struggle for Black Equality* (Princeton, NJ: Princeton University Press, 2001), 66.

federal levels, as well as the passage of loyalty oath requirements. Although they would grow in scope and impact as the decade progressed, they existed throughout, with Congressman Hamilton Fish's Special Committee to Investigate Communist Activities in the United States initiating the surge in governmental anti-Communism in the decade. When Fish, a founder of the American Legion and a congressman from New York, launched his inquiry in June 1930, the first witness was Walsh, who warned of subversion and claimed that faculty who traveled to Russia returned as propagandists for Communism. In New York City, the superintendent of schools reported that there were no Communists in the system but that any found would be dismissed immediately. In all, Fish's committee traveled to 12 cities across the country and heard from more than 275 witnesses, yet was unable to uncover significant Communistic activity in educational systems. Still, it claimed that New York University housed numerous Communists and that further subversion existed at Columbia and Harvard Universities, as well as at the Universities of California, Chicago, Washington, and Wisconsin. Most were unimpressed, including the *New York Times*, which noted that the committee's assertion of Communist infiltration into higher education "implies that it does not know how to take an undergraduate joke."[56] The committee's larger claims of subversion and calls to enhance judicial authority and increase deportations were further derided.

Despite Fish's investigation doing as much to harm anti-Communism as to provide evidence of subversion in schools, legislative efforts to counter Communist teachers and students returned in ensuing years, including Congressional threats to investigate Howard University and African American higher education more broadly.[57] More frequently it was state governments, which were especially susceptible to pressure groups, that launched inquiries.[58] Following years of allegations by newspaper editor and occasional Republican candidate for the U.S. Senate John B. Chapple, the Wisconsin assembly, for example, investigated the existence of "so many communists among the students" of the University of Wisconsin in 1933.[59] At the time, only one

---

[56] Iversen, *Communists and the Schools*, 28–31; "Communists and Criminals," *New York Times*, January 19, 1931; American Civil Liberties Union, "Still the Fish Committee Nonsense! The Answer of the Press to the Fish Committee Proposals to Outlaw Free Speech for Communists" (New York, 1932).

[57] The Department of the Interior did investigate Howard as part of its oversight role, with Secretary Harold Ickes ultimately supporting the institution. Walter Dyson, *Howard University: The Capstone of Negro Education, A History: 1867–1940* (Washington, DC, 1941).

[58] Ellen Schrecker, *Many Are the Crimes: McCarthyism in America* (Boston, 1998), 67.

[59] John B. Chapple, *La Follette Socialism: How It Affects Your Job, Your Savings, Your Insurance Policy, Your Rights, and Your Future* (Ashland, WI, 1931), 79–99; "Says Wisconsin

120 *Little 'Red Scares'*

hearing was held and the findings were inconclusive, but two years later, at the urging of the American Legion and the Hearst press, the state senate launched its own investigation into whether the university and state teachers' colleges were "hotbeds of communism." The committee targeted President Frank, claimed that he harbored Communists, and condemned his dismissal of a dean who had denied tenure to an accused Communist teacher unionist. Though it could not identify any Communists on the faculty, the senate warned that the administration had long conveyed its tolerance of Communism to the great detriment of the institution and demanded that it cooperate with Americanism efforts.[60] In Illinois, following drugstore magnate Charles Walgreen's removal of his niece from the University of Chicago to protect her from Communist indoctrination—an event that was abetted by Hearst, a friend of Walgreen's— the state senate authorized inquiries into Communistic teaching at public and private colleges and universities. Its hearings, which only ever considered the University of Chicago, featured wild accusations by Jung and Dilling, including the latter's claims that Professor Robert Morss Lovett was even more dangerous than Eleanor Roosevelt and that justice Louis Brandeis and U.S. senator William E. Borah were Communists. University president Robert Maynard Hutchins and others successfully countered with a denial of the charges and a defense of academic freedom; the investigative committee exonerated the institution. Moreover, the institution ignored the committee's call that Lovett be dismissed for his off-campus activities, and the sole committee member who sought to extend the investigation was unable to generate any support.[61]

In 1936, New York state senator John J. McNaboe's resolution for a joint committee to investigate Communism and un-American activities by students, teachers, and faculty was approved by a large margin in both houses of the legislature. McNaboe charged widespread subversion, especially at Cornell University, which he termed a "center of revolutionary communistic propaganda."[62] Cornell president Livingston Farrand denied the claim, noting that a few dozen activist

---

University Is Soviet Hotbed," *Chicago Tribune,* May 7, 1932; "Alleged Red at Wisconsin U. to Face Inquiry," *Chicago Tribune,* June 28, 1933.

[60] Iversen, *Communists and the Schools,* 181–4; "Senate Votes Hunt Reds at U. of Wisconsin," *Chicago Tribune,* February 22, 1935; "Senate Find U. of Wisconsin Haven for Reds," *Chicago Tribune,* September 22, 1935.

[61] John W. Boyer, *Academic Freedom and the Modern University: The Experience of the University of Chicago,* Occasional Papers on Higher Education 10 (Chicago, 2002), 23–66; Milton Mayer, "The Red Room," *Massachusetts Review* 16, no. 3 (Summer 1975): 520–50; William H. McNeill, *Hutchins' University: A Memoir of the University of Chicago, 1929–1950* (Chicago, 1991), 63–5; Iversen, *Communists and the Schools,* 188–91.

[62] Lawrence H. Chamberlain, *Loyalty and Legislative Action: A Survey of Activity by the New York State Legislature, 1919–1949* (Ithaca, NY, 1951), 55–8, 57.

Anti-Communists and Education in an "Age of Conflicts" 121

students out of a population of 6,000 was far less troubling than McNaboe's efforts themselves, and student papers at Cornell and elsewhere mocked the senator.[63] McNaboe claimed to be met with "an avalanche of abuse, ridicule and invective," but he continued and expanded his charges.[64] His fellow legislators, though, retreated, and the committee expired without holding a single hearing. McNaboe was only able to continue his anti-Communist efforts by redirecting a committee investigating probation and parole.[65]

McNaboe's efforts would be superseded by the most damaging legislative investigations of the era, the Rapp–Coudert investigation into subversion in New York City schools in 1940 and 1941. Before then, though, the Florida legislature approved a two-year investigation into the state's schools and colleges after pacifist activities at Florida State College for Women led to fears over Communist infiltration.[66] More importantly, the House Un-American Activities Committee, commonly termed the Dies Committee after Representative Martin Dies of Texas, was authorized to investigate subversion throughout the country. Though catalyzed by concerns over Nazism, the committee quickly turned its attention to Communism and eagerly included educators and schools among other foci of investigation. With testimony from superpatriots such as Walter S. Steele and Homer Chaillaux, director of the American Legion's NAC, as well as from liberal anti-Communists within the education profession, the committee heard descriptions of Communist-front student organizations and infiltration of the teachers unions. In Washington, DC, Howard University president Mordecai Johnson was accused of being a Communist, and Warren D. Beatty, director of the Division of Education of the Office of Indian Affairs was thought to be, as well.[67] The committee asked the Kansas legislature for cooperation in uncovering the circumstances leading to University of Kansas student Don Henry's death while fighting in the Spanish Civil War; the legislature largely left the investigation to the Board of Regents, though it did bemoan the influence of the Young Communist League on campus.[68] In Detroit, Wayne University

---

[63] Morris Bishop, *A History of Cornell* (Ithaca, NY, 1962), 493; "Red, White—and McNaboe," *Cornell Daily Sun*, December 1, 1936; "Campaign against College Reds," *Harvard Crimson*, December 1, 1936; "Big Red Reds," *Daily Princetonian*, December 1, 1936.

[64] "More Red Schools Listed by McNaboe," *New York Times*, January 4, 1937.

[65] Chamberlain, *Loyalty and Legislative Action*, 58–63.

[66] "Order Inquiry into Teaching of Communism," [*St. Petersburg*] *Evening Independent*, May 22, 1937.

[67] William Gellermann, *Martin Dies* (New York, 1944), 116–37.

[68] Iversen, *Communists and the Schools*, 190–93; Edwin F. Abels, Clarence P. Oakes, and A.F. Cross, "Transmittal Report to the Dies Committee Accompanying Evidence and Board of Regents' Documentation in the Don Henry Case to the Special Committee on Un-

professor Walter Bergman was accused of being a Communist, and the Detroit Federation of Teachers was alleged to be a front organization. The situation was somewhat defused when Superintendent Frank Cody responded to a charge of "ten red" teachers in the city by claiming, "There are 8,000 teachers in our school system and if 10 of them are Red and the remainder are well read, I would be satisfied." When the Board of Education investigated the charges aired before the Dies Committee, it found no evidence of subversion of Communist Party membership among its teachers, and civil liberties were preserved.[69]

The Dies Committee fostered additional efforts at local and state levels, including in California, where Jack B. Tenney's committee began its work in 1941 with a special interest in the state's colleges, and in Texas, where the committee itself was short-lived but legislative investigations and inquiries continued for a decade.[70] In New York, the legislature formed the Rapp–Coudert Committee in September 1940, shortly after philosopher Bertrand Russell was barred from a professorship at the City College of New York (CCNY). With support from college administrators, evidence provided by former Communists, and testimony from more than 500 educators and 50 students, the committee claimed to find evidence that 69 educators were Communists and implicated more than 400 more faculty and staff members at Brooklyn and City Colleges. In 1941, the Board of Higher Education responded to the legislative investigation by banning its staff from Communist Party membership and, eventually, by dismissing 20 faculty members for conduct unbecoming of a faculty member. Another 11 resigned while their cases were pending. Through its reliance on informers, pressure on witnesses to identify Communists, and reliance on institutions to dispose of uncooperative witnesses, the Rapp–Coudert committee established the precedents that would be followed in the Red Scare of the late 1940s and 1950s.[71]

American Activities, House of Representatives" (Topeka: Kansas House of Representatives, 1939).

[69] The institution is now known as Wayne State University. Jeffrey E. Mirel, "Radicalism and Public Education: The Dies Committee in Detroit, 1938–39," in *Michigan: Explorations in Its Social History*, ed. by Francis X. Blouin, Jr., and Maris A. Vinovskis (Ann Arbor, 1987), 1–22, 9; Jeffrey E. Mirel, "Politics and Public Education in the Great Depression: Detroit, 1929–1940" (Ph.D. diss., University of Michigan, 1984), 264–92.

[70] John Aubrey Douglass, *The California Idea and American Higher Education: 1850 to the 1960 Master Plan* (Stanford, CA, 2000), 207; Susan R. Richardson, "Reds, Race, and Research: Homer P. Rainey and the Grand Texas Tradition of Political Interference, 1939–1944," *Perspectives on the History of Higher Education* no. 24 (2005): 125–71.

[71] Carol Smith, "The Dress Rehearsal for McCarthyism," *Academe* 97, no. 4 (July–August 2011): 48–51; Stephen Leberstein, "Purging the Profs: The Rapp Coudert Committee in New York, 1940–1942," in *New Studies in the Politics and Culture of U.S. Communism*, ed. by Michael E. Brown, Randy Martin, Frank Rosengarten and George

Until the very end of the 1930s, these formal investigations—as well as those that were threatened or proposed but not enacted—rarely resulted in specific action against individuals or institutions. They were, though, just one element of governmental attempts to eradicate Communism from schools and colleges. In Georgia, for example, the governor reorganized the state's governance structure as part of an effort to rid the colleges of Communists.[72] More than two dozen states required patriotic instruction in schools, and many municipalities barred allegedly Communistic organizations from using school facilities.[73] Also prevalent were the requirements that educators (and sometimes students) pledge their loyalty to either the U.S. Constitution or that of a specific state. In 1934, Representative Edward A. Kenney involved Congress in the debates over teachers' oaths by proposing a resolution "memorializing the states of the union to require the taking of an oath of allegiance to the Constitution of the United States by all teachers of the public schools and other institutions of learning." The House Committee on Education held hearings on the resolution but never voted upon it. Still, the efforts demonstrate the connections between anti-Communist activists—Fish and Steele were among those who testified—and highlight the increasing fears of Communism in the schools. Moreover, despite Kenney's claim that he found American teachers to be "the finest body of men and women that may be found anywhere who act as school teachers" and that the disloyalty of students was a far greater concern than that of teachers, many teachers took offense to his and other similar efforts.[74] Why, they asked, were they being singled out and held to standards that frequently did not apply to other employees? The oaths could also be misused. As former Chicago teacher Helen Thayer testified, "an oath puts into the hands of school authorities an instrument for intimidation of teachers on matters quite apart from that of loyalty ... The set-up we have here in city administration is not one that should be entrusted with the administration of such an oath."[75]

Kenney's act was never passed, but at the urging of retired army general Amos Alfred Fries, American Legion vice-commander E. Brooks Fetty, and attorney George E. Sullivan, Congress did act locally by attaching a "red rider" to its 1935 appropriations for Washington, DC. Until it was repealed in 1937, the rider

---

Snedeker (New York, 1993), 91–122; Ellen W. Schrecker, *No Ivory Tower: McCarthyism and the Universities* (New York, 1986), 75–83.

[72] Sue Bailes, "Eugene Talmadge and the Board of Regents Controversy," *Georgia Historical Quarterly* 53, no. 4 (1969): 409–23.

[73] American Civil Liberties Union, *The Gag on Teaching*, 3rd edn (New York, 1937).

[74] "Hearing before the Committee on Education, House of Representatives, Seventy-Third Congress, Second Session on H.J. Res. 339" (Washington, DC, 1934), 1, 5.

[75] Ibid., 2.

124 *Little 'Red Scares'*

forbade the schools from using federal funds "for the payment of the salary of any person teaching or advocating Communism." Despite advice to the contrary and under pressure from business and patriotic groups, the school board interpreted it to mean that teachers could not discuss Communism in the classroom, much less analyze it. Twice a month, teachers had to sign a statement that they had adhered to the law in order to receive their paychecks.[76] Still, most of these efforts took place at the state level: By 1936, 21 states had enacted loyalty oaths of one form or another, at times over the protest of teachers and administrators. Elsewhere, loyalty oaths were considered but ultimately defeated or vetoed.[77] Indeed, many educators thought they were both demeaning and useless; anyone about whom there was legitimate concern, they believed, could have easily lied. Still, as Ellen Schrecker, the leading authority on anti-Communist activity in higher education, noted, "Loyalty oaths for teachers were a popular device. They were cheap and symbolically satisfying."[78]

Loyalty oaths were public statements of legislative anti-Communism; they were joined by both public and private law enforcement efforts that targeted college students across the country. At the local and state levels, these efforts could involve police infiltration into or attacks on organizations and events, including the beating of University of Michigan students who participated in May Day events in 1934—beatings that were lauded by other university students and administrators and resulted in disciplinary action against the injured students.[79] As Robert Cohen detailed, colleges also frequently supplied the Federal Bureau of Investigation (FBI) with information on the activities of allegedly radical and Communist students, and institutional leaders welcomed the efforts of the city police to control student protesters. Cohen identified such activity at more than 20 institutions; by the end of the decade, the FBI had files on more than 2,000 student activists from the University of Chicago alone. Moreover, institutional leaders often worked in concert with local law information officials to gather

---

[76] Lionel Heap, "The Little Red Rider," *Social Frontier* 2, no. 8 (May 1936): 254–5; Hartman, *Education and the Cold War*, 48–9; "Teacher and Communism," *New York Times*, September 22, 1935; "Teaching of Communism in Public Schools of the District of Columbia; Hearings Before the Subcommittee on Education of the Committee on the District of Columbia, House of Representatives, Seventy-Fourth Congress, Second Session on H.R. 10391 and H.R. 11375" (Washington, DC, 1936).

[77] Schrecker, *No Ivory Tower*, 69; Henry R. Linville, *Oaths for Teachers*, [1935]).

[78] Schrecker, *Many Are the Crimes*, 67.

[79] Peter E. Van de Water, *Alexander Grant Ruthven of Michigan: Biography of a President* (Grand Rapids, MI, 1977), 140; Hewitt, *How "Red" Is the University of Chicago?*, 47–8.

information on their students for their own and larger uses, though they often did so covertly to avoid detection and any potential negative publicity.[80]

Educators and Students

While external groups and governmental bodies could pressure schools or impose restrictions, the discussion above highlights that educators and students themselves were often complicit in the efforts against alleged Communist influences. Boards of both public and private institutions were at the junctures of schools and society; indeed, that positioning was central to the roles of said boards. Elected school boards could bear the brunt of attacks on subversion but could also launch them or enact their mandates. The larger legislative inquiries frequently includeD boards' defenses of the schools as being free of Communists, rather than defenses of students' and teachers' rights to be Communists. As in the investigation of Don Henry's education in Kansas, these efforts were at times aimed to circumvent a potentially more damaging governmental investigation.[81] At other times, though, boards themselves were the sources of the anti-Communist activities or, at least, the main proponents of such efforts. And both public and private institutions were frequently, though not always, overseen by those with conservative business and political interests.

Administrators were likewise beholden to larger societal pressures, institutional needs, and their own beliefs. At times, they sought to protect their institutions and faculty from external forces, as Cody did with his defense of Detroit teachers; as Howard University's Johnson did with his call for more, rather than less, political heterodoxy in education; and as numerous institutional leaders did in protesting against the loyalty oaths that were passed throughout the era. At other times, though, school and college administrators were themselves the perpetrators of anti-Communist efforts. Former University of Illinois president David Kinley, for example, wrote to Elizabeth Dilling, praised her work, and claimed, "I agree with you that it is time that parents should look more closely into the influence of the teachers of the schools and colleges which their children attend."[82] Kinley, who had overseen the investigation into un-Americanism at Illinois during and just after World War I, later denounced Communism as "economically unsound, religiously atheistic, socially destructive, ethically indefensible, and morally debasing."[83] Georgetown's Walsh was likewise

---

[80]   Cohen, *When the Old Left*, 98–100.

[81]   Iversen, *Communists and the Schools*, 192–3.

[82]   Dilling, *Red Network*, 6.

[83]   Bruce Tap, "Suppression of Dissent: Academic Freedom at the University of Illinois during the World War I Era," *Illinois Historical Journal* 85, no. 1 (1992): 2–22; "Dr. Kinley

an outspoken opponent of Communism in the schools, as were numerous other administrators, both nationally known and only locally recognized. As Cohen argued, college administrators were the most active opponents of leftist students in the first half of the decade. In New York, a center of Communist activity in education and more broadly, several institutional leaders took pronounced stands and one in particular stood out: CCNY president Frederick B. Robinson, who, with his subordinates, "violated student free speech rights more often than any other college administration in Depression America."[84]

As might be expected during the tumultuous 1930s, administrators' views on the issues could be highly differentiated. So, for example, Alexander Grant Ruthven, president of the University of Michigan, defended his faculty against charges of subversion, denounced loyalty oaths, successfully fought his governing board's efforts to identify and purge Communist faculty, and lectured the Michigan Manufacturer's Association on the importance of academic freedom. In 1938, he insisted not only that colleges were not Communistic but also that they were not even liberal; it was only due to their conservatism that "any evidence of unorthodox thinking, the slightest tinge of pink, becomes conspicuous as a departure from the norm and causes spasms of hysteria in timid souls who are fearful of being disturbed."[85] Yet, at the same time, Ruthven willingly expelled leftist students for disrupting the institution. Though he denied that he did so for political reasons, in 1940, he sought and received the faculty senate's approval to dismiss Communist students before expelling a dozen and suspending five more. Following a mock trial of Ruthven in a local park, the editors of the school's paper were suspended for printing reactions from the ASU, and the local ASU chapter was disbanded.[86] Moreover, shortly thereafter, he told the National Association of State Universities that "administrative officers and professors of colleges and universities should rid themselves of the notion that romanticism, sentimentalism and indiscriminate tolerance are essential constituents of democracy."[87]

The acquiescence of the Michigan faculty to these actions highlights that, although schools and colleges exhibited greater freedom and political diversity than in previous eras, teachers and professors were still frequently conservative in their political beliefs and personal behaviors. As Beale wrote in

---

Hits Communism as Foe of Society," *Chicago Tribune*, February 1, 1937.

[84] Cohen, *When the Old Left*, 108.

[85] Cain, "Academic Freedom," 460–91; Alexander Grant Ruthven, "The Red Schoolhouse," 25 February 1938, Box 63, Alexander Grant Ruthven Papers, Bentley Historical Library, University of Michigan, Ann Arbor, MI (hereafter Ruthven Papers).

[86] Cain, "Academic Freedom," 460–91; Van de Water, *Alexander Grant Ruthven*, 144–9.

[87] "The Little Red Schoolhouse," *Michigan Daily*, Box 58, Ruthven Papers.

Are American Teachers Free?, "one of the most powerful restraints upon teachers is the influence of other teachers. Most teachers are themselves conservative by instinct and are made doubly cautious by long training ... The influence of the old-timer upon the youngster, particularly if he is dependent on the older teacher for advancement, is very strong."[88] Further, K-12 teachers knew little about academic freedom and were even unable to understand principles of freedom that they claimed to hold.[89] The battles within the AFT demonstrate the influence of anti-Communist teachers even more clearly. At first in New York, and then more broadly, teacher unionists struggled with the existence and influence of Communists within their unions, eventually culminating in the expulsion of New York Teachers Union, New York College Teachers Union, and the Philadelphia Teachers Union, and in the ensuing diminishment of other locals with significant Communist presence.

Importantly, the battles over Communism in New York unions have contributed to the perception that New York schoolteachers exhibited a range of leftist political beliefs from liberal to Communist, when, in fact, a much larger variety existed. Beginning in 1938, for example, both the Teachers Alliance of New York City and the American Education Association (AEA) organized conservative teachers in opposition to their liberal and leftist colleagues. Through outlets such as the *Bulletin of the Teachers Alliance* and the AEA's *Educational Signposts*, the associations argued in favor of loyalty oaths and accused those who opposed them of fascism, Communism, and un-Americanism. They supported the Rapp–Coudert investigations into the city's schools and helped provide a broader base of support for anti-Communist efforts. Moreover, although they were largely composed of K-12 teachers, in 1938 the AEA formed a branch at Brooklyn College, with 40 charter members concerned about the open Communism in the City Colleges.[90] Although Beale accurately noted that teachers in small towns were both more conservative and under greater restrictions than those in urban centers, these groups help to demonstrate that in even the biggest cities, conservative anti-Communists were well represented.

Finally, the presence of a growing student movement and increased leftist political activity on college campuses did not mitigate the efforts of students themselves to attack and remove Communists from campus. Even the largest student protests were frequently minority affairs on college campuses, and they

---

[88] Beale, *Are American Teachers Free?*, 599.

[89] National Education Association Committee on Academic Freedom, *The Limits of Academic Freedom: A Report of the Committee on Academic Freedom* (Washington, DC, 1939).

[90] Zoe Burkholder, "Teachers Against Academic Freedom: Right Wing Teachers in Cold War New York City" (paper presented at the History of Education Society Annual Conference, Chicago, IL, November 2011).

128 *Little 'Red Scares'*

sometimes received significant pushback from students. Michigan State College was, for example, "relatively quiescent politically, dominated by an antiradical administration, a powerful Reserve Officer Training Corps (ROTC), and a conservative student body."[91] In 1935, the student newspaper proudly proclaimed that it was "not one of these institutions that is continually faced with the annoying possibility of red 'riots.'"[92] Just more than a month later, a university administrator denounced an impending off-campus peace rally, instituted a requirement that all students take a loyalty oath, and opined, "The administration of the college will have no objection if other students toss these radicals in the river."[93] That night, 200 students taunted suspected pacifists and Communists with anti-Semitic chants and threatened violence against them; the following day, approximately 500 students gathered at the rally, heckled and threw rotten fruit at the speakers, and, with the encouragement of members of the ROTC, stormed the makeshift stage. They deposited the five speakers, including local ACLU leader and Dilling target Rev. Harold P. Marley, into the Red Cedar River.[94] Of course, such student anti-radicalism was not isolated. At the University of Michigan, "100 Michigan Men" threatened members of the NSL, and, at both the University of California and City College of New York, administrators met with conservative students and encouraged them to form vigilante groups to police their campuses. As such, it is not surprising that violence erupted at more than dozen campuses between 1934 and 1936. At the end of the decade, student anti-Communism was emboldened and included student governments' investigations into and decertification of chapters of the ASU.[95] The pressures on educational institutions were real, and they could emanate from a variety of internal and external sources.

---

[91] Kristen Fermaglich, "The Social Problems Club Riot of 1935: A Window into Antiradicalism and Antisemitism at Michigan State College," *Michigan Historical Review* 30, no. 1 (2004): 93–115, 94.

[92] "Collegiate Communists," [*Michigan*] *State News*, March 5, 1935.

[93] "Minutes of the Administrative Group Meeting," 11 April 1935, Michigan State University Archives and Special Collections, East Lansing, MI; "Campus Peace Being Periled by Pacifists," *Lansing State Journal*, April 12, 1935; Madison Kuhn, *Michigan State: The First One Hundred Years* (East Lansing, 1955), 393–4.

[94] Fermaglich, "Social Problems Club Riot"; Wechsler, *Revolt on the Campus*, 306; "Campus Peace Being Periled by Pacifists," *Lansing State Journal*, April 12, 1935; "MSC Students Duck Preacher in Peace Riot," *Detroit Free Press*, April 13, 1935.

[95] Cohen, *When the Old Left*, 106–7, 416–17n115.

Focus of Attacks

As this discussion of the diverse forces attacking alleged Communists highlights, politically heterodox educators faced real pressures, and battles were launched on many fronts. Perhaps the most direct attacks focused on specific educators, on specific institutions, or on the profession as a whole: Teachers, faculty, and administrators were forced to sign loyalty oaths; lived under the threat and reality of surveillance; and understood that even though they possessed more political freedom than educators of previous generations, substantial restrictions remained. As Schrecker noted, "Though the academy then tolerated more left-wing political activity than it did either earlier or later, it did not welcome it. Nor did radical teachers or students feel completely secure in their double commitment to scholarship and left-wing politics. They knew that were they to reveal themselves as Communists in public they might well be expelled or lose their jobs."[96] The Rapp–Coudert investigations and ensuing purges in New York both confirmed and exacerbated these fears, costing numerous City College educators their livelihoods. For Morris Schappes, the toll was worse. Convicted of perjury for denying knowledge of other Communists on staff, he spent more than 13 months in jail before his early release in 1944. Largely forgotten but more tragic, in 1935, William E. Sealock was forced from his position as chancellor at the Municipal University of Omaha amid a controversy over radicalism and his allegations of a "spy system" on campus; he committed suicide several days later.[97] How deep the chilling effect of these and related events was is necessarily unknown, although Paul W. Lazarsfeld and Wagner Thielens's work on faculty views in the 1950s suggests the likelihood of anxiety.[98] Also unknown are the scope of limitations on Communists imposed at the time of hiring. As Alexander Meiklejohn argued when the AAUP first worked on behalf of academic freedom, restraints are more easily applied though hiring decisions than dismissals.[99]

Schrecker's quote about tolerance and fear highlights that efforts to remove faculty were joined by more widespread and easier to undertake attacks on a second group: leftist students. Struggles in the early 1930s were highlighted by sporadic May Day violence, by CCNY's expulsion of more than 40 students

---

[96]   Schrecker, *No Ivory Tower*, 63.

[97]   Altbach, *Student Politics in America*, 61; "Education: Ouster Aftermath," *Time* (July 22, 1935).

[98]   Paul F. Lazarsfeld and Wagner Thielens, Jr., *The Academic Mind: Social Scientists in a Time of Crisis* (Glencoe, IL, 1958).

[99]   Alexander Meiklejohn, "Discussion," *Association of American Colleges Bulletin* 2 (April 1916): 179–87, 179–80.

130

Little 'Red Scares'

for their radical political activities between 1931 and 1934, and by UCLA's suspension of 5 student leftists in 1934.[100] As the mass student movement expanded, administrative restrictions continued, and many more students were suspended or dismissed for their parts in anti-war or anti-military activities across the nation.[101] Colleges and universities routinely banned or limited leftist student groups and barred the Communist, pacifist and socialist speakers they hoped to bring to campus. They also censored student newspapers and removed student editors. In an era of *in loco parentis*, student rights were severely limited, and, with only few exceptions, anti-Communist administrators could act against heterodox students with impunity. Students, too, could and did monitor and regulate each other.

A third key point of contention was the alleged bias in textbooks written by progressive college teachers and used in K-12 schools. Though battles had previously been fought over issues of race, religion, regionalism and ethnicity, it was not until the mid-1930s that the textbook controversies began to focus explicitly on Communism. In 1935, superpatriots claimed that Washington, DC, schools were using books that violated the recently enacted ban on teaching Communism, including Carl L. Becker's world history text and two books from Harold Rugg's Man and His Changing Society series. Despite local and national pressure—the *National Republic* warned that they were part of a larger "program for sovietizing American school children"[102]—the Washington, DC, school board eventually decided to retain the works. Elsewhere concern spread over *Our Economic Society and Its Problems*, written by presidential adviser Rexford G. Tugwell, who was depicted as a Communist infiltrator; Cleveland, Los Angeles, Kansas City, and Delaware schools all discontinued the use of the book. More far-reaching were the end-of-the-decade attacks on Rugg's social studies texts, which were then used in more than 4,000 school systems. Beginning in 1939, the American Federation of Advertising, NAM, American Legion, and Hearst press waged a widespread campaign against the reconstructionist Rugg and his works, using radio addresses, newspaper articles, pamphlets and other means, including O. K. Armstrong's important critique, "Treason in the Textbooks," which appeared in the September 1940 *American Legion Magazine*. The following January, Columbia University professor Ralph Robey, who had been hired by the NAM to analyze more than 600 school textbooks, released a 1,200-page report that was particularly critical of Rugg's books as biased against America. The NAM circulated the report across

---

[100]   Cohen, *When the Old Left*, 108–33.

[101]   ACLU, *Gag on Teaching*, 3rd edn, 43–4; ACLU, *Liberty's National Emergency: The Story of Civil Liberty in the Crisis Year, 1940–1941* (New York, 1941).

[102]   Dan W. Gilbert, "Sovietizing our Children," *National Republic* 24, no. 4 (August 1936): 16–17, 32.

Anti-Communists and Education in an "Age of Conflicts"   131

the nation as local American Legion posts campaigned for the books' removal from schools. At times these attacks were specifically anti-Communist or anti-Soviet but were more broadly anti-New Deal and fearful of a vague notion of un-Americanism. They were ultimately successful, as more than 1,500 school districts dropped the books by 1943.[103]

Joining these concerns over Communism in traditional schools and colleges was fear of Communists in alternative educational settings. Certainly, the Communist Youth Camps of the era were severely critiqued, and professional patriots disparaged a wide array of youth activities, including Dilling's warning that the "C" in YMCA might stand for "Communist."[104] Folk and labor schools, too, were especially vulnerable to accusations and tribulations. Tennessee's Highlander Folk School, for example, was repeatedly attacked in the 1930s, including in statewide papers and publications such as Joseph F. Kamp's sensationalist *Fifth Column in the South*. The FBI investigated the institution, and state officials proposed legislation designed to criminalize its activities. Within the labor movement, its refusal to disassociate with unions believed to be Communist-dominated led some to abandon it, as well. Highlander survived the immediate attacks but succumbed to larger political, racial, and economic pressures two decades later.[105] Other institutions' demises were more imminent, including Commonwealth College, founded in Louisiana in 1923 as a communal labor college and then relocated to Mena, Arkansas, in 1924. By the early 1930s, Commonwealth grew more radical, more active in the labor movement, and more influential in state-level socialist politics. In the middle of the decade, the college was attacked as a bastion of free love, atheism, and Communism, attacks that increased—and became increasingly violent—when it became closely associated with the Southern Tenant Farmers' Union (STFU). In 1935, the institution survived a state investigation and attempts to pass strict sedition laws aimed at the college. In 1937, following provocation by the KKK and publications such as Rev. L.D. Summers's pamphlet "Communism and Commonwealth College Unmasked," a related bill was again proposed and defeated, though the combined assaults took their toll. In 1938, the college split with the STFU and soon faced internal factionalism, financial difficulty, and external pressure. In September 1940, the state raided the institution and charged that the school had propagandized for

---

[103] Jonathon Zimmerman, *Whose America? Culture Wars in the Public Schools* (Cambridge, MA, 2002), 55–80; Joseph Moreau, *Schoolbook Nation: Conflicts over American History Textbooks from the Civil War to the Present* (Ann Arbor, 2003), 215–63.

[104] Dilling, *Red Network*, 250.

[105] John M. Glen, *Highlander: No Ordinary School, 1932–1962* (Lexington: University Press of Kentucky, 1988).

anarchy, had failed to fly an American flag, and had displayed a hammer and sickle. Convicted of the misdemeanors, Commonwealth College closed and had its possessions auctioned to cover its debts.[106]

Finally, teachers' organizations were a significant and persistent focus of concern as even conservative organizations such as the NEA could find themselves critiqued for imagined heterodoxy. Certainly, the PEA raised the ire of anti-Communists, as well, but much of the drama involved the AFT, which grew to new influence during the Depression years but increasingly struggled with how to handle Communism within its ranks. As early as the mid-1920s, Henry R. Linville worried about the presence of Communists within New York Teachers Union; in the early 1930s, as its president, he tried to diminish their influence. When New York-based efforts, including an investigation into factionalism led by John Dewey, failed to remove Communist influence and Linville's appeal to the AFT to revoke the local's charter were unheeded, Linville and liberal anti-Communist teachers left the local and formed their own competing union. As the influence of Communists increased in Local 5 and in its offshoot, Local 537, the national union also moved further left. Under the leadership of Jerome Davis—whom some both inside and outside the union alleged to be a Communist—the union expressed support for the Congress of Industrial Organizations, defended the academic freedom of alleged Communists, and pursued an aggressive agenda in the late 1930s. The union's activist stances and the influence the Communist Party members held and were purported to hold caused significant divides. In 1939, with support of liberal anti-Communists within the union and the AFL, Counts launched a successful effort to unseat Davis from the presidency. The following year, the union's executive committee likewise went to the anti-Communists. In 1941, with the New York locals taxed by the Rapp–Coudert investigations—investigations about which the AFT equivocated—the AFT both expelled the New York and Philadelphia locals and changed its non-discrimination clause to explicitly exclude Communists from membership. In doing so, the union eliminated roughly one-third of its membership and decimated college faculty unionization.[107]

---

[106] Richard J. Altenbaugh, *Education for Struggle: The American Labor Colleges of the 1920s and 1930s* (Philadelphia, PA, 1990), 197–203, 230–44; William H. Cobb, "The State Legislature and the "Reds": Arkansas's General Assembly v. Commonwealth College, 1935–1937," *Arkansas Historical Quarterly* 45, no. 1 (Spring 1986): 3–18.

[107] Murphy, *Blackboard Unions*, 150–74; William Edward Eaton, *The American Federation of Teachers, 1916–1961* (Carbondale, 1975), 79–121; Timothy Reese Cain, "Unionized Faculty and the Political Left: Communism and the AFT in the Late 1930s and Early 1940s" (paper presented at the Association for the Study of Higher Education Annual Conference, Indianapolis, IN, November 2010).

Conclusion

A year removed from his Congressional investigation, Representative Hamilton Fish opined: "Communism is the most important, the most vital, the most far-reaching, and the most dangerous issue in the world" and warned of faculty members' complicity in promoting its doctrines.[108] His concerns were echoed throughout the decade as teachers, students, institutions and organizations found themselves charged with subversion as coalitions of anti-Communists set their sights on schools and colleges as important battlegrounds for the future of the country. Professional patriots warned of "Red Microbes in Our Colleges"; business organizations propagandized against threats to capitalism; cartoonists portrayed Communists as rats, termites and snakes undermining American schools; and the labor movement sought to purge itself of Communists and their locals.[109] Frequently, they were joined by educators themselves, including administrators with vast powers over student activities and progressive teachers fearful that their union policies were being dictated by the Communist Party. Government efforts to control the schools and their teachers included prescribed loyalty oaths, investigations into subversion, and attacks on textbooks. Sporadically throughout the 1930s, these attacks were effective in silencing and removing politically heterodox students, teachers and speakers. On the eve of World War II, in the aftermath of the end of the Popular Front and a split in the American left, they proved more so in New York City, in Mena, Arkansas and elsewhere.

---

[108] Hamilton Fish, Jr., "The Menace of Communism," *Annals of the American Academy of Political and Social Science* 156 (July 1931): 54–61, 59.

[109] E.D. Clark, "Red Microbes in our Colleges," *National Republic* 24, no. 9 (January 1937): 1–2, 32. Anti-Communist cartoons appeared repeatedly in the *National Republic*, Hearst newspapers, and other publications.

Chapter 6

Fighting the "Red Danger": Employers and Anti-Communism

Chad Pearson

Employers representing a diverse set of industries entered the post-World War I period determined to undermine communism as an ideology and to eradicate the Communist Party (CP) as a political organization. They relentlessly denounced communism as a theory, and fought, both covertly and publically, communists in workplaces and in communities. They did so individually and collectively, holding membership in various elite organizations like the National Metal Trades Association (NMTA), the National Association of Manufacturers' (NAM), the American Chamber of Commerce, and the Southern States Industrial Council (SSIC). Employers dismissed communists from workplaces, endorsed red-hating politicians, and disseminated anti-communist propaganda, which, taken together, helped make anti-communism a mainstream force in American society.

Employers' collective, often intense, disdain of communism stems, above all, from their own economic interests. No group had more to lose from a movement that sought to abolish the profit system, eliminate class divisions, and create a worker-run civilization. A system of communism, articulated forcefully by Karl Marx and generations of his followers' voluminous writings, called for the collective ownership of industry, an end to private property, workers' control internationally, and a society based on human need, rather than individual profit. For these reasons, employers, including self-made men, nepotism's beneficiaries, proprietary capitalists, and leaders of major corporations, felt threatened and thus engaged in a decades-long campaign to defend capitalism—rhetorically and by force when necessary—against various waves of left-wing activism.

During the interwar period, employers adopted several strategies designed to contain and ultimately eliminate threats from the left. They built new, and piggybacked on long-standing, organizations. In the area of public relations, they disseminated pamphlets that stressed the supposed deep-seated connections between America and capitalism, and many established hyper-patriotic "American Plan" organizations. Spokespersons described the ideology of communism as atheistic, fundamentally violent, and, above all, deeply un-American. It was, in their collective views, economically unworkable, morally indecent, and ultimately incompatible with humans' desire to attain upward social and economic mobility. Rather than underline their own narrow economic interests, employers generally sought to demonstrate that communism threatened American society and its political institutions as a whole.

Many employers, particularly those active in associations, allied themselves with state authorities, and benefited from local and federal laws intended to protect private property and criminalize radicalism. Their high-profile allies included professional red-hunters like J. Edger Hoover and A. Mitchell Palmer. And throughout the interwar period, they enjoyed mutually supportive relationships with politicians like New York's Hamilton Fish and Clayton Lusk, Texas's Martin Dies, Washington's Miles Poindexter, and Virginia's Howard Smith. Employers donated money to their campaigns, often befriended them as individuals, and covertly cheered on their efforts. In general, politicians, rather than manufacturers, represented the public face of anti-communism. However, as business owners seeking profit, control over labor, and public legitimacy, employers remained the most consistent activists and principle beneficiaries of pre-McCarthyite forms of anti-communism.

This essay explores the numerous ways in which employers, who tended to conduct much of their work secretly, battled communism. They fired communists from their workplaces and shared information about communists with government authorities. In extreme cases, employers dispatched private guards during strikes against leftist activists, and sometimes they got their own hands dirty as they violently confronted labor and left-wing protesters on picket lines. Others felt no need to use private guards or engage in vigilante activities because state authorities, including judges and police forces, typically sided with employers during labor conflicts.

Employers' views of communism remained relatively consistent from the post-World War I period to the end of the World War II. Shortly after World War I, employers were especially concerned about the Bolshevik Revolution's impact on the American working class. Many were acutely alarmed, privately realizing that this revolution had captured the imagination of numerous immigrant and native-born workers. For decades, employers appeared unable or unwilling to disentangle the Russian experiment from communist movements domestically. Some complained that the Russian Revolution inspired domestic workers to disturb the supposedly harmonious relationship between employers and employees. The "Reds," one source complained, have instilled "the spirit of hatred between employers and employees."[1] Such hatred seemed especially clear in 1919 when countless numbers of workers from different industries staged strikes.

Employers defeated most of these strikes, and scores of manufacturers enjoyed prosperity in the 1920s, though many remained concerned about signs of class-based hatreds permeating from numerous shop floors. Employers wanted to put a stop such tensions, and some thought that benevolent forms of management constituted a potential solution. New welfare capitalist programs and company unions, emerging in the aftermath of the 1919 strike wave, were designed, in part, for public relations purposes. By offering health insurance, sponsoring athletic events, giving employees free turkeys during holidays, and listening to workers' suggestions and grievances, managers sought to show that they were hardly the coldhearted bosses depicted by muckraking journalists and Marxist propagandists. In some cases, such programs were designed to kill the appeal of communism, and left-wing ideas generally, with kindness.

In the 1930s, employers faced an uphill struggle. The Great Depression had a profoundly crippling effect on millions of workers, convincing large numbers to organize and, in some cases, question capitalism's legitimacy. Economic theories that challenged the free market's logic, especially Marxism, circulated widely and influenced the views of growing numbers. In this context, CP organizers mobilized aggressively, signing up new members and exploiting what appeared to some to be capitalism's imminent destruction. Domestically, the CP's influence, impacting the nature of unemployed protests and shaping the direction of the labor movement, was much greater than it ever had been, and communists helped launch many of the highly inclusive and combative CIO industrial unions. Some organized manufacturers' believed that an effective way to respond to unions' demands for "collective bargaining" was to engage in what one employer-activist called "collective thinking."[2] A resurgence of NAM and Chamber of Commerce activism, and the establishment of new employers' associations like the Southern States Industrial Council (SSIC), indicated that employers remained stubbornly committed to winning the struggle against radicalism and unionism.

After the US entered World War II, employers' anti-communism became less vocal, but was not muted altogether. With the country allied with the Soviet Union, communist trade unionists supported the war effort, subordinating their domestic interests to the great fight against German Nazis. What did this mean in practice? Answer: CP members supported the government's no-

---

[1]   Joseph J. Mereto, *The Red Conspiracy* (New York: The National Historical Society, 1920), 58.

[2]   John E. Edgerton, "Very Important," speech on October 1, 1934, Box 3, Folder 2, Southern States Industrial Council papers, Tennessee State Archives, Nashville, Tennessee.

138 *Little 'Red Scares'*

strike pledge. Yet employers did not refrain from denouncing communism altogether. Illogically, some equated communism with fascism, suggesting that both ideologies were foreign and therefore un-American. The political economy of World War II was distinctive, but employers' continued to invoke earlier arguments that communism was an alien and thus unwelcome ideology.

The Pre-World War I Decades

Employers enjoyed a long, and somewhat heroic, history of fighting radicalism. In the late nineteenth century, they formed organizations designed to weaken the labor movement and prevent the spread of leftist ideas. At the time, many believed that the labor movement itself was an expression of socialism. Large numbers of radical working class activists had attempted to, as a member of the National Metal Trades Association (NMTA), a leading union-fighting employers' association, put it, "limit industrial liberty" and enforce "demands by violence." "The issue" during periods of labor unrest, the commentator noted, "is between the free citizen and communism."[3] Groups like the NMTA, which offered membership to employers representing both large and small workplaces, recognized communism as a threatening theory that could, based on the rebellious activities of sections of the working class, potentially find expression in practice.

At the turn of the century, employers watched the spread of strikes, left-wing movements, and individual acts of rebellion with anxiety. They pointed to a handful of high-profile cases of anarchist-caused violence: the Haymarket bombing in 1886, Alexander Berkman's attempt to kill industrialist Henry Clay Frick in 1892, and Leon Czolgosz's murder of President William McKinley in 1901.[4] Soon, state and federal authorities criminalized anarchists. New York, New Jersey, and Wisconsin passed "criminal anarchy" laws shortly after jurors sent Czolgosz to die in the electric chair.[5] Coincidently, the head jurist in Czolgosz's trial, Henry W. Wendt, was a Buffalo-based industrialist and a leader of the anti-radical and anti-union National Founders' Association (NFA).[6] In response to various acts of radicalism and labor unrest generally, employers in several cities formed outwardly populist "Citizens' Associations," which

---

[3] Henry Loomis Nelson, "Industrial Liberty, Not Industrial Anarchy," *The Bulletin of the National Metal Trades Association* 3 (June 1904), 264.

[4] On the context surrounding these events, see Beverly Gage, *The Day Wall Street Exploded: A Story of America in its First Age of Terror* (Oxford: Oxford University Press, 2009).

[5] Gage, *The Day Wall Street Exploded*, 67.

[6] Chad Pearson, "'Organize and Fight': Communities, Employers, and Open-Shop Movements, 1890–1920" (Ph.D. diss., SUNY Albany, 2008), 162.

campaigned, often successfully, against strikes and radical protesters while advocating the restoration of "law and order."[7]

Despite an atmosphere inhospitable to labor activism, leftists and union activists continued to organize, strike, protest and demand workplace reforms. The most vocal activists were left-wing revolutionaries of various strips. How did employers make sense of this? Sometimes their deepest fears and anti-radical ideas found expression in works of literature. In 1906, David M. Parry, one-time National Association of Manufacturers (NAM) President and head of an Indianapolis-based carriage manufacturing company, published a dystopian novel entitled *The Scarlet Empire*, which dramatized, even exaggerated, the horrors of living under "social democracy" in the fictionalized community of Atlantis. Parry, who helped turn the NAM into a union-fighting organization in 1902, described an underwater world that was unbearable: food tasted horribly, one could not choose spouses, citizens were forced-feed medicine, feelings of alienation were an unsolvable fact of life, and residents had no ability to express themselves individually. Nightmarish conditions were a permanent feature of Atlantis, a place where signs of mediocrity were superior to acts of excellence; the society punished, rather than fostered, individual ambition. According to a

---

[7]   Self-proclaimed Citizens Associations appeared in communities throughout the nation, and some emerged before the official beginning of the open-shop movement. See Melvyn Dubofsky, *We Shall Be All: A History of the Industrial Workers of the World* (New York: Quadrangle/New York Times Books Co., 1969), 47–50; George G. Suggs, Jr., *Colorado's War on Militant Unionism: James H. Peabody and the Western Federation of Miners* (Norman: University of Oklahoma Press, 1991 [1972]), 68–72, 75, 77, 109, 146, 151–2, 184; Richard Schneirov, *Labor and Urban Politics: Class Conflict and the Origins of Modern Liberalism in Chicago, 1864–97* (Urbana: University of Illinois Press, 1998), 58–63, 87, 142, 163–7, 204, 334; Sven Beckert, *The Monied Metropolis: New York City and the Consolidation of the American Bourgeoisie, 1850–1896* (Cambridge: Cambridge University Press, 2001), 318; William Millikan, *A Union Against Unions: The Minneapolis Citizens Alliance and its Fight against Organized Labor, 1903–1947* (St. Paul 2001); Theresa A. Case, "Blaming Martin Irons: Leadership and Popular Protest in the 1886 Southwest Strike," *Journal of the Gilded Age and Progressive Era* 8 (January 2009): 51–82; Sam Mitrani, "Reforming Repression: Labor Anarchy, and Reform in the Shaping of the Chicago Police Department, 1879–1888," *Labor: Studies in Working-Class History of the Americas* 6 (Summer 2009): 73–96. On "Law and Order", see "The National Founders' Association Meeting," *Iron Age* 92 (November 27, 1913), 1220; San Francisco Chamber of Commerce, *Law and Order in San Francisco: A Beginning* (San Francisco, 1916); Steven C. Levi, *Committee of Vigilance: The San Francisco Chamber of Commerce Law and Order Committee, 1916–1919* (Jefferson, North Carolina: McFarland and Company, 1983); George Gorham Groat, *An Introduction to the Study of Organized Labor in America* (New York: The Macmillan Company, 1920), 269; Sidney Fine, *"Without Blare of Trumpets": Walter Drew, the National Erectors' Association, and the Open-shop Movement, 1903–57* (Ann Arbor: University of Michigan Press, 1995), 78.

140 *Little 'Red Scares'*

dwarf, one of the book's characters, ignorant and inept citizens "make the best officials, the best judges and the best generals in the industrial army."[8]

Parry sought to show, in a not-so-subtle way, socialism in practice. Responding to critics who insisted that his fictitious scenarios were utterly nonsensical, Parry explained that the book demonstrated the dreadfulness of a society in which "private ownership shall be abolished" and replaced by a society run by "the Government." The "Government," Parry warned, "shall run the factories, the farms, the railroads, the ships, the dormitories, and the kitchens, controlling all the activities of man, doing all his thinking for him, and caring for him with paternal solicitude from the cradle to the grave."[9]

Parry died in 1915, but his book continued to circulate and the NAM's anti-union and anti-radical agenda lived on. Employers hardly stopped speaking out against labor and radicalism. Yet the start of World War I brought business leaders and politicians together in unprecedented ways. Revolutionary labor activists, including anarchists and Industrial Workers of the World (IWW) members, were in retreat under the repressive arm of the state while the conservative American Federation of Labor (AFL) promised to refrain from striking. Under Woodrow Wilson's administration, the union, led by the anti-radical Samuel Gompers, promised to conduct its work in responsibly. Employers were in no position to continue their open-shop drive.

World War I, however, was hardly free of labor strife or radicalism. Unofficial work stoppages broke out in several workplaces, and socialists like Eugene Debs spent time in jail for criticizing capitalism and US military intervention. The federal government arrested numerous radicals under the Espionage and Sedition Acts, and elites in general were forced to come to terms with the success of the Bolshevik Revolution, which conservative commentators suggested was even worse than the fictional society of Atlantis.

"Worse than Barbarism": Employers and Communism after World War I

Employers entered the postwar era shaken by the successes of the Russian Revolution yet determined to maintain profits and to re-establish complete control over their workplaces. They challenged the popularity of left-wing ideas by connecting capitalism to the supposed virtues of individual freedom and patriotism. At the same time that they praised the goodness of the nation and its institutions, many kept wages low, and in 1919, roughly 4 million workers,

---

[8]   David M. Parry, *The Scarlet Empire* (New York: Grosset and Dunlap, 1906), 241.

[9]   "Parry, Author of 'The Scarlet Empire,' Replies to Socialist's Criticisms," *New York Times*, April 15, 1906.

frustrated by poverty wages, staged dramatic strikes from coast to coast. Communists played an active role in some of the work stoppages, which were energetic and widespread, impacting cities from Boston, where police officers engaged in an unprecedented citywide protest, to Seattle, where radical labor activists practically shutdown the entire city. The strike wave spread to numerous steel towns, impacting labor-management relations in Buffalo, Chicago, Gary, Pittsburgh and elsewhere.

The employer counter-attack was as intense as the labor unrest, but ultimately more effective. Employers pushed back hard, working with public and private guards, lawyers and judges to destroy the strikes, punish the strikers, and in the process send a powerful message to would-be protesters across the country. In Pittsburgh, future communist leader and chronicler of employer repression, William Z. Foster, recalled that "the Steel Trust went ahead with strikebreaking measures unprecedented in industrial history. It provisioned and fortified its great mills and furnaces, surrounding them with stockades topped off with heavily charged electric wires, and bristling with machine guns. It assembled whole armies of gunmen."[10] Such employers clearly went to great lengths to regain control of their workplaces.

In Seattle, organized employers relied on the local government to suppress the general strike and discipline the demonstrators. Angered by the $44 million cost of the protest, Seattle's Bolshevik-fearing employers, many of whom held membership in the Associated Industries of Seattle, saluted government authorities, including mayor Ole Hanson for, in the words of one spokesperson, promising "to deport most of the strike leaders as alien enemies." This figure thanked government forces for "arresting between fifty and a hundred to date."[11] Edwin G. Ames, a leader of Seattle's employer-led anti-radical campaigns, believed that such dramatic actions were necessary because the strike "was organized more along the lines of a revolutionary activity than to do anything for labor."[12]

Elsewhere, "Chamber of Commerce mobs," as Foster described them, riotously broke up meetings of activists and helped police as they arrested left-wing activists. In Cincinnati, the NMTA chapter helped mobilize a 300-strong person "mob of young businessmen and young rowdies from the best families" in a raid of the city's socialist party headquarters in November. Some of the socialists were International Association of Machinists (IAM) members who had participated in the city's recent strike. According to a source

---

[10]   William Z. Foster, *The Great Steel Strike and Its Lessons* (New York: De Capo Press, 1971 [1920]), 96.

[11]   Quoted in Dana Frank, *Purchasing Power: Consumer Organizing, Gender, and the Seattle Labor Movement, 1919–29* (Cambridge: Cambridge University Press, 1994), 94–5.

[12]   Quoted in ibid., 98.

142   *Little 'Red Scares'*

unsympathetic to the businessmen-led crowd, the "young gentlemen," which included the son of Cincinnati's NMTA secretary, removed left-wing literature from the headquarters and burned it in front of several policemen who "acted as ushers" during this rather chaotic stampede.[13] Spokespersons from other labor organizations complained that elite-led mobs, many of which were organized by flag-waiving employers' associations, disrupted working class activists in numerous states, including Arizona, Colorado, Kansas, Mississippi, and West Virginia, in the aftermath of the 1919 strike wave.[14]

With help from a network of public and private police forces, employers, several of whom harbored painful images of the Russian Revolution in their heads, defeated most of the postwar strikes. Fortunately for them, the messy work of strikebreaking and union-busting had a mostly adverse impact of the labor movement as a whole. Unions went into retreat as businessmen blacklisted strikers, imposed company unions in workplaces, and formed explicitly anti-labor and anti-radical organizations. Many enjoyed large profits, and felt mostly, though not entirely, confident about their future managerial prospects. As one historian put it, "American capitalism consolidated its most sustained victories in the aftermath of world revolution's first partial successes."[15] The period constituted, according to another scholar, a "glorious heyday."[16]

But employers seeking to insure there would be no repeat of the 1919 strike wave or, more alarmingly, a Bolshevik Revolution in the US, hardly put their guard down. In this context, employers' associations enjoyed a spike in recruitment. Groups like the National Association of Manufacturers (NAM) increased its organizing activities as it tapped into employers' fear. This 5,000-person organization continued to prove itself during the decade. Capitalizing on wartime era patriotism, some employers formed American Plan Associations, which joined the NAM in defending the interests of the so-called "free" workers against the evils of closed shop-demanding unionists, supporters of the Bolsheviks, and Industrial Workers of the World (IWW) members.[17] As

---

[13] Joseph W. Sharts, "Inside Story of Cincinnati Raid: American Legion Rioters Led by Professional Strikebreakers; Machinists' Desk Rifled," *Miami Valley Socialist* 7 (December 12, 1919), 1.

[14] "Autocracy and Mobocracy," *Brotherhood of Locomotive Firemen and Enginemen's Magazine* 70 (June 1, 1921), 10.

[15] Bryan D. Palmer, *James P. Cannon and the Origins of the American Revolutionary Left, 1890–1928* (Urbana: University of Illinois Press, 2007), 203.

[16] Howell John Harris, *The Right to Manage: Industrial Relations Polices of American Business in the 1940s* (Madison: University of Wisconsin Press, 1982), 5.

[17] For more on the "American Plan," see M.J. Heale, *American Anticommunism: Combating the Enemy Within, 1830–1970* (Baltimore: Johns Hopkins University Press,

Fighting the "Red Danger" 143

historian Sanford Jacoby explained, the postwar "open-shop movement was able to draw on lingering public suspicion that organized labor was Communist-inspired."[18] Of course, employers, the architects and beneficiaries of the first red-scare, actively sought to generate such suspicion.

Despite their efforts, employers were unable to completely eliminate the presence left-leaning workers or radical thinkers from their workplace and communities. But they tried, using an almost relentless campaign to smear communism as an ideology by drawing attention to the supposedly immoral conditions in Russia, by insisting that leftist thinkers suffered from a mental deficiency, and by arguing that Marxist economics were irredeemably flawed. Other actions fell outside the boundaries of acceptable public relations. Employers engaged in surveillance, fired radical workers, shared information with authorities, and threatened to depart radical immigrants.[19]

We must ask: how did employers make sense of communists in the 1920s? First, they believed that communism was an alien ideology incompatible with American values. "Socialism, syndicalism, communism, and other mental and moral diseases with deceiving names," a member of NAM wrote in 1922, "are among our inheritance from the cesspools of foreign thought." This was not simply a "disease" that inflicted workers; rather, these supposedly foreign ideologies were "breaking out in our schools and colleges, churches and other centers of so-called advanced thought, and in the Congress of the United States."[20] The NAM's magazine, *American Industries*, insisted in 1919 that there were two reasons why the Russian revolutionary fever spread to certain sections of the US. Some blamed the presence of newly arrived immigrants who failed to shed their old world customs. According to Michael J. Hickey, the NAM's head of the industrial department, "first, the presence of a large number of aliens who have not been Americanized, or among whom illiteracy is prevalent and labor skill scarce; second, where any group or class of citizens reside having

---

1990), 83.

[18] Sanford Jacoby, *Employing Bureaucracy: Managers, Unions, and the Transformation of Work in the 20th Century* (Mahwah, New Jersey: Lawrence Erlbaum Associates, 2004), 130. By invoking the words "public suspicion," Jacoby appears to follow Robert K. Murray's position that it was "the people," rather than elites, who were primarily responsible for generating the red scare. See Robert K. Murray, *The Red Scare: A Study of National Hysteria* (Minneapolis: University of Minnesota Press, 1955). For a fine critique of this line of thinking, see Nick Fischer, "The Founders of American Anti-communism," *American Communist History* 5 (2006): 67–101.

[19] Fischer notes that employers were lawfully able to threaten to deport aliens until 1933. See Fischer, "The Founders," 76.

[20] D.M. Edwards, "A Convention of Constructive Ideas," *American Industries* 22 (June 1922), 12.

special or imaginary grievances, such as the farmers of North and South Dakota, where labor is hazardous and education has been limited, such as among the lumbermen and loggers in the Pacific Northwest."[21] Educationally, employers worried that, in the words of NAM president John Edgerton, too many workers have "become more enamored of the ideals of Lenine [*sic*] than of those of Washington, Jefferson, Madison, Hamilton, and Lincoln."[22]

Presumably, employers could successfully respond to the communist problem by effectively teaching employees, immigrants and native-born, about the goodness of America's institutions and the virtuousness of the founders while pointing out the moral bankruptcy of the Russian Revolution. Throughout the 1920s, organized employers spread much anti-communist literature, seeking to demonstrate that the Bolsheviks used unspeakable violence in their quest to establish a living example of Atlantis, the horrendous imaginary community described in *The Scarlet Empire*. According to one employer, "It is important that the American people should obtain a correct vision of the Russian experiment." How did that experiment find expression in practice? Answer: it was, according to critics, shaped by corruption, violence, and crushing poverty. Conditions under the new regime were apparently, in the words of one employer writing in the *Manufacturers' Record* in 1922, "worse than barbarism."[23]

Indeed, trade publications, which were read by businessmen across industries, underlined the nature of such supposed barbarism. Manufacturers, some of whom had enjoyed economic relationships with Russian businesses in the years prior to the revolution, discussed various problems, including high rates of taxation, under the new regime. This, one writer noted, helped cripple the"Russian Utopia's" economy. Citing a government report, another writer for the *Manufacturers' Record* noted the obnoxious reality: "Wholesale suspension of trade and industrial establishments because of excessive taxation under Soviet rule in Free (?) Russia is reported by the Department of Commerce."[24] Some organized employers pitted communism against the open-shop principle. In an article entitled "The Open Shop and Industrial Liberty," one writer explained the necessity of protecting individual rights: "We must strive, that this liberty

---

[21] Michael J. Hickey, "Bolshevism—Old Wine in New Bottles," *American Industries* 19 (February 1919), 14.

[22] "The President's Annual Address." *American Industries* 26 (November 1925), 10.

[23] Courtenay DeKalb, "A Revelation of Sovietism," *Manufacturers' Record* 82 (November 2, 1922), 88.

[24] "Taxation under Soviet Rule," *Manufacturers Record* 82 (November 19, 1922), 56.

withstand the shock of all attacks, whether they emanate from the state or private citizens, the rich or the poor, a Czar of Russia or the Bolshevists of Russia."[25]

Others faulted Russian communists for their godlessness. Some remained frustrated that Christian Europe failed to establish a united front against Russia's atheistic Bolsheviks. "It seems incomprehensible," Courtenay DeKalb, a prominent engineer and businessman noted in 1922, "that the European nations should not unite on a common platform of protection to the Christian faith and to the political institutions that have grown up under it and overthrow the clique of 6,000 radicals in Russia who work through a bare 600,000 doubtful adherents."[26] Writing in the *Annals of the American Academy of Political and Social Science* journal, Henry S. Dennison of the Framingham, Massachusetts-based Dennison Manufacturing Company, stressed the Christian and American goodness of property ownership, which contrasted with communist values. The question, he believed, was settled and unworthy of debate, but communists continued to do so "with high passion and meager profit."[27]

While some underscored communism's incompatibility with Christianity, others sought to dissuade workers from seeing value in the Soviet Union and communism generally by emphasizing the sensibleness of American capitalism and the inherent inadequacy of Marxism as an economic theory. Such appeals coincided with the economic prosperity of the 1920s. Indeed, polemically minded employers engaged with Marxist writings, pointing out its alleged unsoundness. "When Karl Marx wrote his celebrated book 'Das Kapital,'" F. C. Biggert, a NAM activist, noted in 1924, "he gave to the world one of the most exactly logical analysis that has ever been written, but when he came to draw his conclusions from this analysis, some strange mental disturbance must have afflicted him. His conclusions are utterly illogical." Biggert maintained that "the whole world has suffered and still is suffering because" of Marx's ideas.[28] "Marx," Biggert concluded, "argued from an extreme position."[29]

---

[25] Walter Gordon Merritt, *The Open Shop and Industrial Freedom* (New York: The League for Industrial Rights, 1922), 41.

[26] Courtenay DeKalb, "A Revelation of Sovietism," *Manufacturers' Record* 82 (November 2, 1922), 88.

[27] Henry S. Dennison, "An Employer's View of Property," *Annals of the American Academy of Political and Social Science* 103 (September 1922), 58.

[28] F.C. Biggert, Jr., "Making Capitalists out of Workers," *American Industries* 25 (August 1924), 35. Biggert was an executive at Pittsburgh's United Engineering and Foundry Company. The former head of this company, Isaac Frank, served as president of both the NAM and the National Founders' Association (NFA) in the Progressive period.

[29] Ibid., 36.

According to Biggert, Marx's conclusions were inappropriate in the post-World War I period in part because growing numbers of workers had embraced, and ultimately benefited from, capitalism. Prosperity in the mid-1920s, Biggert held, led to wage increases and the introduction of investment opportunities for wage earners. "Marx," he argued, wrote for a nineteenth century readership, one that never witnessed the democratization of the market. As Biggert put it, he "never examined the possibility of converting the Labor element into capital." The rise of individual stock ownership meant more than wealth accumulation: "I believe that the wide distribution of the ownership of stock, which really means the converting of workers into capitalist-workers, is the solution to the capital-labor controversy."[30] Workers, he sought to illustrate, had profited from the free market, and therefore had no reason to harp on the language of class struggle or to look disdainfully at wealthy individuals.

To offer further creditability to their positions, employers' associations published and distributed several gripping stories of ordinary people, including former socialists, who witnessed the ostensibly shocking moral deterioration, economic irrationality, and repressive nature of communism in practice—and lived to write about it. The messages were clear and consistent: young, somewhat idealistic individuals were initially drawn to communism after hearing speeches by rabble rousers or reading books by left-wing theorists. But ultimately, after witnessing *real* communism in Russia, they came to their senses and renounced it. "I preached the theories of 'isms' for many years," one former radical who supposedly came to his senses explained, "simply because I failed to receive the practical education I needed."[31]

Take the case of Jacob Rubin, a one-time socialist from Milwaukee who changed his political orientation after visiting Russia in the immediate aftermath of the revolution. Following his visit, he wrote a detailed, 20-page account of conditions under the Bolsheviks in the *Open-Shop Review* in 1922 that reinforced the appalling picture captured in Parry's *The Scarlet Empire*. The multiple horrors that Parry discussed had, in Rubin's mind, become an abhorrent reality. In Rubin's narrative, conditions were unbearable: homes lacked electricity, elevators were chronically broken, and hot water was scarce. Human rights abuses were rampant, and growing numbers of people died from starvation. To make matters worse, authorities accused Rubin of spying for the US and sent him to prison, where conditions for counter-revolutionaries, he protested, were

---

[30] Ibid., 35.

[31] "A Socialist Who Changed his Mind: Practical Experience Shows James Horn That Socialist Theories Are Unsound," *The Open Shop Review* 24 (October 1922), 469.

thoroughly intolerable. The environment was filthy, temperatures were bitterly cold, and "prison food," Rubin observed, was "repulsive."[32]

Rubin drew comparisons to the United States while describing the hopelessness of life in Russia: "I have never seen or heard of it here in the United States, but in Russia I have seen hundreds of women and children dying of starvation and freezing to death from cold."[33] Moreover, housing conditions, he reported, were awful: "There isn't one house fit to live in—the plumbing defective, the woodwork used for fuel and the people dying like flies from cholera and typhus, and ruled by the most despotic government that has ever ruled, even in Russia."[34] Rubin reminded readers that inhuman conditions and political repression even persuaded anarchist Emma Goldman, certainly no friend of capitalism, that life in the US was superior to conditions in Russia.

Rubin concluded his lengthy, melodramatic article with a warning about the ultimate goals of the communist movement, noting that Lenin, Trotsky, and their comrades had their eyes set on internationalizing their campaign. He believed that the American business community needed to comprehend potential domestic threats and prepare themselves: "I want Capital to understand they should not think for a moment that the germ of Bolshevism is confined to the soil of Russia—it is all over every corner of the world—it is right here in the United States."[35] Editors of the *Open-Shop Review*, seeking to disseminate the jaw-dropping details of Rubin's essay widely, offered readers the opportunity to purchase bulk copies for a discounted rate.

Following the publication of Rubin's essay, employers, particularly those impacted by labor unrest, regularly invoked the threat of communism. This was especially the case during violent conflicts between unionists and scabs on picket lines. Sometimes protesters were actual communists; on other occasions, they were not. Writing about the deaths of strikebreakers in Illinois during a mine strike in 1922, John Edgerton, the Lebanon, Tennessee-based NAM president, cautioned that "a mob" had sought to establish a "Soviet." Such actions were, in his view, un-American: "There can be no support in free America of the theory that any group of workers possesses vested rights to any jobs."[36] His association of unionism with communism was unambiguous, and he insisted that the strikers'

---

[32] Jacob H. Rubin, "A Trip to Russia and Return," *Open Shop Review* 19 (March 1922), 101.

[33] Ibid., 104.

[34] Ibid., 107.

[35] Ibid., 118.

[36] Quoted in "J.E. Edgerton Holds Their Preachings Partly Responsible for Massacre," *New York Times*, June 25, 1922.

148   *Little 'Red Scares'*

use of violence suggested that they had more in common with the revolutionaries in Russia than with law-abiding Americans.

Yet capitalist propaganda, including pamphlets featuring former leftists that equated America with freedom and Russia with tyranny, was never enough to curtail the tide of communist organizing. Employers wanted to demonstrate, not merely argue, the advantages of capitalism over communism. In fact, some sought to dissuade workers from engaging in any type of union or radical activities partially by establishing company unions, employer-controlled representation plans that constituted an alternative to labor unions. Observers, including scholars, are in disagreement about the character and success of such programs, but evidence suggests that reducing the appeal of Marxism was *a* reason why some employers implemented such programs. Employers promoted these innovations because they helped establish what a representative from the American Anti-Boycott Association, an anti-radical association comprised chiefly of employers and attorneys, called "factory solidarity" rather than "class solidarity."[37]

Communist activists argued that company unions were sham organizations designed to dupe workers into believing that their interests were aligned with the company's. Such managerial practices, they argued, were intended to give workers the false impression that they had a meaningful say over their conditions and pay rates. Writing about company unions in a widely circulated pamphlet, communist William Z. Foster maintained that company unions "serve to delude the workers into believing that have some semblance of industrial democracy."[38]

Such stinging criticism displeased employers and the industrial relations experts who they hired to help implement and oversee company unions. Rather than dismiss observations like Foster's, these figures took them seriously, noting in an internal document that "If employee representation is to become efficacious in dealings with employees, the company executives must recognized these [Foster's] charges and examine diligently the means for preventing their foundation in fact."[39] According to this logic, managers needed to implement and oversee employee representative plans that systematically addressed workers' genuine needs. Company union designers sought to prove that company unions were indeed legitimate outlets for the development of bottom-up forms of democracy. To achieve their goals, industrial managers needed to show flexibility, respond to grievances, and make appropriate changes when necessary. In the view of this

---

[37]   Walter Gordon Merritt, "Anti-Social, Militant Methods Condemned," *Iron Age* 104 (July 3, 1919), 10.

[38]   Quoted in Bruce E. Kaufman, *Hired Hands or Human Resources?: Case Studies of HRM Programs and Practices in Early American Industry* (Ithaca: Cornell University Press, 2010), 153.

[39]   Ibid.

industrial relations consultant, comments made by communists like Foster's would be inconsequential provided that managers remained diligent, insuring that workers *did* have a voice in shaping the character of industrial relations.

But sections of the labor movement, including groups with ties to the CP, remained unmoved by employers' public relations efforts or attempts at benevolence. And plenty of employers discovered the stubborn presence of communists in their workplaces, including car manufacturing plants in Detroit, steel mills in Pittsburgh, meatpacking operations in Chicago, and textile factories in the Piedmont. How did they respond? Some fired communists, believing that such individuals represented the chief, if not the exclusive, reason for industrial unrest. Consider the case of Henry Ford. According to communist journalist Robert Dunn, Ford had "said that he himself had discovered a nest of 'Bolshevik' propaganda in the plant. He found out all about it—he said these agitators were preparing for a strike in the plant—and then had all the conspirators fired. He said in answer to a question that mere membership in a union would not be a cause for dismissal but propagandizing would be a sufficient cause."[40] Indeed, the presence of communist papers, which featured regular articles about poor conditions in factories, troubled auto manufacturers. In one workplace, management complained that these papers charged "management with wrongs that never existed or for which they were never responsible."[41]

In Detroit and elsewhere, employers' associations like the NMTA monitored local communists and wrote reports about their activities. One NMTA member was somewhat charitable in his assessment of the organization, explaining that its members have considerable "organizing ability" and are "quick to take advantage of any disaffection among working forces." But why did these figures embrace an ideology that promoted workplace disharmony? The answer, from the NMTA's perspective, had nothing to do with dangerous or oppressive workplace conditions. Workers became communists and engaged in rebellious activities not because of low wages or because of draconian shop rules. Instead, the document, echoing statements made by NAM spokesmen, insisted that left-leaning employees suffered a mental problem and had become "self-deluded almost to the point of fanaticism." Yet communists, the report concluded, could

---

[40]   Robert W. Dunn, "Organizing (and Unionization)," Robert W. Dunn Collection, Box 1, Series 1, "Research Notes," Walter Reuther Library, Wayne State University, Detroit, Michigan.

[41]   Quoted in Roger Keeran, *The Communist Party and the Auto Workers Unions* (Bloomington: Indiana University Press, 1980), 42.

150   *Little 'Red Scares'*

not secure a footing in the city provided that the employers' association was not "careless" and took "ordinary precautions."[42]

But "ordinary precautions" were often not enough. Indeed, when propaganda failed to dissuade workers of communism's supposed ills, employers often backed up their views with force. In the late 1920s employers watched with frustration as communist organizers played a critical role in protests that broke out in several communities, including Passaic, New Jersey, New Bedford, Massachusetts, and in parts of the Piedmont. Consider the 1926 textile strikes in Passaic, where communists, overseeing the creation of a United Front Committee, played an especially critical part. Challenging employers and pro-business police forces, close to 16, 000 workers from several mills demanded improved conditions, higher wages, and union recognition. Predictably, employers denounced the workforce, which included many immigrants, as a motley crew of "un-American" communists.[43] Further, employers sought to isolate one of the leaders, Albert Weisbord, by portraying him as a disconnected communist with no interests in the community's welfare, and in the process employers received help from the law. They benefited from a 1902 anti-anarchist state law, which authorities used to criminalize the strike's communist leadership.[44]

Three years later, communists participated in several dramatic textile strikes in Eastern Tennessee and Western North Carolina. In the face of a large, angry, and determined working class struggle, employers in this region, like those in Passaic, relied on the help of a multilayered anti-labor and anti-red campaign. Massive arrests combined with blacklisting resulted in the defeat of these strikes. Writing about a women-led textile strike in eastern Tennessee, NAM leader Noel Sargent commented, "Communist agitators from North Carolina created a slight flurry Monday."[45]

While Sargent highlighted the issue of communist influence in the NAM's major publication, the southern employers impacted by the protests engaged in the messy and violent work of removing the communist threat from their workplaces. The most remarkable chapter of these communist-led campaigns occurred in Gastonia, North Carolina. Led by the communist National Textile Workers Union (NTWU), workers here confronted hostile forces on several occasions. The 800-member National Guard, rather than a mob of employers,

---

[42] Pamphlet "Employers' Association of Detroit," 10–12, Robert W. Dunn Collection, Box 2, Folder 1.

[43] For examples of such insults, see Vera Buch Weisbord's autobiographical account. Vera Buch Weisbord, *A Radical Life* (Bloomington: Indiana University Press, 1977), 112.

[44] Ibid., 126–9.

[45] "Noel Sargent, "East Tennessee's Rayon Strikes of 1929," *American Industries* 29 (June 1929), 31.

Fighting the "Red Danger" 151

helped suppress that conflict. But the Guard had plenty of support, including unidentified masked men who, on one occasion, assisted employers by destroying union headquarters and physically harassing strikers.[46] Under the leadership of communist organizer Fred Beal, union activists armed themselves in response to such attacks. Violence stemming from both sides led to the deaths of police head Orville Aderholt and union activist Ella May Wiggins. Following the death of Aderholt, several union activists, including communists, were tried and sentenced to lengthy jail sentences.[47]

Southern employers' embroiled in the conflicts of 1929 invoked the race card as part of their campaign against communist activists. In Gastonia, pro-company newspapers published articles designed to stir-up racial distrust. According to one source, the outside communists responsible for the strike demanded "racial equality, intermarriage of whites and blacks, abolition of all laws discriminating between whites and blacks."[48] Another, seeking to encourage a racist and patriotic backlash against the left, called the strike leaders "negro lovers, against America, free lover[ers], northern agitators, Russian reds."[49]

The combined forces of state and private authorities resulted in the failure of these southern strikes and communist organizing campaigns. Southern textile mills remained largely union-free, communist organizers went into temporary retreat, and workers continued to receive low wages and few benefits. And employers and their spokespersons, particularly those in the South, continued to insist that unions were fundamentally inorganic to their communities. All labor activism, they argued, was the work of outside agitators possessed by morally repulsive and utterly foreign ideas.[50]

---

[46] "Anti-Red Mob Raids Union Offices after Gastonia Mistrial," *New York Times*, September 10, 1929.

[47] John A. Salmond, *The General Textile Strike of 1934: From Maine to Alabama* (Columbia: University of Missouri Press, 2002), 21–2.

[48] Quoted in Glenda Gilmore, *Defying Dixie: The Radical Roots of Civil Rights* (New York: W.W. Norton Company, 2008), 82.

[49] Ibid., 87.

[50] For more on CP organizing in this southern region, see Irving Bernstein, *The Lean Years: A History of the American Worker, 1920–1933* (Baltimore: Penguin Books, 1970 [1960]), 1–44. Historians are split on the impact that the anti-union and anti-communist attacks here had on the American Communist Party (CP). Robert Justin Goldstein maintains that "the CP completely ended all organizational activities at Gastonia on September 20." See Robert Justin Goldstein, *Political Repression in Modern America: From 1870 to 1976* (Urbana: University of Illinois Press, 2011 [1978]), 188. Reinforcing Goldstein, historian Robert Korstad maintains that the CP's involvement in the strikes of 1929 "had met with quick repression" and that the Party had "largely faded from view" in the years after. See Robert Korstad, *Civil Rights Unionism: Tobacco Workers and the Struggle for Democracy in*

152   *Little 'Red Scares'*

Not all forms of employer-led anti-communism in the 1920s were rooted in workplace struggles. Culturally, left-wing ideas and the example of the Russian Revolution continued to influence a sizable minority, and perhaps nothing exemplified this more than annual May Day marches, which took places in several major cities and involved heterogonous groups of Marxists and anarchists. Seeking to counter the popular and, at times, militant parades, some organized employers created their own patriotic-tinged parades. In 1920, groups like the New York City-based American Defense Society, which was created by businessmen troubled by the annual May Day parades and the subversive messages that they spread, wanted to rename the holiday "American Day." In an effort to connect patriotism to anti-radicalism, anti-May Day campaigners organized their own marches, which, according to one campaigner, "will be a great discouragement to the disloyal propaganda with which the Communists now strive to destroy our free and independent nation."[51]

Despite triumphing over organized labor and the left in most of the decade's battles, organized employers continued to see communism as a formidable problem. In some instances, it appeared that their struggle against communism took priority and overshadowed the campaign for open-shop workplaces. In fact, the NAM even applauded conservative labor leaders for their anti-communism. According to one writer, "We are glad to commend the American Federation of Labor for keeping subdued the more radical element within its ranks, and for refusing in a truly American manner to cohabit with communism and with Russian sovietism."[52] This comment is telling, above all because the AFL had suffered considerably at the hands of the NAM throughout the Progressive period. Despite their rocky past, the two organizations found common ground on the question of communism.

Employers and the "Red Decade"

In the 1930s, employers throughout the nation were startled by the militancy of working class activists, considerable numbers of whom were influenced by,

---

the Mid-Twentieth Century South (Chapel Hill: University of North Carolina Press, 2003), 265. Glenda Gilmore, on the other hand, insists that "After the Gastonia strike and trials, the Communist Party sustained a permanent presence in the south and committed itself to racial equality in the service of class struggle." See Glenda Gilmore, *Defying Dixie: The Radical Roots of Civil Rights* (New York: W.W. Norton Company, 2008), 96.

[51]   Quoted in Donna T. Harverty-Stacke, *America's Forgotten Holiday: May Day and Nationalism, 1867–1960* (New York: New York University Press, 2009), 115.

[52]   "The President's Annual Address," *American Industries* 26 (November 1925), 14.

or members of, the Communist Party. Several communists throughout the decades played leadership roles in union-building activities and strikes. In 1931, for example, the American CP informed Soviet leaders that it was responsible for one-third of the strikes that broke out that year.[53] Large numbers of working class activists in a variety of industries joined the CP or front groups; indeed, communists, inspired to fight growing economic inequality, helped organize several CIO unions in the second part of the decade. And communists were present in a number of high-profile conflicts, including the so-called Ford massacre of 1932, the massive, multistate 1934 textile strike, and the attention-grabbing sit-down strikes that broke out throughout parts of the industrial Midwest in the second part of the decade. Communists were behind the creation of many protest campaigns and unions, including the umbrella Trade Union Unity League, which brought together workers from different industries. A diverse set of workers, including native-born Kentucky coal miners, African American sharecroppers in Alabama, Mexican American agricultural workers in Texas and California, west coast Filipino cannery workers, and Polish-American auto and steel workers in the Midwest, participated in communist-led actions. Union activists were often successful by establishing solidarity with one another and demonstrating militantly, which in many instances forced bosses to raise wages, improve conditions, and formally recognize labor unions.[54] As the depression deepened, communists expanded their activities outside of workplaces, helping to organize massive hunger marches, defending renters from eviction, and uniting with African Americans in their struggles against the sadistic cruelties of the Jim Crow justice system. Communists were responsible for, in the words of one historian, linking "workers' struggle with community-based mobilizations."[55]

Employers were alarmed by the inclusivity and combativeness of the new unions. In response, they did what they had done previously: they looked to one another for assistance and resumed their activities in organizations like the NAM,

---

[53] James G. Ryan, *Earl Browder: The Failure of American Communism* (Tuscaloosa: University of Alabama Press, 1997), 42.

[54] Robin D.G. Kelley, *Hammer and Hoe: Alabama Communists During the Great Depression* (Chapel Hill: University of North Carolina Press, 1990); Vicki Ruiz, *Cannery Women, Cannery Lives: Mexican Women, Unionization, and the California Food Processing Industry, 1930–1950* (Albuquerque: University of New Mexico Press, 1987); Chris Friday, *Organizing Asian American Labor: The Pacific Coast Canned-Salmon Industry, 1870–1942* (Philadelphia: Temple University Press, 1994), 135–6. For the general context, see Fraser M. Ottanelli, *The Communist Party of the United States: From the Depression to World War II* (New Brunswick: Rutgers University Press, 1991), 139.

[55] Rosemary Feurer, *Radical Unionism in the Midwest, 1900–1950* (Urbana: University of Illinois Press, 2006), 43.

154   *Little 'Red Scares'*

NMTA, and the American Chamber of Commerce, organizations that helped coordinate anti-communist activities. Meanwhile, employers in individual cities held membership in local organizations. They fought communists in workplaces and communities through the continued use of surveillance, by firing members, by blacklisting activists, by dispatching company guards during strikes, and by collaborating with municipal "red squads."[56] Additionally, employers continued to appeal to nationalism and occasionally praised union leaders for distancing themselves from communists. In at least one city, a NMTA branch distributed a disparaging pamphlet called *Join the CIO and Help Build a Soviet America* to employees seeking union recognition.[57]

The decade was shaped partially by ideological polarization. While increasing numbers of workers joined various Marxist organizations and embraced left-leaning ideas, several employers had shifted further to the right. In their quest to rid their workplace and communities of communists, several found inspiration from the growth of far-right movements in parts of Europe. Impressed by the Italian fascists' successful campaigns against the left, the NAM's James Emery, for instance, speaking at one of the group's conferences, praised Mussolini for defending Italy from "the blighted hand of radical socialism."[58] In Minneapolis during the end of the decade, employers' active in the city's American Industries attended meetings of organized fascists because of a shared hatred of communists.[59]

Fascist is precisely the word that communist organizers used to describe the conduct of a group of California growers during a series of labor conflicts in 1933 and 34. In response to Mexican immigrant workers' involvement in the

---

[56] Note Fischer's discussion of the ways in which the Los Angeles-based Better American Federation, a businessmen-led organization, worked with a coalition of "law and order" activists in attacking meetings of left-wingers. See Fischer, "The Founders," 88. Writer Kevin Starr suggests that Los Angeles's Red Squad "was perhaps the most aggressive" in the nation. See Kevin Starr, *Endangered Dreams: The Great Depression in California* (Oxford: Oxford University Press, 1996), 157. For the broader context, see Frank Donner, *Protectors of Privilege: Red Squads and Police Repression in Urban America* (Berkeley: University of California Press, 1990).

[57] Quoted in Feurer, *Radical Unionism*, 63. For a comprehensive account of repression during the 1930s, see Robert Justin Goldstein, *Political Repression in Modern America: From 1870 to 1976* (Urbana: University of Illinois Press, 2011 [1978]), 193–262.

[58] Quoted in Thaddeus Russell, *A Renegade History of the United States* (New York: Free Press, 2010), 246.

[59] According to William Millikan, Associated Industries President George Belden attended meetings organized by the Silver Shirts because the fascist group was "intent on exposing Communism." See William Millikan, *A Union against Unions: The Minneapolis Citizens Alliance and its Fight against Organized Labor, 1903–1947* (St. Paul: Minnesota Historical Society Press, 2001), 337.

Fighting the "Red Danger"

communist Cannery and Agricultural Workers' Industrial Union (CAWIU), which demanded modest wage increases, growers threatened deportation, physically attacked union headquarters, and even murdered striking activists. The growers, intolerant of the presence of communist union activists on their land, gave striking workers an ultimatum: "If the strike continues, it is more than likely that every last one of you will be gathered into one huge bull pen ... And, what will the bull pen mean to you? Many of you don't know how the United States government can run a concentration camp. First of all, every last one of you will be deloused."[60] Such actions, including threats and physical abuse, demonstrate the persistence of the type of businessmen-led savagery that William Z. Foster described in his analysis of the 1919 steel strikes.

Employers did not always enjoy victories. And despite their efforts, they watched communist-led movements in workplaces thrive. Indeed, Marxist organizations played critical roles in the major strikes of 1934. For instance, left-wing ideas helped inspired city-wide strikes in Toledo, Minneapolis, and San Francisco. The CP's influence was greatest in San Francisco, where the Australian-born Harry Bridges led a dramatic, three-month long strike of waterfront workers who challenged what historian Bruce Nelson has called "unchecked employer domination."[61]

It is worth considering the ways in which the waterfront employers' responded to this particular strike. First, they capitalized on their connections to one another, which they developed first in the Progressive years. Their organization, the Waterfront Employers' Union, had confronted several earlier struggles, including post-World War I strikes organized by the Industrial Workers of the World (IWW). They successful crushed these uprisings and enjoyed long periods of relative labor peace with conservative unions.[62] In fact, this employers' association prided itself on its give-and-take bargaining relationship with "responsible" waterfront unions. Unlike most other employers' associations, it publically accepted the closed shop. The organization's president, Thomas G. Plant, stated matter-of-factly that "union recognition is and has been the policy of the employers."[63]

But from the standpoint of waterfront employers, the 1934 strike was more radical and thus more unsettling than earlier struggles. Communist union

---

[60]   Quoted in Mark Reisler, "Mexican Unionization in California Agriculture, 1927–1936," *Labor History* 14 (Fall 1973), 572.

[61]   Bruce Nelson, *Workers on the Waterfront: Seamen, Longshoremen, and Unionism in the 1930s* (Urbana: University of Illinois Press, 1988), 103.

[62]   For a history of anti-unionism in this industry, see Howard Kimeldorf, *Reds or Rackets?: The Making of Radical and Conservative Unions on the Waterfront* (Berkeley: University of California Press, 1988), 60–67.

[63]   Thomas G. Plant, *The Pacific Coast Longshormen's Strike of 1934* (NP: 1934), 3.

activists, unlike leaders of the relatively conservative International Longshoremen's Association (ILA), were uninterested in engaging in class collaborationism. The 1934 conflict was distinctive, Plant complained, because it was "under the domination of radicals and Communists."[64] In their struggle against communist activists like Bridges, waterfront employers formed a complementary organization, the American League against Communism, which distinguished supposedly conservative East Coast union members from West Coast Radicals: "On the East Coast, the GOOD AMERICAN UNION LEADERS can keep out the Communists. On the West Coast the COMMUNISTS ARE IN! Bridges is the dictator! It's up to the public to GET THEM OUT! IT'S UP TO YOU!"[65] Waterfront employers, echoing generations of anti-labor union spokesmen, framed the struggle as not one of workers against bosses, but rather as a communist-inspired conflict that threatened the nation itself. Roger Lapham, Plant's colleague, protested that the strikers were "out and out Communists" determined to "break down the walls of government."[66] Believing that the famous communist from Australia was a dangerous threat to the US, Lapham, following the example of Seattle's employers in the aftermath of the 1919 strike, requested that government officials deport him.

The American Chamber of Commerce, a relative latecomer to anti-radical organizing (the group was formed in 1912), shared the central complaints articulated by San Francisco's waterfront employers. In the face of rising class struggle, it sought to play a leadership role in information gathering and dissemination, and in the mid-1930s established an anti-communist committee. One of the committee's first tasks was to publish a report outlining the nature of the communist problem. The 16-page document outlines the creation of the Communist Party, its relationship to the Soviet Union, compares it to other left-wing groups, provides rough estimates of the total number of members, and offers suggestions about the ways in which the business community should respond. The committee's report offered much context, noting the history of pre-communist threats to American capitalism, including the 1886 Haymarket bombing and the murder of William McKinley in 1901. The committee feared more brutality in the 1930s: "Like anarchism, communism in the United States advocates a program of violence."[67]

---

[64] Ibid., 22.

[65] Quoted in Bruce Nelson, *Workers on the Waterfront*, 217.

[66] Lapham quoted in Howard Kimeldorf, *Reds or Rackets?: The Making of Radical and Conservative Unions on the Waterfront* (Berkeley: University of California Press, 1988), 61.

[67] Chamber of Commerce of the United States, *Combating Subversive Activities in the United States* (NP: Washington, D.C., 1935), 5.

Fighting the "Red Danger" 157

But communism, the document warned, differed in significant ways from anarchism. While anarchism "advocated the elimination of all government and of man-made laws and the substitution of a 'no government' regime—communism has a program for the establishment of its own Soviet type of revolutionary dictatorship." Anarchism, the authors insisted, was characterized by expressions of chaos caused by bomb-throwing immigrants. Communism, a more sophisticated, though equally dangerous "ism," called for a "carefully planned" society.[68] Most distressingly, communists sought to create, as the committee put it, "a world union of Soviet groups with a world capital at Moscow."[69] How would Soviet-led communists achieve this goal? The committee believed that they would carry out their extremism violently, just as Marx predicted. But the CP, the committee warned, had become politically savvy, running candidates in traditional elections. The Chamber believed that such maneuvers constituted a cynical ploy, arguing that the organization "places its candidate on the ballot, not with any actual hope or purpose of electing him, but rather thus to cloak with a semblance of orderly governmental procedure its advocacy of subversive doctrine."[70]

Like other employers' associations, the Chamber was especially concerned about communists' involvement in labor activities. Its members worried that communists would encourage unionists to disobey not only their bosses, but also official labor leaders. Responding to events like the 1934 San Francisco strike, the Chamber, echoing Thomas Plant, complained that "communists" have taken "leadership of strikes out of the hands of organized labor." As a result, communists helped inspire "a spirit of antagonism against the government, the recognized labor unions, and other institutions of American character."[71]

Reinforcing the positions articulated by the NAM and the Waterfront Employers' Union, the Chamber complemented union leaders for their anti-radicalism, and even applauded the temperate position of the AFL's William Green, who allegedly stated that "The purpose of communist labor organizations is not to safeguard and improve the present order but to undermine it and destroy it."[72] While employers presumably preferred workplaces with no unions, they appreciated that the established labor leadership were sufficiently anti-communist and thus partners, rather than rivals, against workplace radicalism. For them, official labor organizations like the AFL, which demonstrated a decades-long commitment to anti-communism, served as a necessary buffer against the rising tide of radicalism.

---

68 Ibid.
69 Ibid.
70 Ibid., 8.
71 Ibid., 13.
72 William Green quoted in ibid., 14.

158   *Little 'Red Scares'*

The Chamber also feared the impact that communists had on the armed services, pointing out that the CP had circulated several papers to servicemen insisting that they "fight against war." Members of the industrial working class would, if the communists had their way, join soldiers in the class struggle. "In time of war," the Chamber warned, "the workers are urged to go on strike particularly in important wartime industries of production and transportation."[73] Here the Chamber, like previous organizations of employers, revealed that its goals—economic growth, industrial stability, and national defense—coincided with the US government's interests. The Chamber, while certainly no proponent of state intervention in the economy, denounced the CP for its supposed "obstruction and discrediting of governmental recovery and relief enterprises."[74] The document's conclusions called for more government intervention, recommending "that a special agency within the Department of Justice be created to investigate subversive activities, with particular attention to the Communist Party and its members and its and their domestic and foreign relationships."[75]

Not all employers during the stormy 1930s called for increased state intervention or sought partnerships with conservative labor leaders. Some linked the New Deal state and the labor-liberal coalition that sustained it to an encroaching red tide. Such figures believed that a greater infusion of old-fashioned American patriotism, articulated by a cross-class section of society, constituted a necessary antidote to both Russian-inspired communism and the expansion of government interference in the national economy. This was certainly the case with respect to the Southern States Industrial Council (SSIC), which was founded in part by former NAM president John Edgerton in 1933. According to speech given L.C. Morrow before one of the group's meetings in 1939, some 150 years ago the patriots who then lived in the New England states found Paul Revere galloping over the roads on his trusty steed to warn of the approach of a regiment, and today throughout the United States thousands of men realize that there is another threat of a red danger far greater than that of the Redcoats upon us, and they are using the ether waves and every other means to educate their people on the approach of that red menace.[76]

Another commentator, speaking in 1940, explained the "red menace" in action, noting that Russian communists had demolished the foundations of a virtuous society: they "have destroyed the Church. They are destroying the homes. There is

---

[73]   Ibid., 17.

[74]   Ibid., 14.

[75]   Ibid., 29.

[76]   L.C. Morrow, "The Wagner Labor Relations Act" January 26, 1939, Box 1, Folder 4, Southern States Industrial Council papers, Tennessee State Archives, Nashville, Tennessee.

Fighting the "Red Danger" 159

no sanctity of the home."[77] Predictably, both commentators, reiterating numerous employer-activists from earlier periods, spoke on behalf of the law-abiding American people, not as businessmen with narrow, money-making interests.

As they strategized about how best to weaken communism domestically, employers continued to collaborate with government officials. Organizations like the NAM, the Chamber of Commerce, the SSIC and city-based employers' associations met regularly with high-level figures from the public sector. Virginia's congressman Howard Smith, known in part for his role in establishing the 1940 anti-communist Smith Act, had worked closely with business organizations including the NAM.[78] And the FBI's J. Edger Hoover, like Smith, periodically made appearances before such organizations, endorsing their position on the communist question. Speaking before the employer-led Detroit Economic Club in 1938, Hoover said "Subversive alien theories and isms are not only a drastic contrast to American ways of thinking, feeling and acting, but they stand for a complete overthrow of established ideals of American life and philosophy of government to which America is dedicated."[79]

Smith and Hoover were hardly the only high-level public figures to address the supposed evils of left-wing "isms." Take the case of Texas Democrat Martin Dies, a staunch anti-communist with strong ties to the business community. Rhetorically, Dies, who chaired the notorious House of Un-American Activities Committee, fought communism in ways that mirrored the language employers commonly used. Speaking before a room full of exuberant SSIC members in 1940, Dies said "we cannot claim success until we have uprooted the forces of Marxism. The aim is to destroy private property and personal initiative in favor of public ownership and planned economy. The destruction of property rights is always followed by the destruction of personal rights."[80] Dies, whose speech contained little more than recycled statements made by an earlier generation, more than proved himself as an unrepentant red-hater. SSIC members wanted to hear the language of support, not grand theories.

---

[77]   E.J. McMillan, "An Address by the President," January 23, 1940, Report of the Proceedings of the Seventh Annual Meeting of the Southern States Industrial Council," Box 1, Folder 4, Southern States Industrial Council papers.

[78]   Bruce J. Dierenfield, *Keeper of the Rules: Congressman Howard W. Smith of Virginia* (Charlottesville: University of Virginia Press, 1987), 60. At a 1941 NAM meeting, members apparently gave Smith "a thunderous ovation" following his speech. See David Witwer, *Shadow of the Racketeer: Scandal in Organized Labor* (Urbana: University of Illinois Press, 2009), 202.

[79]   Quoted in Frank J. Donner, *The Age of Surveillance: The Aims and Methods of America's Political Intelligence System* (New York: Alfred A. Knopf, 1980), 55.

[80]   Martin Dies, "Americanism," Box 1, Folder 4, Southern States Industrial Council papers. For more on Dies's committee, see Richard Gid Powers, *Not without Honor: The History of American Anticommunism* (New York: The Free Press, 1995), 124–9.

160 *Little 'Red Scares'*

Indeed, southern conservatives, several of whom held membership in the SSIC, remained particularly active in challenging communism and in preventing unionization from gaining a meaningful grip in the region. Such figures condemned unions and institutions that legitimatized left-leaning thinking, including worker education centers. In the mid-1930s, Edgerton, denounced the leftist Highlander Folk School in Tennessee for supposedly promoting communist ideas.[81] And southern employers continued to invoke race as they fought expressions of working class radicalism in factories, mines, and on city streets. In Alabama, employers' responded to the activism of multi-racial mine workers' unions by using violence against organizers and by calling one left-leaning labor organization a "nigger union."[82]

Despite setbacks in the South and elsewhere, the CP enjoyed its greatest successes during the so-called "red decade." It saw large membership increases, influenced the direction of the labor movement, and fought Jim Crow racism passionately. The CP spoke to the frustrations of countless numbers of people disillusioned by the economy's collapse. For these reasons, employers redoubled their efforts by continuing to challenge communism as an ideology and by combating communists in workplaces and in communities.

Employers and the "Ism" Problem during World War II

By the second part of the 1930s, the CP's character and political orientation had changed considerably. During the Popular Front period, it focused much attention on the fascist threat abroad, and in the process sought to place itself in the mainstream. It also embraced America's iconic figures, viewing itself, in the words of one writer, as a part of the nation's long democratic tradition expressed most canonically by "Jefferson, Paine, Jackson, and Lincoln, and the Declaration of Independence."[83] Remarkably, CP members had found inspiration from the

---

[81] Kristi Kay Loberg, "An Exploratory Study of Leadership in Social Work Based on the Highlander Approach to Social Leadership," (Ph.D. diss., North Dakota State University, 2008), 48.

[82] Robin D.G. Kelley, *Hammer and Hoe*, 67. Of course, such racism was hardly restricted to the south. Just prior to the start of World War II, the head of the Michigan Manufacturers' Association explained that blacks were unfit for industrial work because they lacked the "speed and rhythm" required for such work. Quoted in Judith Stephan-Norris and Maurice Zeitlin, *Left Out: Reds and America's Industrial Unions* (Cambridge: Cambridge University Press, 2003), 212.

[83] Quoted in Earl Latham, *The Communist Controversy in Washington: From the New Deal to McCarthy* (Cambridge: Harvard University Press, 1966), 19.

bourgeois revolutionary tradition that John Edgerton had insisted that they respect in the early 1920s. Moreover, while it still attracted a sizable minority of people from the working class, the CP had begun to enlist growing numbers of middle class recruits, and many had little personal stake in the class struggle. The organization's leadership welcomed these new members, believing that they were, in the words of historian Paul Buhle, "just as useful, perhaps more useful than, blue-collar workers."[84] Equally notable, after the US entered the Second World War, the CP broke from the traditional Marxist call for class conflict by officially supporting the war effort and the no-strike pledge, which was imposed by the Roosevelt administration and enforced by labor leaders. The Chamber of Commerce's concern that communists would promote labor unrest and industrial sabotage during wartime, articulated with great concern in its 1935 document, did not come to fruition.

During wartime, the Chamber of Commerce publically softened its anti-communist position. In 1944, almost a decade after it issued its call-to-arms report, Chamber President Eric Johnston spent three months in the Soviet Union in an effort to promote, in his words, "understanding and cooperation."[85] He wrote about this grand journey in the pages of *Life Magazine*, and his observations contrasted sharply to those of Jacob Rubin, the scare-monger whose 1922 exposé depicted the Bolsheviks as heartless monsters. While Rubin had nothing affirmative to say about Russian society, Johnston was awed by the nation's industrial efficiency and the kindness of the people he and his companions encountered, including high-level politicians like Joseph Stalin. He applauded Russians for, as he put it, their well-focused campaign to defend "the soil of Mother Russia."[86] Johnston was impressed by their commitment to obtaining victory, which, of course coincided with the US's goals.

At the same time, Johnston found it prudent to walk a fine line, acknowledging the two country's seemingly irreconcilable political distinctions while recognizing common aims. "Although our social and political systems are poles apart," he noted, "we have no insoluble economic or territorial conflicts."[87] In a meeting with "a Communist Party leader," Johnston predicted that the two nations had a strong future together despite ideological differences. Yet, Johnston warned, "there is one way this cooperation can be destroyed. That would be for the Soviet Union to interfere in our domestic affairs by giving direct or indirect support

---

[84] Paul Buhle, *Marxism in the United States* (London: Verso Press, 1987), 187. Also, see Harvey A. Levenstein, *Communism, Anticommunism, and the CIO* (Westport: Greenwood Press, 1981), 156–66.

[85] Eric Johnston, "Russian Visit," *Life* (September 11, 1944), 100.

[86] Ibid., 109.

[87] Ibid., 100.

to American communists."[88] Johnston was hopeful that Soviet leaders would prioritize relationships with US officials and businessmen over the American CP, which remained, in his view, a dissident network with which neither he nor his colleagues sought to make peace or treat as a legitimate organization.

The NAM leadership, like the Chamber's, was eagerly supportive of the war effort, but unwilling to praise the Soviet Union. NAM spokespersons continued to describe communism as a cancerous "ism", and one figure even connected it with political systems that had little to do with Marx's ideas, including fascism. Reiterating Martin Dies and J. Edger Hoover, William P. Witherow, president of Pittsburgh's Blaw-Knox Company and NAM head, claimed "The American people will have no traffic with Socialism or Communism or Fascism if they can identify them."[89] Like other employers, Witherow, who was apparently unmoved by the CP's shift to the right, saw himself as a reasonable spokesperson for the American people, not merely businessmen. Unwilling to jeopardize their financial relationships with the US government, organized employers no longer claimed to find inspiration from European or domestic fascist movements. Indeed, as critical players in the political economy of the wartime state, they were in no position to offend Washington. Employers and their spokespersons may have appreciated the anti-communist work conducted by European fascists, but they did not say so publically because they wanted to demonstrate patriotism and keep politicians content as they secured wartime contracts.

But Witherow faced a potential contradiction in his critique of economic systems run by strong central governments. After all, American industries, including many with links to the NAM, profited handsomely from the wartime state, one directed largely by the federal government, not capitalism's invisible hand. As one scholar explained, "America acquired a planned war economy in which business power was safe, and in which the largest corporations' interests and opinions counted most."[90] Witherow and his NAM colleagues apparently had no problems with *this* type of government intervention, but not all types, including most New Deal policies. Witherow wanted to insure that there were no more liberal New Deal-style reforms on the horizon, warning that "efforts to misuse this war as a means of socializing American industry and our society do not strengthen but weaken this nation for war."[91] The NAM remained more or less content because

---

[88]   Ibid., 116.

[89]   William P. Witherow, "Making America Strong," *NAM News* 9 (December 12, 1942), 20.

[90]   Howell John Harris, *The Right to Manage: Industrial Relations Polices of American Business in the 1940s* (Madison: University of Wisconsin Press, 1982), 42.

[91]   William P. Witherow, "Making America Strong," *NAM News* 9 (December 12, 1942), 20.

the membership enjoyed positions of power and enjoyed high salaries. Their goal then, as before, was to maintain authority, and they did so, in part, by aligning themselves with politicians and by preaching against foreign "isms.'"

Conclusion

Employers remained consistently anti-communist between the First and Second World Wars, and they approached their tasks from multiple angles. At the heart of their struggle was a desire to attain legitimacy and control, and as a result they disseminated propaganda, used surveillance against workers, launched company unions, and periodically unleashed repressive forces against labor and the left. Some engaged in direct attacks themselves, though most conducted their anti-communist activities from the comforts of offices and elite meeting halls. While maintaining profits and power were their chief aims, employers seldom admitted their true motivations. Instead, they presented themselves as protectors of Americans' individual rights and as defenders of the country's supposedly sacred institutions and heroic past. Of course, their communist victims knew much better.

Chapter 7

Leftward Ramparts: Labor and Anticommunism between the World Wars

Markku Ruotsila[1]

"American labor is grappling and fighting communism and will continue to fight and grapple with communism until either the American labor movement is destroyed or communism meets its death." So promised William Green, president of the American Federation of Labor in June, 1925. According to him, Communism posed a menace to all the free institutions of America and was "labor's greatest enemy." Green therefore vowed that "labor organizations as founded upon the American trade unionism and communism both can not live in the same country. It will either destroy us or we will destroy it. There is no compromise, there can be none and never will be."[2]

Green's statement underlines the fact that in the United States as elsewhere, labor and socialist groups were among the very first and most energetic opponents of Russian Communism. Yet the historic record is full of proof also for the contrary fact that labor was among the most prominent victims of the anti-communist campaigns of others. In the Great Red Scare of 1919–20, during the interwar decades and to an only slightly lesser extent in the McCarthyite era of the late 1940s and the 1950s, labor was subjected to constant harassment, intimidation and repression by those in business, in conservative civic associations and in government who conflated labor unionism, in and of itself, with Communism. It is self-evident to the point of mootness that in each of these three eras, labor had, often tortuously, to negotiate between the principled opposition to Communism that characterized a large section of it and its need to defend against "Red-baiting" repression by other anti-communists.

Less generally appreciated has been the level of labor and socialist complicity in the political repression that took place under cover of anti-communism. The history of American anti-communism needs to be conceptualized as one of

---

[1]   I am grateful to Alex Goodall and to Jack Ross for their expert and helpful comments on drafts of this article.

[2]   Address by William Green, June 10, 1925, William Green Papers, RG1–105, box 2, George Meany Memorial Archives, Silver Spring, Maryland.

166   *Little 'Red Scares'*

multiple, mutually contradictory thrusts, and the place of labor in it as a highly ambiguous and conflicted one.[3] Especially in the decades from 1920 to the mid-1940s, when business and other conservative anti-communists focused their campaigns on labor unions in particular, labor straddled the continuum from anti-Communism proper (that is, opposition to the policies and ideologies of Communist parties and states) and the broader assault (or "anti-communism") on all those who dissented or were seen to dissent from the status quo of a free enterprise system.[4] In the course of this prolonged straddling act, labor in fact ended up as the accomplices as much as the victims of the anti-communist campaigns of others.

Labor in the Aftermath of Palmer

American labor and socialist groups had suffered greatly from repression during the First World War and in the Great Red Scare that culminated in Attorney General A. Mitchell Palmer's raids of early 1920. Immediately afterwards they were subjected to yet another attack that used the anti-communist template against them, the so-called "American Plan" campaign for an open shop in industry by the National Association of Manufacturers and other business groups. Faced with this assault, labor was split in two camps, one opting for counter-subversionary work in their own midst and cooperation with those engaged in repression while the other choosing to ignore its reservations about the Communists' ultimate aims and to collaborate with them in defense of dissenters' civil liberties and in industrial organizing.[5] What might have been a powerful united labor and radical front in defense and extension of previously

---

[3]   See Markku Ruotsila, *British and American Anticommunism Before the Cold War* (London, 2001); Richard Gid Powers, *Not without Honor: The History of American Anticommunism* (New Haven, 1998); John Earl Haynes, *Red Scare or Red menace? American Communism and Anti-Communism in the Cold War Era* (Chicago, 1996).

[4]   The conceptual distinction between "anti-Communism" and the broader movement of "anticommunism," but not the argument about labor's position, is from Joel Kovel, *Red Hunting in the Promised Land: Anticommunism and the Making of America* (London, 1997), x–xx, 4–13.

[5]   For general studies of American labor that pay attention to this division, see Robert H. Zieger and Gilbert J. Gall, *American Workers, American Unions: The Twentieth Century* (Baltimore, 2002); James R. Green, *The World of the Worker: Labor in Twentieth Century America* (Urbana, 1998); Nelson Lichtenstein, *State of the Union: A Century of American Labor* (Princeton, 2003); David Montgomery, *The Fall of the House of Labor: The Workplace, the State, and American Labor Activism, 1865–1925* (Cambridge, UK, 1987); Bert Cochran, *Labor and Communism: The Conflict That Shaped American Unions* (Princeton, 1977).

made gains in collective bargaining, wages and unionization rights ran aground on the shoals of Communism.

The initial signs in 1918–20 had seemed to indicate a different course for the American labor movement. The situation was dire and especially so for those sections of labor affiliated with the Socialist Party. Having been both anti-war and, at first, supportive of the Russian Bolshevik regime, the party's activities had been severely curtailed and its image tarnished when the federal government used its wartime power to restrict the distribution of its publications, to harass its institutions and to imprison some of its key leaders.[6] Ever since, some scholars have maintained that the party's terminal decline, begun in these wrought years, resulted from this spate of repression.[7] Labor unions fared better, due to the American Federation of Labor (AFL) alliance with President Wilson and the Democrats that went back to 1913 and also because of its wartime no-strike pledge (not always kept at the grassroots level but in any case politically significant). In the end, only the anti-war anarcho-syndicalist Industrial Workers of the World (IWW) was suppressed – thoroughly, by a concerted campaign of several years' duration jointly undertaken by federal, state and private agencies.[8]

Understandably, wartime and immediate postwar repression worried labor and socialist activists and tended to lead them into alliances with Communists and other radicals, since it could be easily used as a template for new attempts at curbing their activities in the future. To prevent such an eventuality, some of the era's most powerful unions joined with the Socialist Party and with Communist activists in the American Freedom Convention's organized defense of labor's and dissenters' civil liberties in 1919 and in the 1920s in the National Council for Protection of Foreign Born Workers and in Senator Robert LaFollette's Conference for Progressive Political Action.[9] In the immediate postwar years even the staunchly anti-Communist and pro-war section of the

---

[6] For details, see Harry N. Schreiber, *The Wilson Administration and Civil Liberties, 1917–1921* (Ithaca, 1960); William Preston, Jr., *Aliens and Dissenters: Federal Suppression of Radicals, 1903–1933* (Cambridge, MA, 1963).

[7] Robert Justin Goldstein, *Political Repression in Modern America: From 1870 to 1976* (Urbana, 2001), xxi–xxv, 553–8. For a contrary argument, see Seymour Martin Lipset and Gary Marks, *It Didn't Happen Here: Why Socialism Failed in the United States* (New York, 2000), 241–60.

[8] Preston, *Aliens and Dissenters*, 118–51; Michael Heale, *American Anticommunism: Combating the Enemy Within, 1830–1970* (Baltimore, 1990), 54–8; Melvyn Dubofsky, *We Shall Be All: A History of the Industrial Workers of the World* (Chicago,), 423–44.

[9] J. Mahlon Barnes to the secretaries of organizations involved in or interested in the American Freedom Convention, August 6, 1919, Socialist Party of America Papers, reel 9, Perkins Library, Duke University, Durham, North Carolina; National Council for Protection of Foreign Born Workers mass mailing, March 3, 1927, copy in J.B. Matthews

168   *Little 'Red Scares'*

labor and socialist movement participated, and many of its leaders criticized in no uncertain terms the Woodrow Wilson administration's apparent use of anti-communism as a cover for suppression of all socialist, non-AFL labor and other dissenting opinion.[10]

In a few years' time, however, the onslaught by business interests for the open shop forced key sections of the labor movement to reassess these early alliances. The business champions of the "American Plan" used anti-communist smears to link all labor activism to the perceived Communist menace, resorted to blacklists and the use of labor spies and cooperated often intimately with local police "red squads" in what was a sustained campaign to roll back labor's recent gains. From 1921, these business interests successfully imposed the open shop in several key states and industries, and they managed to keep unionization at the meager level of 12 percent of the industrial workforce until the early 1930s.[11] All this was significantly facilitated by the support of the U.S. Supreme Court in a series of key decisions, starting with the *Hitchman Coal and Coke v. Mitchell* (1917) ban on unionization attempts in industries that had already instituted the open shop. Also the secondary boycott was severely limited and the states' right to fix minimum wages practically abolished.[12] For labor to have responded to this twinned Supreme Court and business assault by further strengthening its alliances with just those whom they were accused of colluding with no longer seemed to many to be a prudent strategy for safeguarding their existing rights.

While the defense of (non-Communist) dissenters' civil liberties remained, on the surface, a key aspect of labor activism in the interwar decades, there emerged deep differences of opinion over how best to negate the "American Plan" and how the presence of Communists in unions affected this primary task. The division was also class based, the AFL being composed of skilled craft unionists often deridingly called "labor's aristocracy" while the CIO attracted its recruits from among the less skilled and more poorly paid industrial workers. For those in the unions minded to exploit it, some unexpected room for maneuver was opened up by the fact that there were also those in influential positions in the era's business community also, who, whilst upholding the open shop, ere amenable to some kind of compromise with the sections of labor ready to take

---

Papers, box 21, Rare Books, Manuscripts and Special Collections Library, Duke University, Durham, North Carolina.

[10] See Markku Ruotsila, *John Spargo and American Socialism* (New York, 2006), 95–6; "Insidious Attack on Progressive Organizations Called Real Soviet Menace in U.S.," January 5, 1920, William English Walling Papers, box 2, Wisconsin Historical Society, Madison.

[11] Heale, *American Anticommunism*, 82–3; Green, *The World of the Worker*, 118–21, 133.

[12] Goldstein, *Political Repression in Modern America*, 183–4; Michael E. Parrish, *Anxious Decades: America in Prosperity and Depression, 1920–1941* (New York, 1992), 22–6.

strong measures against Communism. Some unexpected room for maneuver was, however, opened up by the fact that there were also those in influential positions in the era's business community who, whilst upholding the open shop, were amenable to some kind of a compromise with the sections of labor ready to take strong measures against Communists.[13]

Partly the willingness of AFL-affiliated union leaders to abandon their initial tentative alliances with political radicals can be seen in terms of a pre-emptive attempt to inoculate the unions against charges of communism and thus to preserve as much of their gains as possible.[14] Many of those who came to be involved in labor's own repression of known or suspected Communists genuinely believed (as the influential labor lawyer Louis Waldman put it) that "Communists attach themselves like leeches to unions, labor's political parties, with one sure result – disaster to the trade-union or to the political party."[15] Just as important, however, were the considered, deep and insurmountable differences of view over ultimate goals and tactics alike that existed between the Communists and other labor radicals on the one hand and the era's conservative craft union leaders and their Socialist allies on the other. The roots of labor's complicity in interwar political repression lay as much in these ideological, and philosophical differences of conviction and goals as much as they lay in purely opportunistic self-inoculation.

Labor and Socialist Anticommunism

Anti-Communism had been pronounced in the American Federation of Labor (AFL) already during the First World War and it continued to be so in the interwar years. The mold had been set by long-serving AFL president Samuel Gompers in 1917 when he had created the American Alliance for Labor and Democracy (AALD), a propaganda and publicity group by labor union and

---

[13]   See, by Alex Goodall, "Diverging Paths: Nazism, the National Civic Federation and American Anticommunism, 1933–1939", *Journal of Contemporary History* 44 (2009), 49–69; and "The Battle of Detroit and Anticommunism in the Depression Era", *The Historical Journal* 51 (2008), 457–80.

[14]   This has been emphasized to the exclusion of almost all factors in the scholarship that has been influenced by Ellen Schrecker's *Many Are the Crimes: McCarthyism in America* (New York, 1998), 48–9, 69–70.

[15]   Social Democratic Federation of America press release, November 2, 1939, Louis Waldman Papers, box 12, Rare Books and Manuscripts Division, New York Public Library; John Spargo to Robert Maisel, June 30, 1937, John Spargo Papers, box 16, Special Collections, Bailey/Howe Memorial Library, University of Vermont, Burlington; "Green and A.F. of L. Defended", petition sent to the *New York Herald Tribune*, July 27, 1937, Spargo Papers, box 5.

socialist supporters of the First World War. This organization quickly took on a clearly anti-communist coloring. It did not survive into peacetime, but Gompers had the AFL adopt several convention resolutions immediately after the war that resumed from where the AALD had ceased, denouncing in uncompromising terms the Russian Bolshevik regime.[16]

The resultant AFL anti-Communism rested on decades of Gompers' suspicion about attempts at centralizing economic and political power that had ideological roots in his personal life journey away from his Socialist radicalism. To him, Communism was an extreme form of socialism, in all its forms a "cancerous growth" upon the body politic and upon the organized labor movement, but a "freak and a scourge" full of "impracticable and puerile visions." Gompers was certain that it would destroy free labor unions if allowed to spread to the West just as surely as it had destroyed them in Russia, for at its very core lay the undemocratic urge "to build a society where the political and industrial worlds are merged into one." Once power was in the hands of a single Communist "super-union" that controlled the State as well, free labor's story would be at an end.[17]

The conservative craft union leaders who controlled the AFL after Gompers' death in 1924 agreed with this assessment in its entirety. The Teamsters president Dan Tobin, the Metal Trades Department's John Frey and the Brotherhood of Carpenters' William Hutcheson taking the lead, these men saw to it that for the next 28 years the AFL's presidency and vice-presidency remained in the hands of two equally safely anti-communist men, William Green of the United Mine Workers and Matthew Woll of the Typographers' Union. Under these two men's reign, the AFL kept issuing as strongly worded convention resolutions as it had under Gompers that denounced Soviet Russia, the American Communist Party (CPUSA) and all other forms and approximations of Communism. In 1935, they published, too, a detailed investigative report, the *Report on the Communist Propaganda in America*, on Communist activity in the unions. This report took a robust position in opposition to the Trade Union Educational League (TUEL), the CPUSA's principal instrument in the union field that had already infiltrated some AFL unions.[18]

---

[16] Frank L. Grubbs, *The Struggle for Labor Loyalty: Gompers, the A.F. of L., and the Pacifists, 1917–1920* (Durham, 1968); "American Labor's Greatest Convention," *American Federationist* 26 (August 1919), 689–90.

[17] Quotes from Samuel Gompers, "American Labor Is True to Democracy," *American Federationist* 26 (April 1919), 318–20, and "The Truth About Soviet Russia and Bolshevism, No. 2," *American Federationist* 27 (March 1920), 253–6.

[18] George Sirgiovanni, *An Undercurrent of Suspicion: Anti-Communism in America During World War II* (New Brunswick, 1990), 25–31; Harvey A. Levenstein, *Communism,*

Leftward Ramparts 171

Radical critics at the time and some later historians have viewed these actions in the context of the AFL's clear endorsement of the "New Era" capitalist system of the 1920s. Allegedly, there was little difference between business anti-communists and the AFL's position; the latter, too, having accepted the fundamentals of the economic and industrial status quo.[19] This oft-repeated claim had a grain of truth in it, since the 1920s' craft union heads did in fact propose to modify the capitalist system only by some new structures of co-management and co-partnership; they tended to brand as Communist, un-American or otherwise subversive all reform proposals or organizing methods to the left of such a position. The AFL was heavily involved, too, in the National Civic Federation, on the board of which Woll served for many years, a staunchly anti-communist joint labor-business association that pioneered new methods of employee-employer conciliation and collaboration but resisted all other attempts at modifying the free enterprise system.[20]

In making their choice for such a system of collaboration, the Catholic faith of several key AFL leaders played a significant role. This appears to have been the case with Matthew Woll, in particular, and with Green's successor as AFL president in 1952, George Meany. Ever since Pope Leo XIII's 1891 encyclical *Rerum Novarum*, Catholic social theorists had been advocating for some essentially guildist alternative both to unregulated capitalism and to Russian-style state socialism, and the AFL's model seemed to fit this. Whether themselves of the Catholic faith or not, it behooved AFL leaders to take seriously such guildist public theologies, for the union contained a strong Catholic contingent which it was in no aspiring leader's interest to alienate.[21]

In addition to faith-based promptings, fears over centralization of economic power and the need to defend against business accusations, AFL anti-Communism was grounded in a particular rendition of socialist theory. This was devised over many decades by the two right-wing socialist organizations that separated from the Socialist Party in large part over the movement's relations with Communists – the short-lived Social Democratic League (SDL), created in 1917 by a smallish group of pro-war socialist intellectuals, and the Social

---

Anti-Communism and the CIO (Westport, 1981), 118–26; Anders Geoffery Lewis, "Labor's Cold War: The American Federation of Labor and Liberal Anticommunism" (Ph.D. dissertation, University of Florida, 2000).

[19]   Green, *The World of the Worker*, 104, 118–21, 127.

[20]   David Montgomery, *Workers' Control in America: Studies in the History of Work, Technology, and Labor Struggles* (Cambridge, UK, 1979), 26, 93–101; Montgomery, *The Fall of the House of Labor*, 411–20, 423–5.

[21]   Sirgiovanni, *An Undercurrent of Suspicion*, 26–7; David J. O'Brien, *American Catholics and Social Reform: The New Deal Years* (New York, 1968), 13–30, 43–4, 82–3.

172 *Little 'Red Scares'*

Democratic Federation (SDF, 1936–58). The latter was the home of the party's by-then anti-Communist Old Guard after the party itself had been taken over by a militant left-wing faction that was willing to work with Communists.[22] The influence of these groups on the AFL was by no means negligible, for the SDL had been a constituent member in the wartime AALD, and in the 1920s its chairman William English Walling became Gompers' and then Green's adviser, as well as a ghostwriter for AFL publications.[23] The Old Guard, on the other hand, had worked with AFL leaders in pre-1917 attempts at creating a labor party. Although that attempt had failed, it did land control over at least one-third of AFL unions into the hands of the Old Guard Socialists.[24]

Doctrinally, socialist anti-communism can be traced to the polemics by future SDL and SDF leaders in decade preceding the First World War that challenged the anarcho-syndicalist models for industrial unionism then being proffered by the IWW. Russian Bolshevism was subsequently placed into the interpretive matrix that was developed during these polemics and the attendant faction fights that were eventually (but only for a brief while) won by the right-wingers.[25]

In their rendition, Bolshevism was a false claimant to the name of scientific socialism or Marxism in that its adherents proposed to effect the hoped-for transition into socialism through the employment of methods that Karl Marx himself had condemned in the 1840s – through catastrophic, undemocratic and violent means that disposed of the gradual building of a socialist consciousness and refused to wait for the maturation of capitalist industrial structures. Use of such methods would destroy the workers' ethically higher consciousness, the right-wingers believed, and render them unfit to wield power were they perchance to gain it, while concentrating power in the hands of a single hierarchical industrial union ran entirely unacceptable risks of future oppression at the hands of unscrupulous union operatives. To the right-wing Socialists, the coming of

---

[22] Markku Ruotsila, "Neoconservatism Prefigured: The Social Democratic League of America and the Anticommunists of the Anglo-American Right, 1917–1921," *Journal of American Studies* 40 (August 2006), 327–47, and "Communism as Anarchism: The Pro-War Socialists, the Old Guard, and the Forging of Socialist Anticommunism in the United States," *The International History Review* 31 (September 2009), 499–520.

[23] See Kenneth E. Hendrickson, Jr., "The Pro-War Socialists, the Social Democratic League and the Ill-Fated Drive for Industrial Democracy in America, 1917–1920," *Labor History* 2 (Summer 1970), 304–22; James Boylan, *Revolutionary Lives: Anna Strunsky & William English Walling* (Amherst, 1983), 253–4, 262.

[24] James Weinstein, *The Long Detour: The History and Future of the American Left* (Boulder: Westview Press 2003), 46; Lipset and Marks, *It Didn't Happen Here*, 103–106; Eric Thomas Chester, *The Mission: Socialists and the Labor Party Question in the U.S.* (London: Pluto Press 2004).

[25] Ruotsila, "Communism as Anarchism," 508–14.

the "co-operative commonwealth" was a long drawn-out, gradual, peaceful and above all a democratic process, and they believed (as the SDF's Charles Edward Russell put it) that "changes instituted by force must be sustained by force and inevitably fall by the means they have invoked."[26]

These convictions predated but were significantly further strengthened by the suppression of the Menshevik and Social-Revolutionary rivals of the Bolsheviks that took place in Soviet Russia in the 1920s. American Socialists who watched the show trials from afar were appalled and disgusted but rarely surprised, for they had already concluded that such repression was the logical and inevitable outcome of a system based on anarcho-syndicalist and insurrectionary models of governance.[27]

Into this interpretive matrix, Socialist anti-communists placed both the interwar CPUSA *and* the Socialist left-wing enthusiasts for a Popular Front with Communists who came to control the party in the 1930s. As they put it in their 1934 manifesto, *The Crisis in the Socialist Party*, the Old Guardists did not believe that "Socialism can be established as a result of confusion and chaos" brought about by violent acts of revolt and sabotage as proposed by Communists and their left-wing Socialist allies.[28] Labor and socialists, it was believed, could build a sustainable "cooperative commonwealth" only through rational argument and the acquisition of parliamentary majorities by democratic means. All that calls to violent insurrection or proletarian dictatorship could produce was a regimen of government repression that used labor spies and agents provocateurs to repress union organizing.[29] Right-wing labor and socialists came to believe, too, that Communists were "only vociferous for civil liberties within democratic countries as an issue behind which to operate in order to secure power to better destroy civil liberties."[30]

---

[26] James Oneal, *Sabotage, or Socialism vs. Syndicalism: A Critical Study of Theories and Methods* (St. Louis: The National Rip-Saw Publishing Company 1913), 1–13; John Spargo, *Syndicalism, Industrial Unionism, and Socialism* (New York: B.W. Huebsch 1913), 14–15, 39–40, 60–65, 75–9; Charles Edward Russell, "Toward the American Commonwealth. VIII. Social Democracy," *The Social Frontier* 5 (October 1938), 22.

[27] James Oneal, "Militancy's Record of Wreckage," *New Leader*, May 22, 1926, 3; "The Revolution Devours Its Own Children," *New Leader*, November 26, 1927, 3; James Oneal, *American Communism: A Critical Analysis of Its Origins, Development and Progress* (New York: The Rand Book Store 1927), 13–18, 23–4, 147–56.

[28] *The Crisis in the Socialist Party* (New York: Committee for the Preservation of Socialist Party, nd. [1934]), 6.

[29] *The Crisis in the Socialist Party*, 6; "Statement to Our Readers by the New Leader Board of Directors," *New Leader*, March 9, 1935, 1; "No Compromise with Infantile Sickness of Armed Insurrection," *New Leader*, March 9, 1935, 2.

[30] Louis Waldman to the editor of the *New York Times*, October 11, 1939, Social Democratic Federation of America Records, reel 15, Tamiment Institute Library and Robert

174   *Little 'Red Scares'*

The syllogism was clear and genuinely believed: were Communists allowed to gain power, they would repress labor, and if labor allied with Communists in the pursuit of its own, non-Communist aims, then government would repress them. It was this conviction that in 1936 propelled the Old Guard to leave the Socialist Party and create the SDF, and this conviction that propelled them into anti-communist work in the unions. The proper term for their position was and is, in fact, socialist anti-Communism – rather than mere anti-Bolshevism or anti-Stalinism – for the entire syllogism that guided these right-wingers rested on the assumption that "democratic Socialism and totalitarian Communism are opposites. They have nothing in common either in ends or means."[31]

In between the 1910s and the start of the Cold War, labor and socialist groups had developed, then, a considerable corpus of anti-Communist exegesis. In the decades between the two world wars, this body of exegesis solidified into a non-negotiable for a large and influential section of the labor union movement. Much as AFL craft union heads and the Socialist Party/SDF Old Guard deprecated the use of anti-communism as a cover for repressing political and labor union activism that was unconnected with any actual Communists or Soviet agendas, they could not escape their own equal urge, rooted in a multiplicity of compelling motives, to fight the Communists themselves. From this duality in approach and sentiment issued the prolonged, bitter struggle for control of labor unions that shaped the era. In the course of these fights right-wing labor and socialist leaders themselves engaged in significant repression of those in their movements whom they suspected of or knew to have Communist leanings.

Labor's Repression of Communists in the Unions

Labor-on-labor and socialist-on-socialist repression impacted upon many unions but centered on those associated with the Congress of Industrial Organizations (CIO). For the AFL's and the SDF's publicists, it was easy to represent CIO organizing in terms of the anti-syndicalist interpretive matrix that had been developed to deal with the Wobblies, for the resemblance between Wobbly sabotage and the CIO's new sit-down strikes was striking. As labor anti-communists eagerly pointed out, there was, too, an apparent direct linkage between the CIO, the Communists and the Wobblies, for among the CIO's leaders was William Z. Foster, the Communist head of the TUEL, a former

---

F. Wagner Labor Archives, Elmer Bobst Library, New York University.

[31]   "The 'New' Communist Line: Another Bolshevik Fraud and Danger," pamphlet by the Social Democratic Federation, nd [1941], 3.

Wobbly who had founded the Syndicalist League before the First World War.[32] Other syndicalists, as well, were involved in setting up the CIO, and several known Communists were given top positions within its leadership. It is now known that by the late 1940s Communists controlled outright some 20 percent of all CIO unions and had major influence in some 40 percent. In some cities and key industries the majority of its organizers came from that party.[33]

Initially, right-wing anti-Communist Socialists did not think that Communists could ever become a "dominating influence" in the CIO, but by 1936–37 they were forced to revise this estimate as they came to better knowledge of the makeup of the CIO's staff.[34] The more that business and other conservative anti-communists focused on the CIO's actual Communists, many labor anti-Communists started to fear that government repression would soon befall on all unions if any of them kept allowing Communists to use them as instruments of class strife and violence (or in support of Soviet foreign policy). Such being the perceived stakes, a bitter and prolonged faction fight between Communist and anti-Communist labor was well-nigh inevitable.

One of the earliest and most bitter locations for this faction fight was in the CIO affiliated needle trades in New York City. In these unions, Communist TUEL influences were considerable. Consequently, both AFL and SDF organizers fought relentlessly (sometimes with their fists) in the late 1920s to the mid-1930s to keep more Communists out of these unions or to purge union locals that Communists had already infiltrated. Much of their success was due to the efforts of Morris Sigman and David Dubinsky, the successive presidents of the International Ladies Garment Workers Union (ILGWU) in these years, both equally staunch anti-Communists and equally close to the SDF circle. By 1926, control of the ILGWU had reverted into anti-Communist hands and the union became a center of anti-Communist resistance elsewhere in New York.[35]

---

[32] Oneal, *American Communism*, 28.

[33] Robert H. Zieger, *The CIO, 1935–1955* (Chapel Hill, 1995), 253–73; Bert Cochran, *Labor and Communism: The Conflict That Shaped American Unions* (Princeton, 1977), 95–8; Harvey Klehr, *The Heyday of American Communism: The Depression Decade* (New York, 1984), 238. See also Levenstein, *Communism, Anti-Communism and the CIO*; Steve Rosswurm (ed.), *The CIO's Left-Led Unions* (New Brunswick, 1992).

[34] Algernon Lee to Adolph Germer, March 12, 1936, Adolph Germer Papers, box 3, Wisconsin Historical Society, Madison; Julius Gerber to Adolph Germer, August 21, 1936, Germer Papers, box 3; James Oneal to [Sarah?] Limbach, February 22, 1937, Social Democratic Federation of America Records, reel 15.

[35] See Robert Parmet, *Master of Seventh Avenue: David Dubinsky and the American Labor Movement* (New York, 2005); Morris Sigman, "The Communist Plague in Our Union," *New Leader*, July 4, 1925, 4. See also David Garowsky, "Factional Dispute within the ILGWU, 1919–1928" (Ph.D. dissertation, State University of New York – Binghampton, 1978).

176   *Little 'Red Scares'*

In the smaller Amalgamated Clothing Workers, on the other hand, an alliance was forged between the Communists and the union's non-Communist president Sidney Hillman, and in the still-smaller Fur Workers Union, Communists seized complete control. The AFL responded by starting to cooperate with local police in an attempt to undermine the unions in question.[36]

Similar turn of events on an even greater scale awaited in the United Auto Workers (UAW) once this union, originally in the AFL, had joined the CIO in 1936. Especially once the onetime Socialist Party trekker to Soviet Russia and a pioneer of the sit-down strike, Walter Reuther, had been appointed as organizer, Communists gained ever more influence in UAW locals. Reuther may himself have been a CPUSA member at this time or earlier; it is now known that he continued to attend party meetings as late as 1939. In any case Reuther forged a solid alliance with the union's Communists that lasted until after the Second World War.[37] Communists came to control one of the CIO's largest unions, the United Electrical Workers, as well, and the small but very powerful New York Transport Workers Union and two maritime and longshoremen's unions.[38]

In addition to these unions, bitter fighting gripped the American Labor Party (ALP) as well. This New York organization was the latest (and last) organizational expression of the right-wing socialists' pre-World War I attempt at the creation of a socialist and labor coalition, but among its founders and activists were some leading Communists, too, such as the Transport Workers Union's Mike Quill and the National Maritime Union's Joe Curran. The more powerful as a local electoral force that the ALP became in the late 1930s and the 1940s, the more controversial did its inclusion of Communists become. A prolonged, bitter faction fight between its Communist and non-Communist labor members ensued in the late 1930s and early 1940s.[39] The SDFers were encouraged in their attempt to oust all known or suspected Communists by the

---

[36]   For details, see Steve Fraser, *Labor Will Rule: Sidney Hillman and the Rise of American Labor* (New York,1991). For AFL countermeasures, see Frank Sullivan to William Green, June 14, 1927; Green to Sullivan, June 15, 1927; Joseph Warren to Green, June 17, 1927; Green to Warren, June 18, 1927, each in the Green Papers, reel 6, Ohio Historical Society, Columbus, Ohio.

[37]   Victor G. Devinatz, "Reassessing the Historical UAW: Walter Reuther's Affiliation with the Communist Party and Something of Its Meaning – a Document of Party Involvement," *Labour/Le Travail* 49 (Spring 2002), 223–46. For further details, see Martin Halpern, *UAW Politics in the Cold War* (Albany, 1988); Nelson Lichtenstein, *The Most Dangerous Man in Detroit: Walter Reuther and the Fate of American Labor* (New York, 1995).

[38]   See Ronald L. Filipelli and Mark McColloch, *Cold War in the Working Class: The Rise and Decline of the United Electrical Workers* (Albany, 1995); Bruce Nelson, *Workers on the Waterfront: Seamen, Longshoremen and Unionism in the 1930s* (Urbana, 1988).

[39]   Cochran, *Labor and Communism*, 235–7, 243.

research director of the House Un-American Activities (or Dies) Committee, the ex-Socialist Benjamin Mandel, lest they be held to account for the "Communazi espionage and propaganda" that was, according to him, flowing through the ALP.[40] When no such purge took place, the SDF leader Algernon Lee resigned his city chairmanship and his colleague Louis Waldman left the entire organization.[41]

Power in the ALP's headquarters did remain in the staunchly anti-Communist hands of the ILGWU's David Dubinsky, but the New York section came to be ruled by Communists. This situation proved untenable when during the Second World War, the CIO's new Political Action Committee (CIO-PAC), in which Communists held commanding positions, proposed a reorganization that would have given even more powers to their faction. This prompted a final round of faction fighting during which accusations flew about regarding the ALP's alleged subservience to "alien interests" and "Communist infiltration" – all of it to no avail, for in the end the right-wingers lost and the ALP ended up in full Communist control.[42] The labor anti-Communists promptly retaliated by creating their own alternative, the even smaller Liberal Party – which immediately resumed the attack upon those left in the ALP, Communists or not.[43]

What happened in the ALP, the needle trades and the UAW were but the most prominent examples of late 1920s, 1930s and early 1940s labor turning against labor for political reasons and of the unions' right-wingers using repression against known or suspected Communists in their midst. The repression was extensive and supported even by some of the most previously radical union organizers. In the 1920s, for example, even such a legendary Wobbly as "Mother" Jones was party to efforts at preventing Communist United Mine Workers officials from being funded from their locals' treasuries. These people were, she maintained, engaged in "sowing the seed of ... [a] philosophy which is not very wholesome for those unsophisticated men" and which ought

---

[40] Benjamin Mandel to Louis Waldman, September 1, 1939, Waldman Papers, box 11; Benjamin Mandel to Algernon Lee, January 18, 1940, Algernon Lee Papers, reel 59, Tamiment Institute Library and Robert F. Wagner Labor Archives, Elmer Bobst Library, New York University.

[41] Social Democratic Federation of America executive conference minutes, September 17, 1938, Social Democratic Federation of America Records, reel 15; Louis Waldman to Algernon Lee, November 6, 1941, and Lee to Waldman, November 27, 1941, ibid., Social Democratic Federation of America Records, reel 17.

[42] Cochran, *Labor and Communism*, 235–7.

[43] Sirgiovanni, *An Undercurrent of Suspicion*, 177; Cochran, *Labor and Communism*, 235–7.

therefore to be stopped.[44] Similarly, repression was championed by some of the Socialists who had been among the most prominent victims of the 1919–20 Red Scare – such as the labor lawyer Louis Waldman, denied his seat on the New York state assembly in 1920 because of his (falsely) alleged Communist sympathies. Throughout the 1930s and 1940s, Waldman insisted that it was the Communists in the CIO unions and the left-wing of the Socialist Party – rather than the employers who tried to suppress these two – who were out to "undermine our country and our way of life." To allow these people to have any say in labor matters would, according to Waldman, be tantamount to the labor movement's "suicide", for it would surely turn the capitalists against all labor.[45]

These kinds of accusations did have merit, yet they need to be balanced by the fact that some CIO top officials were in fact staunch and long-serving anti-communists whose reliability and credentials not even the bitterest AFL or SDF critic could deny. Not unjustifiably, such men took exception to portrayals of the CIO as dominated by Communists. One such man was Adolph Germer, a veteran of the labor movement and of the Socialist Party since the beginning of the century, whom CIO head John L. Lewis brought out of retirement into the union's leadership. Germer had begun his organizing career with the Wobblies in the early 1900s but had soon turned against them, having come to see them as nothing but a collection of "nuts, freaks, [and] impossibilists."[46] Just two years before taking his post in the CIO, he had left the Socialist Party, too, after 34 years of membership, because he could not abide its new leaders' willingness to work with Communists. "I was fighting the Communist type", he told one young SDF critic in 1940, "while you were still rocking in the cradle and I have no more in common with them now than I had then."[47]

It was the presence of men such as Germer in the CIO leadership that made it possible for CIO unions eventually to purge Communists from their leadership. This, however, did not take place until the late 1940s. The United Auto Workers acted first, passing a convention resolution in 1940 that denounced all "brutal dictatorships" and barred from union offices individuals who were members in

---

[44] "Mother" Jones to William Green, July 23, 1923, and Green to Jones, July 25, 1923, Green Papers, reel 3, Ohio Historical Society.

[45] Louis Waldman, *Labor Lawyer* (New York, 1944), 71–5, 260–63, 271, 278–80.

[46] Adolph Germer to Harvey [Freming], November 20, 1935, Germer Papers, box 2. See also Lorin Lee Cary, "Institutionalized Conservatism in the Early CIO: Adolph Germer, A Case Study," *Labor History* 13 (Fall 1972).

[47] Adolph Germer to Sol Levitas, October 8, 1935, Germer Papers, box 2; Adolph Germer to Jim Maurer, July 8, 1936, Germer Papers, box 3; Adolph Germer to Victor Riesel, September 12, 1940, Victor Riesel Papers, box 7, Tamiment Institute Library and Robert F. Wagner Labor Archives, Elmer Bobst Library, New York University.

any organization that had been designated "illegal by the government" because of its subversive activities. After this, UAW president Walter Reuther finally turned against his erstwhile Communist allies, completing their purging by 1947. The CIO itself had passed resolutions at its 1939 and 1940 conventions announcing that it was now "unalterably opposed to any movement or activities of subversive character, Trojan horses, or fifth columns which are aimed against our nation and government" and that it rejected policy propositions emanating from "totalitarianism, dictatorships and foreign ideologies such as Nazism, Communism and Fascism." Despite the apparent clarity of the statements, no concrete measures were, however, taken to expel any Communist members until 1949.[48]

The Dies Committee and its Labor Collaborators

While anti-communist labor and socialists preferred to set their house in order, as they saw it, by their own independent efforts, they were not unwilling to cooperate in often intimate ways with selected governmental agencies. In the first instance, this meant working with the Fish Committee of 1930 and, more significantly, with the Special House Committee on Un-American Activities, better known as the Dies Committee, that existed in 1938–45 (whereupon it was made permanent and took the new name, the House Committee on Un-American Activities).[49] Since the latter's Democratic chairman, Representative Martin Dies of Texas, made it known from the beginning of its work that a large part of his committee's investigations would center on the CIO, this willingness by anti-communist labor to collaborate was not at all surprising.

According to his own later testimony, Dies had tried privately (and failed) to convince CIO president John L. Lewis into a housecleaning under the committee's supervision. Instead of gaining the hoped-for cooperation, Dies had been thrown out of an irate Lewis' offices.[50] Such an experience (coupled with the fact that Dies and Lewis had been flanked at the meeting by the CIO's legal counsel Lee Pressman, a Communist) imparted a certain a priori hostility to Dies' interactions with this union. Contrary to later portrayals, however, Dies insisted that he was not himself anti-labor but regarded a "strong and vigorous" labor movement as one of the major historic bulwarks of American

---

[48] Cochran, *Labor and Communism*, 152–3, 263–90, 304–12; Green, *The World of the Worker*, 194–203.

[49] See Walter Goodman, *The Committee: The Extraordinary Career of the House Committee on Un-American Activities* (New York, 1968), 3–23; for labor and the Fish Committee, see also Alex Goodall's article in this book.

[50] Martin Dies, *Martin Dies' Story* (New York, 1963), 43–4.

democracy. Such a publicly oft-reiterated position was a good sign as far as anti-Communist labor was concerned – and even more promising was Dies' public call for all American workingmen and women to support only what he called the "responsible leaders and conservative groups" in their midst.[51]

These "responsible leaders" included the AFL's William Green and John Frey, both of whom gave public endorsements to the Dies Committee's work. Some AFL officers testified at its hearings, as did key SDF members.[52] Committee investigators received lists of suspected Communists from Frey and other AFL and SDF officials and, in turn, they sent copies of their own materiel to such labor anti-communists as the ILGWU official and future head of the AFL's International Affairs Department, the former Communist Jay Lovestone, and to the SDF's Louis Waldman. As has been seen, the Committee's research director Benjamin Mandel also advised these men on how to purge Communists from the ALP and affiliated unions. Regularly, too, Dies' men coaxed the SDF's paper, the *New Leader*, into responding to attacks that labor and socialist groups were making against the committee.[53] Some of its Socialist critics thought that in this way the entire paper had turned, by the early 1940s, into nothing but the "Martin Dies official organ."[54]

This characterization was unfair, since not all *New Leader* contributors were willing to endorse Dies' work. The supporters, too, always coupled their statements of appreciation with caveats about the dangers involved in "smearing liberals, trade unionists, and socialists, in one inclusive amalgam with communists" in which they saw some of the committee's most "foul-mouthed witch-hunters" at times engaging.[55] Even the onetime SDL chairman John Spargo, by now a Republican anti-communist, insisted that he was "disgusted" by many things the Dies Committee had done (even if his own daughter was one of its investigators).[56] The other former SDL leader Charles Edward Russell, now a member of the SDF's executive committee and *New Leader* columnist, denounced Dies' "comedy work" as a "roaring farce" and supposed that the man was secretly dreaming of full-scale press censorship and the outlawing of

---

[51] Dies, *Martin Dies' Story*, 51–2.

[52] Powers, *Not Without Honor*, 126; Dies, *Martin Dies' Story*, 66–7, 82.

[53] Benjamin Mandel to J.B. Matthews, October 5, 1939, February 21 and April 19, 1940, and July 30, 1946, Matthews Papers, box 692; Jerry Voorhis to Leo Meltzer, June 9, 1939, Social Democratic Federation of America Records, reel 15; Gerhart H. Seger to Leo Meltzer, September 17, 1939, Social Democratic Federation of America Records, reel 16; Benjamin Mandel to Louis Waldman, September 1, 1939, Waldman Papers, box 11.

[54] Adolph Germer to Victor Riesel, July 17, 1941, Riesel Papers, box 7.

[55] "What Kind of a Dies Committee?," *New Leader*, January 13, 1945, 16.

[56] Ruotsila, *John Spargo and American Socialism*, 227.

Leftward Ramparts   181

all strikes. According to Russell, "Dies would have us practice nothing that has been invented since 1787"; to him, supposedly, all those were communists who did go in for such inventions.[57]

Similarly, the SDF's first executive secretary and longtime *New Leader* editor James Oneal warned in 1938 about Dies' propensity at branding as communists many among the labor movement who were either "innocents" or "semi-innocents." At the same time, Oneal did feel that labor unionists were failing to address the very real threat posed by the actual Communists in their midst and that something much more substantive ought to be done.[58] By the summer of 1939, all ambiguity had vanished: in that month the SDF had a Dies Committee member (the former Socialist Jerry Voorhis, later to be branded a Communist fellow-traveler himself by Richard Nixon) appear at an event of theirs where Louis Waldman called for new federal legislation to "curb subversive groups." From this moment onwards, regular calls to strengthen the Dies Committee and to make it permanent were a staple in SDF discourse.[59]

Though initially qualified, SDF and AFL leaders did, then, give support to the most controversial of governmental "Red-baiters" of the interwar decades. In so doing they aided and abetted in the harassment and repression of sections of the labor movement that were uninvolved in Communist subversion, no matter how much they tried to insist that the "preservation of civil liberties" must not be endangered as the Committee's investigators went about their work.[60] For as the Dies Committee went about its investigations, it did unquestionable harm to legitimate labor organizing.

Dies' investigators worked closely with many local "red squads", and they raided the headquarters of CPUSA front organizations, often in blatant violation of the law.[61] In their reports, the committee claimed that the spate of CIO sit-

---

[57] Charles Edward Russell, "The News Reel," *New Leader*, October 29, 1938, 1, and "The News Reel," *New Leader*, November 26, 1938, 1.

[58] James Oneal, "Dies Confuses Fight on C.P.," *New Leader*, December 10, 1938, 7; James Oneal to Leo Meltzer, August 16, 1938, Social Democratic Federation of America Records, reel 16.

[59] Victor Riesel, "Dictatorship of Left and Right Hit at Tamiment," *New Leader*, July 1, 1939, 1, 7; Louis Waldman, "Boycott All Soviet Goods and "Stooge Fronts"," *New Leader*, September 2, 1939, 10; "Statement on War and Neutrality Adopted at the National Executive Committee of the SDF," October 1, 1939, Social Democratic Federation of America Records, reel 15; Social Democratic Federation of America executive committee minutes, January 6, 1940, Waldman Papers, box 11; "Tamiment Speakers Urge War on Fifth Column, Back Defense," *New Leader*, June 29, 1940, 2.

[60] Social Democratic Federation of America executive committee minutes, January 6, 1940, Waldman Papers, box 11.

[61] Schrecker, *Many Are the Crimes*, 91, 96, 109.

182   *Little 'Red Scares'*

down strikes in 1936 in Atlanta, Georgia, and in Detroit and Flint, Michigan, was engineered by the CPUSA – and then used this claim as justification for further repression. Most of the committee's assertions in its 1939 and 1940 reports about the level of Communist infiltration in specific CIO unions *were*, in fact, accurate, and the conclusion – that "most of its largest organizations are free of Communist control, domination or even serious influences" – was eminently reasonable.[62] Dies was also essentially correct in his accusations about the CIO-PAC (it did include 18 CPUSA members on its executive committee and its legal counsel and co-counsel were both Communists).[63]

There were aspects in Dies' work that appealed especially to anti-communist labor. Most prominently, these included his 1938 and 1939 investigations into the Communist-led National Maritime Union, which they had been combating for some time on their own, and his exposure of the American Youth Congress, a Communist front organization. Anticommunist labor leaders gave strong public support to efforts at suppressing these organizations that followed in the wake of Dies' investigations.[64] However, suspicions were raised once the committee began to focus on federal agencies and to suggest that a total of some 1121 "Communists, Socialists and fellow travelers" had infiltrated key New Deal agencies through the 1935 National Labor Relations Act. Dies' rather indiscriminate equating after about 1939 of Communists, New Deal liberals and some of anti-Communist labor supportive of the New Deal did not sit well with any of the three and least of all with anti-Communist labor.[65]

Repression of Labor by Federal Agencies

For added effectiveness, Dies would have required Justice Department assistance, and he asked for it. Not surprisingly in light of his attacks on the New Deal

---

[62] Goodman, *The Committee*, 43–54, 75–86; Dies, *Martin Dies' Story*, 43–4; Cochran, *Labor and Communism*, 121; Schrecker, *Many Are the Crimes*, 22, 27–31.

[63] Cochran, *Labor and Communism*, 231–4; Dies, *Martin Dies' Story*, 29–40; Sirgiovanni, *An Undercurrent of Suspicion*, 55–67.

[64] See Lawrence McRyn, "Joe Curran's Maritime Union Is Comintern Agency on U.S. Waterfront," *New Leader*, May 4, 1940, 4; Charles Yale Harrison, "Red Maritime Union Plans Sabotage of U.S. Defense," *New Leader*, July 27, 1940, 9; "Smash the Fifth Column!," *New Leader*, January 18, 1941, 8.

[65] Schrecker, *Many Are the Crimes*, 110–11. For anti-communist labor comment, see "What Kind of a Dies Committee?," *New Leader*, January 13, 1945, 16; Christopher Emmet, "Rankin and the Communists: How Not to Fight Totalitarianism," *New Leader*, August 11, 1945, 5.

bureaucracy, the request was denied.[66] This fact highlights the relatively limited role played in the interwar decades' harassment of labor by the Federal Bureau of Investigation (FBI). As much as some historians have portrayed the FBI as the principal instigator of a later, Cold War climate of intolerance and repression,[67] in the decades between the world wars its bureaucrats were strikingly reluctant to get involved. The Palmer raids had seriously damaged the Bureau's reputation, and director J. Edgar Hoover's own personal beliefs about labor and Communists aside, he was unwilling to re-enter into full-scale labor repression. In the early 1920s, there were only few major incidents of FBI repression of labor activity under the cover of anti-communism, and in each such case Hoover acted on the specific instructions of superiors in the Justice Department.

The most famous and egregious of these cases involved the national railroad strike of 1922. Having obtained a sweeping injunction from the courts three weeks after the strike had begun, forbidding the striking union members from doing anything in word or in deed that hindered the operation of the railroads, then-Attorney General Harry J. Daugherty instructed the FBI to gather evidence to prove that Communist influences were behind the strike. Federal agents and informants were sent to the picket lines and they managed to amass sufficient hearsay evidence to persuade a judge. The Justice Department arrested 1,200 union members for inciting a rebellion and the railroad strike was broken.[68] Also in 1922, FBI agents and informers sought to undermine the TUEL on the assumption of its subservience to Soviet Russia (which was not unreasonable to suppose, since it was a member of the Profintern, the Kremlin-controlled and Comintern-linked Red International of Labor Unions). TUEL meetings were regularly disrupted and, in August, 1922, in cooperation with local police, a raid was conducted on a joint TUEL-CPUSA strategy session in Bridgman, Michigan, during which 17 Communists present were arrested.[69]

While no friend of the TUEL or its leader Foster, even Samuel Gompers took these incidents as proof of the existence of a "conspiracy against labor" in the FBI that had, according to him, unleashed "the mightiest onslaught

---

[66] Dies, *Martin Dies' Story*, 60–61, 64–5, 138–43.

[67] Schrecker, *Many Are the Crimes*, 203; Michael J. Heale, "Beyond the "Age of McCarthy": Anticommunism and the Historians," 133–8, in Melvyn Stokes (ed.), *The State of U.S. History* (Oxford, 2002); Kenneth O'Reilly, "The FBI and the Origins of McCarthyism," *Historian* 45 (May 1983); Frank J. Donner, *The Age of Surveillance: The Aims and Methods of America's Political Intelligence System* (New York, 1980).

[68] Schmidt, *Red Scare*, 332–3; Powers, *Secrecy and Power*, 139–40.

[69] See David K. Williams, ""They Never Stopped Watching Us": FBI Political Surveillance, 1924–1936," *UCLA Historical Journal* 2 (1981), 13.

of reaction through which the nation has ever passed."[70] Such a statement is especially striking in light of the fact that when he made it Gompers had already turned against the FBI's ostensible target, the syndicalist-to-become-Communist William Z. Foster. This man had started his organizing some four years earlier, in a committee that was originally chaired by Gompers himself. His actions had, however, been such that Gompers informed him that it was "impossible for him to be sincere or that he had any honest purpose in so far as the trade union movement or the A. F. of L. was concerned."[71]

After 1924, however, the AFL did not need to grapple much with the inherent contradictions in its position, since for the next 12 years there were no repressive measures by the FBI directed against labor. That year the newly appointed, reformist Attorney General (and future Supreme Court Justice) Harlan Fiske Stone issued new instructions for the Bureau to desist from political investigations and to concentrate on crime alone. The General Intelligence Division, the principal FBI section engaged in political surveillance and harassment operations, was abolished.[72] It is apparent that J. Edgar Hoover did not follow these instructions to the letter; he did continue general surveillance of some labor unions (including the UMW and the IWW). Yet even in the TUEL the FBI kept only one infiltrated agent after 1924. The file that Hoover kept on suspected subversives (reputedly containing 2500 names) was not used to institute criminal proceedings against the individuals named or their organizations.[73]

Just as importantly, from 1924 to 1936, Hoover remained opposed to any re-authorization of the abolished GID – despite the repeated demands by conservative politicians and patriotic societies, as well as by key AFL leaders. In these years even the American Civil Liberties Union, formerly a key critic (and unbeknownst to its leaders, itself still under FBI investigation)[74], came to praise Hoover's stance on civil liberties. The AFL's Matthew Woll, on the other hand, publicly denounced what he felt was the ACLU's deleterious influence on the Bureau and demanded that the GID be reestablished.[75]

---

[70] Gompers cited in Powers, *Not Without Honor*, 70.

[71] Samuel Gompers, *Seventy Years of Life and Labor: An Autobiography*, vol. 2 (New York, 1925), 515–18.

[72] Regin Schmidt, *Red Scare: FBI and the Origins of Anticommunism in the United States, 1919–1943* (Copenhagen, 2000), 324–5; Rhodri Jeffreys-Jones, *The FBI: A History* (New Haven, 2007), 83–8.

[73] Schmidt, *Red Scare*, 326–9; Williams, "They Never Stopped Watching Us," 5–28; Richard Gid Powers, *Secrecy and Power: The Life of J. Edgar Hoover* (London, 1987), 229–30.

[74] Williams, "They Never Stopped Watching Us", 9–11.

[75] Powers, *Secrecy and Power*, 147–8, 148n12, 165–7.

When President Franklin Roosevelt finally did reestablish the GID (in 1936), he specifically instructed Hoover to resume investigations of suspected subversives. The initial authorization was expanded after the outbreak of the Second World War in September, 1939, to cover "investigative work related to espionage, sabotage, and the violations of neutrality regulations, and any other subversive activities." Propaganda "opposed to the American way of life" was further specified, as was all public talk that might stir up "class hatreds."[76] There remains disagreement among scholars over whether Hoover in his subsequent actions overstepped his presidential instructions or not.[77] The end result in any case was the same: the FBI returned to domestic spying and repression of selected labor unions.

In his own memoranda and public testimony on the key meetings with the President that led to this reversal of the 1924 policy, Hoover said that he had stressed the subversive potential of the International Longshoremen's Union, the United Mine Workers and the Newspaper Guild; these, he maintained, could "at any time paralyze the country." Each of the three included a sizable contingent of known Communists in leadership positions, making Hoover's claims not unreasonable. Once authorized to resume GID operations, Hoover however issued instructions for his agents to start investigating and infiltrating not only the specified Communist-led organizations (and several Fascist ones) but all of the coal, garment, maritime and newspaper industries. He specified that "activities in Organized Labor organizations" were of particular interest – regardless of actual subversive activity in the present, for it was the *future* potential of said labor groups that concerned to him.[78]

On this basis, informants and infiltrators were placed in several major labor unions. In 1940, President Roosevelt himself further instructed the Bureau to employ so-called "suicide squads", that is, special FBI units engaged break-ins, wiretapping and the stealing of union documents. Their employment was to take place specifically in connection of labor disturbances. On this authority, constitutionally highly suspect wiretaps were placed, among others, at the CIO, UMW and UAW offices and break-ins were conducted at the CPUSA and

---

[76] The words are Hoovers. See Powers, *Secrecy and Power*, 232–3.

[77] Studies maintaining that the resumption of surveillance of radical labor groups took place on Roosevelt's orders include Jeffreys-Jones, *The FBI*, 120–25, Schmidt, *Red Scare*, 341–2, and Powers, *Secrecy and Power*, 229–30. Theoharis, *The FBI and American Democracy*, 45–6, claims that Hoover overstepped his instructions.

[78] Theoharis, *The FBI and American Democracy*, 45–6; Powers, *Secrecy and Power*, 232–3.

the American Youth Congress' offices.[79] Most notoriously of all, in February, 1940, the FBI conducted raids at the homes of several members of the Abraham Lincoln Brigade, a group of volunteers in the Spanish civil war. Those arrested were then publicly paraded before representatives of the press as dangerous Communist subversives. While some three-quarters of the Brigade's 2,800 members were, in fact, Communists, most of those arrested appear not to have been. They were non-Communist members of the CIO's UAW union.[80] What happened to the Abraham Lincoln Brigade, then, was a prime example of union members being targeted, *cum* union members, because of the perception deeply entrenched in the FBI that labor unionism somehow equated with communism.

The FBI's post-1936 repression of labor should not be overstated, however. In fact episodes such as the arresting of the Abraham Lincoln Brigade members on false basis continued to be exceptional. For the most part, after 1936 and into the second Great Red Scare of the 1940s, the FBI was simply engaged in gathering information by way of infiltrators and informants, information that was placed on file rather than used for actual prosecuting of union members. This information gathering, too, was facilitated by SDF and the AFL members who kept sending information on specific known or suspected Communists in the unions. Even the legendary émigré leader of the Russian Mensheviks Raphael Abramovitch participated in this exchange of gossip and accusation with Bureau agents.[81] Another key group of labor informants could be found in the Jesuits who worked as labor priests in CIO unions and in the staunchly anti-communist Association of Catholic Trade Unionists, created in 1936.[82]

The two other major government agencies that were involved in surveillance of suspected radicals – the so-called Negative Branch of the Military Intelligence Division (MID) in the Department of War and the Office of Naval Intelligence (ONI) – were just as active as the FBI. In 1922, a leak exposed the MID's assumption that the AFL as well as the IWW and the CPUSA were "organizations or elements hostile to or potentially hostile to the government of

---

[79] Schmidt, *Red Scare*, 341, 358–9; Theoharis, *The FBI and American Democracy*, 58; Jeffreys-Jones, *The FBI*, 125.

[80] Jeffreys-Jones, *The FBI*, 132, 138.

[81] P.E. Foxworth to Sol Levitas, February 12, 1940, New Leader Records, box 1, Tamiment Institute Library and Robert A. Wagner Labor Archives, Elmer Bobst Library, New York University.

[82] For details, see Steve Rosswurm, *The FBI and the Catholic Church, 1935–1962* (Amherst, 2009), 240–50, 253–6; Douglas Seaton, *Catholics and Radicals: The Association of Catholic Trade Unionists and the American Labor Movement from the Depression to Cold War* (Lewisburg, 1981).

this country."[83] While the MDI ceased its domestic surveillance in 1924 (until the beginning of the Second World War), the ONI stayed in the field, watching Communist aliens as well as several radical African American organizations. In 1924 it committed a burglary of the Federal Council of Churches, a key ally of organized labor at the time, and five years later they did the same at the New York City headquarters of the CPUSA. From 1940, both agencies actively infiltrated communist front organizations, radical student groups and selected CIO unions.[84]

Local and Private Agencies' Repression

While not insignificant, federal surveillance and repression of labor radicals paled in comparison with that practiced by state, county and municipal authorities and by the varied patriotic societies and vigilante groups. In many instances, federal agencies supported, facilitated and sometimes inspired these actions. J. Edgar Hoover, for one, decided soon after the Palmer raids to transfer as many of his open cases as possible to states where wartime anti-sedition or prewar anti-syndicalist laws remained still in force, or where new ones had been instituted. It behooved the FBI to effect such a transfer since once the First World War had ended (and before the new federal anti-subversive legislation of the 1940s), the federal government did not have the authority to prosecute subversives.[85] On this basis, considerable sharing of information took place with the "red squads" of local police departments (which often were funded by business groups) and with the patriotic societies that had campaigned for increased FBI powers throughout the 1920s and 1930s.[86]

Given that probably most of the "red squad" and patriotic societies members were not anti-Communists in the strict sense but rather *anti-communists* – that is, not concerned with the activities of actual Communist Party members or Soviet spies only but representatives of a much broader anti-collectivist pro-free enterprise worldview – it was a foregone conclusion that they would use the materials provided to repress and intimidate all non-accommodationist labor.

---

[83] Roy Talbot, Jr., *Negative Intelligence: The Army and the American Left, 1917–1941* (Jackson, MS, 1991), 216–17, 221.

[84] Talbot, *Negative Intelligence*, 223–35, 260–66; Kornweibel, *"Seeing Red,"* 16, 174–7; Jeffery Dorwatt, *Conflict of Duty: The U.S. Navy's Intelligence Dilemma, 1919–1945* (Annapolis, Naval Institute Press 1983).

[85] Goldstein, *Political Repression in Modern America*, 171–5, 177–9.

[86] Williams, "'They Never Stopped Watching Us,'" 10–11, 14–15; Theoharis, *The FBI and American Democracy*, 30–31; Schrecker, *Many Are the Crimes*, 50–52, 61–9.

There were significant interconnections, too, between many of the patriotic societies and the key federal agencies engaged in domestic surveillance, given that some of the latter (and the umbrella group speaking for most of them, the American Coalition of Patriotic Societies) were led or advised by former FBI or MID agents.[87]

In several key labor struggles in the Southern states, appeals to racial prejudice were also used to great effect by local authorities and business groups, as well as by vigilante organizations such as the Ku Klux Klan, the White Knights of Mississippi and, on occasion, by the AFL itself (it was a segregated organization at this time). In some regions KKK and similar organizations were deputized by company owners and local authorities in place of or side by side with hired deputies and local police. Employment of racial prejudice to buttress conservative anti-communism was particularly glaring during the prolonged corporate resistance to the Southern Tenant Farmers Union and the Sharecroppers' Union that rocked the South in the 1930s. In both of these cases, the Communist Party was, in fact, behind some of the industrial action and unionization efforts that were launched by these unions, but that did not mean that the majority of those striking were themselves Communists or engaged in subversion. However, the ranks of labor could effectively be divided (in the South particularly but not only there) by appeals that combined race (and sometimes religion, as well) with anti-communism.[88]

The most widely noted of all the interwar era's instances of labor repression by state and private agencies took place in the Harlan County, Kentucky, coalfields in 1931. In "Bloody Harlan", as the region was to be known in labor lore forever after, union organizing had been practically non-existent for decades and the open shop enforced, often brutally, by the coal industry in alliance with local officials and police forces. Into this situation came the non-Communist United Mine Workers organizer William Turnblazer, and under his initial direction a strike of some 11,000 workers began for better living and working conditions and higher wages. That strike was brutally suppressed by the coal companies' armed deputies who engaged the (equally if less impressively) armed strikers in pitched battles that left three deputies and one miner dead. The anti-communist argument was used to justify all this repression and the state's anti-syndicalism laws invoked to indict the strikers. Communists had *not* been the

---

[87] Powers, *Not Without Honor*, 79–81; Kornweibel, *"Seeing Red,"* 81.

[88] For details, see Donald Grubbs, *Cry from the Cotton: The Southern Tenant Farmers Union and the New Deal* (Chapel Hill, 1971); Jeff Woods, *Black Struggle, Red Scare: Segregation and Anti-Communism in the South, 1948–1968* (Baton Rouge, 2004); Paul Harvey, *Freedom's Coming: Religious Culture and the Shaping of the South from the Civil War through the Civil Rights Era* (Chapel Hill, 2005).

main instigators of what had taken place – but they *did* take the lead in what followed after the invoking of anti-syndicalism laws frightened the UWM away and the CPUSA's National Miners Union took over.[89]

The new round of repression that met the NMU-organized follow-up strike in 1932 was, once again, argued in terms of anti-communism (and, given the CPUSA's actual lead role, rather more persuasively than during the initial strike). However, even in this second Harlan County strike, most of the workers who initially had flocked to the Communists' standard peeled away once their local leaders discovered and began broadcasting the fact, apparently unknown to Kentucky's highly religious miners until then, that the Communists were atheists and admirers of Soviet Russia.[90]

Genuine concerns about Communist infiltration of unions undoubtedly played a role in what took place in Harlan County. But much else was at work, as well, both in this outbreak of repression and elsewhere in similar incidents. The industrialists and local officials who unleashed the repression were uninterested in the minutiae of whether a Communist was actually in charge of a given industrial action and whether the action sought only concrete improvements in wages and work conditions rather than the wholesale undermining of the capitalist system. For at least some of those responsible for the repression, all labor organizing was anathema. This reality was shown clearly in the three major strikes of the 1920s (and two in the early 1930s) that were organized not by CIO Communists but by the staunchly anti-Communist AFL.

The Elizabethton, Tennessee, textile strike of 1929 and the near-simultaneous Marion county, South Carolina, textile strike were put down by local authorities with injunctions that were obtained against the AFL as an alleged subversive organization. State troops, hired deputies and local vigilante groups were used to drive clearly non-subversive organizers out of the areas involved. A similar fate befell the 1934 truck drivers' strike that was led by the AFL Teamsters in Minneapolis, falsely accused of being Communist initiated and aimed at overthrowing the government, as well as the AFL automobile workers strike in Toledo and a major West Coast maritime strike, both in that same year. In each of these cases, the amassed powers of special deputies, National Guardsmen and company-hired strike-breakers were used in the name of anti-communism to put down a strike that originally had little connection with any Communist Party affiliated group. Trotskyists *were* involved in Minneapolis and Toledo and the leader of the West Coast maritime strike, Harry Bridges, would later join the

---

[89]   See John W. Hevena, *Which Side Are You On? The Harlan County Coal Miners, 1931–1939* (Urbana, 1978); Alessandro Portelli, *They Say in Harlan County: An Oral History* (New York, 2010); Theodore Dreisel et al. (eds), *Harlan Miners Speak* (New York, 1970).

[90]   Cochran, *Labor and Communism*, 55.

Communist Party, but there is scant evidence to support the charges made at the time (and later in court proceedings) about these strikers having had secret plans for mass revolutionary insurrection.[91]

In each of these cases, non-Communist unionists were harassed as alleged Communists. In other places this fate befell the Socialist Party's members. The KKK and other vigilante organizations disrupted their organizing in a major way and not only in the South.[92] Local police forces often cooperated with vigilantes – as in Old Forge, Pennsylvania, in 1923, when they kidnapped and deported several Socialists after a public meeting of theirs. In Boston a year later the local authorities banned all public meetings by Socialists. During the California maritime strike of 1922, the Passaic textile strike of 1927 and the Gastonia textile strike of 1929, as well as during several miners' strikes in 1920–27, injunctions were used liberally, anti-syndicalism laws invoked and police and privately hired detectives employed in great numbers. Each of the named strikes did include IWW and/or CPUSA organizers but Socialists as well and many who were neither.[93]

All in all, it has been estimated that in 1920–30 federal and state courts issued over 900 injunctions against labor unions engaged in industrial action (this would have constituted about half of *all* injunctions issued in the 50 years after 1880). It has also been estimated that up to nine-tenths of National Guard active duty in 1920–24 alone related to the suppression of strikes that allegedly involved the CPUSA.[94] While most of this repression was by state and local authorities, it did have U.S. Supreme Court backing through the Hitchman doctrine and subsequent decisions on the secondary boycott. Finally, the state anti-syndicalism laws of the World War I era that had been largely dormant since the early 1920s were once again employed against significant numbers of labor, and deportations of known or alleged radical aliens increased from one in 1929 to more than 50 in 1932 and to 74 in 1933. With the beginning of the Second World War, more new anti-syndicalism laws and other legislation curbing labor rights was passed on the local and state levels than had been the case even in 1919.[95]

---

[91] Goldstein, *Political Repression in Modern America*, 190–91; Cochran, *Labor and Communism*, 36–8, 88–9; Bud Schultz and Ruth Schultz (eds), *The Price of Dissent: Testimonials to Political Repression in America* (Berkeley, 2001), 34–43.

[92] Wilbur Sheron to Socialist Party National Office, September 12, 1923, Socialist Party of America Papers, reel 10.

[93] Goldstein, *Political Repression in Modern America*, 178–9, 186–90.

[94] Montgomery, *The Fall of the House of Labor*, 271; Goldstein, *Political Repression in Modern America*, 183–4.

[95] Goldstein, *Political Repression in Modern America*, 197, 202, 255, 259–60.

Towards the Cold War

By 1941, there was little to differentiate the counter-subversive Right's onslaught upon suspect labor from that of the anti-Communist Left. While the AFL had suffered from the repression in places such as Toledo, Minneapolis and Elizabethton, by the time the United States joined the Second World War, they, too, were fully behind the new spate of counter-subversive legislation that was put on the books and much less given than ever before to joining civil liberties campaigns. The same can be said about the right-wing Socialists gathered in the SDF and the *New Leader*, for by the early 1940s some of them had come to think that it would be "foolish and sentimental" to afford civil rights to Communists, given that a Communist would only use such rights in an attempt to gain power to destroy all democratic institutions.[96] By the early Cold War, both of these labor groups' anti-Communism was much closer to that of the political Right than to the Cold War liberals.

While anti-Communist labor's sentiments did not in themselves generate the triumvirate of new counter-subversive acts (the Hatch Act of 1939, the Smith Act of 1940 and the Voorhis Act of 1940) that would be used for the duration of the world war against all groups suspected of planning or supporting a violent overthrow of the government, they did contribute to the wide public acceptance of these laws. The SDF's Algernon Lee, for example, gave his strong endorsement to the wartime imprisonment of the CPUSA leader Earl Browder under the Smith Act. When so doing, he emphatically denied that this man had been jailed for his opinions; rather, Browder was in jail as an "agent of the Russian government" who was engaged in an attempt to use American freedoms to undermine democracy, something that democracy had every right to prevent.[97] In the case of the Voorhis Act (it compelled the registration of organizations advocating the violent overthrow of the government or were otherwise subservient to a foreign power), there was even a direct linkage to labor anti-communism, given that the drafter of this particular piece of legislation was a former Socialist and a close collaborator of the SDF circle.

The AFL having already been purged of Communists, its leaders started now to focus on foreign affairs. There was a logical progression at work here, for the men who led the AFL's new International Affairs Department and the American Institute for Free Labor Development were the same ones who in the interwar years had fought against Communists in CIO unions and cooperated

---

[96] August Claessens to D. Shier, August 30, 1943, Social Democratic Federation of America Records, reel 16.

[97] Algernon Lee's notes for a radio address, April 11, 1942, Lee Papers, reel 61.

with federal investigators.[98] They had never compartmentalized the domestic Communist threat and the global, nor did they do so now. In February, 1944, the SDF for example called on the federal government to give all possible aid to the "traditional liberal and labor forces in Europe", none to Communists or those sympathetic to Communists – *and* to make sure that all government agencies be "thoroughly cleaned of all totalitarian communist elements who may have succeeded in penetrating into them." With this demand went the accompanying call for labor unionists to beware of Communists in their midst and to refuse all united fronts with CPUSA members or fronts.[99]

These kinds of demands paved the way to the labor and socialist participation in the postwar years' McCarthyite Red Scares. There was a continuity between what anti-Communist labor had done in the interwar years and what they did during the Cold War, a continuity in perceptions of the enemy, in goals – and in the willingness to cooperate in repression by government agencies. By the late 1940s and early 1950s, the SDF was in frequent touch with the FBI, cooperating with agents that the Bureau sent to its offices, while the AFL cooperated with congressional investigators and encouraged them to expose what Matthew Woll continued still to call "the Russian worldwide Fifth Column outfit" in the labor unions.[100] The SDF's erstwhile national secretary James Oneal even proposed in 1950 that a new federal law be passed that would penalize the leaders and declare illegal any political party, social club *or labor union* that had for a specified number of years followed the "policy of any foreign dictatorship."[101] In that same year, the SDF's Esther Friedman thundered that "sheer self-preservation demands that all Communists be liquidated." The Korean War being by then underway, she and like labor right-wingers felt that "there is no hope for Social Democracy until all peoples are freed from the fear of the aggressor."[102]

---

[98] See Ted Morgan, *A Covert Life: Jay Lovestone, Communist, Anti-Communist, and Spymaster* (New York, 1999).

[99] Resolution adopted at the Social Democratic Federation's executive committee meeting, February 19–22, 1944, Social Democratic Federation of America Records, reel 15.

[100] August Claessens to Leo Meltzer, January 5, 1952, Social Democratic Federation of America Records, reel 15; August Claessens to Harry Lerner, February 11, 1953, ibid., reel 15; Matthew Woll to Abraham J. Multer, June 11, 1947, Jay Lovestone Files, box 15, AFL International Affairs Department, RG 18–003, George Meany Memorial Archives, Silver Spring, Maryland.

[101] James Oneal to the editor of the [Los Angeles?] *Mirror*, August 31, 1950, Oneal Papers, box 1.

[102] "Greetings from Esther Friedman," *Social Democratic Federation U.S.A. 14th Anniversary Celebration Souvenir Journal* (1950), np.

Conclusion

All in all, then, key leaders of the American Federation of Labor and of some of its strongest craft unions, as well as the major right-wing socialist organizations of the interwar era, the Social Democratic League and the Social Democratic Federation, ended up complicit in much of the repression of labor radicals that took place in the 1920s through the mid-1940s. These labor anti-communists did, indeed, protest against counter-subversive excesses but more often than not they accepted what local and state officials were doing and hoped that the FBI and the Dies Committee would have done much more than they did. Conversely, and despite their many protestations to the contrary, by the mid-to-late 1930s some of the radical unions in the CIO and local labor organizations such as the ALP ended up under Communist leadership.

The repression of the latter (and those suspected or claimed to have belonged to the latter) by federal, state and private agencies could not have taken place in the degree and in the ways that it did take place had the leaders of the AFL and the right-wing socialist groups not accepted the core assumptions about the immensity of the Communist threat that cohered the interwar era's varied counter-subversive drives. The purposes and ultimate aims of anti-Communist labor groups were different from those responsible for the bulk of interwar political repression, and for this reason we can justifiably call these groups anti-Communists proper rather than anti-communists. At the same time, we need to recognize the fluidity of the demarcation lines between the two groupings and acknowledge that labor opponents of Communists sometimes did cross over.

It is impossible to draw a firm, fast and simple line between the repressors and the repressed in the 1920s through the mid-1940s where employers and government bureaucrats would somehow have stood all on one side and labor and socialists all on the other. In the repression of non-Communist political and labor union activism that did take place between the world wars large parts of the labor and socialist movement, too, were complicit. They were complicit because they so thoroughly agreed with the period's conservatives that Communism was an immediate and massive threat to all free American institutions, including labor unions, and to the survival of the United States itself, that it had to be resisted even if the resistance ran the risk of hurting some unintended and undeserving people.

Chapter 8

Premature McCarthyism:
Spanish Republican Aid and the Origins
of Cold War Anti-Communism

Eric Smith

In the early morning hours of February 6, 1940 orchestrated home raids by the FBI in Detroit and Milwaukee resulted in the indictments of 11 activists formerly associated with the Medical Bureau, an organization that had been deeply involved in raising relief aid for the Spanish Republic, which had finally succumbed to Francisco Franco's forces nearly a year before. The charges stemmed from accusations that the 11 had recruited men into a foreign army. In many respects the event marked the beginning of a new phase in American politics that would call men and women to account for their earlier associations even when based on false information. Yet the Loyalist Indictments as they are often called (because sympathizers to Spain's Republic were dubbed Loyalist by the press) were but one egregious manifestation of a much larger trend then underway.

Many of the Spanish Republic's supporters in the United States faced retribution later on. The more famous cases involved International Brigade veterans during World War II and Hollywood 10 defendants Alvah Bessie and Herbert Biberman, both of whom were actively involved in activities for the Spanish Republic (the former serving in the International Brigade, the latter in relief aid). Anti-Communist intimidation of the Spanish Republic's defenders, however, dates back to early in the war, and the 1940 raids marked a turning point in the consequences of Popular Front activities. While Communists formed a large segment of those involved in Spanish Republican activities, they were by no means the only ones concerned. They were also not the only ones targeted later for their premature antifascism.[1]

---

[1]   A Library of Congress electronic subject search conducted in December 2006 turned up 4,977 entries under "Communism," 2,058 for "World War, 1939–1945," 1,704 on the "United States History Civil War, 1861–1865," followed by 1,148 for the "Spain History Civil War, 1936–1939." This put the Spanish conflict ahead of "Roosevelt, Franklin D. (Franklin Delano), 1882–1945" at 968 entries, "Cold War" at 879, and "Depressions 1929,"

The Spanish Relief Activities

The activities in question stemmed from the political effort to raise relief aid for the embattled Spanish Republic. These were not volunteers to fight in Spain, nor necessarily Communists, though there were plenty of party members. These were members of the foreign policy public concerned about the course of events in Europe where the conflict in Spain that erupted in July 1936 appeared to be the first phase of an anticipated general war. The conflict was far more complicated than a first battle of World War II and the complexities were easily exploited in this "low dishonest decade" by those who sought to gain political currency with partisan constituencies.[2]

A short sketch of the course of events in Spain should suffice in illustrating the contours of the period. Spain had entered the Depression decade by establishing a republic after nearly seven years of dictatorship. The new democratic secular government rested upon a precarious foundation in a state long-dominated by the Catholic Church and where the military had intervened 13 times in the previous century. The Second Republic underwent three elections cycles in its eight-year history, beginning with a center-left government, followed by a center-right coalition in 1934, and finally by its final Popular Front coalition in 1936. That last government had only three Communist ministers but aroused the indignation of the far right with its increased pushes for secular education and the increasing attenuation of traditional privileges of the church.

In July 1937, half of the Spanish army rose in rebellion, assisted by Mussolini's fascist air force. Short of backing by the Nazis and Italy's fascists, the rebellion would have been quickly retired. Instead the internationalization of the conflict had two consequences. The first was that the British feared the ire of Hitler and Mussolini if they were actually to be punished for their roles, so in the name of appeasement, the League of Nations following Britain's lead chose to isolate the Spanish government under the auspices of neutrality legislation that undermined the traditional rights of nations to put down insurrections. The second consequence stemmed from the Nazi-fascist backing of Franco's insurgent forces and that was the decision of Joseph Stalin to begin assisting the Republic in October (after several months of insisting that Spain's was nothing

---

which generated 157 entries. For details on the inaccuracy see Eric S. Smith, American Relief Aid and the Spanish Civil War (Columbia: University of Missouri Press, 2103), 109–27.

2   Quote from W.H. Auden, "September 1, 1939," *The New Republic*, October 18, 1939, available at: http:// harpers.org/ archive/2010/06/hbc-90007252.

but a bourgeois revolution). Having been sold down the river by the Western democracies, Spain's democratic fate hinged upon Stalin's opportunistic whims.[3]

To conclude this cursory sketch, it is crucial to emphasize that Soviet Communists were meddling in the affairs of the Spanish state and the Spaniards had few options other than to cooperate. A civil war within the civil war emerged early on as the Communists sought to purge the military of non-Communists. Yet by the end of the conflict those Communists were also being purged by the faltering Republic. This was a war with many dimensions.

These complexities found few sympathizers in this era. The Hearst Press, in particular, characterized the Republic as Communist. Hearst wrote in July 1936 that "Spain today is prey to the same forces of national disintegration that are working in France and Belgium. This force is Communism ... And what has happened in France and Spain can happen here ... To be conscious of this danger is to tighten up our Americanism."[4] "Red Spain" became the short cut pejorative for which no further consideration was necessary.

On the political left, an international aid effort quickly coalesced around the defense of the Republic. This movement was politically broad in the United States if not very deep. Communists provided the footwork – the activists and organizational structures – as they had with the CIO in this period but generally permitted broad representation. The Medical Bureau and North American Committee to Aid Spanish Democracy emerged as the forerunners of the effort, though there were other organizations as well. This movement labored under immense pressures both internal and external that limited its achievements. Its sympathies for the Republic were its original sin with the Medical Bureau populated by party members from the outset.

McCarthy Era Spanish Cases

In the era of McCarthy Spanish aid activities were wheeled out as treasonous indiscretions, though a 1942 Civil Service Commission directive indicated

---

[3]   See, for example, Paul Preston, *The Spanish Civil War: Reaction, Revolution and Revenge* (London and New York, 2006), 135–62. For Stalin's opportunism see especially Geoffrey Roberts, "Soviet Foreign Policy and the Spanish Civil War, 1936–1939," in Christian Leitz and David J. Dunthorn, *Spain in an International Context, 1936–1959* (New York, 1999), 83.

[4]   O.W. Riegel, "Press, Radio, and the Spanish Civil War," *The Public Opinion Quarterly* 1, No. 1 (Jan., 1937): 131–6. Hearst quote from Rodney Carlisle, "The Foreign Policy Views of an Isolationist Press Lord: W.R. Hearst and the International Crisis, 1936–41," *Journal of Contemporary History* 9, No. 3 (Jul., 1974): 217–27.

assuming that associations of the Spanish Civil War "having any bearing on pro-communism" is better "scrupulously avoided."[5] This did not deter other legal battles, particularly among three major organizations (the Joint Anti-Fascist Refugee Committee, Veterans of the Abraham Lincoln Brigade, and the Abraham Lincoln Brigade).[6] Of the American veterans of the Spanish war only one was arrested in the United States upon his return, and his story is peculiar. A POW for seven months in one of Franco's prisons, Leo Hecht was a seaman prior to going off to Spain. He later turned informant for the government when it investigated the Veterans of the Abraham Lincoln Brigade (VALB). After his arrest, a Brooklyn grand jury refused to indict him. So no one as far as scholars have been able to determine no one was ever imprisoned for involvement in Spanish Civil War activities in the immediate aftermath of the conflict.[7]

Moreover, consider the cases of Paul Draper and Larry Adler to illustrate the McCarthy era's obsession with the Spanish Civil War period. Muriel Draper had been chair of the Women's Committee of the North American Committee. During the thirties, her husband Paul was the country's leading vaudeville dancer. He recalled later that his "political awareness had nothing to do with the Depression. It was the Spanish Civil War. It was around 1937, '38. I danced to raise money for the Spanish Loyalists." This landed him in trouble when he was blacklisted as a "Communist sympathizer." Draper and harmonica player Larry Adler filed a libel suit in 1949 against the accusers who put them on the list, but the jury was hung.[8] Adler moved to England while Draper was forced into retirement, never to work again.[9]

For José Rubia Barcia, a Spanish Republican exile who initially fled to Cuba, his opposition to Franco was enough to bring early McCarthyism down upon him. In 1943 he was able to enter the U.S. due to the intervention of a Princeton University professor. He was employed under the name Andrés Aragon by the Department of War Information but fired for refusing to translate a pro-Franco

---

[5] Quotes from Robert Justin Goldstein, *American Blacklist: The Attorney General's List of Subversive Organizations* (Lawrence, 2008), 105.

[6] The VALB and ALB were the only organizations ever ordered de-listed by the courts from the Attorney General's list of subversive organizations. See ibid., 314.

[7] Carroll, *Odyssey*, 305.

[8] Studs Terkel, *Hard Times: An Oral History of the Great Depression* (New York, 1986 [1970]), 372.

[9] This outline of Adler's story is available at: http://www.time.com/time/magazine/article/0,9171,805203,00.html;http://rmoa.unm.edu/docviewer.php?docId=wyu-ah08198.xml. An obituary can be found at: http://www.nytimes.com/2001/08/08/arts/larry-adler-political-exile-who-brought-harmonica-concert-stage-dies-87.html?pagewanted=all. See also John Cogley and Merle Miller, *Blacklisting: Two Key Documents* (New York, 1971), 150.

Premature McCarthyism 199

speech for re-broadcast in Spain. He then worked for Luis Buñuel, the Spanish surrealist film director. But when Buñuel left for Mexico in 1946, Aragon's visa forbade him to follow. Aragon found employment at the University of California – Los Angeles and was urged by immigration authorities to go to Canada to get a re-entry permit that would lead to permanent residency. The Dies Committee, in the meantime, accused Aragon of being a Communist probably because he had friends like Edwin Rolfe for whom he had once translated a poem to Spain ("Elegia"). This led to Aragon's arrest in Canada and jail in Seattle as he awaited deportation to Franco's Spain, where he certainly would have endured the caudillo's wrath. Only the intervention of the chancellor at UCLA forestalled deportation and permitted his eventual citizenship.[10]

The most famous early case of legal sanctions came in January 1946. It was now HUAC (the postwar successor to the Dies Committee) that began exerting pressure and demanding the donor list for the Joint Anti-Fascist Refugee Committee, one of the successor organizations to the North American Committee. Edward Barsky and the organization's secretary, Helen Bryan, refused to furnish the request. They were both jailed as were others who refused to assist the investigation. During the war in Spain, Barsky led a contingent of medical personnel forming a sort of International Brigade of doctors and technicians. He had been and remained an activist party member. People with ties to the JAFRC lived under the shadow of HUAC's demands, and the Supreme Court refused protection in such cases when it heard Barsky's appeal in 1948. The ties of Communists to the JAFRC were reason enough to attract official suspicion to the group. Aggravating the problem, Gerhart Eisler, who was under investigation by the FBI for a range of activities, was also making frequent visits to the New York office of the JAFRC and was one of numerous recipients of refugee aid from the group (and its "Julius Eisler" fund, named after a dead German Communist). By 1946 FBI mistakenly had made Eisler out to be the leader of the C.P. in the US. With Barsky and Bryan already imprisoned and now further aggravated by the Eisler case, the group was forced to sever its connection with Eisler. Later appeals by the JAFRC to be removed from the FBI's list of subversive organizations ended up all the way at the Supreme Court along with appeals by the International Workers Order and National Committee on American–Soviet Friendship. The Supreme Court was unmoved.[11]

---

[10] Gladys Nadler Rips, *Coming to America: Immigrants from Southern Europe* (New York, 1981), 120–21; see also June Namias *First Generation: In the Words of Twentieth-Century American Immigrants* (Boston, 1978), 99–108; Roberta Johnson, "Jose Rubia Barcia: Ethical Humanist," *Hispania* 80 (May 1997): 290–92.

[11] Robert Justin Goldstein, "The Grapes of McGrath: The Supreme Court and the Attorney General's List of Subversive Organizations in Joint Anti-Fascist Refugee

200   *Little 'Red Scares'*

Another high profile figure to face federal investigation for his Spanish Republican sympathies was Adlai Stevenson, the Illinois Senator who went on to be Illinois governor and presidential candidate. Following from Stevenson's 1937 application for an appointment to the Justice Department, the FBI had taken special interest in his activities in the 1930s, recording his affiliations with "subversive organizations." The FBI's collection on him was aired in a "summary memorandum" in 1952 just as Stevenson considered his presidential run.[12] According to the Church Committee, "Army Intelligence maintained files on Senator Adlai Stevenson and Congressman Abner Mikva because of their participation in peaceful political meetings under surveillance by Army agents."[13]

Anti-Communism

The broad brush of anti-Communism assumed McCarthyist form during the Depression when radical politics emerged to offer solutions to the era's ills. In the late thirties, the American Legion and anti-Communist Roman Catholics emerged as united forces resisting activities associated with Spanish aid efforts, which served as an obvious target. By far, Catholics were the major force resisting the formation of local aid networks. Legion activists provided intelligence services to the FBI and were a lesser organizing force. While not all Roman Catholics were predisposed to such activities, one particularly anti-Communist cross-section backed Franco and accepted without question the prevailing assumptions of Catholic writers on the benevolent nature of Franco's regime and the allegedly atheistic and Communistic Popular Front government in Spain. Often these Catholics also advanced isolationist sentiments within a

---

Committee v. McGrath (1951)," *Journal of Supreme Court History* 33, No. 1 (March 2008), 68–88. On Eisler see Ellen Schrecker, *Many Are the Crimes: McCarthyism in America* (Princeton, 1998), 124–8.

[12] Athan G. Theoharis, "Dissent and the State: Unleashing the FBI, 1917–1985," *The History Teacher* 24, No. 1 (Nov. 1990), 41–52; Kenneth O'Reilly, "Adlai E. Stevenson, McCarthyism and the FBI," *Journal of the Illinois State Historical Society* 81, No. 1 (Spring 1988): 45–60; Naftali Bendavid, "From FBI Files: Hoover's Grudge Match with Stevenson," *Chicago Tribune*, May 30, 1999, accessible at: http://articles.chicagotribune.com/1999–05–30/news/9905300183_1_fbi-files-hoover-governor-stevenson.

[13] *Intelligence Activities and the Rights of Americans, Book II, Final Report of the Select Committee to Study Governmental Operations with Respect to Intelligence Activities (Church Committee Report), United States Senate Together with Additional, Supplemental and Separate Views, April 26 (legislative day, April 14), 1976* citing 1973 Senate Judiciary Subcommittee on Constitutional Rights Report. Available at: http://www.icdc.com/~paulwolf/ cointelpro/cointel.htm.

context of anti-Communism.[14] The American Legion too, the historic purveyor of "Americanism," was one of the loudest voices opposing Spanish aid. In 1938 one local Legion post "raised hell and seemed to have scared everybody around" to the point that no one wanted to be involved in Spanish activities.[15] The case of aid to the Spanish Republic demonstrates that many Americans, if not disposed to what Malcolm Cowley characterized as the American right, nonetheless preferred sympathizing with Franco to sympathizing with the left.

The Roman Catholic anti-Communist impulse was officially sanctioned as the Vatican had re-iterated its historical position on Communism in Pope Pius XI's 1937 encyclical under the self-explanatory title, "On Atheistic Communism."[16] Combined with the view that Franco's army partook in communion every day and so could not possibly "indulge in rapine, mutilation and slaughter," it was little wonder that the insurgents were the Vatican's protagonists in Spain, and their transgressions were ignored. The Knights of Columbus, League of Catholic Women, and others all fell in line. The Social Action Department of the National Catholic Welfare Conference even formed a grassroots network to track the activities of Communists and the Popular Front organizations in the United States.[17] Supporting this resistance, Catholic media praised Franco's supposed defense of liberalism and democracy; meanwhile, the secular media offered targets for Catholic derision.[18]

Catholic activists threatened boycotts of the *Philadelphia Record* for an editorial in support of the Republic and the *New Orleans Times-Picayune* and *St. Louis Post-Dispatch* for their pro-Loyalist war coverage. The *New York Times*'s Lawrence Fernsworth, a Catholic, admitted being pressured by the church hierarchy to skew his writing. The pro-Republic documentary *Spain in Flames* was barred by a censor board in Pennsylvania; and the *Spanish Earth* in Detroit. The syndicated column by Westbrook Pegler, a Catholic, was dropped from many papers for his comment that "If I were a Spaniard who had seen Franco's missionary work among the children I might see him in hell but never in the Church." And Catholic priest Peter Whiffen was severely indicted for

---

[14]   Allen Guttman, *The Wound in the Heart: American and the Spanish Civil War* (New York, 1962), 25–51.

[15]   Harold Siegel to Jack Sherman, November 2, 1938, Harold Siegel folder, Part B, Box 31, Spanish Refugee Relief Organizations, Rare Book and Manuscript Library, Butler Library, Columbia University (SRRO).

[16]   Donald F. Crosby, "Boston's Catholics and the Spanish Civil War: 1936–1939," *New England Quarterly* 44, no. 1 (1971): 86, 99.

[17]   From *The Pilot*, cited in ibid., 87, 95; Reeves, *America's Bishop: The Life and Times of Fulton J. Sheen* (San Francisco, 2001), 104.

[18]   Guttman, *The Wound in the Heart*, 33.

202 *Little 'Red Scares'*

his criticisms not just on the church's stance toward the Spanish Civil War, but also for his claims that perhaps something is deeply wrong with the Catholic Church if a few Communists were able to do so much damage to the entrenched Catholic institutions of Spain.[19]

Among the most politically active Catholics were the Knights of Columbus. In Washington, D.C., each member of the Knights received a letter warning him that friends of "'Leftist Spain' and Communists were at work to lift the embargo."[20] After all, "Lifting the embargo would be a positive act of giving aid and comfort to a regime that bore the responsibility for one of the most cruel persecutions in modern times." It had, the writers perceived, denied religious freedom to its citizens, claims that found popular appeal. At least 4,000 people gathered together on January 9, 1939 in Constitution Hall where the first speaker of the evening was Martin Conboy of the Knights of Columbus and later Irwin Laughlin, American ambassador to Spain from 1929 to 1933. He told the audience that the Communists were so deeply entrenched in Spain that only Franco could restore Spanish democracy. Monsignor Fulton J. Sheen, a Catholic University professor and later one of the country's most popular Catholic theologians, was "perhaps the most effective speaker of the evening." He claimed he did not support Franco but did not want the U.S. involved in someone else's war. Combining isolationism and anti-Communism Sheen explained that the embargo should be kept because the groups who wanted it lifted were Communists, and the Spanish government, even if not red, still bore responsibility for the deaths of 11,000 Catholic clergy and the burnings of 20,000 churches and chapels by virtue of being unable to prevent these tragedies.[21] Aileen O'Brien, an Irish writer who had been in Franco's Auxilio Social (the social services of the insurgents) and had written of his commitment to liberal democracy, attested to the common sight of half-buried nuns and priests set aflame. Reportedly, 400,000 signatures filled petitions as a result of this meeting.[22]

On January 15, Father Charles Coughlin took to the airwaves on his radio show in Michigan to lambaste the organizations supporting the "Loyalist-Communists" and the claims of the "League for War and Dictatorial Communism" telling tales of how Franco's territories had no starvation or religious persecution, but "peace and order." Coughlin called Franco a "rebel for Christ, a rebel for humanity's sake" and claimed that Loyalists killed not just

---

[19]   F. Jay Taylor, *The United States and the Spanish Civil War* (New York, 1956), 150–1, 153–4.

[20]   J. David Valaik, "Catholics, Neutrality, and the Spanish Embargo, 1937–1939," *The Journal of American History* 54, no. 1 (June 1967): 73–85.

[21]   For additional context on the violence from both sides see Helen Graham, *The Spanish Republic at War 1936–1939* (Cambridge, UK and New York, 2002), 84–92.

[22]   Valaik, "Catholics, Neutrality, and the Spanish Embargo," 77–9.

12,500 clerics but also 300,000 women and children.[23] Thousands more appeals arrived to legislators after Coughlin's broadcast.[24]

Active resistance was also evident in Springfield, Illinois where local Catholics organized their own "non-partisan" – in this case pro-Franco – effort with Reverend James Griffin, bishop of Springfield, in alliance with Father Joseph Moisant. Moisant was not only chair of the American Spanish Relief Organization (ASRA) and pastor of St. Joseph's in Springfield, but also chaplain to the American Legion. The ASRA was one of four pro-Franco aid organizations in the United States during this period.[25]

Further north in the heartland in Davenport, Iowa, a city of 62,092, the story was similar.[26] (Incidentally, Herbert Kline, the director of the Spanish Civil War propaganda film *Heart of Spain*, and radio propagandist in Madrid, grew up there.)[27] Due to its proximity to Illinois, Davenport proponents of Spanish aid worked with peers in Rock Island, Illinois, but also other more distant small cities like Madison, Wisconsin. Again the local Catholic Church and American Legion along with the local Chamber of Commerce erected so many barriers to Spanish aid efforts that the North American Committee found it impossible to form a permanent organization in the tri-cities region. As one local aid organizer reported, "[The tri-cities community of 150,000] is virulently open shop, the Catholic Church is very much a power, and the Chamber of Commerce, the Manufacturers Association, the Knights of Columbus, and the American Legion are perfect types of what such groups should be."[28]

---

[23]   The phrase is a play on the Communist organization the American League against War and Fascism which by that time had been renamed the American League for Peace and Democracy. From *Brooklyn Tablet*, January 21, 1939, cited in ibid., 81–2.

[24]   Ibid., 82.

[25]   The material on pages 202 and 203 is borrowed from Smith, American Relief, 81–83, 89; "Program to Aid Victims of War in Spain Organized," *Illinois State Journal*, December 21, 1937, 9; News clipping, December 21, 1937, Illinois, Springfield, Part K, Box 11, SRRO.

[26]   The area is now called the quad-cities but at the time earned its name from the actually quite dispersed cities Davenport, Rock Island, and Moline. Population statistics are from "Davenport's Population is 62,092," *Davenport Democrat and Leader*, September 27, 1936.

[27]   William Alexander, *Film on the Left: American Documentary Film from 1931 to 1942* (Princeton, Princeton University Press, 1981), 159.

[28]   Reissig to Horace Kallen, January 7, 1937; Kallen to Hodgson, January 5, 1937; Reid to Reissig, May 20, 1937, all in Iowa, Davenport, Part K, Box 11, SRRO. Quote from Blything to Reissig, May 15, 1937.

The American Legion and the Origins of Government Interest in Spanish Aid

The Legion's intelligence activities were another matter and had greater consequences than shutting down political organizing. In Massachusetts, Senator Thomas Burke chaired a state version of HUAC – the Special Commission to Investigate Communistic, Fascist, Nazi and Other Subversive Groups, founded in 1937. Its search for Communist involvement in Spanish issues was based on the intelligence gathering of James Rose and Leo Halloran, former commanders of the American Legion in the state. Burke's commission had access to insider information on the party, one source of which was the National Guard, which had been investigating Communists for 10 years. The other source was local police. The committee published hundreds of names of people labeled Communists or sympathizers and thus "made it extremely difficult for Popular Front activities in Massachusetts to continue in 1937 and 1938." Among those who made use of this naming of names were the local Knights of Columbus, who managed to pressure local governments into censoring pro-Loyalist films. Pro-Franco meetings were permitted, however, including one in Fall River attended by the governor. Smith College professor Oliver Larkin, who was active in the Massachusetts Committee to Aid Spanish Democracy, was among those caught in the net of the investigations.[29] In this instance nothing came of the revelations that Larkin, like many others who joined the party during its anti-fascist period, had also became disillusioned with it.

At the federal level, early interest in Spanish aid was also evident in the Dies Committee hearings. In October 1939, Francis Henson, the former treasurer of the Committee on Fair Play in Sports and a former activist in the Medical Bureau, testified before HUAC on the Communist involvement in the republican aid movement. Henson contended that the Medical Bureau had been from the outset a Communist organization and that Browder initially opposed its merger with the NAC because the NAC was not party dominated.[30] "[A]

---

[29] Judith Larrabee Holmes, "The Politics of Anticommunism in Massachusetts, 1930–1960" (Ph.D. diss., University of Massachusetts Amherst, 1996), 79–89, 91–2. Larkin was already famous; he went on to win a Pulitzer for his 1949 book *Art and Life in America*. On Larkin see: http://sophia.smith.edu/blog/ smithipedia/smith-and-politics/ mccarthyism-at-smith/.

[30] There are good reasons to dispute Henson's claim of the NAC as a Communist organization, which are taken up in Eric R. Smith, "The Communist Party, Cooptation, and Aid to the Spanish Republic," *American Communist History* 8, No. 2 (2009): 137–64. The NAC was later designated a Communist organization anyway. See Goldstein, *American Blacklist*, 141–2.

very considerable amount [of funding] was spent for administrative purposes in raising the money," Henson contended. "It was largely spent on a very large office staff and office set-up." No figures were cited but the Dies Committee wanted prosecutions. "I think that a most thorough audit of the books of many of these organizations for relief purposes throughout the country is going to disclose a shocking situation of the misappropriation of the funds and of their use by certain people." J.B. Matthews, who was working with HUAC, tried to argue that Colonel William J. Crookston, a World War I veteran who had been at the founding meeting of the American Legion and was later involved in the Medical Bureau, was a Communist by his professional connections to Louis Gibardi, a Communist Party member involved in the MB. Other people involved in the aid movement, including President Roosevelt's Secretary of the Interior, Harold Ickes, were painted as Communist dupes. In all, the same broad brush that painted many of the later McCarthy era figures was already being used here.[31]

While Harry S Truman's executive orders have been characterized as partly responsible for the rise of McCarthyism, Franklin Roosevelt opened opportunities, as well, by sanctioning anti-Communist activity in this period. Roosevelt met with FBI Director J. Edgar Hoover in August 1936 to discuss domestic security threats. Hoover was prepared to counter concerns about the FBI's appropriations statute which limited bureau activities to criminal investigations by justifying his intent to include subversive activities in this endeavor by referencing a 1916 statute permitting investigations if they originated at the request of the State Department.[32] By coincidence, Spanish Civil War activities began that same month. The president then expanded the FBI's domain again on June 26, 1939 just as the general war was about to erupt when he issued a confidential memorandum that authorized all intelligence services – the FBI, Military Intelligence Division, and Office of Naval Intelligence – to investigate "all espionage, counter espionage, and sabotage matters." Subversive activities were not explicitly stated as the directive intended to limit FBI investigations to

---

[31] "Statement on the Description of the Spanish Refugee Relief Campaign in the Dies Committee Report to Congress," undated [probably December 1940], Dies Committee, Box 10, Part B, SRRO; Griffin Fariello, *Red Scare: Memories of the American Inquisition* (New York, 1995), 348, 442, 443; Carroll, *Odyssey of the Abraham Lincoln Brigade*, 285–8; Schrecker, *Many Are the Crimes*, 124–8; U.S. Congress, House of Representatives, Special Committee on Un-American Activities, *Investigation of Un-American Propaganda Activities in the United States*, 76th Cong, 2nd Sess., vol. 11 (October 24, 1939), 6370–6377.

[32] Frank J. Donner, *The Age of Surveillance: The Aims and Methods of America's Political Intelligence System* (New York, 1981 [1980]), 53.

206 *Little 'Red Scares'*

violations of federal statutes.[33] In May 1940, FDR wrote his Attorney General, Robert Jackson, that while he accepted the recent Supreme Court rulings that upheld the 1934 Telecommunications Law precluding intelligence gathering with new technologies, he didn't think those prohibitions applied to "grave matters involving the defense of the nation," which were arguably existent given the outbreak of war in Europe. In any case, Roosevelt ordered Jackson under executive privilege to proceed with the clandestine use of bugs and wiretaps to monitor "persons suspected of subversive activities ... including suspected spies."[34] "You are authorized and directed in such cases as you may approve ... to authorize investigating agents that they are at liberty to secure information by listening devices direct to the conversation or other communications of persons suspected of subversive activities."[35] All of this activity had the hallmark of a later era and gave FBI Director J. Edgar Hoover all of the ideological space he required for a broad interpretation of the orders.

The Detroit Cases

On the night of February 6, 1940 the FBI coordinated home raids in Detroit and Milwaukee to arrest a dozen activists who had been involved in the Medical Bureau. The case against the Detroit activists rested upon evidence compiled by the same sources as those who had assisted the Dies Committee, originating with activists of the Knights of Columbus and local police red squad. Knights of Columbus's John D. McGillis told Dies in October 1938 that "As secretary of the Detroit Council 305, of the Knights of Columbus, it has been part of my work to investigate un-American activities. I have been asked to do that." These activities included "recruiting of American youth for the Loyalist cause in Spain" based upon interviews with recruits. The most substantial source of information was an affidavit signed by Paul Padgett in June 1938.

Padgett, who was just 18 and unemployed at the time he volunteered (or at the time of "his recruitment" as the Dies Committee affidavit stated it), claimed that he was "induce[d] to attend the YCL [Young Communist League] school

---

[33]   Donner, *Age of Surveillance*, 57; Neal Katyal and Richard Caplan, "The Surprisingly Stronger Case for the Legality of the NSA Surveillance Program: The FDR Precedent," *Stanford Law Review* 60, No. 4, 1023–1078, accessible at: www.stanfordlawreview.org/system/files/articles/KatyalCaplan.pdf.

[34]   David Greenberg, "Let 'Em Wiretap!", July 6, 2002, *History News Network* at: http://hnn.us/articles/366.html.

[35]   Ward Churchill, Jim Vander Wall. *The COINTELPRO Papers: Documents from the FBI's Secret Wars against Dissent* (Boston, 1990), n 26, 338.

Premature McCarthyism

in Mena, Arkansas" by Mary Paige. The affidavit seems to suggest that induce should be read as "seduce" given the later incarnations of this line of argument. As the affidavit explains Padgett's recruitment to the IB: "Young Paul talked to [Phil] Raymond, who told him that he would make the arrangements and instructed him to go to the offices of Dr. Eugene Shafarman, 5320 John R. Street." It was there that he:

> ... was examined by Dr. Frederick C. Lendrum who, incidentally, was a candidate for coroner at our latest election and failed of nomination. He was also sent to see Dr. Verne C. Piazza, a dentist, with offices on the corner of Forest and Mount Elliott. Dr. Piazza pulled two of his teeth and filled others. He paid neither of these doctors. Neither asked him for money, and to this day he does not know who paid them for their services. Padgett returned to Raymond's office and was told by Raymond that they were having some difficulty in securing passports, and in order for him to leave at once it would be necessary that they fake a passport by using another name. This Padgett hesitated to do, and his hesitation saved him from becoming "lost" in the Spanish war.[36]

The line of argument is obvious here. A young innocent was duped into the recruitment process for the International Brigades but was saved from the fate of others less fortunate. McGillis's private vigilance of documenting health records showing that the doctors checking the volunteers for Spain charged the city for shots and other services, which the patients were entitled to under Detroit law, permitted an air of scandal to the claims. Supporting testimony to the committee by two Detroit police officers in that city's red squad permitted the pouring of a foundation that would build the affairs as red subversion.

The connection to the Medical Bureau rested upon spurious claims. The group had intended to remain apart from the Friends of the Abraham Lincoln Brigade (FALB), though its members knew people at the other organization. People who expressed interest in fighting in Spain were sent there from the MB. The witnesses called before Dies even admitted that the MB (the group's Sol Green, for example) didn't know how people went to Spain only that they did. Mitchell Webb, Secretary of the Detroit Medical Bureau had written to the New

---

[36] Block quote and foregoing paragraphs all from U.S. Congress, House of Representatives, Special Committee on Un-American Activities, *Investigation of Un-American Propaganda Activities in the United States*, 75th Cong, 3rd Sess., vol. 2 (October 11, 1938), 1241–45.

208   *Little 'Red Scares'*

York office requesting permission to merge the group's operation with Lincoln Brigade activities but was told not to do so.[37]

The raids the night of February 6 targeted a distinct Communist network. The accused included two Lincoln Battalion veterans, two doctors active in the local Medical Bureau, one female activist, and assorted others.[38] Harold Hartley, chaired the Detroit chapter of the International Labor Defense. Joseph Cohn was the editor of the YCL newspaper and served as the organization's national Educational Director. Frank Feldt, Jr. was active with the FALB, while Leon Davis and Robert Taylor both fought in the International Brigades. Taylor would go on to have a battle even in his death as the family attempted to have him interred in Arlington National Cemetery to the opposition of the political establishment. Philip Raymond ran for governor on the Communist Party ticket. Peter Kowal and Rudolph Schweir both were active in the Workers Alliance, the former as vice-president and the latter had been secretary. Three doctors directly tying the Medical Bureau to alleged IB recruitment were Eugene Shafarman, John Rosefield and Frederick Lendrum. Lendrum was practicing in Milwaukee at the time of the arrests. The only woman among the group was Mary Paige whose case attracted particular attention. Paige was the daughter of the former mayor of Dickersville, Michigan. Since July 1939, she had suffered from a medical condition in need of constant physician attention and consequently Paige's conditions of incarceration elicited widespread sympathy.

In his memoirs Communist leader Earl Browder recalled the Detroit incident: "The ensuing storm of public indignation was great enough to cause Washington to quash the indictments promptly. No official wanted to test how deep American sympathy was for the beleaguered Spanish Republic."[39] The Michigan Civil Rights Federation formed a support committee following the arraignment and later issued a white paper FBI Detroit (its title a play on FOB Detroit – "free on board" – a popular phrase at the time due to the transport of cars from the region and suggesting that the cars were free but the people were not).

Correspondence in the papers of the Medical Bureau to Aid Spanish Democracy suggests that there were other targets the federal authorities did not intend to arrest but rather sought only information from and intended to

---

[37]   Martha Fainaru to John Sherman, February 20, 1940, Detroit, Michigan folder, Box 16, Part K, SRRO; in the same folder see also Mitchell Webb to Sherman, March 23, 1939; Sherman to Webb, March 25, 1939; Sherman to Webb, March 25, 1939.

[38]   Ernest Goodman, "The Spanish Loyalist Indictments: Skirmish in Detroit," *The Guild Practitioner* 36 (Winter 1979): 1–13; *FBI Detroit: The Facts Concerning the FBI Raids in Detroit* (Detroit, 1940), 1–16.

[39]   Rita James Simon, *As We Saw the Thirties: Essays on Social and Political Movements of a Decade* (Urbana, 1967), 235.

intimate. Because of the Legion's claims, the local office appears to have been under FBI surveillance as early as 1938. Martha Fainaru wrote the Medical Bureau in New York that the Detroit offices had been raided.[40] Joe Clark, who does not show up on the list of the Detroit 12, was also arrested, as his wife Ruth called lawyer Ernest Goodman and set the legal defense of the 12 in motion.

None of the arrested was told what the charge was. It turns out they were being prosecuted under an 1818 statute that stated: "An act to prevent citizens of the United States from privateering against nations in amity with, or against the citizens of, the United States," which seems to leave open the Spanish case. Curiously, an 1896 case *Wiborg v. the United States* was later used to defend the very same type of recruitment by President Kennedy for the Bay of Pigs invasion with his brother Attorney General Robert F. Kennedy arguing that "the neutrality laws were never designed to prevent individuals from leaving the United States to fight for a cause in which they believed. Nor is an individual prohibited from departing from the United States, with others of like belief, to join still others in a second country for an expedition against a third country."[41]

Attorney General Robert Jackson, who had taken office on January 18, moved to dismiss the case on the grounds that every case of alleged recruitment would need to be prosecuted and this one was therefore inappropriate.[42] This disclaimer had the irony of laying the groundwork for exactly the opposite scenario in the coming years, though as demonstrated above, the systematic search for Spanish Republican supporters pointed in no particular direction. Once Jackson dismissed the case his District Attorney in Detroit refused to follow through on the dismissal, and Jackson was forced to send a special assistant to make the request to the judge, who was also irritated at the quashing of charges. The fact that the raids were made at all seems to hinge on the appointment of Jackson's predecessor to the Supreme Court (Frank Murphy), a point made by both contemporary reports and later by the defendants' attorney in the 1970s.[43]

---

[40]   Martha Fainaru to John Sherman, February 20, 1940, Detroit, Michigan folder, Box 16, Part K, SRRO; in the same folder see also Mitchell Webb to Sherman, March 23, 1939; Sherman to Webb, March 25, 1939; Sherman to Webb, March 25, 1939.

[41]   Edward K. Kwakwa, *International Law of Armed Conflict: Personal and Material Fields of Application* (Dordrecht, 1992), 116.

[42]   An excellent analysis of anti-Communism in Detroit in this period can be found in Alex Goodall, "The Battle of Detroit and Anti-Communism in the Depression Era," *The Historical Journal* 51, No. 2 (2008): 457–80.

[43]   Again see Goodman's piece and Goldstein as above. A Freedom of Information request by the author in late 2009 for the original investigation files (and for material on the other cases mentioned herein) has not yet led to the release of any further material from the Department of Justice that might shed light on Murphy's motivations.

210 *Little 'Red Scares'*

If one accepts Murphy's reputation as a civil libertarian, his role in this episode appears very strange indeed. Murphy's position on the court, however, evolved over time and his vehement anti-Communism was evident as much during his time as Attorney General as in his court decisions. Therefore, Murphy's civil liberties credentials would seem overplayed. The attorney for the Detroit case later argued that Murphy's decision to go ahead with these prosecutions (held in abeyance for over a year due to Dies Committee investigations) paved the way for his unanimous confirmation to the Court and also assured FDR of Catholic votes in his quest for an unprecedented third term as president. FDR may have had Catholic voters in mind in putting Murphy on the high court, but Murphy needed no prompting to pursue the Detroit case.

Furthermore, the blatant violation of rights suggests that the FBI and US Attorney did not expect the case to actually lead to jail time. This sort of use of official intimidation, which has a long history that has reached into the present, creates a chilling effect whose purpose, therefore, would seem to lie more in gaining public attention (for both active opponents of the Communists and their supporters) and in sending a message to others involved in such activities. In other words, heavy-handed tactics are not intended for any purpose other than as psychological operations.[44]

The case drew such attention that Senator Frank Norris, an old Progressive, made his last act as Senator an attack upon J. Edgar Hoover before the convened Senate. He criticized the return of the General Intelligence Division, which had been the source of the Palmer Raids in 1919 before the FBI was born. Nobody went after Hoover, but Norris was convinced the Director of the FBI had now grabbed entirely too much power and had to go: "I think a fair conclusion from the evidence taken ... must bear out the charge that the Federal Bureau of Investigation was guilty of conduct which ought not to be approved by the Attorney General, and which will not be approved, when understood, by all those who believe in justice and in the fair treatment of every man charged with a crime, be he black or white, great or small ... It is my humble judgment ... that

---

[44] Frank Donner lays out a theory for repression in which the consequences of intimidation are weighed over intelligence value in what he refers to as "the politics of deferred reckoning" (i.e. the costs of a trial are worth the value of stopping the progress of organizing). This would seem to be the same thinking that emerges later during the era of COINTELPRO when the FBI planned to "disrupt" and "neutralize" alleged subversives. This disruption thesis requires much more study to realize the extent to which it is official policy rather than existing as an ideological disposition. In any case, its basic premise seems easily illustrated in the above instances. See Donner, *The Age of Surveillance*, 3–7. See also the introductory discussion in Robert Justin Goldstein, *Political Repression in Modern America From 1870 to 1976* (Urbana and Chicago: University of Illinois Press, 2001 [1978]), xxi–xxxiv.

Mr. Hoover is doing more injury to honest law enforcement in this country by his publicity-seeking than is being done by any other one thing connected with his organization."[45] Norris's was a cry in the wind. The Senate enacted the Smith Act not long after.

Historians have trod upon this Catholic ground before. Roosevelt had shown a propensity to bend to a Catholic voting bloc, one that appears in the opinion of the president and administration insiders as monolithic in its behavior. But the treatment of the Catholics as a bloc dismisses any possibility of a varied opinion among Roman Catholics, an aged stereotype that has still not been shaken in American political culture.[46]

Just as important, the Detroit case originated with the convergence of several anti-Communist forces that in the thirties were just beginning to find institutional backing and supportive organizational structures. These included grassroots patriots trying to thwart "un-American" activities, the sanctioning of Congressional investigations, the return to counter-subversive measures on the part of the US's domestic police arm (the FBI), and the growing international crisis that offered legitimacy to concerns about subversion. Add the character of the FBI's chief to the maelstrom and the stage was set for the Detroit raids. Joseph McCarthy provided the encore.

---

[45] Rhodri Jeffreys-Jones, *The FBI: A History* (New Haven and London, 2007), 138–9; quote in Steve Babson, Dave Riddle and David Elsila, *The Color of Law: Ernie Goodman, Detroit, and the Struggle for Labor and Civil Rights* (Detroit, 2010), 79.

[46] See in particular Harold L. Ickes, *The Secret Diary of Harold L. Ickes* (New York, 1953) vol. II, 470; Valaik, "Catholics, Neutrality, and the Spanish Embargo, 1937–1939," 73–85.

Chapter 9

Laying the Foundations for the Post-World War II Red Scare: Investigating the Left-Feminist Consumer Movement

Landon R.Y. Storrs

In May 1939, a front-page story in the *Chicago Tribune* warned that a "Communist front" group called the League of Women Shoppers (LWS) was threatening to boycott the products of employers who did not comply with the National Labor Relations Act. Asserting that LWS members were "innocently or not ... fellow travelers of the communist party," the article stressed that many LWS activists were married to New Deal officials.[1] Two weeks later, the daughter-in-law of Interior Secretary Harold Ickes told the woman next to her at a luncheon that "the League of Women Shoppers is the fashionable thing to belong to in Washington now." Unbeknownst to Mrs. Ickes, her lunch companion was an undercover agent, whose report on the league soon reached the Special House Committee for the Investigation of Un-American Activities (also known as the Dies Committee).[2] In December 1939, the Dies Committee

---

[1]   "Bare Campaign of Intimidation on Wagner Act," *Chicago Tribune*, May 7, 1939, p. 1. The story hinted that fellow travelers at the National Labor Relations Board (NLRB) were leaking information to their wives in the LWS in order to generate the appearance of grassroots support for the NLRB. It named Washington DC LWS sponsors and officers Mrs. Mordecai Ezekiel (wife of the economic adviser to Secretary of Agriculture Henry Wallace), Mrs. William O. Douglas (wife of the Supreme Court justice), Mrs. Leon Henderson (whose husband had just moved from the Temporary National Emergency Council to the Securities and Exchange Commission), Mrs. John Collier (wife of the Commissioner of Indian Affairs) and her daughter-in-law Nina P. Collier (whose husband worked in the Department of Agriculture), Mrs. Ernest Gruening (wife of an Interior Department official), Miss Josephine Roche (National Youth Administration), Representative Caroline O'Day, D-NY ("great friend of Mrs. FDR"), Mrs. Ernest Lindley (wife of FDR's biographer), and Mrs. Donald Richberg, Mrs. Dean Acheson and Emily Newell Blair, whose husbands were former New Deal officials (Emily Blair herself had headed the Consumer Advisory Board to the National Recovery Administration).

[2]   Report of Helene Abbott, May 23, 1939, exhibit to report of Thomas J. Nash, Aug. 31, 1939, LWS-Chicago file, F&R: Orgs, Dies Committee Records, National Archives,

charged that most of the consumer groups that had burst onto the political scene since 1935—including the League of Women Shoppers, Consumers' National Federation, and several others—were controlled by Communists. Dies Committee researcher J.B. Matthews claimed that the Communist Party was exploiting consumer protests against "real or fancied abuses" in order to discredit "free enterprise in the United States."[3]

This was an early skirmish in a 30-year war against the consumer movement, waged in the name of anti-Communism by conservative business interests and their allies in government. This anti-Communist campaign damaged the movement by undercutting its grassroots support, pressuring its leaders to moderate their objectives, and, until recently, hindering its visibility to scholars. But the effect on the consumer movement is only the beginning of the story. Consumer activists had access to federal policymakers and in some cases obtained jobs in federal agencies. This article argues that in the late 1930s, right-wing hostility to these consumer advocates was an important source of the crusade against "Communists in government." At its peak in the late 1940s and early 1950s, that crusade would reshape the terrain of partisan politics and cramp the development of U.S. social policy. But the groundwork was laid earlier, well before Soviet espionage became a national concern. The anti-Communist attack on the New Deal—sometimes understood as triggered by the rise of mass production unionism under the CIO—also was a reaction against the emergence of a pro-labor, anti-racist and feminist consumer movement. Indeed it was the very conjunction of these movements—sit-down strikers demanding higher wages at the same moment that housewives demanded lower prices and higher quality—that was so alarming to American conservatives.[4]

Although some men were important to the consumer movement and some women were important to the labor movement, each movement's respective icon, the housewife and the male factory worker, did reflect an actual gender division of economic and political labor. Not only were most grassroots constituents of the consumer movement housewives, as observers then and since have recognized, but women also ran most of its non-governmental organizations and were among its key allies in government. A core group of thinkers, activists and policymakers was crucial to a succession of consumer initiatives that stretched from the 1930s through the 1960s, including women like Persia

---

Washington DC, hereafter Dies Records.

[3] "Dies Investigator says Reds Utilize Consumer Groups," *New York Times*, Dec. 11, 1939, 1.

[4] We have countless studies of the labor movement and of specific unions, strikes and activists, but only a handful of monographs on the consumer movement, and those studies have not been integrated into general syntheses on the New Deal or McCarthyism.

Investigating the Left-Feminist Consumer Movement   215

Campbell, Caroline Ware, Mary Dublin Keyserling and Esther Peterson. They provided a thread of continuity through voluntary associations including the National Consumers' League (1898–), League of Women Shoppers (1935–49), Consumers' Union (1935–), Consumers' National Federation (CNF, 1937–41) and National Association of Consumers (1946–54), in addition to consumer divisions of groups such as the American Association of University Women. Pressure from these organizations helped produce a series of consumer-oriented government agencies. During the New Deal, these included the Consumers' Advisory Board of the National Recovery Administration, the Office of the Consumers' Counsel in the Department of Agriculture, and the Temporary National Economic Committee. These initiatives were sustained during World War II through the National Defense Advisory Council and its successor, the sprawling and controversial Office of Price Administration. The government bodies were headed by men, but they were staffed chiefly by women from the voluntary organizations, who created a dense web of associations between private and government consumer groups.[5]

Although they did not use the term, these women were left feminists. Their pursuit of a vision of women's emancipation that insisted on class and racial justice as well as gender equality quickly drew the attention of anti-Communists.[6] Research in newly opened records reveals that counter-subversives investigated all the women named above and many others, often at great cost to their careers. Furthermore, many of those women were married to government officials— including prominent consumer-oriented economists such as Gardiner Means,

---

[5]   On a more modest scale after the war, the Consumers' Advisory Committee to the President's Council of Economic Advisers and similar committees under Presidents Kennedy and Johnson tried to keep consumer interests on the agenda. Campbell's major consumer associations were as follows: Consumers' National Federation, NCL, and New York State Consumers' Advisory Council. Ware's were the American Association of University Women consumer program, National Consumers' League, LWS, chair of Consumers' Advisory Committee to OPA, chair of Consumers' Clearing House, National Association of Consumers (NAC), chair of Consumers' Advisory Council to Council of Economic Advisers, and President's Consumer Advisory Council. Keyserling's were: LWS, NCL and NAC. Peterson's were the Consumers' Union, NCL, NAC and Special Assistant on Consumer Affairs to President Johnson.

[6]   Thus they differed with the National Woman's Party, which focused single-mindedly on the Equal Rights Amendment; left feminists opposed that amendment because it would have invalidated labor laws for women. To invoke Ellen DuBois's definition, left feminists fused "a recognition of the systematic oppression of women with an appreciation of other structures of power underlying American society"; DuBois, "Eleanor Flexner and the History of American Feminism," *Gender and History* 3 (1991), 84.

216 *Little 'Red Scares'*

Leon Keyserling, Leon Henderson, and Mordecai Ezekiel—who faced charges of Communist sympathies based at least in part on their wives' associations.[7]

Since the 1910s, a vanguard of consumerist thinkers—academics, reformers, and a few liberal businessmen and labor leaders—had argued that increasing "mass purchasing power" was vital to the nation's economic and political health. Raising the living standard of the working-class majority, they believed, was not only a matter of social justice, it was good economics. The Great Depression illustrated the U.S. economy's vulnerability to under-consumption and brought "purchasing power progressives" into office in Washington. They encouraged the burgeoning labor movement and implemented public works, public assistance, social insurance, minimum wage laws, and other measures to get money into the hands of the people. Significantly, they also encouraged consumer involvement in policymaking and implementation, to facilitate grassroots civic engagement and to ensure that employer concessions to labor unions did not come at the public's expense in the form of high prices or poor quality. An alliance of organized labor, consumers, and sympathetic policymakers challenged business prerogatives during the New Deal and World War II years, working through agencies such as the National Labor Relations Board (NLRB) and the Office of Price Administration (OPA). NLRB decisions sought to democratize the workplace and did much to strengthen the CIO, which was more welcoming to women and minorities than the older American Federation of Labor. The OPA, whose activities included mobilizing consumers to enforce price controls and rationing, melded technocratic planning with participatory democracy. The NLRB and OPA offered models of a strong interventionist state that were as alarming to the right as they were inspiring to the left. After the war, however, congressional and media conservatives took advantage of inflation to divide organized labor and consumers against each other, facilitating the OPA's demise and the weakening of the National Labor Relations Act with the Taft–Hartley Act of 1947.[8]

---

[7]   Caroline Ware was married to the New Deal economist Gardiner Means. Esther Peterson's husband was on the OPA labor advisory committee and later worked for the State Department. Mary Dublin Keyserling and Mrs. Leon Henderson (first name unknown) belonged to the NCL and LWS. Lucille Ezekiel was president of the Washington LWS. Donald Montgomery, consumers' counsel for the Department of Agriculture in the 1930s, married two consumer activists, first the Communist Sarah Adamson and then the socialist Mary Taylor.

[8]   The phrase "purchasing power progressives" is from Meg Jacobs, *Pocketbook Politics: Economic Citizenship in Twentieth-Century America* (Princeton, 2005). See Steve Fraser and Gary Gerstle (eds), *The Rise and Fall of the New Deal Order* (Princeton, 1989); Landon R.Y. Storrs, *Civilizing Capitalism: The National Consumers' League, Women's Activism, and Labor Standards in the New Deal Era* (Chapel Hill, 2000); Lizabeth Cohen, *A Consumers' Republic: The Politics of Mass Consumption in Postwar America* (New York, 2003); and Lawrence

To demonstrate the importance of the consumer movement in the reaction against the New Deal, this chapter focuses on the League of Women Shoppers, the Consumers' National Federation, and the fate of members of these groups who became government employees, particularly in the Office of Price Administration. The LWS and CNF have been studied less than the Consumers' Union, the other major consumer group of their day.[9] These organizations vividly demonstrate the ties to government officials that were a key source of strength before the Second Red Scare intensified in the late 1940s but an Achilles' heel thereafter. The LWS, which unlike the Consumers' Union was a women's organization, also stands out for its distinctly feminine direct action tactics and for the anti-feminist response it provoked. Left-feminist consumer groups should be included along with the better-known labor, antifascist, and civil rights causes as associations that were the kiss of death for individuals facing allegations of disloyalty. The stories of the LWS and CNF indicate the conservatives' gendered resistance to the consumer movement was one source of the federal employee loyalty program and the wider Red Scare.

In the spring of 1939, the Consumers' National Federation and one of its member groups, the League of Women Shoppers, did several things that antagonized powerful conservatives. The CNF filed a complaint against *Good Housekeeping* magazine that led the Federal Trade Commission to cite its owner, Hearst Magazines, for guaranteeing fraudulent advertising. CNF executive Persia Campbell also testified before the Temporary National Economic Committee (TNEC), a key platform for purchasing-power progressives. She warned that representatives of various industries were setting up bogus consumer groups in an effort to co-opt the "widespread consumer impulse to organize independently."[10] At that very moment, the Chicago LWS chapter was backing the American Newspaper Guild-CIO strike against Hearst's Chicago newspapers that culminated in an injunction against Hearst.[11] Meanwhile, the national LWS undertook its pro-National Labor Relations Act campaign,

---

Glickman, "The Strike in the Temple of Consumption: Consumer Activism and Twentieth-Century American Political Culture," *Journal of American History* 88, no. 1 (2001).

[9]   On the Consumers' Union, see Kathleen Donohue, *Freedom from Want: American Liberalism and the Idea of the Consumer* (Baltimore, 2003); Glickman, "Strike in the Temple of Consumption"; and Norman Silber, *Test and Protest: The Influence of Consumers' Union* (New York, 1983).

[10]   Confidential statement by Persia Campbell to TNEC, May 11, 1939, in folder 10, box 59, Helen Hall Papers, Social Welfare History Archive, University of Minnesota, Minneapolis, hereafter Hall Papers.

[11]   On LWS support of the Newspaper Guild strike, see House Special Committee on Un-American Activities, *Investigation of Un-American Propaganda Activities in the United States, Appendix IX* (Washington: Government Printing Office, 1944), 1002–17.

218 *Little 'Red Scares'*

sending questionnaires about compliance with the law to employers and threatening to boycott violators.

Conservatives responded immediately. Although the anti-Communist right in the late 1930s was not the mighty force it would become in the Cold War era, it commanded enough leverage to put left-leaning New Dealers on the defensive and thwart their hopes for extending the welfare state. Employers in labor-intensive industries bitterly resented New Deal initiatives to raise wages by recognizing union rights and reducing employment discrimination. Martin Dies, before become chair of the Special House Committee on Un-American Activities, had distinguished himself as one of the most vociferous opponents of the CIO sit-down strikes and of the Fair Labor Standards Act (he argued that "you cannot prescribe the same wages for the black man as for the white man").[12] Also hostile to the Roosevelt administration were the so-called "press lords," including William Randolph Hearst and Robert McCormick, whose media empires dominated major markets and whose syndicated columnists enjoyed unprecedented popularity in the 1930s and 1940s.[13] Joining forces with congressional conservatives, these employers and newspapermen used the close associations between the consumer groups and government agencies to portray a Communist conspiracy. The May 1939 article in McCormick's *Chicago Tribune* that labeled as fellow travelers LWS officers and, by implication, the New Deal officials who married them, was only the public face of a much broader effort. In April, soon after CNF filed its complaint against *Good Housekeeping*, Hearst Magazines hired an undercover agent to investigate CNF's Persia Campbell. Another undercover investigator attended meetings of the Chicago LWS and obtained bank statements and arrest records of its officers. Lengthy reports on Campbell and the Chicago LWS soon reached Dies Committee files.[14]

Dies Committee researcher J.B. Matthews used these and other materials when he unveiled his full case against the consumer movement in December 1939. In a highly irregular proceeding, Matthews, whose authority rested on his credentials as a self-proclaimed "former fellow traveler" of the Communist

---

[12] James T. Patterson, *Congressional Conservatism and the New Deal* (Lexington, 1967), 195.

[13] David Witwer, "Westbrook Pegler and the Anti-Union Movement," *Journal of American History* 92, no. 2 (2005).

[14] I discovered these reports after the Dies Records were opened to researchers in 2001. It is unclear who ordered the investigation of the Chicago LWS, but it was probably Hearst Magazines or someone at the *Chicago Tribune*. Francis Gosling report, Oct. 5, 1939 (he was hired April 20), General Consumer Movement file, box 81, series 11, Dies Records. Reports of Helene Abbott, May 1939, exhibits to report of Thomas J. Nash, Aug. 31, 1939, LWS-Chicago file, F&R: Orgs, Dies Records.

Party USA, testified before a subcommittee consisting solely of Martin Dies. Before other Dies Committee members had seen the report, Dies released it to the press—on a Monday, an old trick designed to maximize coverage since Monday was a slow news day.[15] Headlines all over the nation publicized Matthews's testimony that the Communist Party had decided in 1935 to use the consumer movement as a "Trojan Horse" for winning middle-class support. According to Matthews, the Communist Party leader Earl Browder himself had told the Dies Committee that the LWS, CNF, and other consumer groups were Communist "transmission belts."[16] Matthews linked criticism of the advertising industry with Communism. Because "advertising performs an indispensable function" in the "capitalist system of free enterprise," Communists had targeted advertising as a "revolutionary tactic." He claimed that "the current government procedures against advertising and advertising media have been instigated and are being aided by these consumer organizations which are under the control of communists." His primary example was the cooperation between the Department of Agriculture's consumer counsel, Donald Montgomery, and the CNF in the complaint against Hearst's *Good Housekeeping*. Only with additional funding, Matthews concluded, would the Dies Committee be able to undertake the thorough investigation that was urgently required.[17]

The Matthews report provoked a storm of protest. Consumer movement leaders did not deny that Communists participated, but they emphatically denied that Communists controlled their organizations. Eleanor Roosevelt announced at a press conference that she had been a member of the League of Women Shoppers, President Roosevelt scolded Martin Dies, and angry letters from distinguished citizens poured in to the Dies Committee. Many suspected a brazen scheme to increase Dies Committee funding. Journalists also

---

[15]   See Morris Ernst to Dies, Dec. 21, 1939, folder 5, box 60, Hall Papers.

[16]   Matthews distorted Browder's testimony. Browder had said the CP tried to use mass organizations to propagate its views just as Republicans, Democrats and Socialists did; see Browder to Roger Baldwin, Sept. 8, 1939, copy to Helen Hall, Nov. 2, 1939, folder 5, box 60, Hall Papers. In addition to LWS and CNF, Matthews named the Consumers' Union, Milk Consumers Protective Committee, and United Conference against the High Cost of Living. He singled out Susan Jenkins, Arthur Kallet, and Meyer Parodneck as Communists (which they may have been) who were involved in most of the consumer groups.

[17]   Subcommittee of the Special Committee to Investigate Un-American Activities, *Un-American Propaganda Activities in the U.S.*, Dec. 3, 1939, 7189–94, copy in Consumers' Union file, box 81, Dies Records. At the insistence of other members of the Dies Committee, this published version was much watered down from what the newspapers first got; *New York Post*, Jan. 5, 1940. For more evidence of the advertising industry's involvement in redbaiting the consumer movement, see the untitled Jan. 1940 and 1967 reports in box 5, Esther Peterson Papers, Schlesinger Library, Cambridge, MA, hereafter Peterson Papers.

220   *Little 'Red Scares'*

discovered that Matthews had ties to an LWS rival. He had been among the principals of Consumers' Research back in 1935 when its employees went on strike; the fledgling LWS had investigated and found in favor of the strikers, and the National Labor Relations Board forced Consumers' Research to rehire some of them. That outcome led to the formation of the pro-labor Consumers' Union, and it also was the catalyst for Matthews's sharp swing from left to right and his decades-long vendetta against the LWS and Consumers' Union.[18] Next it came out that only days before his subcommittee appearance, Matthews had met with top advertising and corporate executives at the home of George Sokolsky, a Hearst columnist and paid lobbyist for the National Association of Manufacturers. (The accused organizations later discovered that the official copy of Matthews's report had been stenciled at Hearst Magazines.) Consumer activists who already had been calling for abolition of the Dies Committee intensified their efforts. Matthews took a drubbing in the press and before the full membership of the Dies Committee, and all in all it seemed he and Dies had made fools of themselves.[19]

J.B. Matthews was wrong that the consumers' movement was a Communist plot, but he was right that it was ambitious, influential, and innovative in its tactics. The umbrella group for progressive consumer organizations, the Consumers' National Federation, served as a two-way communication medium between ordinary consumers and government officials. On one hand it developed educational materials for housewives (on the cost of living, prices, quality standards and cooperatives, for example), and on the other it offered

---

[18]   *Washington Evening Star*, Dec. 11, 1939, 1; Glickman, "Strike in the Temple of Consumption." In 1938 Matthews had labeled the LWS and the Consumers' Union Communist fronts during his first appearance before the Dies Committee. Dies promptly hired Matthews as the committee's chief investigator, a position Matthews held until 1945 (later he worked for Senator McCarthy's subcommittee). See Walter Goodman, *The Committee: The Extraordinary Career of the House Committee on Un-American Activities* (New York, 1968); Nelson L. Dawson, "From Fellow Traveler to Anticommunist: The Odyssey of J.B. Matthews," *Register of the Kentucky Historical Society* 84, no. 3 (1986).

[19]   For protest letters, see box 81, series 11, Dies Records; also Morris Ernst for CNF to Dies, Dec. 21, 1939, folder 5, box 60, Hall Papers; and statement by Hall and Lynd, *New York Times*, Dec. 11, 1939, 1. On the Nov. 30, 1939, meeting at Sokolsky's house, see "The Dies Plot, Detail," excerpt from *Space and Time, Newsletter of Advertising*, Dec. 18, 1939, folder 5, box 60, Hall Papers. On the stenciling by Hearst, see Katharine Armitage to LWS local presidents, Apr. 3, 1947, DC League of Women Shoppers Papers, Schlesinger Library, Cambridge, MA, hereafter DC LWS Papers. The above-cited Hearst report on Persia Campbell in Dies Committee files further demonstrates the Hearst–Matthews tie. For the embarrassment of Matthews by Dies Committee Democrats, see "Dies Sleuth Failed to Produce a Single Red When Challenged," *New York Post*, Jan. 5, 1940.

expert representation of "the consumer point of view" in government councils. Ultimately, the CNF wanted consumer agencies in local, state and national governments, but its leaders recognized that vocal grassroots support was critical to creating and sustaining such agencies. As CNF leader Helen Hall put it, the group tried to create a "widespread expression of a buyers' demand to which administrators can refer ... this is not to disparage administrative leadership itself. But these agencies can function best when the groups they are set up to serve are articulate." So the CNF tried to stimulate in cities across the nation a "conscious, educated, and [effective] consumer movement as a decentralized force in American democracy."[20] CNF objectives also included distinguishing "bona fide" consumer organizations from business fronts. Opposing the campaign of "captive" consumer groups to blame high prices on union-driven wage increases, the CNF yoked consumer and labor interests together in a march against unchecked corporate profit-seeking.[21]

The Consumers' National Federation enjoyed easy access to the corridors of power, a fact unnoticed by historians but not by conservatives at the time. After meetings with President Roosevelt and Secretary of Agriculture Henry Wallace in 1938, Persia Campbell reported that "'CNF' is an 'open sesame' in Washington. I never have the least difficulty in making appointments in or out of the government."[22] The CNF believed its efforts were at least partly responsible for the creation of the Temporary National Economic Committee, a body whose challenge to big business has led some scholars to reperiodize New Deal policy. Recent scholarship on American state development has stressed the mutually reinforcing, dynamic interaction between grassroots and government initiatives, with particular emphasis on the effort of (male) state actors to mobilize (female) ordinary citizens as "consumers." The example of the CNF qualifies that interpretation by underscoring that voluntary organizations, often run by female experts, were essential instigators and mediators between government and grassroots, both during and between periods when purchasing-power progressives were ascendant.[23]

---

[20] See first issue of CNF's *The Consumer*, June 2, 1937, folder 10, box 59, and Helen Hall, funding application to Marshall Field Foundation, Mar. 15, 1945, pp. 23, 19, box 60, both in Hall Papers.

[21] The federation's membership criteria required dedication to protecting consumers "in the purchase of goods and services *and* in the conditions under which such goods and services are made, performed, and distributed." From first issue of CNF's *The Consumer*, June 2, 1937, in folder 10, box 59, Hall Papers (emphasis in original).

[22] Persia Campbell to Helen Hall, Oct. 16, 1938, folder 9, box 59, Hall Papers.

[23] For the claim that CNF helped created TNEC, see statement by Helen Hall and Robert Lynd [n.d., early 1940], p. 4, folder 5, box 60, Hall Papers. On TNEC's importance,

The consumer movement attracted the most prominent left and liberal women of the day, as well as thousands of less famous ones. They included New Deal Democrats, independent leftists, and Communists. A 1936 list of prospective CNF members illustrates its inclusive impulse. The list featured mainstream women's clubs; left/liberal groups such as the Women's Trade Union League, the Amalgamated Clothing Workers, and the NAACP; and Communist-affiliated groups such as the International Workers' Order, National Negro Congress, and Progressive Women's Council. Contrary to Matthews's suggestion, the original executive council of the CNF was hardly Communist-dominated; one or perhaps two of seventeen members were Communists.[24]

Of the CNF members, the LWS pulled in the greatest star power. Virtually every well-known woman radical and liberal of the 1930s seems to have been on its letterheads, and many of them participated actively. Founded in 1935 and claiming 25,000 members in 13 chapters by 1939, the LWS mobilized middle- and upper-class women to "use their buying power for social justice, so that the fair price which they pay as consumers will also include an American standard of living for those who make and market the goods they buy." The LWS initially specialized in investigating labor disputes and supporting female strikers in boycotts and picketing. LWS expertise on labor matters was acknowledged by the National Labor Relations Board, which occasionally asked the LWS to mediate disputes or monitor union elections. LWS members also were appointed to the boards that implemented state minimum wage laws for women. During and after World War II, price control became a second major strategic focus. But the LWS always conceived its agenda broadly: "We work for high wages, low prices, fair profits, progressive taxation, adequate health protection and housing for all and the ending of racial, religious, or sex discrimination in employment."[25]

In the late 1930s and early 1940s that agenda attracted big names whose presence generated abundant newspaper coverage for the LWS, particularly in Washington and New York. "Mrs. Dean Acheson entertained the League of Women Shoppers at a membership tea at her home, with nearly 100 attending," was the caption for a typical *Washington Post* photograph of three elegantly dressed LWS officers holding teacups. The District's chapter quickly grew to

---

see Alan Brinkley, *The End of Reform: New Deal Liberalism in Recession and War* (New York, 1995); and Jacobs, *Pocketbook Politics*.

[24] See Dec. 28, 1936 list, folder 9; and *The Consumer*, June 2, 1937, folder 10, box 59, Hall Papers.

[25] The national and its locals produced frequent digests of pending legislation in all these areas. First quotation from "The League of Women Shoppers" [Dec. 1939]; second quotation from "Statement to be used if ... LWS is on Attorney General Tom Clark's Blacklist," April 3, 1947, both in DC LWS Papers.

about 500 members, including female legislators, government officials, and journalists, as well as wives of men in those occupations. The Washington newspapers covered its activities regularly, on and off the women's pages.[26] In another typical event, Lillian Hellman, national league vice president, addressed the D.C. chapter at the home of Cornelia Bryce Pinchot, the prominent feminist and wife of the former governor of Pennsylvania. Also present was the star of Hellman's play *Little Foxes*, Tallulah Bankhead (daughter of the speaker of the House), while those who took turns pouring tea included two female judges, a congresswoman, peace activist Dorothy Detzer, and several New Deal wives.[27]

For these women, the consumer movement's goal of raising the living standards and political participation of ordinary people had a feminist dimension. They demanded women's rights in the workplace, but they also recognized that women, whether wage-earners or housewives, usually did the shopping and often worried as much about the price and quality of household goods as about wage rates. The Consumers' National Federation sought to "make the pay envelope, whatever it is, count for more" by fighting inflated prices and shoddy goods on many policy fronts. Helen Hall believed the movement had added "some understanding and some dignity to the job of the low-income housewife." Not only living standards but political democracy was enhanced: "Local leadership sprang up as women became aware that they could play some part in changing their conditions of life."[28] Professional women too were taken more seriously when they spoke as "consumers" than when they spoke as representatives of labor or business. By the 1930s the political discourse increasingly cast "consumers" as the working-class masses, eroding the Progressive-era association between upper-class women and consumption. Still, although consumers were no longer *only* women, they clearly *included* women—more indisputably than "workers"

---

[26] *Washington Post*, Jan. 19, 1938; in the photograph were Mrs. Marquis Childs, Elizabeth Wheeler Colman and Nina Collier, whose husbands were, respectively, a prominent journalist, a U.S. senator and an official in the Dept. of Agriculture. Dean Acheson had been undersecretary of the Treasury and soon would rise to fame in the State Department. Clippings file, DC LWS Papers.

[27] *Washington Post*, Feb. 7, 1940. In addition to those named so far, prominent women who belonged to the LWS: Josephine Herbst, Mary Heaton Vorse, Leanne Zugsmith, Freda Kirchway, Dorothy Day, Mary Beard, Virginia Durr, Jessie Lloyd O'Connor, Eveline Burns, Frieda Miller, Helen Gahagan Douglas and Catherine Bauer.

[28] First quotation from Helen Hall, CNF funding application, Mar. 15, 1945, folder 5, box 60, Hall Papers; second from Helen Hall, *Unfinished Business in Neighborhood and Nation* (New York, 1971), 332, and see 345.

224   *Little 'Red Scares'*

or "employers" did. Women of all classes had greater access to the public stage when they represented themselves as consumers.[29]

The left-feminist consumer movement also challenged white supremacy. LWS chapters demonstrated against stores that refused to hire African Americans. The Washington league surveyed 600 women about wages and hours of their household employees and then arranged for a domestic worker, laundry worker, and hotel waitress, all African American women, to address the group. When a House committee refused to consider extending Social Security coverage to household workers, the LWS protested the racially discriminatory impact of their exclusion.[30] The wider consumer movement shared the league's convictions. African American groups joined the Consumers' National Federation. The civil rights feminist Ella Baker was an active member of the Consumers' Advisory Committee to the Office of Price Administration and later to the President's Council of Economic Advisers, and she also was a founding officer of the postwar National Association of Consumers. Frances Williams, who was African American, and Caroline Ware, who was white, cooperated in desegregating OPA offices.[31] This racial egalitarianism only deepened anti-Communists' suspicions about the consumer activists.

The consumer movement used a gendered style to get results. Members of the Councils against the High Cost of Living projected a working-class feminine image, presenting themselves as simple housewives on tight budgets.[32] By contrast, the LWS deliberately took advantage of its members' class and gender status as "ladies." Its fundraising and publicity stunts included a mink coat raffle and silk-free fashion shows in support of a controversial boycott of Japanese silk. The abundant newspaper coverage of the Washington league's fashion show, attended by 600 in January 1938, featured titillating close-ups of the cotton-stockinged legs of Capitol socialites.[33] Cornelia Bryce Pinchot assured members

---

[29]   For more on feminism and consumer activism, see, Storrs, *Civilizing Capitalism*, esp. 18–23, 211–19.

[30]   "League Deplores Low Servant Pay," *Washington Post*, Nov. 9, 1938; Nina Collier Op-Ed, *Washington Post*, Mar. 23, 1939.

[31]   The 1936 list of prospective CNF members included Marion Cuthbert of the Harlem YWCA, Thyra Edwards of the National Negro Congress, Louise Thompson of the IWO and Mary Ovington (white) of the NAACP. For a recent synthesis of scholarship on black boycott tactics in the 1930s, see Cohen, *Consumers' Republic*, 41–53. On desegregating the OPA, see Caroline Ware interview by Susan Ware, 1982, 94–9, Oral Histories of Women in the Federal Government, Schlesinger Library, Cambridge, MA, hereafter Ware interview.

[32]   See report of Alice Belester's testimony before TNEC, *New York Times*, May 11, 1939.

[33]   Most articles on the DC LWS referred to members' class status, for example, as "fur-coated New Deal wives," *Washington Post,* Mar. 18, 1937. On the mink coat raffle, see NY LWS minutes, Nov. 1, 1937, LWS Papers, Sophia Smith Collection, Smith College,

that picketing was not "unladylike." Lucille Ezekiel, "wife of one of the original brain-trusters," led a group of LWS members in evening gowns in picketing the Harrington Hotel to protest its lay-off of 16 waitresses.[34] Another stunt that generated plenty of newspaper photographs was picketing on roller skates, as Washington LWS members did in June 1939, bearing placards that read, "We used to be patrons, now we're pickets."[35] A few years later, when Capitol Hill police interfered with a women's delegation to present legislators with pro-price control petitions, LWS officers traded on their femininity by protesting the rough handling, which they claimed had sent a pregnant woman into shock.[36]

Conservatives noticed and deprecated the femininity of the consumer movement. They also highlighted the presence of upper-class women whenever possible. An article in *Consumers' Digest*, the bulletin of J.B. Matthews's old group, entitled "Halfway to Communism with the League of Women Shoppers," ridiculed women who went from a tea party to picketing. "Truly, this sets a new style in teas ... We may expect to see worthy matrons cut short their bridge parties and teas to dash off to some strike headquarters." The author suggested that women were as fickle in their politics as they were in their shopping tastes: "The fashion forecasters, however, predict ... it will in time be fashionable to be a lady once again."[37] After a sarcastic editorial in the *Pittsburgh Press* made fun of lady picketers, the local league's executive retorted that there was nothing illogical about a group of fortunate women "opposing the unwise and anti-social activities of others in similar position who oppose the legitimate objectives of organized labor." In fact, she continued, "women who can afford to lunch at the Mayflower Hotel" should be "commended for not being impervious to the needs and welfare of waitresses and chambermaids."[38]

Northampton, MA. On the silk boycott, which divided labor groups, see Jan. 1938 clippings, DC LWS Papers.

[34] Hotel management contended it had replaced the white waitresses with black men because it could not afford to comply with the DC minimum wage law for women; the waitresses charged the hotel with trying to break their union. *Washington Times*, June 16 and 23, 1938. On Pinchot's talk, see *Washington News*, Apr. 10, 1940.

[35] *Washington Evening Star*, June 21, 1939.

[36] "OPA Women say Capitol Cops Shoved 'Em Around Like Nazis," *Washington-Times Herald*, Apr. 14, 1946. Mrs. Leon Henderson, wife of the former OPA head, was among the protesters.

[37] M.C. Phillips, "Half-Way to Communism with the League of Women Shoppers," *Consumers' Digest*, Apr. 1940. Phillips and her husband F.J. Schlink remained close allies of J.B. Matthews.

[38] Katherine Ruttenberg, Letter to the Editor, *Pittsburgh Press*, n.d. [May 1939], DC LWS Papers. For other examples of conservatives' gendered hostility to consumer activism, see Cohen, *Consumers' Republic*, 57, 134.

226   *Little 'Red Scares'*

Critics were wrong that the LWS was a fad, an indulgence of bored ladies who joined for the parties and publicity. No doubt the group acquired a certain cachet, which helps explain why hundreds of prominent people turned out for its events. But many of the big names on its letterheads were dedicated activists, and they did not melt away at the first sign of a shift in political climate. The District of Columbia league was not intimidated by the Dies Committee allegations. In May 1940 it threw a benefit party attended by 400 on the roof of the Washington Hotel. Leading New Dealers participated in satirical skits, one of which featured league president Lucille Ezekiel (whose husband was the economic adviser to Secretary of Agriculture Henry Wallace) mocking the Dies Committee with a "Martin Pies" magician act. Other distinguished performers included Abe Fortas (Interior Department) and Carol Agger (a NLRB lawyer and Fortas's wife), Leon Henderson (TNEC), Metcalfe Walling (Labor Department), and Supreme Court justice William O. Douglas.[39]

The LWS also was adept at more conventional, less glamorous tactics. Many of the "fur-coated New Deal wives" knew a lot about social policy and legislative politics, and they were hard workers. They staffed the Washington chapter's nine committees (including living standards, legislation, education and collective bargaining), and they churned out savvy legislative digests, letters to editors and press releases. In 1940 and 1941, the D.C. league's work included creating a 13-part radio series on consumer and labor issues, boycotting a Disney film in support of striking cartoonists, organizing conferences on household employment, housing and defense issues, lobbying on national and district legislation, and investigating the dismissal of a woman from the War Department. Despite the Dies allegations, female New Dealers like Caroline Ware, Eveline Burns, Elizabeth Wickenden, Charlotte Tuttle Lloyd, and Josephine Roche remained members, and New Deal wives continued among its active officers. Between 1943 and 1946, the District league followed the national organization in focusing primarily on price control, earning recognition from the Office of Civilian Defense and the OPA for its advisory and educational efforts.[40]

But Matthews and the Dies Committee did not go away. In fact, they intensified their attack. The League of Women Shoppers, after being cited as a Communist front group several more times, eventually did begin to lose its most distinguished members, increasing the influence of lesser-known women,

---

[39] "Skytop Fair," *Washington Post*, May 1, 1940.

[40] Annual report for 1940–41, DC LWS, in House Special Committee on Un-American Activities, *Appendix IX* (Washington: Government Printing Office, 1944). On the Disney boycott, see postcard in Dies Records; Disney would testify against the LWS in 1947. Chester Bowles and Paul A. Porter, OPA, to Katharine Armatage, May 14, 1946, DC LWS Papers. On OCD, see Armatage to local chapters, Apr. 3, 1947, DC LWS Papers.

Investigating the Left-Feminist Consumer Movement 227

some of whom were Communists.[41] As government employees began to be screened for loyalty in 1941 and 1942, they grew more circumspect about their affiliations and those of their spouses. This affected all LWS branches, as federal workers were scattered around the country, but it was particularly devastating for the D.C. branch. In 1939, such had been that league's respectability that a Washington advice columnist had recommended joining the LWS as an antidote to one young wife's temptation "to flirt and carouse."[42] That day was long past by 1947, when the expansion of the federal loyalty program prompted still more resignations. Under further pressure from anti-Communists, the national LWS dissolved in 1949. The Consumers' National Federation had folded in 1941, and its postwar successor, the National Association of Consumers, never generated widespread support. The Consumers' Union, also under constant anti-Communist fire, distanced itself from leftists and moderated its program.[43]

Conservative anti-Communists had bigger fish to fry than the consumer movement. Far from being chastened, they took New Dealers' indignant defense

---

[41] The LWS was cited by J.B. Matthews in 1938 and 1939, in the 1943 report of the California Un-American Activities Committee, p. 100, the Dies Committee report of Mar. 29, 1944, 121, 181, and in the latter committee's *Appendix IX*, 1004–17. Communist Party members were involved in the LWS from the outset but were not dictating the agenda, at least not before 1939; thereafter, some chapters seem to have been more CP-oriented than others (Philadelphia and New York more than DC, for example). I base my estimate of increase in CP influence over time on study of letterheads, newsletters, minutes and internal correspondence. The Dies Committee stressed indications that the national LWS may have "followed the CP line" during the Hitler–Stalin Pact (1939–41) and also that a card-file obtained through surveillance of the Philadelphia Communist Party listed three members of the local LWS as a CP "fraction.".

[42] "Mary Haworth's Mail," *Washington Post*, Apr. 8, 1939. Another indication of the LWS's prominence and mainstream status is that it was listed with five much older and larger national women's groups in a Jan. 1939 ad for the *Ladies Home Journal*; copy in clippings folder, DC LWS Papers.

[43] For example, see resignations of Laura Somers, Sept. 30, 1948, and Asho Ingersoll Craine, Dec. 3, 1948, folder 7, DC LWS Papers. Craine's husband worked in the Interior Dept. Kitty Gellhorn, whose husband held a series of government positions later including an OPA job, resigned in 1940. Some said they resigned not because of the group's CP association but because they differed with the group's direction or thought it was no longer effective, but the increasing influence of Communists (as a result of the redbaiting) certainly contributed to these internal rifts; see Caroline Ware, reply to interrogatory, Apr. 24, 1954, p. 7, Caroline Ware investigation file, Record Group 478, National Archives, College Park, MD, hereafter Ware file, RG 478, and Craine's resignation letter cited above. The LWS folded into Congress of American Women in about 1949, according to Glickman, "Strike in the Temple of Consumption," 125. On the move to the center by Consumers' Union, see ibid.; and Silber, *Test and Protest*.

of the consumer movement in December 1939 and their close ties to its member groups as evidence that Communists had penetrated the federal government. Despite the fact that most liberals still did not take the Dies Committee seriously, its use of the "Communists in government" issue substantially increased the political leverage of congressional conservatives during and after the war. In September 1941 Martin Dies declared in an open letter to FDR that Communists had infiltrated the Office of Price Administration. Dies claimed that OPA head Leon Henderson and four other prominent employees had Communist affiliations, and that at least 50 others (whom he did not name) also had subversive records. Henderson called the charges ridiculous but said he would ask the Civil Service Commission to investigate, and he promised to dismiss any OPA employee found to be a Communist.[44] One of the many things Dies held against Henderson (although Dies did not publicize it) was the fact that Henderson's wife was an active officer of the Washington chapter of the LWS.

Congressional conservatives particularly disliked the OPA's Consumer Division, which was run by women experienced in using the consumer cause to promote social reform.[45] Under the OPA's predecessor, the National Defense Advisory Commission (created in May 1940), the responsibility for price issues was shared between Leon Henderson (wholesale prices), and Harriet Elliott (retail prices). Elliott, a Democratic Party worker who had organized women to fight inflation during the First World War, hired the formidably talented Caroline Ware as her assistant. Ware was the real force at the Consumer Division.[46] A professor of social economy and history, Ware had been on the Consumer Advisory Board to the National Recovery Administration (1933–35), in charge of the AAUW's consumer program, and a member of the LWS and National Consumers' League. Elliott and Ware enlisted a team of consultants that included Mary Dublin Keyserling of the Consumers' League, the African American YWCA worker Frances Williams, the Texas women's leader Minnie Fisher Cunningham, and the labor leader and housing expert John Edelman. This group embarked on an ambitious program to involve consumers as volunteers in the price control program. It also pressed to make the OPA a model of racial egalitarianism, forcing the integration of the secretarial pool, promoting college-educated African Americans out of the mailroom, and involving minority groups in OPA enforcement. In 1941, Harriet Elliott

---

[44] "Henderson, Aides Accused by Dies of Links to Reds," *New York Times*, Sept. 8, 1941..

[45] Imogene Putnam, *Historical Reports on War Administration, Office of Price Administration: vol. 14: Volunteers in OPA* (Washington, 1947), 33.

[46] See Ware interview, 78, 91. A hostile FBI informant also described Ware as the one running the show at the Consumer Division; report of Robert Welton, Sept. 1, 1953, Ware file, RG 478.

was effectively demoted by two OPA reorganizations. In November, after OPA head Leon Henderson announced that her division's function would be further reduced to communicating OPA directives to the public, Elliott resigned. Much of her staff soon did the same.[47]

Gutting the Consumer Division seems to have been Henderson's attempt to appease congressional conservatives even as he publicly maintained a defiant attitude toward them. Dies Committee staffers had been tracking Harriet Elliott's appointments from the start. All four of the OPA employees who Dies publicly named on September 7, 1941 were in the Consumer Division. (Two also had ties to the Consumers' Union.)[48] Further suggesting that allegations of subversion had something to do with the Division's demotion is the fact that just before Dies made his charges, the FBI began an investigation of Caroline Ware. According to Ware's FBI file, the August 19 investigation was "predicated upon a review of the indices of the Washington Field Office," which claimed she was "affiliated with the American Association of University Women, the National Federation for Constitutional Liberties, the Washington Committee for Democratic Action, and the League of Women Shoppers." It likely was Dies Committee staffers who prompted the FBI to check its Washington office indices on Ware. On September 15, FBI Director J. Edgar Hoover notified the Attorney General's office of Ware's affiliations.[49]

---

[47] When the National Defense Advisory Committee became the Office of Price Administration and Civilian Supply (OPACS) in Apr. 1941, Elliott became associate director under Henderson as well as head of the Consumer Division. When OPACS became OPA in late August, Elliott's authority was further reduced. "Assigned to Staff of Defense Board," *New York Times*, June 29, 1940; "Miss Elliott and Co.," *Business Week*, Dec. 6, 1941, 77–80; and Putnam, *Volunteers in OPA*, 12. On the fight to integrate OPA, see Ware interview, 94–9; Frances H. Williams interview, 1977, *Black Women's Oral History Project* 10 (Westport, 1991), 275–307; and Frances H. Williams, "Minority Groups and OPA," *Public Administration Review* 7 (Spring 1947), 123–8.

[48] Dies Committee staff flagged the names of Mary Dublin (soon to be Keyserling) and Frances Williams as soon as they were appointed; see "Assigned to Staff of Defense Board," *New York Times*, June 29, 1940, marked copy in box 82, series 11, Dies Records. Dies named Robert Brady (Consumers' Union), Mildred Edie Brady, Dewey Palmer (Consumers' Union), and Tom Tippett.

[49] Ware might have caught J.B. Matthews' eye when she wrote a letter protesting his report on the consumer movement; see Ware to Martin Dies, Dec. 11, 1939, box 81, series 11, Dies Records. See FBI report of Sept. 22, 1941, summarizing investigation done on Aug. 19, and Hoover to Matthew McGuire, Assistant to the Attorney General, Sept. 15, 1941, both in FBI file of Caroline F. Ware obtained by Freedom of Information Act (FOIA) request, hereafter Ware FBI file.

230 *Little 'Red Scares'*

In October, Dies turned up the pressure on the Roosevelt administration by sending the Attorney General a list of 1,124 alleged subversives in federal positions. Dies claimed that more than 25 percent of these "subversives" held high-paying executive and policymaking positions. Suggesting that the Attorney General's office had been lax, Dies wrote that "the retention on the Federal payroll of several thousand persons who, to put the matter mildly, have strong leanings toward Moscow will confirm the widely held suspicion that a large and influential sector of official Washington is utilizing the national emergency for undermining the American system of democratic government."[50] Scaling back the Consumer Division seems to have been a way for Henderson to ease out some employees with controversial associations—many of whom were, not incidentally, women whose interest in using the OPA to increase housewives' civic participation and to fight race discrimination was irritating to other OPA divisions.

The circumstances of Caroline Ware's resignation support this hypothesis. Ware and Henderson both later described her resignation as a response to her division's demotion, but allegations of subversion also were part of the story. Henderson wrote Ware in early December: "Your choice in not tendering a formal resignation is, of course, a personal choice ... The responsibility for the Consumers Division is clearly mine ... [and I will] make the best disposition as to personnel and policies as seem sound in my own judgment."[51] FBI documents indicate that Ware was responsible for hiring some controversial employees, including Robert and Mildred Edie Brady (who would be the only OPA employees publicly dismissed in response to Dies's charges). Ware protested what she saw as Henderson's capitulation to Dies, and in turn Henderson invited her to resign, which she initially refused to do. But on December 19 a Civil Service Commission examiner was assigned to interview Ware about the "derogatory information" on her record. On January 31 she resigned after all. She cited "agency reorganization," but the ongoing investigation must have been a factor in her decision.[52]

---

[50] "Dies Charges 1,124 in Federal Posts Help Communists," *New York Times*, Oct. 20, 1941. This list did not include war agencies and thus did not include OPA employees, but Dies's accompanying letter to Attorney General Francis Biddle pointedly referred to subversives at the OPA. By "several thousand" Dies presumably meant the 1,124 plus others in war agencies. I have been unable to locate the list of 1,124 names, but I can make educated guesses about who many of them were.

[51] Henderson to Ware, Dec. 11, 1941, cited in US CSC investigations report, June 26, 1942, Ware FBI file.

[52] US CSC investigators formally requested the Bradys' dismissal in late December 1941; see FBI report of Sept. 1, 1953, p. 11, Ware file, RG 478. Ware was still defending Mildred Brady in 1954; see her reply to interrogatory, Ware file, RG 478. See also Ware interview, 89A.

If Leon Henderson hoped that firing the Bradys and phasing out the Consumer Division would appease the Dies Committee, he was wrong. Although the Consumer Division indeed had employed many of Dies's suspects, others were scattered throughout the agency, and the Dies Committee had no intention of letting up. Dies's hitherto little-noticed attack on the OPA, which originated from conservative hostility to the consumer movement, was critical to the prehistory of the formal federal employee loyalty program that President Truman would create in 1947.[53]

In response to Dies's fall 1941 allegations, the Civil Service Commission (CSC) created a loyalty board, which proceeded to review employees whom Dies had called subversive. When many of these employees were retained, the Dies Committee attacked the Civil Service Commission, going so far as to subpoena CSC case files. Many of the disputed cases involved OPA employees.[54] Dies staffers charged that OPA head Leon Henderson had pressured the CSC loyalty board to reverse negative decisions on certain cases. Association with the League of Women Shoppers was among the indicators that the Dies Committee took as evidence of Communist sympathies; not only Henderson but also his protégé Tom Emerson, in whose case Henderson reportedly intervened, were married to LWS activists.[55] In 1942, the CSC had adopted standards that expressly forbade inquiry about membership in the LWS (or the ACLU, Socialist Party, and several other groups) in order to avoid catching liberals and non-Communist leftists in a net officially intended for Communists. The Dies Committee believed that the CSC loyalty board members were far too tolerant. Professing outrage that CSC standards were even looser than those of the employing agencies, the Dies Committee now shifted its attention from the

---

[53] The basic studies of the Dies Committee only briefly note its attack on the OPA, and two new treatments of the OPA do not mention it. See August Ogden, *The Dies Committee* (1943, 1945), Goodman, *The Committee*, Cohen, *Consumers' Republic*, and Jacobs, *Pocketbook Politics*. Also see Eleanor Bontecou, *The Federal Loyalty-Security Program* (Ithaca, 1953), 8–10.

[54] I have been unable to find any list of 50 other subversives at OPA, but the subpoenaed CSC files and other materials indicate that Dies's suspects included John Edelman, Walter Gellhorn, Tom Emerson, Paul R. Porter, Oliver Peterson, Rose Eden, Esther Rosenberg, Marcus Rosenblum, Robert Sessions, Aaron Werner, Ed Scheunemann and Teresa Liss.

[55] Lawyer Tom Emerson was suspect on the basis that he was friends with CP member Nathan Witt at the NLRB and also that his wife Betty, a Labor Department employee, was active in the LWS; see Ben Mandel to J.B., May 20, 1941 (list of alleged subversives in government), box 692, J.B. Matthews Papers, Duke University, Durham, NC. The Dies Committee believed Henderson also had meddled in the case of Tom Tippett. LWS associations were further noted in the subpoenaed files of Jean Lenauer and Josephine Herbst, who did not work at the OPA.

232   *Little 'Red Scares'*

OPA to the Civil Service Commission.[56] After a few more years of relentless right-wing alarms about Communists in government—which several espionage cases seemed to corroborate—Truman authorized the sweeping program requiring all federal workers to pass loyalty tests.[57]

Many of the people most prominent in the consumer movement of the 1930s and 1940s, as well as many others who had been associated with it but not leaders, were investigated under the auspices of the federal loyalty program. Affiliation with the LWS (directly or through a wife) came up in investigations of the following officials: Mary and Leon Keyserling, Dorothy Kenyon, Frieda Miller, Thomas Blaisdell, Mary Taylor Montgomery, Thomas Emerson, Mordecai Ezekiel, Walter Gellhorn, David Demarest Lloyd, Elizabeth Wickenden and Tex Goldschmidt, in addition to Caroline Ware.[58] The LWS noticed that its members and their husbands were being targeted for dismissal and protested immediately. The league president cited government officials' earlier praise of the LWS and denounced the loyalty program as an effort to silence opposition "to the present reactionary leadership of both major political parties" (a tack that probably helped seal the group's fate).[59] For other federal employees the albatross was a connection to the Consumers' Union or Consumers' National Federation. Many of these investigations lasted for years and forced their subjects out of government service, at least for a time. Other federal employees resigned rather

---

[56] Bontecou, *Federal Loyalty-Security Program*, 15. See CSC loyalty investigations, boxes 188–91, series 11, Dies Records. I have not found secondary sources that discuss the conflict between Dies and the CSC.

[57] The best study of the loyalty program remains Bontecou, *Federal Loyalty-Security Program*. Big spy stories leading up to its formalization in 1947 include the 1945 discovery of secret government documents in the office files of *Amerasia* magazine, and the 1946 exposure of a Russian spy ring in Canada.

[58] Most of those named here have loyalty case files in Record Group 478 that I obtained by FOIA request. Emerson's FBI file is with his papers at Sterling Library, Yale University, New Haven, CT. On David Lloyd's case, see the following sources at the Harry S Truman Library, Independence MO: Lloyd folder, box 110, President's Secretary's File; loyalty program folder, box 23, White House Confidential Files; and Lloyd folder, box 10, Charles S. Murphy Papers. According to Jeffrey Kisseloff, Priscilla Hiss's LWS activism was part of the early case against Alger Hiss. Dean Acheson, too, was asked to explain his wife Alice's work in the LWS.

[59] Katharine Armatage, "Statement to be used if [LWS is put on Attorney General's] 'Blacklist' of Subversive Organizations," Apr. 3, 1947, DC LWS Papers. The "security risk" concept, as distinct from the loyalty question, did not apply only to the homosexuals discussed by David Johnson's *Lavender Scare* (Chicago, 2003); it probably produced even more dismissals of spouses. On married left-liberals as a trigger of right-wing hostility long before the Clintons' day, see Landon Storrs, "Attacking the Washington 'Femmocracy': Antifeminism in the Cold War Campaign against 'Communists in Government,'" *Feminist Studies* 33 no. 1 (Spring 2007): 118–52.

than undergo investigation.[60] Other citizens found that affiliation with these groups made it harder to get hired into government service in the first place. Helen Hall, the executive of CNF and its successor the National Association of Consumers, was nominated for a CSC regional loyalty board but then rejected; HUAC's file on her made reference to her LWS sponsorship.[61] As word of the investigations spread, others who were or had been affiliated with the "subversive" consumer groups presumably did not even bother applying for government jobs.

Of course, many people who were not associated with the LWS, CNF or Consumers' Union underwent loyalty investigations, and for many who did have ties to those groups, those ties were only part of a long list of charges against them. Typically a loyalty case was not decided by one charge but rather by a series of charges that, however insignificant alone, together could be seen by investigators as evidence of a pattern that warranted dismissal. The consumer movement was not the only thing, or even the most important thing, that got these individuals in trouble. However, left-feminist consumer groups rank right alongside the labor, civil rights and antifascist causes—which have received much more attention—as associations that got federal employees in trouble. The League of Women Shoppers in particular merits recognition as a group that was sensitive to the interconnections between class, gender, race and international inequalities and whose visibility helped trigger the alarm about "Communists in government."

The investigation of federal employees associated with consumer groups continued long after the demise of the League of Women Shoppers, the Consumers' National Federation, and the OPA. Data gathered by J.B. Matthews in the late 1930s would haunt his consumer movement nemeses years after his own star had waned. Commerce Department economist Mary Dublin Keyserling was suspended in the early 1950s after a protracted investigation; the charges against her also fed an investigation of her husband Leon, then President Truman's chief economic adviser.[62] Truman White House aide David

---

60   Donald Montgomery was hired by the United Auto Workers in 1942, perhaps with a push from his agency. Colston Warne of Consumers' Union in 1947 insisted on paying his own expenses as a government consultant rather than sign the loyalty oath, provoking an outcry from the right; *Washington Daily News*, Nov. 3, 1947; and *Washington Post*, Nov. 14, 1947.

61   On Hall's disqualification, see "Reports of Investigation" file, box 5, Records of the Loyalty Review Board, Record Group 146, National Archives, College Park, MD, and Helen Hall file, F&R Name Files, Records of the House Un-American Activities Committee, Record Group 233, National Archives, Washington DC. Many other LWS associates were accused in one context or another, but here I am focusing on federal loyalty program cases and prominent consumer activists.

62   Storrs, "Red Scare Politics."

234 *Little 'Red Scares'*

Demarest Lloyd was investigated repeatedly in the early 1950s on grounds that included his wife's LWS membership and his own appearance at an LWS event.[63] Esther Peterson's husband Oliver, a labor attaché in the State Department, faced successive loyalty investigations from 1949 through 1955, eventually losing his position and his health. The case against him was built in part on Esther's associations, which included the Consumers' Union. Esther Peterson's later appointment as President Lyndon Johnson's Special Assistant on Consumer Affairs might suggest a triumph over the anti-Communist right. Throughout her tenure in that position, however, the old allegations against her were raised frequently, constraining her agenda and tactics.[64]

The FBI kept tabs on Caroline Ware into the 1960s. After she resigned from the OPA in 1941, she joined the faculty of Howard University, where she taught until 1961 (she later credited Howard for shielding her from the worst of McCarthyism). Ironically, in late 1943, when the OPA's new administrator, Chester Bowles, recognized the necessity of consumer involvement and created the Consumer Advisory Committee, he asked Caroline Ware to chair its executive committee. Since this was an unpaid position, it was not subject to loyalty review procedures. She did an enormous amount of crucial work for the OPA, but without getting paid for it.[65] In the early 1950s she began applying for government consulting positions, chiefly with the Pan American Union of the Organization of American States. These were short-term assignments, and each time Ware started a new one she had to get loyalty clearance again. The FBI investigated her extensively and repeatedly from 1951 to 1955, which cost her some assignments and delayed others. She was cleared in 1955, but unbeknownst to her, the FBI continued to track and report on her activities. In 1960 the FBI warned that she was on the Coordinating Committee for Enforcement of D.C. Anti-Discrimination Laws; in 1962, the FBI reported its discovery that she had attended the (pro-labor, anti-racist) Highlander Folk School a few years earlier.[66] In spite of the allegations that never died, Ware led

---

[63] See David Demarest Lloyd FBI file, obtained by FOIA request.

[64] On the Petersons' case, see unidentified 1940, 1965, and 1967 reports, apparently by advertising interests with access to FBI reports, files 66–73, Peterson Papers, and Esther Peterson, *Restless*, 84–8.

[65] In addition to chairing its executive committee, Ware was secretary of the larger CAC, and its minutes suggest she was the key player; copies in box 103, Hall Papers. For a glimpse of Ware's OPA work, see Jacobs, *Pocketbook Politics*, chap. 5; and Putnam, *Volunteers in OPA*. For an abbreviated description of her encounter with McCarthyism, see Ware interview, 121L-P.

[66] From Ware's FBI and RG 478 files.

Investigating the Left-Feminist Consumer Movement 235

an intensely busy and productive life, but her ability to contribute her expertise through government service was limited.

Female experts like Caroline Ware were central to the left-feminist consumers' movement that emerged in the 1930s, and their success in achieving influence within the federal government was an important stimulus to the crusade against alleged Communist sympathizers in government. Years before fears of Soviet espionage crystallized in the mid-1940s, right-wingers in and out of Congress responded to the challenge posed by the consumer movement by highlighting its network of allies (and sometimes spouses) in sympathetic government agencies. Furthermore, information gathered by the Dies Committee and the FBI in this early period—before federal employees became cautious about acknowledging the slightest association with left-wing groups or people— became the derogatory evidence that was recycled repeatedly when employee loyalty standards tightened (as they did several times between 1946 and 1955).

Federal employees with associations to the consumer movement became prominent among the victims of the postwar Red Scare. Although they had participated in groups that had Communist members, they were neither agents nor dupes of a Communist plot. They were independent leftists whose brief period of policymaking influence suggests that the New Deal had more social democratic potential than most scholars since the 1960s have believed—and thus that red scare political repression did even more damage than we thought.

Chapter 10

The Dies Committee v. the New Deal: Real Americans and the Unending Search for Un-Americans

Kenneth O'Reilly

"Not one of us," Sarah Palin said of Barack Obama during the 2008 campaign.[1] After Obama's election as the nation's first African-American President, Congresswoman Michele Bachmann (R., MN) called for a vetting of her colleagues "to find out if they are pro-America or anti-America"; Congressman Spencer Bachus (R., AL) claimed he had a list of 17 socialist members of the House; and former Vice President Dick Cheney's daughter said the Justice Department had been infiltrated by seven or more al-Qaeda sympathizers and/or dupes. The specificity recalled Senator Joseph R. McCarthy's Lincoln Day 1950 claim to have a list of 205 (or whatever number of) communists in the State Department. The general tenor brought things back to where they started in 1938 with the birth of the House Special Committee to Investigate Un-American Activities.

That body was known during its seven-year run (1938–45) as the Dies Committee in honor of its chair, Martin Dies (D., TX).[2] Its predecessors included a Senate Judiciary Subcommittee that investigated German and Bolshevik propaganda in 1919 and more recently a Special Committee to Investigate Un-American Activities in 1934–35. The Dies Committee had its successors, too. In 1945 the House reconstituted the Committee as a standing Committee (known by the phonic friendly acronym HUAC),[3] and that Committee is best remembered for the Alger Hiss case and the Hollywood blacklists. Richard

---

[1]   *Newsweek* (Nov. 24, 2008) considered even the most extreme version of the formulation as if it were reasonable: "The people who believe Obama is the Antichrist are perhaps jumping to conclusions, but they're not nuts."

[2]   Martin Dies's papers are in the Sam Houston Center, Texas State Library and Archives Commission, Austin.

[3]   Dies Committee records (and those of its successor committees) are in the National Archives (RG 233).

Nixon, a freshman member of the House in 1948 who had managed a HUAC appointment, led the pursuit of Hiss. Ronald Reagan, who testified before HUAC as a cooperative witness during the Hollywood Ten hearings of 1947, was president of the Screen Actors Guild at the time and known to the FBI and its director as "Confidential Informant T-10." In 1969, the same year that then California Governor Reagan solicited FBI aid for a "psychological warfare" campaign against campus radicals,[4] the House renamed HUAC as the Committee on Internal Security. In 1975 the House abolished the Committee.[5]

The Dies Committee marked a line of demarcation. Prior to 1938 congressional investigation of "un-American" activities was episodic. After 1938 the pursuit was sufficiently institutionalized to survive HUAC's death. Sarah Palin et al. have made it perfectly clear that the hunt for un-American activities has penetrated the nation's value set to the point where it no longer requires a fully credentialled entity formally devoted to the matter. That is the Dies Committee's true legacy; namely, a political culture that casually accepts as a norm most any attempt by any and all conservative inhabitants of "the real American" to equate advocacy of liberal reform with disloyalty. Palin's point of emphasis was plain enough. Would one mention the "pro-America areas of this great nation" for any reason other than calling attention to the inhabitants of the allegedly anti- or un-American areas of this great nation?

When Martin Dies proposed an Un-American Activities Committee in 1938, a conservative coalition of Republicans and southern Democrats concluded that he intended to discredit the New Deal's programs, personnel and constituency. Such recent events as the Supreme Court packing fight, the sit-down strikes by automobile workers, and the onset of a recession in the midst of the still ongoing Great Depression increased dissatisfaction with the New Deal. Ironically, the House overwhelmingly approved Dies's resolution because the conservative coalition merged with dozens of liberal congressmen who assumed the new committee would investigate anti-Semitism and not the New Deal.

---

[4]   DeLoach to Tolson, July 17, 1969, 100-151646-348, FBI University of California File.

[5]   In its later years the Committee mostly labored in obscurity. An exception occurred when Richard H. Ichord (D., MO), the Committee's last chair, had a Pentagon Papers cameo on the matter of President Nixon's search for "somebody to be a [Joe] McCarthy" and pursue Daniel Ellsberg et al. Maybe a "pipsqueak" congressman, White House Chief of Staff H.R. Haldeman suggested. "Sonofabitch could make himself a Senator overnight," Nixon replied. The thought started an "Ichord is the man" chant. Another plus was the Committee's GOP minority ("two Birchers"). "But you know what's going to charge up an audience," Nixon added. "Jesus Christ, they'll be hanging from the rafters ... Going after all these Jews. Just find one that is a Jew, will you." *Abuse of Power: The New Nixon Tapes*, ed. Stanley I. Kutler (New York, 1997), 5, 11–12, 19–20, 26.

The Dies Committee paid some attention to organizations like the German American Bund. On August 12, the very first day of its public hearings, the Committee received testimony from two brothers, one of whom had infiltrated the Bund on behalf of the *Chicago Tribune* and the other on behalf of the FBI. Eventually Bund leader Fritz Kuhn was arrested for misappropriating Bund funds and quickly deported (along with other Bund functionaries). Kuhn's successor, William Kunze, was among 30 native fascists indicted under the Espionage Act and the Smith Act during the war years. Justice Department prosecutors selected some 900 documents from Dies Committee files when preparing their case against Kunze.[6]

Many native fascists supported Congressman Dies's work despite his occasional foray into their affairs. The Committee's constituency included, at one time or another, William Dudley Pelley's Silver Legion; Nazi apologist George Sylvester Viereck; Father Charles Coughlin, "the Little Flower radio priest" who railed against Reds, Jews and New Dealers; Gerald L.K. Smith, widely referred to as "the minister of hate"; and Gerald Winrod, the self-styled "Jayhawk Nazi." The Committee had a particularly close relationship with Joseph P. Kamp of the Constitutional Educational League. While Dies was hiring Kamp's secretary as an investigator, the Justice Department was declaring the group "an instrument of the Axis powers." After the League published a pamphlet entitled *The Fifth Column versus the Dies Committee*, President Franklin D. Roosevelt hoped to have "the mails forbidden to [them]."[7]

Dies intended to alert the American public to the dangers of subversive organizations. "Primarily," he told FDR in 1940, "you educate innocent people so that they will get out."[8] He preferred to apply this model to left-wing groups rather than right-wing groups and recruited accordingly. In addition to Kamp's man, he hired fellow Texan Robert Stripling as Committee secretary (who would go on to Hiss case fame as Nixon's de facto sidekick); and four investigators (three of whom were quickly fired). After the Senate Civil Liberties Committee (the so-called Lafollette Committee) revealed chief investigator Edward F. Sullivan's record as a labor spy for an anti-Semitic outfit, the man signed on with the Ukrainian Nationalist Federation—an entity hoping that the Third Reich

---

[6] Dies to Cummings, July 6, 1938, 235343 (13), RG 60, Numerical Files, Justice Dept. Central Files, National Archives; Dies to FDR, Aug. 24, 1938, 235343 (14), ibid.; Jackson to Dies, Aug. 13, 1938, in Dies Committee, *Annual Report*, H. Rept. 2, 76th Cong., 1st sess., 1939, 3–4. For the informants, see serials 61-7582-4 and -5, FBI HUAC File.

[7] See the correspondence in 663, OF 10-B, Roosevelt Papers, Franklin D. Roosevelt Presidential Library, Hyde Park, NY.

[8] Transcript, President's Conference with Dies, Nov. 29, 1940, OF 320 (Dies Committee 1940–1941), ibid.

240   *Little 'Red Scares'*

would soon annex Ukraine. Sullivan had also once shared an office with the inventor of a club marketed as a "Kike Killer."

The House General Accounts Committee scaled down Dies's requested $100,000 budget for a more modest $25,000 because it was assumed that the FBI would do much of the work for the Un-American Activities Committee. Dies did receive some assistance from "G-men" and the occasional Army G-2 agent. But FBI Director J. Edgar Hoover approved dissemination of information only on an informal and case-by-case basis. In hope of preventing further staff embarrassments, he did allow FBI agents to investigate applicant Committee employees. Dies certainly appreciated the FBI's recommendation that he hire Rhea Whitley, a 10-year bureau veteran, as Committee counsel.[9]

Dies was equally pleased with J. B. Matthews, Sullivan's successor, who had been recommended by newspaper columnist and FBI confidant George Sokolsky. Matthews wrote his own book, *Odyssey of a Fellow Traveler* (1938), and ghost wrote one of Dies's books, *The Trojan Horse in America* (1940). Matthews even returned for a cameo 15 years later on the staff of Senator McCarthy's Permanent Subcommittee on Investigations before things crashed with his wild charge that Protestant clergy were the "largest group supporting [communism]." Richard Rovere, author of the *New Yorker's* "Letter from Washington" and eventually a book on McCarthy, dubbed Matthews "a political psychopath."[10]

The FBI deemed Matthews's investigative techniques sophisticated enough to consult his personal files. On the other hand, his method was simple enough to require only a scissors. The Dies Committee's chief investigator and his staff indiscriminately clipped names from the left-wing press. When Matthews discovered that the *Daily Worker* had erroneously listed him, during fellow travelling days, as an associate of an obscure anti-Nazi commission, he noted the standard communist practice of inflating party fronts. Having unburdened himself in defense of himself, Matthews continued clipping names. After he named America's child film icon as a communist dupe, Secretary of the Interior Harold L. Ickes said the Committee had raided "Shirley Temple's nursery."[11]

Vigilante imagery was appropriate. Dies Committee investigators, usually accompanied by local police, often entered CPUSA or other target organizations' headquarters, according to one of those investigators, and "confiscate[d] anything that they wanted."[12] The most spectacular raids were carried out against the American League for Peace and Democracy. Communist

---

[9] See serials 61-7582-6, -120, -123, 126, -131, and 938X, FBI HUAC File.

[10] "J.B. Matthews—The Informer," *The Nation*, Oct. 3, 1942, 315.

[11] Harold L. Ickes, *The Secret Diary of Harold L. Ickes*, vol. 2, *The Inside Struggle* (New York, 1954), 455.

[12] Glavin to Tolson, July 6, 1938, 61-7582-6, FBI HUAC File.

party records were also seized in at least seven cities.[13] The courts condemned these forays in May 1940 following a raid on CPUSA and International Workers Order (IWO) offices in Philadelphia. Escorted by a squad of motorcycle police and eight detectives, Dies Committee investigators filled a two-ton truck with documents and fled across the Delaware Bridge into New Jersey. After the CPUSA and the IWO filed a petition in U.S. District Court asking that their files be returned, Judge George A. Welsh requested Dies not to make use of the purloined documents until he had ruled on the complaint. He also ordered the arrest of a police lieutenant and two Committee investigators.

Dies had anticipated this judicial interference. The documents were seized late in the afternoon and rushed to that New Jersey "hideout," he explained 14 years later. "We spent all night making copies of this stuff. The next morning the federal judge issued an injunction, and so I hid out in a blind office until we completed the photostating." Judge Welsh ruled the raid in violation of the Fourth Amendment. Dies shrugged, explaining that he could not always obtain the best documentation of un-American activities by legal means. If Welsh's ruling tempered the chairman's ache for highway adventure, old habits die hard. In late 1940 Committee staff raided the New York and Chicago offices of 19 organizations of various political persuasions.[14]

Local and state police department "Red Squads" were equally productive sources of information. The Dies Committee heard testimony from a variety of seasoned red-hunters, including a Detroit police officer who claimed to be running 40 operatives in the local communist branch. That city's police superintendent helped out by inserting into the Committee record a series of intelligence memoranda on recent labor unrest (147 sit-down strikes and 40 walk-out strikes).[15] Most of the "Red Squad Intelligence" was submitted in confidence through the efforts of Dies Committee investigator Stephen W. Birmingham, a former detective with the New York Police Department safe-and-loft squad and then a private detective with a strike breaking business. Birmingham maintained

---

[13] For these (and other) Dies Committee raids, see Starling to Early, Mar. 30, 1940, PPF 1-A, Roosevelt Papers; Hutchinson to Wilson, Mar. 25, 1940, ibid.; Hoover to Watson, Mar. 5, 1941, 666-A and Mar. 7, 1941, 672, OF 10-B, ibid.; FBI Rept. No. 66, May 10, 1940 (summary only), ibid.; "The Dies Offensive," *The Nation*, Apr. 13, 1940, 465; Ickes, *Secret Diary*, vol. 3, *The Lowering Clouds, 1939–1941*, 33.

[14] *Cong. Record*, 78th Cong., 3rd sess., Apr. 17, 1940, 2184; Martin Dies, "They Tried to Get Me, Too," *U.S. News and World Report*, Aug. 20, 1954, 66; *Reeve v. Howe*, 33 F. Supp. 619 (1940); *Detroit Times*, Nov. 20 and 22, 1940; Hoover to Jackson, Sept. 14, 1940, 61–7582–470X1, FBI HUAC File.

[15] Dies Committee, *Public Hearings* (17 vols, 1938–1944), 75th Cong., 2nd sess., 1938, 2: 1605–32.

242   *Little 'Red Scares'*

his NYPD contacts while working for Dies and routinely received reports on such targets as actor Melvyn Douglas, writer Waldo Frank, and New York Municipal Judge Dorothy Kenyon—which he leaked to columnist Westbrook Pegler, among other New Deal adversaries. Pegler once said the assassin who killed Chicago Mayor Anton Cermak while he was shaking hands with Franklin Roosevelt had shot the wrong man.[16]

Like the Dies Committee, local red squads did not completely ignore the right. The Committee persuaded the Pennsylvania State Police to plant two undercover operatives, along with a Committee mole, in German America Bund camps in New Jersey. A check of license plate numbers with the State Motor Vehicle Department in Trenton revealed the names of those attending. Additional data, including social security numbers and places of employment, were received from the Social Security Board. As a final step, Dies turned over the names of 3,500 Bundists to the State Department. The department then forwarded the names to the FBI. At President Roosevelt's direction, the FBI then sent the names of those working in any defense connected industry to their employers.[17] This was routine. The FBI designated a liaison agent and assigned up to 15 agents who consulted Committee files "almost every day." This crew even reviewed Committee files when checking special agent applicants.[18]

These files were no more than a supplement to the FBI's voluminous files. Bureau agents were engaged in extensive electronic surveillance (i.e., wiretaps and microphones) and break-ins (i.e., burglaries). Moreover, the FBI often leaked any derogatory information gathered either to expose communists and their sympathizers or to alert management to potentially subversive employees. FBI field agents also had sources of information in the communications industry that allowed them to monitor most long-distance messages. In 1941, for example, a "very confidential contact at Postal" gave the special agent in charge of the Washington, D.C., field office copies of telegrams sent by a *New York World Telegram* city editor to a reporter. The newspaper had claimed that an unnamed

---

[16] Ibid., 14: 8467; Barker to Birmingham, Feb. 22, 1941, and NYPD Alien Squad Report, Sept. 4, 1941, Communism ... Dies Committee 1934–1942, Westbrook Pegler Papers, Herbert Hoover Presidential Library, West Branch, Iowa; NYPD Report no. 695, Oct. 14, 1941, ibid.

[17] SAC New York to Director, Oct. 4, 1940, 61-7582-478, FBI HUAC File; Hoover to McGuire, Oct. 11, 1940, 61-7582-484, ibid.; Hoover to Jackson, Oct. 21, 1940, Dies Folder, Hoover O&C FBI File; J. Parnell Thomas, "Sabotage? You Haven't Seen Anything Yet," *Factory Management and Maintenance*, Dec. 1940, 46.

[18] Dies, "They Tried to Get Me, Too," 66–7; Dies Committee, *Annual Report*, H. Rept. 2748, 77th Cong., 2nd sess., 1943, 3; memo, for the File, Jan. 14, 1947, President's Temp. Commission on Employee Loyalty—vol. II (1), Stephen J. Spingarn Papers, Harry S. Truman Presidential Library, Independence, MO.

The Dies Committee v. the New Deal 243

bureau agent had provided it with information concerning the suicide of former Soviet intelligence officer Walter Krivitsky, once a bureau informant and more lately a Dies Committee witness.[19]

With a 30-man investigative staff directed by Matthews and Whitley and operating out of six branch offices, it was not surprising that the Dies Committee and the FBI had a relationship. By quoting the often reckless Dies, the bureau could spread tripe while maintaining a (largely) false aura of higher standards. The Committee's first published volume of hearings, for example, listed some 640 organizations and 438 newspapers as communist controlled and 284 labor organizers and perhaps 1,000 other individuals as CPUSA members. John P. Frey, who headed the AFL's Metal Trades Department, personally named nearly 300 rival CIO organizers as Reds. The FBI quoted Frey's testimony in its own reports while Dies sent the names of those CIO organizers to the chiefs of every police department operating a Red Squad.

Since the mid-1930s if not earlier, Frey's operatives had been infiltrating the CPUSA and the Young Communist League and photostating or simply stealing "confidential Communist documents." Following his testimony, Frey continued to send the Committee "an immense amount of documentary evidence" and to place his investigative services at the Committee's disposal. He performed similar services for such others as Senator Arthur Vandenberg (R., MI). After Frey accused FDR's nominee to the Maritime Labor Board of associating with communists, Vandenberg asked Frey for a detailed report on the man's activities. Frey produced enough "derogatory information" to help Vandenberg kill the nomination during hearings before the Senate Commerce Committee.[20]

Even more spectacular charges were leveled by Dies Committee witness Walter Steele, editor of the far-right *National Republic* magazine, an advisory board member of an anti-Semitic coterie (the Paul Reveres), and chair of the National Security Committee of the American Coalition of Patriotic, Civic, and Fraternal Societies. He described himself as the spokesman for 20 million patriots, and when testifying named hundreds of individuals as CPUSA members and hundreds of organization as communist "infested." Dies devoted over 400 pages in his initial volume of hearings to Steele's revelations.

Dies Committee member J. Parnell Thomas (R., NJ) interrupted Steele's testimony to announce that he had just been handed an FBI report on CIO organizer Harry Bridges of the International Longshore and Warehouse Union. Dies called this report "evidence of the fact that they [FBI officials] desire to

---

[19]   See the documents in the Krivitsky Folder, Nichols Official and Confidential (O&C) FBI File.

[20]   Frey to Vandenberg, Aug. 16, 1938, Box 7, Dies Committee (1), John P. Frey Papers, Library of Congress; Vandenberg to Frey, Aug. 18, 1939, ibid.

cooperate." Both men were mistaken. Thomas actually received a document from the file on Paul Edwards, the Federal Arts Administrator in New York and yet another Dies Committee target. The file was made available after bureau officials consulted with Assistant Attorney General Alexander Holtzoff, who later served as Hoover's personal counsel and then a federal judge. When Gordon Dean, then with the Justice Department and later chair of the Atomic Energy Commission, attempted to find out through Holtzoff's office the name of the Dies Committee contact who received the bureau document, an FBI agent told Holtzoff's secretary "that I did not recall the name and I do not know how we could locate it." Hoover commended the lie: "Right. We of course do not want to give publicity to such requests."[21]

One reason for Hoover's reluctance to publicize "such requests" was his desire to remain at arm's length from the Dies Committee's unabashed and unapologetic effort to discredit the New Deal. Committee interest in Bridges arose from a charge, first leveled by chief investigator Sullivan before he was fired, that a high-level Labor Department official was protecting the Australian-born Bridges, a controversial figure given his role in the West Coast Longshore Strike of 1934. The government launched what was to become a marathon deportation case against Bridges in the aftermath of that strike (that included on the tail end a four-day general strike in San Francisco and the greater Bay Area). Dies and Thomas used Sullivan's charge to accuse Secretary of Labor Frances Perkins of coddling communists. Actually, President Roosevelt had no real objections to harassing communists. "How does Sam Darcy get in and out of this country?," he asked Perkins about a key organizer of the San Francisco general strike. "Is he not another alien?" Roosevelt also told Perkins that "we can prove propaganda directed at the destruction of the Government [in the Bridges deportation case]."[22] Regardless of FDR's interest, Perkins had no power to evict Bridges because of a recent U.S. Court of Appeals ruling in the *Strecker* case,[23] which held that CPUSA membership alone did not provide adequate grounds for deportation.

Solicitor General Robert Jackson invited Dies to help prepare the government's appeal of *Strecker* to the Supreme Court. (Jackson would go on to serve as Attorney General, chief U.S. prosecutor at the Nuremberg Trials, and as a Supreme Court justice.) Dies responded by sending Jackson a 24-page attack on Perkins. The affair, moreover, refused to fade, with Thomas periodically calling for Perkins's removal and Hoover declaring Bridges a card-carrying communist.

---

[21] See serials 61-7582-12, -12X, -13, and -43, FBI HUAC File.
[22] FDR to Perkins, Aug. 29 and Sept. 18, 1935, OF 1750, Roosevelt Papers.
[23] *Strecker v. Kessler*, 95 F. 2d 976 (1938).

The Dies Committee v. the New Deal 245

And J.B. Matthews read into the Dies Committee record what he said was an FBI report on "Harry Bridges' right-hand man." The case dragged on until 1945 when the Supreme Court overturned Bridges's deportation order.[24]

The Dies Committee's telescopic focus on New Deal personnel and such constituencies as organized labor extended into the White House, with the First Lady a particularly alluring target. Eleanor Roosevelt had supported such left-wing organizations as the American Youth Congress (AYC), and was a close friend of Joseph P. Lash, then national secretary of the American Student Union (ASU). When the Committee heard testimony from Lash, Mrs. Roosevelt attended the hearings to provide moral support. She declined an invitation to sit with the inquisitors and instead sat with Lash and other Committee targets. During a break in the hearings, she took six of the young men back to the White House for lunch. That evening they dined with both Eleanor and Franklin.

Nonetheless, Mrs. Roosevelt was not oblivious to the communist front charges leveled against the AYC and the ASU. Before the Dies Committee hearings opened, she requested an FBI file check on the Youth Congress. When it arrived she privately ridiculed it. (On the other hand, she solicited additional FBI reports on subjects ranging from the International Ladies Garment Workers Union to the ubiquitous Westbrook Pegler.)[25]

Mrs. Roosevelt supported the AYC until the group's ideological gymnastics in the wake of the Nazi–Soviet Pact in 1939 and then the Nazi invasion of Russia in 1941. She continued to support Lash, however, and in 1942 interceded on his behalf with the FBI and the Dies Committee. (Lash was seeking a commission in Naval Intelligence. He did not receive it and instead enlisted in the Army.) That same year, FBI agents burglarized the AYC's New York offices and photographed the First Lady's correspondence. Hoover mistakenly thought she might be having an affair with Lash because she closed her letters with "Love, Eleanor."[26]

Dies Committee efforts to discredit the New Deal were assisted as well by the private sector—as when one Harper L. Knowles testified in October 1938 and received front-page coverage in the *New York Times*. Knowles introduced himself as chair of the American Legion's Radical Research Committee. He did not note his work on behalf of Associated Farmers, Inc., a vigilante organization

---

[24]   Dies to Jackson, Oct. 29, 1938, OF 320 (Dies Committee 1938), Roosevelt Papers; Dies Committee, *Public Hearings*, 14: 8563–64.

[25]   See the correspondence in alphabetized folders Hom-Hoz 1939, Hez-Hoz 1940, He-Ho 1942, and Ho-Hi 1943, Eleanor Roosevelt Papers, Roosevelt Library. See also Hoover to Watson, Dec. 28, 1942, 2294, OF 10-B, Franklin Roosevelt Papers; [Tully] to Thompson, Jan. 8, 1943, ibid.; Tully to Hoover, Dec. 11, 1942, PSF-Justice Department (J. Edgar Hoover), Roosevelt Papers.

[26]   See the documents in the AYC Folder, Nichols O&C FBI File.

246　　　　　　　　　　　　　　*Little 'Red Scares'*

that on one hand hired thugs to terrorize farm workers and on the other ran a peaceful campaign to ban John Steinbeck's *Grapes of Wrath*. Knowles accused U.S. Senator Sheridan Downey and various other California politicians of being communist tools. The Republican nominee for Downey's seat, a millionaire landowner, sat on the Associated Farmers board. The FBI later quoted from Knowles's testimony when dispensing derogatory information to the press. Knowles (with the help of an ex-FBI agent) went on to establish the Western Research Foundation, an entity that provided a political dossier service for the Dies Committee's successor and various corporations.[27]

Perhaps the most explicit example of Dies's preferences involved J.B. Matthews's investigation of Reds in the consumer movement. Matthews had been a vice president of Consumers Research and in 1934 he co-wrote, with CR president Fred J. Schlink, *Partners in Plunder*, an indictment of profit-gouging manufacturers. But when Schlink's own employees tried to unionize, Matthews denounced their strike as a communist ploy. The strikers then broke off and formed the rival Consumers Union. Matthews compiled his exposé four years later, charging communist infiltration of every consumer group except his former employer's and his wife's current employer. With Dies's backing, Matthews released his report to the press—a decision that enraged Jerry Voorhis (D., CA) and several other Committee members who were not even aware of the report's existence.[28]

Voorhis, who would lose his House seat to Nixon in the 1946 elections, thought Matthews's report was simply the unsubstantiated opinion of a disgruntled ex-consumer activist seeking revenge against imagined enemies. But there was more to it than that. The release and accompanying publicity were arranged to neutralize a Federal Trade Commission (FTC) decision to cite the Hearst Corporation's *Good Housekeeping* for fraudulent advertising practices. The FTC challenged the magazine's "use of Good Housekeeping seals," concluding they were "calculated to ... mislead and deceive." One manufacturer claimed a seal of approval could be obtained simply by advertising in *Good Houskeeping*. But if a manufacturer cancelled an ad, the seal was summarily withdrawn. Though the FTC acted in response to pressure brought by retailers and manufacturers and not by communists, the Hearst press and its Dies Committee allies responded by red-baiting its critics.

---

[27]　Shortly before the 1938 elections, six other Dies Committee witnesses smeared Minnesota Governor Elmer Benson and his Farmer-Labor party. This testimony, in the service of GOP gubernatorial candidate Harold Stassen, was coordinated by an attorney whose brother served as Stassen's campaign manager. Dies gave him six blank subpoenas.

[28]　A copy is in Consumers, Gardner Jackson Papers, Roosevelt Library.

Under Hearst executive Richard Berlin's direction, the company launched an advertising blitz. In a telegram to 2,000 businessmen and 1,000 publishers and editors sent on the day the FTC cited *Good Housekeeping*, Berlin warned of a communist-dominated consumer movement that "must now be publicly exposed." When the FTC hearings opened that same month, Dies threatened to investigate "Communist influence" in consumer groups and called on "business leadership" to purge "racketeers who are able to sway the emotions of an uninformed people and teach them the damnable doctrines of socialism and communism."[29]

This strategy of red-baiting consumer activists and their New Deal benefactors was further refined during a dinner hosted by NAM trouble-shooter George Sokolsky. Matthews attended and so did executives from Young and Rubican, Bristol-Meyers, and the Association of National Advertisers, among others. Fred Schlink, Matthews's former boss and still president of the pristine Consumers Research, also attended. Though all guests claimed the dinner was strictly a social gathering, a specific course of action had in fact been agreed upon. Matthews's ill-fated report was released to the press six days later. For his part, Berlin had read and approved this (supposedly) official congressional publication before most Dies Committee members had even heard about it.

However much Martin Dies and associates were troubled by the communist associations of the (mostly) young men and women who flocked to Washington to staff the alphabet agencies both new and old (the FTC was created during the Progressive Era), there was a more fundamental reason for their concern. Quite simply, many congressional conservatives were troubled by the growth of presidential power, with the Dies Committee sounding the alarm about the "creeping totalitarianism" of the executive's "effort to obliterate the Congress of the United States as a co-equal and independent branch of government."[30] Though clearly partisan, the Committee also had an anti-executive strain.

The Roosevelt administration attempted to counter the Dies Committee on every front, however partisan or not. During the consumer movement uproar, for example, the President urged the First Lady and Secretary of Agriculture Henry A. Wallace to publicize Matthews's conflicts of interest and the embarrassing dinner party hosted by Sokolsky.[31] FDR even collected the missives sent to the White House by hard-boiled Dies haters and showed them to House Democratic majority leader Sam Rayburn of Texas, among others. The Democratic National Committee also arranged for an attack on Dies Committee procedures broadcast by NBC radio. Shortly thereafter, Harold

---

[29] See the documents in Series 1, Box 3, Donald Montgomery Papers, Archives of Labor History and Urban Affairs, Wayne State University, Detroit.

[30] Dies Committee, *Annual Report*, H. Rept. 2277, 77th Cong., 2nd sess., 1942, 2.

[31] See the correspondence in OF 320 (Dies Committee 1939), Roosevelt Papers.

248   *Little 'Red Scares'*

Ickes secured a certified statement alleging that Dies had paid no taxes on his home and lot in Texas for eight years; and further that a Committee witness was "probably" financed by "certain pro-Nazi groups." That witness had denounced Commission of Indian Affairs John Collier for "Communist sympathies," a charge picked up by a Nazi press anxious to compare U.S. policy on Indians with the Reich's policy on supposed *Untermenschen*.[32]

Attorney General Jackson passed on a rumor to Hoover that Dies's father had been pro-German during the last war and that the government had compiled "a large dossier on him." Following Dies's unsuccessful bid for a Senate seat in 1941, moreover, Roosevelt ordered the FBI to investigate for election fraud. According to Lyndon Johnson, another unsuccessful candidate in the special election for that Senate seat, the bureau demonstrated that a proportion of Dies's vote was shifted to the eventual victor, Texas Governor W. Lee ("Pappy") O'Daniel (the only person who ever defeated LBJ in an election).[33] On another occasion FDR directed the FBI to investigate a rumor, forwarded to the White House by Supreme Court Justice Felix Frankfurter, that Dies's campaign manager had received $20,000 from a German agent. "This is so important," the President wrote to Attorney General Francis Biddle (Jackson's successor). But the FBI's "painstaking investigation" came up dry.[34]

At the same time, the FBI volunteered intelligence data on the Dies Committee itself. Hoover even forwarded editorial cartoons critical of Dies to FDR's aides. In response to a request for a dossier on Gerald L.K. Smith, Hoover outlined the man's contacts not only with Dies but Henry Ford and Senators Robert Reynolds (D., NC) and Gerald Nye (R., ND). Hoover and his senior executives, however, did not share the administration's sometimes uncompromising opposition to the Dies Committee. They opposed Dies's style and not his goals.[35]

Such FBI services may help explain Roosevelt's restrained public position on the Dies Committee. The President believed he could best contain Dies not by public confrontation but by working behind the scenes to limit his Committee's appropriations. With Rayburn's help, the President also tried

---

[32]   Roosevelt to [McIntyre], Nov. 23, 1938, ibid.; Martin Dies, *Martin Dies' Story* (New York, 1963), 254–5; Ickes, 526.

[33]   Dies made a second unsuccessful run for the Senate in 1957.

[34]   Jackson to Hoover and Allen, Nov. 29, 1940, 61-7582-819X, FBI HUAC File; memo, for the President, Apr. 15, 1942, CF D, Roosevelt Papers; FDR to Biddle, Apr. 16, 1942, ibid.; Biddle to FDR, Apr. 20, 1942, ibid.; Ronnie Dugger, *The Politician* (New York, 1982), 225–6, 233, 333, 442n.

[35]   FBI Report No. 54, Apr. 10, 1940 (summary only), OF 10-B, Roosevelt Papers; Hoover to Watson, Jan. 28, 1941, 616, and Mar. 26, 1941, 700, ibid.

to pack the Committee with New Dealers (something vaguely similar to the Supreme Court packing plan). These schemes failed, though Roosevelt did work with Voorhis to moderate the Committee's behavior. For example, in December 1940, after the House passed a bill calling for the registration of foreign agents and containing an amendment proposed by Dies that required CPUSA functionaries to register, Roosevelt devised a strategy to defeat the amendment in the Senate. Neither the role of the White House nor that of another helper—South Carolina Senator and soon to be Supreme Court Justice James F. Byrnes—in initiating this strategy was revealed.[36]

Yet another strategy to contain Dies was to have the Justice Department and the FBI investigate the various organizations he had been attacking. This we're-already-spyin'-on-'em approach was conceived by Attorney General Frank Murphy (Jackson's predecessor), a staunch liberal who, according to Ickes, "weakened under pressure from Hoover." Murphy reasoned that if a grand jury convened and handed down indictments for espionage (or whatever), Congress would see that the administration was acting responsibly and conclude that there was no reason to renew the Dies Committee's appropriation. Unknown to Ickes, Hoover's pressure on Murphy might not have been routine. The FBI opened a file on Murphy and kept it open even after Murphy had moved to the Supreme Court.[37]

The Roosevelt administration began to implement Murphy's strategy in January 1939 following FDR's announcement that the Justice Department would prosecute anyone who had been named by Dies and had in fact violated any federal law. Murphy, for example, ordered the FBI to investigate Dies's charge of communist influence in the Federal Writers Project.[38] In addition, Roosevelt acceded to some of Dies's demands. When Ickes issued a permit in June 1939 to the Workers Alliance Congress (WAC) to use a Labor Department auditorium for a meeting, the President ordered this permit withdrawn because an FBI report seemingly confirmed Dies's charge that the WAC was a communist front. Acting on the advice of Voorhis and Murphy, the President also acceded to Dies's request that the Committee be permitted to examine income tax returns.[39]

---

[36] FDR to McIntyre, Jan. 13, 1942, OF 133 (Immigration 1942), Roosevelt Papers; [Byrnes] to FDR, n.d. (*c.*Jan. 1942), ibid.

[37] The FBI kept files on other justices too, including Felix Frankfurter (captioned with the name of his brother). See the Otto N. Frankfurter Folder, Nichols O&C FBI File.

[38] See serials 61-7582-46 and -46X, FBI HUAC File; and the Murphy-Dies correspondence in 23677 (1–2), Justice Dept. Central Files.

[39] Ickes, *The Inside Struggle*, 642; Murphy to FDR, Mar. 30, 1939, OF 320 (Dies Committee 1939), Roosevelt Papers.

250   *Little 'Red Scares'*

Roosevelt was even more tolerant of the Dies Committee after the German advance in Europe in early 1940. A few liberals even began to champion the Committee's work as complementing the FBI's. "The Committee, not the FBI," Voorhis said, "had to tell the country the story of un-American activities. But the FBI, not the Committee, had to discover the basic facts on which the story could be built."[40] None of this had any effect on Dies. He continued to assail the New Deal. Over his Committee's seven-year lifespan, he claimed to have submitted the names of 5,000 government employees "with questionable records" to the administration. Indeed, the Committee was only a few months old when Dies first pressured Roosevelt about the federal employment of alleged subversives. In December 1938 he presented to the State Department a list of supposedly un-American organizations (that included the ACLU) and asked the department to treat members of these groups as agents of a foreign government. Roosevelt understood this raw strategy of submitting "evidence" and then criticizing the administration for not acting on it.

In late 1938, for instance, J. Parnell Thomas asked the FBI for a list of communists employed by federal agencies. Hoover said the bureau had no such list. Less than a year later, however, Dies claimed that the Justice Department was investigating 2,850 known communists in government and that FDR had ordered a purge of all those named. According to a *Chicago Tribune* story (apparently based on a leak), this list had been prepared by the FBI. But the President had ordered no such purge and the *Tribune* later reported that the list was suppressed and Hoover rebuked. Similarly, Eleanor Roosevelt recalled "one occasion [where] my husband and I were given a confidential list of organizations which were communist or subversive or un-American, a list compiled by the FBI for the use of the Dies Committee." Secretary of War Henry L. Stimson, Secretary of the Navy Frank Knox, Mrs. James Roosevelt (FDR's mother), and other prominent figures close to the President were listed as financial contributors to two or more of the suspect groups.[41]

By 1941 pressure brought by the Committee began to have an effect. In February Hoover forwarded information to the White House regarding Dies's plans to investigate government employees. In early summer Congress approved a rider adding $100,000 to the Justice Department appropriations bill to enable the FBI to investigate (and report to Congress on) "employees of every department, agency and independent establishment of the Federal Government who are members of subversive organizations." This rider, together

---

[40]   *Cong. Record*, 76th Cong., 3rd sess., Dec. 12, 1940, 13912–13, and 77th Cong., 1st sess., Feb. 11, 1941, 887, 889; Jerry Voorhis, *Confessions of a Congressman* (Garden City, NY, 1947), 224.

[41]   Eleanor Roosevelt, *This I Remember* (New York, 1949), 202–03.

with provisions of the Hatch Act of 1939 (which prohibited federal employee "membership in any political party which advocates the overthrow of our constitutional form of government"), also inspired creation of the first Attorney General's List of Subversive Organizations. At the beginning in June, only eight organizations made that list. In September the FBI began to distribute the list to its local field offices. By February 1942 the bureau had investigated 22 additional groups and recommended their inclusion on the list. By May the list had grown to 12 communist or communist front groups, 14 domestic fascist groups, and 21 pro-Japanese groups. Membership in any of the proscribed organizations was grounds for dismissal from federal employment.[42] Except for the CPUSA, the Silver Legion, and the German American Bund, the listed organizations were kept secret—though a copy of the list somehow leaked to Dies.

Regardless, the Roosevelt administration's loyalty program remained relatively moderate. More than 1,300 job applicants were rejected, but fewer than 200 federal employees lost their jobs or were subjected to disciplinary action during the war years. Intending to limit abuses, FDR requested that journalist John Franklin Carter, who wrote the "We, the People" syndicated column under the name "Jay Franklin," compile a confidential report on "Blacklisting Government Employees." This was somewhat ironic. Carter served as the President's personal "spook," working closely with the FBI and occasionally furnishing "intelligence" on such prominent Republicans as Wendell Willkie and Thomas E. Dewey. Operating a unit closely connected with a reluctant State Department, Carter's "specialized investigative work" received hundreds of thousands of dollars from the President's Emergency Fund. By late 1941 Carter had a staff of 11, and the "jealous" FBI began to spy on the President's private spy—advising Biddle that Carter recently spent 350 taxpayer dollars on cocktails for New York's "upper crust."[43]

An affinity for political intelligence aside, Roosevelt's loyalty program was restrained; and this frustrated both Dies and Hoover, who had hoped the new loyalty program would legitimize the bureau's effort to gather "comprehensive information ... through a program of progressive intelligence and not through isolated investigations of overt acts." In an effort to undercut Dies charges and "to prevent recurrences of situations like the Dies-[Leon] Henderson controversy" (where FDR's choice to head the Office of Price Administration was accused

---

[42] *Report of the F.B.I. Relative to Investigation of Government Employees Charged with Un-American Activities*, H. Doc. 833, 77th Cong., 2nd sess., 1942, 12–13; Hoover to Watson, Feb. 27, 1941, 661, OF 10-B, Roosevelt Papers; Whitehead, *The FBI Story*, 434 n1.

[43] John Franklin Carter, "Report on 'Blacklisting' Government Employees," June 11, 1942, 61-7582-1160, FBI HUAC File. See also the documents in PSF (John Franklin Carter), Boxes 120–37, Roosevelt Papers.

252 *Little 'Red Scares'*

of membership in five CPUSA fronts),[44] Biddle asked Dies for information relating to federal employee membership in subversive organizations.

The FBI had ample files on the (real and imagined) subversive associations of federal employees and was quite willing to publicize information from these files if it could be done without "embarrassing the Bureau." At least one federal employee named by Dies as a subversive, for instance, was the subject of a FBI "blind" memoranda (i.e., unsigned and sans letterhead) connecting him to the allegedly subversive Consumers Union. Bureau officials, however, were reluctant to provide Biddle with much of the information contained in their files because it had been obtained illegally by break-ins or other questionable means. While considering Biddle's request, Dies solicited the advice of Albert C. Mattei, president of the San Francisco-based Honolulu Oil Company, financial backer of GOP candidates in northern California, and close friend of Herbert Hoover. After checking with another close friend (FBI official Louis B. Nichols, who would later serve as Nixon's point man on the Alger Hiss case), Mattei advised Dies to send his list of names to the Attorney General and to the bureau. Dies promptly forwarded a list of 1,124 allegedly subversive federal employees.[45]

Biddle directed Hoover to compile "all available information concerning [each of] the [accused] employee's participation in un-American activities." The FBI was also authorized to investigate complaints of un-American activities on the part of federal employees received from other sources (in all 4,579 complaints were received by late August 1942). Only 149 federal workers were in the vague un-American category. Most were accused of communist associations. Of the thousands of workers whose names had been referred to the FBI during this first round of the loyalty investigations, only 36 were discharged. That number included a mere 2 from Dies's original list of 1,124.[46]

Dies charged a cover-up, claiming possession of an FBI report revealing that Biddle had allowed the bureau to investigate only a few of the persons on his list. Under procedures established by the Attorney General, the FBI forwarded 1,579 complaints to the appropriate department or agency chiefs. But there were only 193 requests for follow-up FBI work during the program's first three months. This lack of response and Dies's continual criticism pressured Biddle into revising the original procedure. Thereafter, the FBI was authorized to investigate solely on the basis of complaints received. The results of its probes were then turned over to department heads for individual evaluation. The new standards please Dies in theory. But the Roosevelt administration still

---

[44] Hoover to Biddle, Apr. 5, 1941, 61-7582-966, FBI HUAC File.

[45] Voorhis, *Confessions*, 224. For Mattei, see Nichols to Tolson, Oct. 14, 1941, Dies Committee Folder, Nichols O&C FBI File.

[46] *Report of the F.B.I ...* (1942), 11, 13–17.

refused to initiate a sweeping purge in practice. By the end of 1942, the FBI had investigated 601 persons on Dies original list, forwarding unevaluated reports to the department heads where the suspect federal employees worked. In 101 cases, the FBI's reports were not even acknowledged. Only two more people on Dies's list were fired, bringing the grand total to four. Two other federal employees were disciplined.[47]

If the Roosevelt administration intended these FBI investigations to deprive the Dies Committee of its most volatile issue and further demonstrate a responsible attitude toward the communists-in-government issue, the immediate result was quite different. "A department report clearing the man and a decision not to fire him," as Ickes advised Roosevelt, "may simply serve to prove Dies' main point, that your Administration cherishes men who want to subvert the government."[48] And if New Deal officials did not then have to pay a major political price for ignoring FBI loyalty reports, in the long run they would. Dies responded to the administration's condescending effort to investigate his cover-up charges by arguing that those department heads who had refused to purge their staff were abetting communism.

In response to Dies's charges, FBI officials first obtained "access to confidential records" of 47 "subversive groups," then identified suspect federal employees by name, and finally submitted a detailed four-volume report to the Attorney General with a recommendation that it be made available to Congress. According to these FBI executives, the President "was primarily interested in having the Bureau's summary report discredit the Dies Committee." Thus after consulting with Sam Rayburn, Biddle ordered a reluctant FBI to prepare for Congress a brief 20-page report, "anonymous in nature both as to names of the persons investigated and the organizations which had been declared subversive." In contrast to Biddle, Rayburn, and Roosevelt, Hoover wanted to name each and every suspect federal employee and all 47 groups on the Attorney General's List of Subversive Organizations. Dies, for his part, was aware that the original report "had been sent back to the FBI to be 'toned down.'"[49]

Dies did not allow the communists-in-government issue to lapse. His March 1942 denouncement of 35 Board of Economic Warfare (BEW) employees prompted Vice President (and BEW chair) Henry Wallace to say the effect on civil service morale "would be no less damaging if Mr. Dies were on the Hitler

---

[47]   *Cong. Record*, 77th Cong., 2nd sess., Sept. 24, 1942, 7442–48; *Report of F.B.I. Relative to Investigation of Government Employees Charged with Un-American Activities*, H. Doc. 51,78th Cong., 1st sess., 1943, 4–5.

[48]   Ickes to FDR, June 3, 1943, OF 1661-A (1941–45), Roosevelt Papers.

[49]   Hoover to Biddle, Sept. 1, 1942, Martin Dies Folder, Hoover O&C FBI File; Ladd to Hoover, Nov. 27, 1953, ibid.; Timm to Ladd, Sept. 24, 1942, 61-7582-1186, FBI HUAC File.

254 *Little 'Red Scares'*

payroll." Still, Wallace promised that the FBI would investigate all 35. Even when Dies inspired a libel lawsuit (he confused a BEW worker with someone with the same name), the House paid Dies's court costs and the chair continued to name names. He supplemented another list of 19 suspect government employees with the names of 39 "irresponsible, unrepresentative, crack-pot, radical bureaucrats" on February 1, 1943. After an abortive attempt to withhold one unfortunate's salary, the House established a special committee, chaired by John H. Kerr (D., NC), to investigate the charges.

The Kerr Committee, described by Ickes as part of "a vicious political campaign" led by "a small group of men determined to smear ... the Administration, irrespective of the cost to the war," ultimately investigated nine people. It cleared six and deemed the remaining three unfit for government service: Robert Morss Lovett, secretary of the Virgin Islands; and two Federal Communications Commission officials, Goodwin Watson and William E. Dodd, Jr. Its findings were based primarily on evidence presented to the Civil Service Commission by the FBI, with the Dies Committee preparing detailed charges supported by its files. FBI officials monitored Kerr Committee proceedings and furnished it with at least two "blind" memoranda. One included data on the ACLU. The other included data, submitted to the bureau by the State Department "in the strictest of confidence," on a film entitled *The Negro in America*.[50]

Whether the FBI worked through Kerr Committee staff or had direct contact with Kerr and the other congressmen is not known. By 1945, nonetheless, Kerr was certainly serving the FBI as a conduit. On one occasion he called Hoover with a request for bureau "material 'to get some things over to the public.'" The bureau responded by preparing a speech for Kerr that was read into the *Congressional Record* and reproduced in the *FBI Law Enforcement Bulletin*. Kerr, in turn, thanked FBI Associate Director Clyde Tolson for the "splendid statement."[51]

Although the FBI covertly assisted the Kerr Committee in order to support Dies's charges, Dies and Hoover did not always work in harmony. In January 1939, after the Philadelphia special agent in charge attended Dies's luncheon address at the Penn Athletic Club, Hoover issued a directive: "I think it is undesirable for our agents to attend such affairs. There can be placed misinterpretation upon such attendance to our embarrassment." Another senior FBI executive rebuked

---

[50] Ladd to Callahan, May 4, 1943, FBI ACLU File; Goodman, *The Committee*, 132; Robert E. Cushman, "The Purge of Federal Employees Accused of Disloyalty," *Public Administration Review* 3 (Autumn 1943): 306, *passim*; Ickes to FDR, May 15 and June 3, 1943, OF 1661-A, Roosevelt Papers. In *U.S. v. Lovett*, 328 U.S. 303 (1946), the Supreme Court held the congressional attempt to strip the salaries of Lovett, Watson, and Dodd to be a bill of attainder.

[51] See the correspondence in the Kerr Folder, Nichols O&C FBI File.

the Philadelphia agent, "*pointing out that Mr. Dies has been accusing the [Justice] Department of investigating him* and ... even alleging that the Bureau is being used by the White House to whitewash the purportedly astounding conditions that he has uncovered."[52]

These strained relations developed into a full-blown feud between Dies and Hoover in 1940 after the chairman reportedly referred to the G-men as "a bunch of boy scouts." He then labeled bureau efforts to contain sabotage in defense plants inadequate and said the Committee could help by exposing prospective saboteurs. According to Dies, there were some 5,000 of these types—Bundists, communists, and German and Japanese aliens—in Detroit alone. Hoover responded to Dies's call for formation of a Home Defense Council by advising the White House that it was unnecessary—because the President had already designated the FBI as the central coordinating agency and the FBI was already spying on all groups espousing "un-American principles."[53]

Dies concern with sabotage seemed well founded. In September 1940 the Hercules powder plant in New Jersey blew up, killing 51. Two months later, three other East Coast powder plants exploded within an hour of each other. Public concern was further heightened in November by the Vultee strike. Many suspected that this action, led by the United Automobile Workers Union (labeled a communist front by Dies Committee witness John Frey), was intended to cripple America's aircraft production. Then, after Committee investigators raided the headquarters of German and Italian organizations in New York and Chicago, Dies claimed that a confessed Gestapo agent had identified several official representatives of foreign governments in the United States as espionage agents. The November 20 release of a Committee "white paper" detailing these alleged espionage activities was considered premature and led to Justice Department criticism and a public rebuke from Hoover.[54]

The white paper consisted of staff reports on Nazi activities in the United States, supplemented by facsimiles of documents seized during the recent raids. The overall focus was on one Manfred Zapp, director of the Transocean News Service, and Zapp's personal correspondence. The material did show that high-ranking Nazis were interested in spreading propaganda throughout Central America and South America. Overall the white paper exaggerated the extent of German espionage and propaganda activities in the United States. Because the press went

---

[52] Tracy to Tamm, Jan. 26, 1939, 61-7582-49X, FBI HUAC File; Tamm to Hoover, Jan. 30, 1939, 61-7582-52, ibid.

[53] Hoover to Watson, June 3, 1940, 109, OF 10-B, Roosevelt Papers.

[54] For the white paper, see Dies Committee, Appendix II, *A Preliminary Digest and Report on Un-American Activities ... Including Diplomatic and Consular Agents of the German Government*, 76th Cong., 3rd sess., 1940.

along with this exaggeration, the implication was that the Dies Committee knew more about the espionage/sabotage problem than the FBI did.

The white paper appeared to catch the FBI off guard. Upon learning that Dies was investigating Zapp and Transocean, Hoover demanded to know why his agents "weren't ... on top of this?" The affair also raised the prospect of criticism from a source normally supportive of both the FBI and the Dies Committee. Paul Mallon, an editor and columnist for the Hearst-owned King Features Syndicate, responded to Dies's revelations by sending a confidential letter critical of the bureau to several (perhaps all) newspaper editors associated with Hearst's International News Service. Hoover countered by contacting Edmond D. Coblentz, publisher of the *San Francisco Call Bulletin* and supervisor of the editorial division for the entire Hearst publishing conglomerate, for advice and assistance in "straighten[ing] Mallon out."[55]

The Justice Department responded by condemning the Dies Committee's interference with an ongoing criminal investigation. (The bureau had filed a report with the White House on Zapp's activities nearly four weeks after learning of Dies's interest in Transocean.)[56] Complaining on November 24 that premature publicity might prevent successful prosecution of Zapp and cohorts, the Justice Department dismissed the Committee's chief witness as a "professional and unreliable" informer/grifter who had been investigated twice for white slavery. Then to head off another promised Dies Committee probe, the Justice Department announced that there was no need for a congressional exploration of the Vultee strike because the FBI had already concluded it was orchestrated by communists.

Hoover responded by disseminating Justice Department criticism "to all friendly newspaper contacts" and other friends of the FBI (e.g., the American Legion's Homer Chaillaux and the ACLU's Morris Ernst). The FBI also escalated its surveillance of the Dies Committee. After approving a suggestion "that each and every employee of the Dies Committee be checked out," Hoover forwarded reports on at least three employees (J.B. Matthews, Benjamin Mandel and Stephen Birmingham) to the Attorney General. The rational for these investigations was a bizarre "suspicion" that the CPUSA had infiltrated the Committee and turned it into a front with a mission to destroy the FBI. Hoover might not have believed

---

[55] Hoover to Coblentz, Oct. 19, 1940, Paul Mallon Folder, Nichols O&C FBI File; Nichols to Tolson, Oct. 19, 1940, ibid.; Tamm to Hoover, Oct. 3, 1940, no. 61–7582–483X, FBI HUAC File.

[56] By November 18 the FBI had agents from 19 field offices working on the Zapp case.

such nonsense but he did say: "The Dies attack smells and there is certainly something in back of it other than that which appears on the surface."[57]

Dies did not criticize the FBI when responding to Jackson. Instead, he complained of "technical limitations," alluding to "many cases in which the Attorney General has failed to act, in spite of evidence furnished by the FBI." Dies offered as an example the dismissal of indictments against the Spanish Civil War veterans arrested *en masse* by the bureau in February 1940 during predawn raids in Detroit, Milwaukee, and New York. Nor did Dies hesitate to redbait the Attorney General. He cited Jackson's support of such alleged communist fronts as the League of American Writers and the American League for Peace and Democracy (which sold anti-Dies Committee Christmas cards).[58]

Dies also-called for more assistance across the executive branch, a plea that led Roosevelt to inform the chairman that the only problem was the Committee's interference in ongoing criminal investigations. "As soon as this distinction is clearly recognized," the President explained, "there is no reason why there should not be complete harmony between your committee and the executive branch." Roosevelt, who had been receiving FBI reports on Dies's alleged criticisms of the bureau even before he had made them public, then met face to face with Dies (with a stenographer present) on November 29.[59] FDR refused to consider Dies's sweeping seven-point countersubversive program, but did concede the need for "education ... just so long as you don't hurt human lives." He suggested that Dies "go to the Attorney General" and "work out a *modus operandi* ... leaving in large part to the committee the very excellent and essential work which is arousing the country to the potential dangers that exist in our midst everywhere. That is perfectly all right."

Jackson negotiated the *modus operandi* that FDR had suggested. But he did so with Voorhis and not Dies (who went off on a speaking tour after meeting with the President). The Attorney General promised to "comply" with requests "to furnish the committee information which ... is not involved in probably prosecutive action." Thus, the department would "informally" forward FBI reports to the Dies Committee. Such a procedure, Jackson added, had already been implemented on an ad hoc basis. At least three committee members ("and perhaps others") had been given "specific information" and "any limitations we have asked on publicity ... have in each instance been faithfully observed."[60]

---

[57] See serials 61-7582-517, -536, -583, -692, -673, -683, -693, -700, -785, and -841, FBI HUAC File; Nichols to Hoover, Nov. 25, 1940, Martin Dies Folder, Nichols O&C FBI File..

[58] Ogden, *The Dies Committee*, 224; Dies, *Martin Dies' Story*, 73.

[59] The transcript is in OF 320 (Dies Committee 1940–41), Roosevelt Papers.

[60] *Cong. Record*, 76th Cong., 3rd sess., Dec. 12, 1940, 6847; *New York Times*, Dec. 11, 1940.

258 *Little 'Red Scares'*

Hoover was not a willing partner in this arrangement. The director had submitted a report on November 28 (the day before Dies met with FDR), that rebuked Dies for holding "the F.B.I. up to ridicule." At the same time, Hoover conceded that there was a place for the Committee. His report branded Dies Committee adversary Harry Bridges a communist and indirectly praised the committee's Appendix I (also released on November 28) that sought to document the CPUSA's advocacy of violent revolution. Hoover also revealed the existence of a "defense index" of some 6,000 persons judged by the FBI to be "potential enemies of the nation."[61] Dies was more apologetic, at least in private. He had already confided to FBI confidant and GOP politico Albert Mattei that his attack on the bureau was "unwarranted." The repentant Dies "now wants to right himself," according to Mattei's briefing of Nichols, "and if anybody goes after the boss [Hoover], he in turn is going after him."[62]

The Voorhis–Jackson agreement had little effect on the Committee's fortunes and did not change Hoover's opinion of Dies as a rank amateur. (In February 1941, after J.B. Matthews revealed Committee plans for a round-up of Soviet agents, Hoover noted: "Now that it is announced that the hunt is on I imagine the OPGU agents will sit and wait for Buck Dies and his merry men to arrive.")[63] The Dies Committee quietly expired in December 1944 at the end of the Seventy-Eighty Congress. Seven months earlier and in the midst of a protracted battle with the CIO's National Citizens Political Action Committee, Dies had announced that he would not stand for re-election.[64] He cited poor health and a desire to resume his law practice. When Dies returned to the House in 1953 he remained too controversial for the new generation of red-hunters to accept. His own party refused to appoint him to HUAC, an affront which prompted Dies to unearth yet another list (of 100,000 subversives this time) and to threaten to "move independently" if necessary. Senator McCarthy was one of the few congressional anti-Communists to support Dies's efforts to get back into the game—though an Eisenhower aide suggested, perhaps facetiously, that the President appoint Dies to be his "personal representative in assembling

---

[61] This "defense index" was part of the FBI Custodial Detention list (later renamed several times and best known as the FBI Security Index).

[62] Nichols to Tolson, Oct. 14, 1941, Dies Committee Folder, Nichols O&C FBI File.

[63] See Hoover's notation on newspaper clipping, Feb. 17, 1941, 61-7582-928, FBI HUAC File.

[64] The Dies Committee's main assault on the CIO took the form of *Appendix IX*, a seven-volume tome compiled in 1944 by a subcommittee and deemed so irresponsible that the full Committee expunged it and ordered existing copies destroyed. The FBI used its copy to cross-index the 22,000 names listed.

information and data from all sources relative to Communist activities in government circles."[65]

In his autobiography, published in 1963, Martin Dies made his last public pronouncements on the communist threat. "Lest I be asked on Judgment Day," he explained, "Why did you sin by silence when you knew the truth?" Filled with Christian revivalist rhetoric and gloomy predictions for the capitalist West, Dies's account of his life lends some credence to Walter Goodman's characterization: "[Dies] represented ... an aching nostalgia for pre-World War I America ... for a style of life that was being shaken by industrial unions, by the Negro awakening, by revolutionary currents of every sort. He stood for fundamentalist enthusiasm against the radical enlightenment ... for capitalism and the Constitution and God, and these were under attack from Pennsylvania Avenue and from New York City as much as from Moscow."[66]

Dies may or may not have resented his loss of status. John Nance Garner, Roosevelt's first Vice President (and Dies's mentor), offered a prediction in 1939 that was probably closer to the mark: "The Dies Committee is going to have more influence on the future of American politics than any other committee of Congress."[67] Under the direction of Dies's heirs, and with more systematic assistance from the FBI, HUAC nearly proved Garner right for much of the Cold War era. Dies and his Committee refined many of the means and methods later identified with McCarthyism. They mined the communists-in-government issue, strove to legitimize guilt by association, championed the veracity of ex-communist witnesses, and worked diligently to open a direct pipeline to the FBI and its files. Dies named "more names in a single year," as Robert Griffith said, "than Joe McCarthy did in a lifetime."[68] Dies and his Committee certainly institutionalized the practice of naming names, and it is equally certain that the practice of identifying and then separating "un-Americans" from "real Americans" continues in our own times.

---

[65] Memo, re suggested Statement for President Eisenhower, n.d., Whiteman File-Brownell 1952–54 (1), Dwight D. Eisenhower Papers, Dwight D. Eisenhower Presidential Library, Abilene, KS.

[66] Goodman, *The Committee* (New York, 1968), 163.

[67] Quoted in Harry S Truman, *Memoirs*, 2 vols (Garden City, 1956), 2, *Years of Trial and Hope*, 275.

[68] *The Politics of Fear* (Lexington, 1970), 32–3.

Chapter 11

The Long Black and Red Scare: Anti-Communism and the African American Freedom Struggle[1]

Robbie Lieberman

They allowed her to see him—he's in the southside jail—and he's all beat up. He told his wife to go out and tell all them that wont members of them Reds, they might as well to join them, "because they done near beat me to death here, trying to make me say I'm a Red, and I ain't nary one. If you ain't in it, you might as well get in it, cause they going to beat you up anyhow if they get you." And he wasn't a Party member, wont involved at all ... He changed his mind when they put him in jail and they beat him up.

Narrative of Hosea Hudson[2]

Mac Sloane, white man, said, "You stay out of it. That damn thing will get you killed. You stay out of it. These niggers runnin around here carryin on some kind of [union] meetin—you better stay out of it.
I said to myself, "You a fool if you think you can keep me from joinin. I went right on and joined it, just as quick as the next meetin come ... he done just the right thing to push me into it—gived me orders not to join.

All God's Dangers[3]

The classical civil rights narrative begins with the 1954 Supreme Court decision in *Brown v. Board of Education* that called for desegregation of schools and ends with the passing of the Voting Rights Act in 1965. In the popular version of this history, the movement is a domestic, nonviolent struggle led by charismatic

---

[1] Thanks to Clarence Lang and Nathan Brouwer for comments on an earlier draft of this piece and to Nathaniel Davis and Andrew Barbero for research assistance.

[2] Nell Irving Painter, *The Narrative of Hosea Hudson: His Life as a Negro Communist in the South* (Cambridge, MA, 1979), p. 172.

[3] Theodore Rosengarten, *All God's Dangers: The Life of Nate Shaw* (New York, 1984), p. 297.

262   *Little 'Red Scares'*

men, focused on desegregation and voting rights in the South. In recent years scholars have forcefully challenged this narrative, highlighting its omissions and sketching the contours of a more expansive black freedom movement. That movement's primary focus included concerns about housing, employment and economic justice, as well as self-defense against arbitrary violence, in the North and South; labor unions and not just churches provided a base. Moreover, important roles were played by women in organizing around these "survival issues" as well as by liberal-radical coalitions around civil rights, labor rights, civil liberties, and foreign affairs, coalitions that had influence in the 1930s but which dissolved in the wake of Cold War anti-Communism.

Though there are reminders from the classical period that economic justice and survival issues were at the center of the black freedom struggle, as in the March on Washington for Jobs and Freedom, this point is far more evident when we begin the narrative in the World War I era. Black expectations were high, determination to survive and push for greater equality were evident in the growing militancy of the black press, migration to the North, organizing for labor rights and soon for unemployment relief. By the Depression era a host of organizations that included labor advocates, liberals, socialists and Communists took for granted the ties between racial and economic justice, and by the latter half of the 1930s and into World War II many linked the struggle against fascism abroad to the battle against racism at home. At the same time, however, defenders of the racial status quo had much practice using red-baiting— frequently combined with violence—as an effective means of undermining the black freedom struggle. The combination of red scares and race riots that followed World War I enabled opponents of "Negro rights" to use the 'red' label "to delegitimize blacks' desire for peace, security and liberation from the racial status quo" as they brutally suppressed attempts to organize around these issues.[4]

If we define a "red scare" broadly as an attack on civil liberties in the name of Americanism aimed at undermining movements for justice and equality, then

---

[4]   Theodore Kornweibel, Jr. *"Seeing Red": Federal Campaigns against Black Militancy 1919–1925* (Bloomington, IN, 1998), pp. xiv–xv. See also Nikhil Singh, *Black Is a Country: Race and the Unfinished Struggle for Democracy* (Cambridge, MA, 2004), who argues on p. 31 that "Following World War I, the combination of Red scares and race riots fueled a countersubversive imagination that would inextricably link antiblack racism and anti-radicalism for years to come." Glenda Gilmore, *Defying Dixie: The Radical Roots of Civil Rights, 1919–1950* (New York, 2008) notes on page 9 "the complexity of a drive to eliminate the economic injustices wrought by slavery, debt peonage, and a wage labor system based on degraded black labor." Such injustices hardly escaped the attention of the Southern Conference for Human Welfare, Southern Tenant Farmers Union, and Highlander in the South or those who worked to get employers and unions to accept African Americans as equals in the North.

perhaps this was the norm after 1918 while the periods in between were the anomalies. The most intense red scare periods followed U.S. involvement in war, when higher expectations for black rights confronted post-war reaction, including suppression of civil liberties. Opposition to racial equality did not simply disappear between wars, however, and neither did the violence that met struggles for black rights. In the first phase of the long "black and red scare,"[5] which began in the World War I era, federal intelligence agents and so-called patriotic organizations inextricably linked their support for the racial status quo with anti-radicalism, and through the 1920s, 30s and 40s, a significant part of their efforts was directed toward suppressing black organizing, especially where it was tied to struggles for greater economic equality.

In order to suggest the profound effect of anti-Communism on the black freedom movement prior to the Cold War era, this chapter summarizes the impact of World War I and the Red Summer of 1919, briefly explores the connections between blacks and Communists, and documents some of the fierce (and frequently violent) opposition to those connections, both real and imagined. Violent attacks in the name of Americanism on those who organized for black rights were merely the tip of an iceberg that included a variety of other means of defending the racial status quo.

World War I and Red Summer

African American participation in World War I, a war President Wilson argued would make the world safe for democracy, did not lead to racial equality on the home front. To the contrary, as the *Chicago Defender* explained more than a decade later, "although black men were good enough to risk their lives in the common cause against the enemy, they are today more abused and more insulted than they ever were before the war."[6]

Where W.E.B. Du Bois had called on African Americans to "close ranks" and support the U.S. war effort, after the war he urged black veterans to carry on their struggle at home. But this had become an increasingly perilous proposition. In the South, lynchings and violence, which increased during the

---

[5]   The phrase "black and red scare" is used by James Goodman, *Stories of Scottsboro* (New York, 1995), p. 205, but is easily applicable to the broader period covered in this chapter.

[6]   The *Chicago Defender* from September 30, 1933, is quoted in Beth Bates, *Pullman Porters and the Rise of Protest Politics in Black America, 1925–1945* (Chapel Hill, 2001), pp. 122–3.

war, increased still more in the immediate post-war period.[7] In the North, race riots broke out as black workers—who were given menial and low paid work when they could find jobs at all—competed for jobs with white workers. Racial violence coincided with demands for loyalty. Suppression of antiwar and anti-draft activities during the war helped pave the way for a larger red scare that followed the Russian Revolution; not only peace activism but labor strife and racial tension could now be blamed on "Bolshevism." On the eve of the Red Summer of 1919—an extended period of race riots, red scare and bloodshed—as conditions for African Americans grew worse than ever, the *Crusader* claimed that black people "exist in a Hell on earth, where mob murder, court injustice, inequality, and rank, widespread prejudice are the rule."[8]

As African Americans sought equal rights and a federal lynch law to protect them from mobs, becoming more militant in their demand that the U.S. live up to its professed values, the federal government led the way in erasing the distinction between black discontent and actual subversion. The *Pittsburgh Courier* explained: "As long as the Negro submits to lynchings, burnings and oppressions—and says nothing, he is a loyal American citizen. But when he decides that lynchings and burnings shall cease even at the cost of some human bloodshed in America, then he is a Bolshevist."[9] Even short of taking up arms, challenging the status quo opened one up to being dismissed as a dangerous radical. J. Edgar Hoover played a central role in this process, targeting black activists and organizations as Communist-inspired. Those supposedly linked to "Bolshevik" influences and ideas included black nationalist and anti-Communist Marcus Garvey (and the *Negro World*), socialist labor organizer A. Philip Randolph (and *The Messenger*), the NAACP (and *Crisis*), the *Chicago Defender*, and many others. For the "crime" of calling for equal and democratic rights, such activists, organizations, and publications were subject to surveillance, intimidation, and "the prospect of prosecution, all because their beliefs were anathema."[10]

While the NAACP later came to be viewed as the more conservative, middle-class wing of the Black Freedom Movement, in this era Southerners intent on preserving the racial status quo saw it as highly subversive. A July 1919 editorial in the *Charlotte Observer* claimed that the NAACP was dominated by

---

[7]   For examples of incidents, see Maria Hohn and Martin Klimke, *A Breath of Freedom: The Civil Rights Struggle, African American GIs, and Germany* (New York, 2010), p. 13, and Robert Whitaker, *On the Laps of gods: The Red Summer of 1919 and the Struggle for Justice that Remade a Nation* (New York, 2008), p. 45.

[8]   Whitaker, *On the Laps of Gods*, p. 48.

[9]   Quoted in ibid., p. 51, n.d. Whitaker suggests that some black people took up arms for self-defense "only after a long history had made it clear that they had no other option left."

[10]   Kornweibel, *Seeing Red*, pp. 180–81, xii.

the "most dangerous class of agitators ever brought together in this country" whose goal was "disruption of the friendly relations so long existing between the whites and the blacks of the south."[11] In 1919 NAACP leader Walter White had volunteered information to the FBI about the organization, explaining that it did not have guns and was not interested in "social equality," but this did not end the Bureau's efforts to monitor and suppress the NAACP and its publications. Working with local "red squads," investigating people who had violated no federal statutes, and using paid informers, the federal intelligence community, according to Theodore Kornweibel, "persisted in harassing individuals engaged in legal, if unpopular, activities, establishing "a pattern of hostility to racial and civil rights that persisted for the next fifty years."[12]

The events of 1919 foreshadowed some of the ways in which activities aimed at racial equality would be suppressed in the name of Americanism over the next several decades. The FBI tried to prove that Bolshevik propaganda was responsible for the riots in Chicago and Washington that July, even though its own investigating agents suggested otherwise. (In fact, white mobs brought on the violence in both places.) A typical article based on material supplied by the Justice Department, called "Enrolling American Negroes under Banners of Bolshevism," warned that there was "well-planned, well-executed and well-financed propaganda among the Negroes of this country to-day for an absolute overthrow of the present form of government and the substitution of governmental ideas as carried out by Trotsky and Lenin in Russia."[13]

Like the second major red scare, then, the post-World War I attacks on civil liberties were first and foremost a top-down phenomenon.[14] But anti-Communist networks of people and organizations that opposed organizing

---

[11]   Quoted in Steven A. Reich, "The Great War, Black Workers, and the Rise and Fall of the NAACP in the South," in Eric Arnesen (ed.), *The Black Worker: Race, Labor, and Civil Rights since Emancipation* (Urbana, 2007), p. 167.

[12]   Kornweibel, *Seeing Red*, pp. 62–3, 67–74, 182. The State Department and military intelligence continued to view the NAACP's *Crisis* as red propaganda, and federal agencies cooperated with the wave of terror in the South that destroyed a number of local NAACP branches. See Reich, "The Great War" and Patricia Sullivan, *Lift Every Voice: The NAACP and the Making of the Civil Rights Movement* (New York, 2009), pp. 85–7.

[13]   Kornweibel, *Seeing Red*, pp. 22, 82. An editorial writer in the *New York Times* suggested there could not be "an outbreak of violent racial animosity" in two cities so far apart from each other without outside influence and argued that "Bolshevist agitation has been extended among Negroes, especially those in the South." As quoted in Jeff Woods, *Black Struggle, Red Scare: Segregation and Anti-communism in the South, 1948–1968* (Baton Rouge, 2004), p. 17.

[14]   Ellen Schrecker, *Many Are the Crimes: McCarthyism in America* (Boston, 1998), p. xiii.

around labor and black rights developed outside of the federal government as well. Local statutes demanded that people apply for permits in order to stage a rally, demonstration, or picket line, punished people for expressing radical ideas or possessing radical literature, and prosecuted them for defending themselves against violence. As Robert Korstad argues, "State and local prohibitions on 'subversive' organizations became the twentieth century's black codes."[15] The anti-Communist networks that shaped the Cold War red scare developed in the 1920s and 1930s, and they included journalists, "patriotic" organizations, businessmen, local officials and law enforcement, and others who routinely branded black people's struggles for economic and racial justice as "Communist."

The way such forces worked together to suppress black claims for equality was evident during the worst racial violence of the first red scare, which took place near Elaine, Arkansas. Here were laid bare the fear that white supremacy was threatened by African American attempts to form unions, the assumption that Communists were behind such attempts, and the willingness to use violence to keep black people in their place. The real disloyalty displayed by African Americans was to a tradition of racial and economic inequality, making accusations of subversion somewhat beside the point. Whether truly a concern or a convenient excuse, however, such accusations played on long-held fears of a black insurrection to create a potent blend that led to horrific violence.[16]

Middle aged black farmers mainly from Louisiana and Mississippi, poor cotton sharecroppers, began meeting during World War I under armed guard as the Hoop Spur Lodge of the Progressive Farmers and Household Union. Robert Lee Hill and other founders of the union in 1918 took their cue not from Marx or Lenin but the teachings of Booker T. Washington: "The object of this organization shall be to advance the interests of the Negro, morally and intellectually, and to make him a better citizen and better farmer."[17] Lodge members used secret fraternal organizations as their model, and took care to register their organization with the state. From the beginning, their meetings, which began with a prayer and ended with a song, were met with threats and rumors that they would be attacked by white people. In the wake of the "cauldron of hate and unchecked violence" that came to be called Red Summer, a local American Legion post had been founded "to maintain law and order" and "to foster and perpetuate a 100 percent Americanism," and plans were laid for

---

[15]   Robert Rodgers Korstad, *Civil Rights Unionism: Tobacco Workers and the Struggle for Democracy in the Mid-Twentieth Century South* (Chapel Hill, 2003), p. 417.

[16]   The brutal suppression of non-Communist black organizations may help explain how Communists were able to come to the forefront a decade later, playing a significant role after all in the struggle for black rights.

[17]   Whitaker, *On the Laps of Gods*, pp. 10–11.

organizing armed posses to put down any black insurrection.[18] Union organizing, especially by black people, flew in the face of "100 percent Americanism." Thus it was that at the third meeting of Hoop Spur Lodge, on September 30, 1919, an attack by white men ended in the massacre of black men, women, and children.[19]

Rather than signifying an end to the Red Summer of 1919, the Elaine massacre suggested that those who were concerned about "Negro rights," which in many cases literally meant a fight for survival, would continue to face an uphill, often dangerous, battle. The difficulty of defending black communities against arbitrary violence and injustice were once again evident in the deadly and destructive attacks on African Americans in Tulsa, Oklahoma, in 1921, and Rosewood, Florida, in 1923. (In the latter, an entire town was virtually wiped off the map.) As the Depression intensified competition for jobs, and poverty and unemployment led to demands for relief, struggles for labor and civil rights continued to be met with violence, whether from local authorities or from white workers who felt their jobs or unions threatened. In the wake of World War I and the ongoing Red Scare that followed it, white supremacists had a powerful new weapon. They could gain support for their cause by branding any campaign for black rights as "Communist" or "subversive," and therefore illegitimate and unpatriotic.

African Americans and Communists

While black activists' commitment to "Bolshevism" was clearly exaggerated in order to suppress legitimate demands and challenges to oppression, African American radicals did indeed receive inspiration from Communists in the early twentieth century as the latter aggressively challenged colonialism and racism. In his transnational history, subtitled "Booker T. Washington, the German Empire, and the Globalization of the New South," Andrew Zimmerman points out that "Though it is perhaps counterintuitive to describe emancipatory aspects of the Soviet Union, the new Communist parties founded across the globe after the October Revolution challenged American racism and European colonialism more fundamentally and consistently than liberalism ever did."[20] In the period between the two world wars, Communists viewed American racism in a global

---

[18] Ibid., pp. 1–3, 77–9.

[19] Whitaker claims that while the killing fields can be plotted and various testimonies tell of a massacre, no accurate numbers are possible—it could be that hundreds were killed. See ibid., pp. 86–7, 99, 118, 121–2, 125, 144, 156–7.

[20] Andrew Zimmerman, *Alabama in Africa* (Princeton, 2010), pp. 9, 240–41. Zimmerman also posits a "Segregationist International," a tantalizing concept that calls for further investigation.

context, agitating on issues of race and class and linking the two together in theory and practice as they sought the demise of capitalism and the liberation of black Americans. Although their approach was always problematic, not least because the CPUSA looked to Moscow for guidance, Communists waged "some of the most daring, uncompromising, and ground-breaking battles" for black rights, occasionally meeting with success.[21]

Black Communists had an impact on the Comintern's formulation of the "Negro Question," attracting black radicals to the CP by emphasizing social, economic, and political equality. In practice, this meant focusing on getting unions to admit black workers and promoting the idea that internationalism should include liberation movements around race and nation as well as working class solidarity. While the Communists' call for "self-determination in the Black Belt" (i.e. the U.S. South) was seriously flawed, Mark Solomon highlights its importance, which was to suggest a path to black liberation that combined the idea of African American control of their own communities with black-white cooperation on the basis of a relationship among equals.[22]

To the extent that the CPUSA attracted African Americans, however, it was less due to its ideology than to Communists' determined efforts to challenge systematic racial oppression. As one African American Communist put it, "The question of the right to self-determination was the final goal. But all these economic questions we struggling for each day ... that was immediate."[23] A number of observers pointed out that in contrast to the NAACP's legalistic approach, the CP was a "fighting organization." Communists were the most willing to take action and work longest and hardest for a cause. In addition to their demonstrated commitment, Communists gave African Americans a way to understand their own oppression. As Robin Kelley suggests, Communism gave black people a "framework for understanding the roots of poverty and racism, linked local struggles to world politics, and created an atmosphere in which ordinary people could analyze, discuss, and criticize the society in which

---

[21]   Mark Solomon, *The Cry Was Unity: Communists and African Americans, 1917–36* (Jackson MS, 1998), p. xxiv.

[22]   Ibid., pp. xvii–xix, 86–7. Minkah Makalani, *For the Liberation of Black People Everywhere: The African Blood Brotherhood, Black Radicalism, and Pan-African Liberation in the New Negro Movement, 1917–1936* (Ph.D. dissertation, University of Illinois, 2004), pp. 21–3, 152–4. See also Minkah Makalani, "Internationalizing the Third International: The African Blood Brotherhood, Asian Radicals, and Race, 1919–1922," *Journal of African American History* (Spring 2011), pp. 151–78.

[23]   Painter, *Narrative of Hosea Hudson*, p. 103.

they lived."[24] A range of black activists later commented on the education they received working in or with the CP. Hosea Hudson, an illiterate iron worker in Birmingham, traveled from Alabama to be educated at the workers School in New York in 1934 and came home feeling like, "... I'm somebody ... I'm talking about political economy, about the society itself ... I'd be discussing socialism in the barber shop." Dorothy Height, who was a leader of the Christian youth movement and later president of the National Council of Negro Women, was always certain she would not be a Communist, but she appreciated the opportunity to get to know and work with leaders of the Young Communist League. "To me the important thing was that in the early thirties we were in an era of the United Front" she said. "I learned so much from the Communists."[25]

African Americans who were drawn to the CP during the Depression era were not "dupes" used by the Party for its own ends. To the contrary, as Robin Kelley has argued, African Americans "put their own stamp on the Party, especially locally, and turned it into an important site of black working-class politics"[26] Historian St. Clair Drake claims that "nearly all of the younger black intellectuals and artists became Marxists of one sort or another between 1929 and 1936." Though black workers and intellectuals never joined the CP in large numbers, many did cooperate with Communists in particular struggles, including some savvy black leaders who, according to Drake, "used" the Communists and then "deftly disengaged."[27] Despite the party's shortcomings—its internal struggles with "white chauvinism" and a changing party line that was not consistent in its emphasis on racial equality—the CP's interracial work, openness to black nationalism, serious interest in social equality (including interracial marriage),

---

[24]   Robin D.G. Kelley, *Race Rebels: Culture, Politics, and the Black Working Class* (New York, 1994), p. 124.

[25]   Hudson is quoted in Robin D.G. Kelley, *Hammer and Hoe: Alabama Communists during the Great Depression* (Chapel Hill, 1990), p. 95. Reminiscences of Dorothy Height (1974), pp. 17, 18 in the Columbia University Oral History Research Office Collection, Black Women Oral History Project Records, Schlesinger Library, Radcliffe Institute.

[26]   Kelley, *Hammer and Hoe*, p. 10.

[27]   St. Clair Drake, "A Note On the Intellectual Climate among Black Americans Between 1929 and 1945 with Special Reference to their Relations with the Communist Party and Kwame Nkrumah's Probable Relations with Them," unpublished manuscript, p. 17, in St. Clair Drake Papers, Box 23, Schomburg Center for Research in Black Culture, New York Public Library, Astor, Lenox and Tilden Foundation. Drake notes people such as Ralph Bunche, A. Philip Randolph and Coleman Young who in his view "used" the Communists. Scholars who explore the relationship between African Americans and Communists include Solomon, Singh, Kelley, Bates, Kate Baldwin, Bill Mullen, James Smethurst, Alan Wald, and Barbara Foley. For a dissenting view, see Earl Ofari Hutchinson, *Blacks and Reds: Race and Class in Conflict, 1919–1990* (East Lansing, 1995).

and especially its courageous and vociferous defense of black rights (discussed below) brought it much respect in black communities, especially in the 1930s.[28]

African American activists had little problem holding onto multiple affiliations, working with the NAACP and the CP, for example, while still being active in their churches, and seeing no contradictions in these loyalties. A few examples of those who worked with a number of organizations include Thyra Edwards and Thelma Wheaton in Chicago, Rev. Charles Andrew Hill in Detroit, and Charlotta Bass in Los Angeles. Bass, who successfully fought for black workers to be hired in several institutions in Los Angeles in the pre-World War II period (and by all accounts was not a Communist at the time), and Hill were red-baited fiercely in the post-war period, but both were noted by observers to love their God, church, community and country. Chicago activist Thelma Wheaton, who organized women workers through the YWCA's labor education program in cooperation with the Brotherhood of Sleeping Car Porters (BSCP), later recalled that she "never knew a Communist who was not also a Christian. I'll bet over a third of my church was Communist."[29]

Multiple affiliations, including work with the CP or CP-led organizations such as the League of Struggle for Negro Rights and the Southern Negro Youth Congress, were widely accepted among activists during the Depression years as Communists took up the issues that the New Deal failed to address, including lynching, and helped make the issue of racial equality prominent in the emerging Congress of Industrial Organizations (CIO).[30] At the same time, efforts to address these issues met with fierce attacks, especially where

---

[28] Drake, "A Note on the Intellectual Climate," discusses the party's appeal at length, including the fact that Communists lived a sort of social equality to which others only paid lip service. The highest number of black CP members was in Chicago; one observer growing up on the South Side believed that any white person who talked to an African American was a Communist. See Randi Storch, *Red Chicago: American Communism at Its Grassroots, 1928–1935* (Urbana, 2007), pp. 39, 78.

[29] Biographical notes, 1959, author unknown, Box 2,; "Biographical Notes on Mrs. Charlotta Bass," The Progressive Party of Ohio, 1952, Box 1 Additions, Charlotta Bass Papers, MSS 002, Southern California Library for Social Studies and Research, Los Angeles, California; Regina Freer, "L.A. Race Woman: Charlotta Bass and the Complexities of Black Political Development in Los Angeles," *American Quarterly* 56 (September 2004), http://lion. chadwyck.com/display/printView.do?area=abell accessed: August 6, 2009. Dillard, *Faith in the City*, pp. xviii–xix; Bates, *Pullman Porters*, pp. 113–18, 122–5, 138–42; Gregg Andrews, *Thyra J. Edwards: Black Activist in the Global Freedom Struggle* (Columbia, 2011), chapter 5.

[30] On the New Deal's failure to address minority rights, see Ira Katznelson, *When Affirmative Action Was White: An Untold History of Racial Inequality in Twentieth Century America* (New York, 2005). John L. Lewis, head of the CIO, knowingly worked with Communists since it was well-known that they were dedicated and effective organizers.

Communists were involved. Attacks took place North and South, but before focusing in on the high level of violence that met those who organized around labor and black rights, it is worth pointing out how hard it is to measure all the losses that resulted from the intimidation, harassment, and self-censorship that anti-Communism brought to such organizing efforts. We have not heard all the voices of people who were intimidated and shrank from participating in these efforts out of fear.

Southern Violence

The Southern economy in the twentieth century continued to be dependent upon cheap black labor. Labor unions found it difficult to penetrate the South, and when they did they usually neglected black workers or at best organized them into separate locals. The 1929 strike of mill workers in Gastonia, North Carolina, reveals the violence and intimidation that met interracial union organizing as well as a Southern "black and red scare" seemingly without end.[31] Glenda Gilmore, who argues for putting race at the center of this strike, calls Gastonia "the first southern skirmish in what became a long Communist battle for black equality."[32] Communist interracial organizing in Gastonia sent some white strikers back to the mill early on while the governor (who was a mill owner) called in the National Guard. The Guard troops left after a week of relative order, and a group of local World War I veterans were deputized for the purpose of breaking the strike. When a mob attacked union headquarters and tore it down, police arrested the strikers who ran out of the building and ignored the mob. Another group of deputized, armed troops beat up and stabbed a reporter from a Charlotte newspaper. Strikers had difficulty holding picket lines because Gastonia required a permit to "parade," and deputies enforced the law with violence, even though many of the pickets were women.[33]

The Communists brought all sorts of problem with them, including infighting at the top, lack of financial support, and unrealistic demands that assured a long

---

[31] Solomon's *The Cry Was Unity* includes numerous stories of arrests and violence against protesters and organizers in the 1920s even in instances where people had received permits ahead of time. Scholars have commented on red scares in 1919–1920, 1930–1932, 1934, and 1939–1941; one cannot help but ask whether these are each separate events or one long red scare, and it is noteworthy that African Americans were singled out for attention each time. Even during the Popular Front era (roughly 1935–1939), violence against "red and black" was not uncommon.

[32] Gilmore, *Defying Dixie*, p. 69.

[33] Ibid., pp. 80–83.

strike. Nonetheless, their strategy met with some success as African American organizer Otto Hall joined forces with local (white) striker Ella May Wiggins to build an interracial base in Bessemer City where most of the millworkers were black. When a shootout at union headquarters left a striker and the chief of police dead, white millworkers drove Hall—who was not involved in the shootout but in danger of being lynched as a scapegoat—to the train station in Charlotte in the trunk of a car. Workers arrested and tried for murder were set free after the judge declared a mistrial, but a week later a band of armed men shot and killed Ella May Wiggins. Fourteen men were indicted and five eventually put on trial, but defense attorneys paid by the mill owners argued that because Wiggins believed in Communism their clients should be found not guilty. The jury reached a verdict of not guilty after 30 minutes of deliberation. The red scare that began in Gastonia spread through the South as economic conditions got worse, but Communists continued to challenge the norms of Southern society, "brooking no compromise with full social equality," Gilmore argues. "It was Communists who stood up to say that black and white people should organize together, eat together, go to school together, and marry each other if they chose." Among their opponents by this time were American Fascisti, Order of the Black Shirts, who invited people to join "If you are opposed to social equality and amalgamated marriages; and if you are in favor of white supremacy and the enforcement of law, against Communism in the United States."[34]

Communists working for black rights in the South met extreme violence, but by the early 1930s they had gained credibility and support in many circles. The turning point was the Scottsboro case of 1931, in which nine young black men were falsely accused of raping two white women on a train in Alabama, a case that eventually cast an international spotlight on Southern injustice. Communists had been organizing against lynching and drawing growing audiences to protest meetings based on the understanding that ultimately African Americans were kept in their place through terror.[35] It was the Communists' legal defense and mobilization of public opinion around the "Scottsboro boys," as they were known at the time, which convinced many black people that the CP was the most militant and effective force for racial justice. This was true in spite of, or perhaps because of, "the tremendous hostility of whites, stiff new criminal syndicalism laws, grave warnings against associations with agitators, and the palpable danger for those who failed to take heed ..." in the South. Even Southern black churches

---

[34]   Ibid., pp. 6, 88–95, 109, photo following 114.
[35]   Ibid., pp. 98–9.

flooded the International Labor Defense, the Communists' legal arm, with requests for speakers on Scottsboro.[36]

Many white Southerners viewed the Communists' defense of the Scottsboro boys as a "third crusade," the first two being Abolition and Reconstruction. P.W. Campbell, editor of the *Jackson County Sentinel*, was among those who expressed this outlook: "Today, in 1933, the 'Reds of New York' march into the South ... and again say 'The Negro is your equal and you will accept him as such.'" Responses to this alleged invasion included violence—such as the double-lynching in Tuscaloosa, where the ILD was defending three men accused of rape and murder of a white woman—espionage, and intimidation, since as James Goodman explains, "every gathering of Negroes was suspected to be a Communist gathering, including 'every one of the large number of religious gatherings and lodge meetings.'"[37]

In September 1932, the ILD announced plans for an All-Southern Scottsboro and Civil Rights Conference to be held in Birmingham the following month; issues such as abolition of the chain gang and the poll tax would be on the agenda in addition to freeing the Scottsboro defendants. The evening of the announcement, police in Birmingham raided the ILD office and arrested three people, photographed and fingerprinted them, then held them incommunicado for more than 24 hours while they were questioned. They were released without charges after an ILD attorney threatened to institute habeas corpus proceedings. When authorities learned from ILD files they had confiscated that Otto Hall was scheduled to arrive in Birmingham a few days later, they made preparations for him. "When he stepped off the bus, police bundled him into a car, drove beyond the city limits, pushed him out, and suggested he 'keep going.'"[38] The KKK held a midnight demonstration the night before the conference was scheduled to begin, posted placards in Birmingham's black neighborhoods with such slogans as "The Klan Rides Again to Stamp Out Communism," and passed out handbills warning African Americans to stay away from the "Bolsheviks." City officials told those who assembled the next day—more than 300 blacks and 50 whites—that they could not meet indoors unless they were segregated. Mrs. Viola Montgomery (mother of one of the Scottsboro boys) made a few remarks and the group planned to meet the following week. That larger meeting—900 blacks and 300 whites— was also disrupted as police in New Orleans arrested a scheduled speaker, Mrs.

---

[36] Goodman, *Stories of Scottsboro*, p. 29.

[37] Ibid., pp. 113–15, 203–204. These are the events Goodman refers to as a "black and red scare."

[38] Dan T. Carter, *Scottsboro: A Tragedy of the American South* (Baton Rouge, 1969), pp. 151–2; Kelley writes that Hall was arrested and beaten first; see *Hammer and Hoe*, p. 85.

274 *Little 'Red Scares'*

Montgomery stayed away after receiving several threats, and hostile whites threw stink bombs that caused the meeting to dissolve in chaos.[39]

Though many people, then and later, accused the Communists of manipulating the Scottsboro case for their own political advantage, there is no question that the ILD succeeded in saving the young men's lives and getting them a new trial.[40] The black press came down squarely on the side of the Communists bold and decisive action, even chiding the NAACP for its attempts to fight for control of the case. Charles Hamilton Houston, who was chief legal counsel for the NAACP, fully understood the import of Scottsboro, which "set a new standard for agitation for equality." As he explained it, "The Communists have made it impossible for any aspirant to Negro leadership to advocate less than full economic, political and social equality." At the NAACP convention in 1934, Houston argued that Southern blacks should form alliances with poor whites: "Together they can win against the forces which are seeking to exploit them and keep them down. Separately they will lose and the other fellow will continue to win."[41]

African Americans who sought to organize such alliances, especially in the South, were taking a great risk, as illustrated in the case of Angelo Herndon, a black Communist arrested in Atlanta in 1932 on charges of inciting insurrection. Only 19 years old at the time, Herndon had organized 1,000 families of the unemployed (600 of them white) to appeal for relief. Herndon was quickly convicted by an all-white jury. Even before his trial, an assistant solicitor had declared that "As fast as Communists come here, we shall indict them, and I shall demand the death penalty in every case."[42] Though Herndon was sentenced to 18 to 20 years on a chain gang rather than being put to death, the point was clear. The law under which he was charged, which dated back to slavery times, defined any attempt "to induce others to join any combined resistance" to the state as an attempt to "incite insurrection." (Six other people had been awaiting trial in Atlanta for 3 years on similar charges.) The State's case was based on Herndon's possession of literature distributed by the Communist Party—the *Daily Worker*, William Montgomery Brown's "The Communist Position on the Negro Question," and George Padmore's "The Life and Struggles of Negro Toilers." Such publications, as the defense pointed out, were widely available

[39] Carter, *Scottsboro*, pp. 152–3; Kelley, *Hammer and Hoe*, pp. 85–6.

[40] Carter, *Scottsboro*, p. 173.

[41] Patricia Sullivan, *Days of Hope: Race and Democracy in the New Deal Era* (Chapel Hill, 1996), pp. 87–9.

[42] *The Case of Angelo Herndon* (New York, 1935), p. 5. The same prosecutor took advantage of the 1934 textile strike, which had nothing to do with Communism, to raid the ILD office, the Urban League, the black YMCA, and meetings in private homes. See Gilmore, *Defying Dixie*, pp. 180–81.

The Long Black and Red Scare 275

including in the public library and at Emory University in Atlanta. Herndon's lawyer, Ben Davis, who had attended Morehouse prep school, Amherst College and Harvard Law School, later credited the judge in Herndon's case for turning him into a Communist: "So crude and viciously unconstitutional and anti-Negro were his rulings that my instant joining of the Communist Party was the only effective reply I could give."[43]

Herndon's conviction was thrown out by the Supreme Court five years later, but in the meantime challenges to the constitutionality of Georgia's insurrection law had not stopped police in Atlanta from continuing to arrest people for possessing Communist literature. In November 1934, the *Chicago Defender* related the story of police arresting alleged Communists on this charge and then arresting a group of African Americans for good measure. The headline tells the story: "Red Scare Brings New Wave of Terror to Atlantans: Jesse O. Thomas Reveals Facts on Police Activity; Many Innocent Persons Thrown in Jail."[44] Similar ordinances curtailed the civil liberties of activists elsewhere. In the spring of 1934, police in New Orleans arrested 15 men on charges of possessing Communist literature, distributing leaflets without a permit, and "being dangerous and suspicious in being Communists." A *New York Times* editorial raised concerns about this "dangerous and suspicious" ordinance, under which authorities could arrest people on suspicion of vagrancy or unemployment as well as for displaying a controversial ideology or appearing wealthy without just cause.[45]

Unlike Herndon, black Communists and union activists in the South were not always fortunate to escape with their lives. An incident in Camp Hill, Alabama, in July 15–16, 1931, left dozens of victims in a story that echoes the 1919 Elaine massacre in some of its particulars. About 150 sharecroppers in Tallapoosa County, Alabama, met in a vacant home that also served as a church to organize a branch of the Croppers' and Farm Workers' Union. Their meeting was raided by the sheriff and a posse that had been deputized for the purpose of breaking up the gathering. A verbal confrontation led to an exchange of gunfire that left a number of people wounded, including the sheriff, several black sharecroppers and some of their family members. The posse murdered the group's leader, Ralph Gray, and enraged vigilantes went on to terrorize African Americans in the surrounding area, killing and wounding dozens of people.

---

[43] Gilmore, *Defying Dixie*, pp. 165–6.

[44] *The Chicago Defender* (National Edition), November 3, 1934. http://www.proquest.com/ Accessed May 7, 2010.

[45] George N. Coad, Editorial Correspondence, *New York Times*. "New Orleans Fears for Civil Liberties: Series of Events Leads to Belief Constitutional Rights are Endangered. Radicals in Disfavor: Socialist Candidate Arrested and Suspicion of Communism Jails 15 Men." *New York Times*, June 3, 1934, http://proquest.com/ Accessed May 9, 2010.

Police held black Communists responsible for the violence and arrested more than 30 black men.[46]

In response to these events, the *Chicago Defender* published an editorial from the *New York World Telegram* that stressed the "deep-seated" and legitimate economic grievances of black sharecroppers that created "rich soil for Communism." The editorial admonished readers to "break away from the theory that in these United States even wrong becomes right when Communism points a finger at it and speaks to those who suffer by it. That theory is worse than foolish, worse than illogical. If carried too far it will end by destroying the very institutions it pretends to cherish. Have done with it."[47]

Editorials in Northern newspapers were hardly enough to cause the terror to subside. In Greenville, South Carolina, interracial groups of workers and unemployed worked to prevent evictions, packed city council meetings and marched by the thousands to protest against discrimination in relief. Two days after a protest at a city council meeting, the KKK showed up at an interracial meeting of the Unemployed Council and "began to beat up the African Americans there. When white Communist workers jumped in to defend them, a free-for-all ensued, while three police officers watched." A few months later Klansmen broke up a similar meeting and organizer Clara Holden was kidnapped and beaten. In Charlotte, where 1,000 people held an integrated march to City Hall to demand relief from the mayor, police beat them up with baseball bats.[48]

Another violent incident took place at Reeltown, Alabama, where an armed standoff between the Sharecroppers' Union (SCU) and police on December 19, 1932, led to the deaths of three black sharecroppers. Party member and union leader Clifford James was indebted to a local merchant for the value of his farm. When the merchant sought to evict James from his land and seize his livestock in order to satisfy the debt, armed members of the SCU stood with James to resist the eviction. The violence that ensued took the lives of James and two other SCU members, and then, similar to Elaine and Camp Hill, white vigilantes carried on a reign of terror. Black families fled to the woods, numerous black homes were violated, and more people were killed. The *Chicago Defender* announced, "Toll of Dead in Alabama Riots Still Mounting; Farmers Believed Killed by Sheriff's Lynch 'Posse.'" Several people were arrested whose only connection with the

---

[46] Kelley, *Hammer and Hoe*, pp. 41–3.

[47] "In Alabama," *The Chicago Defender* (National Edition) (1921–1967); Aug. 1, 1931; Proquest Historical Newspapers *The Chicago Defender* (1910–1975), p. 13.

[48] Gilmore, *Defying Dixie*, pp. 130–31.

affair was that their names appeared in "Communistic" literature discovered by the police in the home of Clifford James.[49]

The response of Southern planters, local authorities, white supremacist organizations, and journalists to the Scottsboro and Herndon cases and to organizing in Camp Hill, Reeltown, and elsewhere in the South illustrate a black and red scare that used or condoned terror against Communist efforts to organize unions and the unemployed and defend African Americans against injustice. But such scares were not only aimed at Communists, and they were not limited to the Deep South. In Memphis, for instance, an Unemployed Citizens League formed without Communists to help people find food and jobs was destroyed by red-baiting from within and without. Throughout the 1930s black and white labor organizers in Memphis were harassed and beaten, forced to leave town, and on occasion murdered or "disappeared." Such activity did not cease after the 1935 Wagner Act gave labor organizers some legal protections and the Senate's La Follette Committee investigated serious violations of civil liberties by employers. One tragic and dramatic case was that of Tom Watkins, a militant and effective union organizer, who was nearly killed after an effort to get black construction workers into the American Federation of Labor (AFL) in Memphis. Forced to flee the city in 1939, Watkins survived another attempt to kill him in St. Louis in 1942, where he was trying to get black officers elected in the International Longshoremen's Association. Watkins left his old life and his family behind, and moved to the West coast. Although he "never regained his place as a natural leader of workers," the FBI was still investigating him in the 1970s for his alleged "procommunist tendencies."[50]

Communists played a significant role in organizing the CIO, where African American workers were generally more welcome than in the AFL. Many workers did not distinguish the CP from the CIO, since both organized around labor and black rights. Besides, in a context in which "everybody who wants a home or a loaf of bread is a red," some of the red-baiting fell on deaf ears, at least the ears of those who were desperate for work. In Memphis, however, as in other Southern cities, red-baiting did succeed in driving off liberal and middle-class support, especially since many Southern whites equated such terms as Communist, agitator, and "nigger lover." Southern journalist Wilbur Cash put

---

[49]   Kelley, *Hammer and Hoe*, pp. 49–53. *The Chicago Defender* (National Edition) (1921–1967), Jan. 7, 1933. http://proquest.com/ Accessed May 2, 2010.

[50]   Michael K. Honey, *Southern Labor and Black Civil Rights: Organizing Memphis Workers* (Urbana, 1993), pp. 1–6, 100–101. After Watkins barely escaped with his life, a local reporter in Memphis wrote "They will kill him if he comes back and tries to organize poor people to struggle for a life with human dignity ... They will kill all the new Tom Watkins!"

278 *Little 'Red Scares'*

the equation this way: "labor unions + strikes = Communists + atheism + social equality with the Negro."[51]

Even where Communists were not at the center, Southern defenders of the status quo used violence and other means to put down any movement promoting labor and black rights. Reactions to the Southern Tenant Farmers Union and Highlander School illustrate this point. Founded in 1934 to challenge the system of sharecropping and tenant farming that left many people poor and homeless, the STFU had a socialist outlook, a large black membership, and women and African Americans in leadership positions. In the Arkansas Delta, once again, white planters and their allies responded to such threats to the social order.[52] On the orders of a prosecuting attorney, police arrested organizer Ward Rodgers on charges of criminal anarchy after he spoke at a STFU rally. Testimony against Rodgers included the charge that he was advocating "racial equality right here in Arkansas." It took the local jury only 10 minutes to find him guilty; he was sentenced to six months in jail and fined $500 plus court costs. When radical groups in the area staged rallies in his support, local whites reacted violently, beating up speakers and shooting into the homes of STFU members. The support of local newspapers for such activity is illustrated by the understated headline that appeared in the *Marked Tree Tribune*, which read "Citizens Ask Reds to Leave."[53] At a STFU organizing meeting in early 1935, armed white men broke in and ordered the African Americans present to leave, telling them that they would be lynched if they were caught at another union gathering. Other union members were beaten and threatened with guns. Buffeted by such anti-Communist attacks and then by Communist attempts to take over the union, the STFU was a shadow of its former self at the end of the decade.[54]

Highlander's existence was also threatened right from the start. Founded in 1932 in Grundy County, Tennessee, for the purpose of educating and organizing poor Southern workers, white and black, it was immediately accused of being a "breeding ground for 'radical social agitators whose baneful influence is felt throughout this section.'"[55] Industrialists, journalists, and members of the American Legion commonly branded Highlander's staff, including founder Myles Horton, as Communists, and the attacks became more intense as Highlander gained support for its efforts and worked with other progressive groups. Along with other organizations, Highlander scheduled an All-Southern

---

[51] Ibid., pp. 128, 129.

[52] Whitaker, *On the Laps of Gods*, p. 313.

[53] Woods, *Black Struggle, Red Scare*, pp. 23–4.

[54] Ibid, p. 24; Donald Grubbs, Cry from the Cotton (Arkansas, 2000).

[55] John M. Glen, *Highlander: No Ordinary School 1932–1962* (Lexington, 1988), pp. 40–41.

Conference for Civil and Trade-Union Rights in Chattanooga for May 1935. Planned as an interracial meeting to discuss labor organizing, abolishing lynching and the poll tax, and repealing anti-union and sedition laws, among other issues, the conference was attacked even before it began. In March a local paper reported that Highlander's staff was part of a "radical group of agitators" who publicly advocated unionization, "equal rights for Negroes and unity of white and Negro workers," and a "united front movement" of Communists and Socialists in the South. These "charges" were not untrue, but this was clearly an inflammatory piece aimed at stirring up white Southerners to defend the social order. The Americanism committee of the Chattanooga American Legion, which saw the conference as a meeting of "reds," successfully pressured those who had agreed to rent a hall for the conference to cancel. The Legion used physical harassment as well, attacking one integrated group and chasing them into the countryside and organizing a statewide rally in July for the purpose of further intimidating Highlander. Horton was not a Communist, but his interest in interracial organizing made him one in the eyes of conservative Southerners. As Highlander's staff worked to persuade Southern white union members that racially integrated unions were practical and employed what Horton called a "method of natural exposure" to battle racial prejudice, "conservatives raised the specter of 'Communism' to undermine the school's challenge to Southern labor, political, and racial customs."[56]

Northern Repression

Race and class issues came together outside the South as well, as discrimination and poverty led to protest, and protest not infrequently led to violence. In Chicago, broad coalitions formed to defend the rights of black workers, with participants well aware that it was "Injustice, not Reds," as the *Defender* explained, that inspired such activity.[57] Support for Angelo Herndon and the Scottsboro defendants brought people together, but so did local issues such as unemployment. Communists were active in the Unemployed Council (UC), which challenged landlords who evicted unemployed African Americans. In one such incident, where the UC organized a large group of people to protect the furniture of an unemployed South Side resident, the police came and arrested

---

[56] Glen, *Highlander*, pp. 68–9; Frank D. Durham, "Anti-Communism, Race and Structuration: Newspaper Coverage of the Labor and Desegregation Movements in the South, 1932–1940 and 1953–1961," *Journalism and Mass Communication Monographs*, 2002, pp. 75–6.

[57] Quoted in Bates, *Pullman Porters*, p. 123.

280   *Little 'Red Scares'*

several men. As Beth Bates relates, "Eventually the police fired into the crowd, killing three black men. An estimated 5,000 to 8,000 people joined a funeral procession, led by the Unemployed Council and Communists through the heart of black Chicago, while many thousands more looked on."[58]

Communists also played an important part in organizing the Unemployed Council in St. Louis, the first integrated protest movement there, which had an "especially visible and militant core" of African Americans, many of them women. (The police called these women "ringleaders," while the press referred to them as "girl agitators.")[59] As in Chicago, the UC organized neighborhoods to prevent evictions and press for relief. Challenging one of the more miserly relief systems in the country, the UC led a number of demonstrations beginning in January 1930. Hershel Walker, who had come up from the South, "recalled the moving effect of 'black and white demonstrating together before city hall, going to jail together, and getting food to eat together' in a city that was still fully segregated."[60] The first sit-down of the 1930s took place at City Hall in St. Louis in January 1931. Contingents from the north and south sections of the city came together in a huge march that symbolized racial unification. Five thousand strong by the time they reached City Hall, the marchers refused to leave until their demands, including aid to the unemployed, were addressed by the Board of Aldermen. They were met with police clubs, tear gas, bloodshed and arrests.

The repression curtailed but did not prevent further activity. When the relief rolls were cut in July 1932, another large demonstration took place at City Hall. A group of women charged the doors, and again the police response relied on clubs and tear gas. Demonstrators were beaten and trampled, one person was fatally wounded, and dozens were arrested on charges of rioting. Here was yet another incident in which, as Clarence Lang suggests, "antiradicalism had collided with white supremacy, and with explosive results."[61] Commenting more broadly on his experience as a labor organizer in St. Louis in the 1930s, Bill Sentner suggested it was "Jim Crow and Red Scare" that led to the defeat of the "working-class civil rights movement in St. Louis."[62]

Across the Mississippi River, in East St. Louis, Illinois, by the early 1930s African Americans made up about 20 percent of the population, many of them

---

[58]   Ibid., p. 111. See also Storch, *Red Chicago*, pp. 99–103, which places the crowd estimates much higher.

[59]   Clarence Lang, *Grassroots at the Gateway: Class Politics and Black Freedom Struggle in St. Louis, 1936–75* (Ann Arbor, 2009), p. 27; Rosemary Feurer, *Radical Unionism in the Midwest, 1900–1950* (Urbana, 2006), p. 32.

[60]   Walker is quoted in Feurer, *Radical Unionism*, p. 33.

[61]   Lang, *Grassroots at the Gateway*, pp. 27–9; Feurer, *Radical Unionism*, pp. 33–4.

[62]   Feurer, *Radical Unionism*, p. 40.

migrants who faced fierce competition for jobs and inadequate relief programs. A number of them supported the CP in spite of constant repression by local authorities. The first demonstration for unemployment relief, in 1931, was met not only with significant police presence but also members of the American Legion who had been deputized for the purpose of helping to prevent the demonstration. Police carried guns loaded with "tear gas bombs" and arrested people for demonstrating without a permit. They also raided a local pool hall in the city's black district, which they believed to be the local CP headquarters, and several other gatherings. Following a raid on a Communist meeting at which all those who attended were arrested, Police Chief Leahy issued a ban on all radical activities within the city. The East St. Louis post of the American Legion, the largest in the Southern Illinois region, organized a massive membership drive in order to curtail Communist activity. Some of the city's police officers were Legion members as well.[63] Similar alliances were found around the country, for example in Memphis, local police joined forces with the Legion for "a drive against Communists and public expressions of belief in racial equality."[64] In East St. Louis, the repression reached a peak in a raid on a private residence in the African American section of the city. While reports on the details were conflicting, a few facts were not disputed—the raid was conducted without a warrant and police had used tear gas to break up a meeting in the home. An editorial in the *St. Louis Post-Dispatch* concluded that the actions of the East St. Louis police had "shattered the first amendment to the Constitution" and "grossly violated the Fourth Amendment."[65]

Arbitrary and discriminatory treatment of African Americans was clearly a Northern as well as a Southern phenomenon. One successful challenge to the systematic criminalization of black people was the 1934 case that African American Communist Harry Haywood called "Detroit's Scottsboro." A black World War I veteran, James Victory, accused of slashing a white woman's face and stealing her purse, was defended by local attorney Maurice Sugar with support from the League of Struggle for Negro Rights and the ILD. Racial tension in Detroit had been increasing, due in no small part to the activities of local white supremacist groups—both the KKK and the Black Legion had a significant presence in the city. The police commissioner contributed to the tension; in the face of a "race-baiting" drive by the press that depicted black people as "natural rapists, voodooists, murderers, and all-around thugs who

---

[63] "Police Prevent Communist Meet," *East St. Louis Journal*, Feb. 26, 1931, p. 1. Articles on the Legion's membership drive and activities are in the *East St. Louis Journal*, Nov. 9 (p. 8), 17 (p. 1), and 22 (p. 4C), 1931.

[64] "Three Held as Reds in Memphis are Freed," *New York Times*, June 8, 1930, p. 22.

[65] "Notes on a Raid," *St. Louis Post-Dispatch*, Dec. 14, 1931, p. 2C.

were conspiring to assault white women" he boasted that his force averaged 50 arrests a day of black criminals. The police arrested Victory using faulty witness identification methods and ignored his solid alibi and lack of a criminal record. Sugar succeeded in his defense of Victory before an all-white jury, arguing in his closing statement that African Americans had the same hearts, pleasures, joys, pains and agonies as other people. But he also wanted the jury to acknowledge the effects of racism, which meant that the "Negro is doubly exploited. He is exploited as a worker and he is further exploited as a colored worker."[66]

This view was at the heart of the National Negro Congress, a quintessential Popular Front organization that provided an organizational base at the local level in order to bring together a variety of efforts aimed at increasing black working class rights. To the extent that it succeeded, it was based on collaborative efforts that took place under a new, more militant leadership, challenging the NAACP's perceived lack of vigor and building on the CIO's drive to increase black union membership. Blending nonviolent direct action with Popular Front alliances grounded in the black working class, the NNC brought together labor leaders—A. Philip Randolph of the BSCP helped organize and became president of the organization—Communists, and liberals (black Communist John P. Davis and Howard University's Ralph Bunche were the other two who put out the initial call). Challenging the shortcomings of the New Deal, the NNC platform pointed to the need for measures that would aid black working class families—"full relief, social security and unemployment insurance, living wage jobs, and full union membership for African Americans." Organizing not just in the workplace but in homes and community organizations, the NNC had several local successes to show in the late 1930s in Chicago, St. Louis, and other Northern cities including important struggles led by women.[67]

Though Haywood and other black Communists were concerned about the Popular Front diluting antiracist efforts, events in Detroit (among other places) broadened the issue of civil rights and brought together new coalitions to work for racial equality. In the wake of the sit-down strike against General Motors in 1936–37, Detroit's Conference for the Protection of Civil Rights defined the issue to include "the rights of free speech, press, assembly and worship as granted in the Bill of Rights ... the right of labor to organize ... and equal rights with all others in the community of religious, racial and political minorities." A bill introduced in the state legislature aimed at preventing the exercise of these rights "under the guise of stopping 'subversive activities'" was watered down

---

[66] Dillard, *Faith in the City*, pp. 77–8; Harry Haywood, *Black Bolshevik: Autobiography of an Afro-American Communist* (Chicago, 1978), pp. 437–8; Harry Haywood, *The South Comes North in Detroit's Own Scottsboro Case* (New York, 1934).

[67] Lang, *Grassroots at the Gateway*, pp. 35–6; Bates, *Pullman Porters*, pp. 135–42.

considerably, signaling a success for the Conference and encouraging coalitions of those concerned about labor organizing, civil rights, and civil liberties.[68] These same coalitions splintered a few years later as liberals joined the anti-Communist consensus, encouraged by the Cold War and a shifting Communist Party line.[69]

International Affairs and Red Scare

International affairs had always been important to black radicals and their opponents. Government agents and so-called patriotic organizations suspected black disloyalty during both world wars, but African Americans who linked the struggle for equality at home with anti-colonial and anti-fascist struggles abroad during the interwar years also faced political repression and racial persecution. In the face of ongoing injustice, unemployment and lack of relief from New Deal programs, and violence, African Americans responded with anger to Mussolini's invasion of the only independent black African nation in 1935. Robin Kelley argues that black Communists and sympathizers, "[a]wakened by Italy's invasion of Ethiopia ... fought Franco as a backhanded response to Mussolini."[70] Popular black newspapers were outspoken in their support for the Spanish Republic's fight against fascism, and a number of individuals and organizations contributed time and money to the cause. Some African Americans volunteered to fight in Spain, defying the official U.S. policy of neutrality; they found respect and dignity in the Abraham Lincoln Brigade, the primarily American battalion that fought on the side of the Spanish Loyalists. One battalion leader was the first black officer to command white troops in any American army.[71] Those who managed to return found themselves facing continued discrimination. Lincoln Brigade veteran James Yates, who could not get a room in the New York hotel in which his comrades had planned to stay, said "The pain went as deeply as any bullet could have done." Many Lincoln Brigade vets faced harassment from the FBI and had their passports revoked by the State Department. Those who enlisted in World War II faced "the double burden of military racism as well as

---

[68] Dillard, *Faith in the City*, pp. 81–3.

[69] While the Popular Front muted some of the most intense anti-Communism, struggles for racial equality and labor rights still brought attacks, as in the 1938 pecan shellers strike in Texas. See Zaragosa Vargas, *Labor Rights are Civil Rights: Mexican American Workers in Twentieth Century America* (Princeton, 2005), pp. 134–43.

[70] Kelley, *Race Rebels*, pp. 10–11.

[71] Peter Carroll, *The Odyssey of the Abraham Lincoln Brigade* (Stanford, 1994), pp. 134–5.

284   *Little 'Red Scares'*

Communist persecution," meaning they were subject to segregation, given the most menial tasks, and physically assaulted.[72]

Just prior to U.S. entry into the war, a national Red Scare led to concerted attacks on "subversives" in every part of the country. (During this period of the Nazi–Soviet pact, 1939–41, the Communist Party took an antiwar position and characterized World War II as an imperialist war.) The New York legislature created the Rapp–Coudert Committee to investigate "subversive activities" in public schools, while Memphis authorities used fears of an alien-led Fifth Column to inhibit CIO organizing among black and white workers. Governor Talmadge in Georgia burned books and threatened to fire any university professor who "dissents from the proposition that the white man is by nature the superior of the black man," a threat on which he followed through.[73] In January 1941 two state representatives introduced a criminal syndicalism bill into the Tennessee legislature as another means to prosecute the Highlander school. They withdrew the bill under pressure, but the Grundy County Court then passed a resolution asking state authorities "to direct the district attorney to indict Highlander as 'the largest center of Communistic teaching in the South.'"[74] These attacks and others took their toll on the school, forcing it to curtail its activities and devote scarce resources to defending its existence.

African Americans took a different approach to the Second World War than they had to the first, lending strong support to the "Double V" campaign promoted by black newspapers, which linked victory against fascism abroad to victory in the struggle against racism at home. The *Crisis* proclaimed, "It must be that we declare the life blood of our fighters and the sweat of our workers to be a sacrifice for a new world which not only shall not contain a Hitler, but no *Hitlerism*. And to the thirteen millions of American Negroes that means a fight for a world in which lynching, brutality, terror, humiliation, and degradation through segregation and discrimination shall have no place *either here or there*."[75]

The most notable efforts to combat discrimination at this time were led by A. Philip Randolph, who had broken with the NNC and the Communists, over their opposition to Roosevelt and the war. The NNC's demise symbolizes the foundering of such coalitions in the early years of World War II, when the shifting party line (against war during the Nazi-Soviet pact era, and then all for it when the U.S. entered the war as an ally of the Soviet Union), public scrutiny by the House Committee on Un-American Activities, and outspoken anti-

---

[72]   Ibid., pp. 151, 153.

[73]   Gilmore, *Defying Dixie*, pp. 350–52; Honey, *Southern Labor and Black Civil Rights*, pp. 146–7.

[74]   Glen, *Highlander*, p. 65.

[75]   Hohn and Klimke, *A Breath of Freedom*, p. 19.

Communism, in this case on the part of Randolph—signaled the end of such Popular Front successes.[76]

J. Edgar Hoover continued to believe that those who spoke out for black rights were Communist subversives. The FBI kept tabs on Randolph, for example, even after his public break with the Communists. Both the FBI and the CP opposed Randolph's organizing of the all-black March on Washington Movement, which held large meetings to protest discrimination in hiring and in the armed forces. The threat of a huge march in the capital led Roosevelt to establish the Fair Employment Practices Committee to address these issues, and Randolph called off the march.[77]

As in World War I, the FBI and army intelligence questioned the loyalty of black newspapers, including the *Crisis*. The black press did indeed report on segregation in the military and abuses suffered by black G.I.s on trains and buses, in training camps and cities near military bases. Army intelligence considered such coverage "inflammatory" and blamed the press for lowering black morale and causing race riots. In February 1942, Military Intelligence charged seventeen black publications with "carrying abnormally inflammatory articles, sponsored by Communists."[78] Hoover shared this outlook, and FBI agents visited a number of black newspapers with the clear intent of intimidating them. After the *Atlanta Daily World* received a second visit from the FBI, columnist Cliff McKay observed wryly: "One gathers that ... some white people would like to read 'sedition' and 'subversive activity' into the determination of Negroes to achieve democracy here at the same time they are called upon to fight for its preservation abroad."[79] There were limits on what Hoover could do mainly because of the demands of the war and the government's desire for unity on the home front. The Justice Department refused to prosecute mainstream black newspapers even when pressed by Hoover to do so, but the FBI continued

---

[76] Lang, *Grassroots at the Gateway*, p. 45; Bates, *Pullman Porters*, pp. 145–6.

[77] Maurice Isserman, *Which Side Were You On? The American Communist Party during the Second World War* (Middletown, 1982), pp. 141–3, 168. When the CP line changed to all out support for war after Germany attacked the Soviet Union in June 1941, Party leaders condemned the MOWM as a disruptive force. Isserman argues that, while promoting wartime unity, Communists did not simply abandon the struggle for black rights. Concentrating on unions that were important to the war effort, they helped win important victories for black maritime workers, fighting discrimination in hiring in several instances, and defending equal employment opportunities even when white union members violently opposed them. During the war years, Communists also succeeded in getting the first black member of the New York city council elected, and after a deadly riot in Detroit helped prevent New York from experiencing similar violence and destruction.

[78] Washburn, *A Question of Sedition*, pp. 58–9.

[79] Ibid., p. 83.

286 *Little 'Red Scares'*

its elaborate surveillance of African Americans and its search for foreign and domestic sources of "agitation among the Negroes," even looking into the formation of Eleanor Roosevelt Clubs.[80]

The End of Civil Rights Unionism

If urban race riots sparked by overcrowded housing and competition for wartime jobs were not ascribed to Communist agitation this time around, labor struggles certainly were, even though the CP supported a no-strike pledge in order not to disrupt the war effort. On the ground, there were still instances in which interracial, left-led CIO unions continued to challenge racial discrimination and second-class citizenship in the context of battles for labor rights. Robert Korstad has labeled such struggles, illustrative of the broad social movements of the Popular Front era, "civil rights unionism." His account of the tobacco workers' strike in Winston-Salem, North Carolina, in 1943, a strike by a work force that was mainly African American, with important leadership by women, is a dramatic example—perhaps one of the last—of those sorts of broad struggles for democracy that characterized the Popular Front era.[81] Movements such as these did not survive, becoming prime targets of the Cold War red scare.

World War II era attacks on New Deal liberals foreshadowed what was to come, led by Southern congressmen who carried on the legacy of the first Red Scare, namely the idea that black protest was Communist-inspired and that its ultimate aim was social equality.[82] Those ideas motivated John Rankin (MS), who played a key role in getting HUAC to become a standing committee, its chairman Martin Dies (TX), and Mississippi Senator Theodore Bilbo, who led the way in opposing a bill to abolish the poll tax because it would leave the white South with "no way to prevent negroes from voting." Fears of a conspiracy were evident in his charge that it was "the Negroes, the C.I.O., the American Federation of Labor, the Railroad Brotherhoods, the Communist Party, and Mr. Browder" [head of the CP] who were trying to subvert the Constitution. The bill was tabled as a result of such opposition.[83]

---

[80]   One report to Hoover from Assistant Director D. Milton Ladd noted that complaints had been received attributing the cause of agitation among black people in South Carolina and Georgia "to the encouragement given Negroes by Mrs. Roosevelt." Athan Theoharis (ed.), *From the Secret Files of J. Edgar Hoover* (Chicago, 1991), pp. 93–4. See also Gilmore, *Defying Dixie*, pp. 354–5.

[81]   Korstad, *Civil Rights Unionism*; Vargas, *Labor Rights are Civil Rights*.

[82]   Kornweibel, *Seeing Red*, p. xii.

[83]   Sullivan, *Days of Hope*, p. 120.

The 1942 elections brought other like-minded Southern Democrats to the Senate, including James Eastland (MS) and John McClellan (AK). Support of black rights was often the reason for anti-Communist attacks on New Deal liberals, attacks that succeeded in driving people out of government and a variety of organizations. One example was the concerted attack on the Farm Security Administration, which had provided direct aid to thousands of families, white and black. The FSA outraged Southern Democrats by allowing families to use loan money to pay poll taxes; the agency also worked with the STFU and CIO, and had union members and African Americans on its local committees. Southerners who charged that FSA director C. B. "Beanie" Baldwin and his policies were Communist succeeded in destroying the agency and getting Baldwin to resign. Similar attacks were mounted against Clark Foreman, a founder of the Southern Conference for Human Welfare who served as director of the Division of Defense Housing, which was part of the Federal Works Administration. Foreman's support for making the Sojourner Truth housing project in Detroit open to black defense workers was seized on by his opponents, who began what Patricia Sullivan calls "an organized and determined campaign to drive him from government because of the stand which he took on behalf of the Negro."[84]

Even before the end of World War II, organizations such as SCHW argued over whether to adopt policies that excluded Communists; after the war liberals became hopelessly divided over such issues. As the Cold War red scare took hold, the Ford Foundation established the Fund for the Republic in order to undermine alleged Communist influence on African Americans, the CIO refused to work with the SCHW and Highlander, and Popular Front organizations dissolved, leading to the marginalization of a number of committed activists. Patricia Sullivan points out that the black freedom struggle became isolated in the 1950s, underscored by another wave of terror that swept the South early in the decade, beginning with the gruesome assassination of NAACP leader Harry T. Moore and his wife Harriet. Events such as this brought international attention to the contradiction between U.S. claims to stand for freedom abroad while African Americans continued to lack basic democratic rights at home. More to the point, however, was that growing concerns about disloyalty undermined the important groundwork that was laid in the prewar period, to the extent that "little, if any, memory of the New Deal years informed the civil rights movement of the 1960s."[85] The long black and red scare had done its job, disrupting the

---

[84] Ibid., pp. 123–9.

[85] Ibid., pp. 274–5. On the continuities and ruptures between the pre-World War II era of black radicalism and post-World War II movements, see for example, Kelley, *Hammer and Hoe*, pp. 228–31; Robbie Lieberman and Clarence Lang (eds), *Anticommunism and the African American Freedom Movement: "Another Side of the Story"* (2009); Erik McDuffie,

movement in profound ways, destroying organizations, driving out committed activists, and separating issues of black liberation from economic justice, civil liberties, and foreign affairs. In the wake of the more intense scare that set in along with the Cold War, outright repression was not always necessary, as people who had jobs and positions in the community to protect censored themselves.

Scholarly debates about the chronology and goals of the civil rights movement remain unsettled: can we posit one "long" movement that begins in the 1930s and continues through the Cold War era, or does the "long" black and red scare cause us to see several movements that differ in focus, strategy, and personnel? One book chapter can only scratch the surface in discussing the effects of anti-Communism on the black freedom movement. The "civil rights" movement that emerged in the 1950s, generally understood as a nonviolent struggle focused on desegregation, was like the pre-World War II movement in that it also entailed great sacrifice and courage, and it was met with anti-Communist attacks. Coming after the long black and red scare described in this chapter, and further delayed by the Cold War political climate, this more familiar struggle had a substantially different character and makeup than the earlier movements that had emphasized the ties between racial and economic justice. Despite some of the successes of these earlier struggles, the movement of the 1950s and 1960s took place in a Cold War context in which the left-led CIO unions that had concerned themselves with racial equality had been purged, dedicated and effective organizers had been driven out of many organizations by red-baiting, the links between working class, minority, and women's issues had been muted, and foreign policy issues were often avoided.[86] Whether we categorize the struggles of the interwar years as a separate movement or as a stage in one long black freedom movement, the impact of anti-Communism on the movement(s) should not be overlooked or underestimated.

Sojourning for Freedom: Black Women, American Communism, and the Making of Black Left Feminism (Durham: Duke University Press, 2011).

[86] See Lieberman and Lang, *AntiCommunism and the African American Freedom Movement*.

Chapter 12

Shooting Rabid Dogs:
New York's Rapp–Coudert Attack
on Teachers Unions

Stephen Leberstein

Speaking before a Republican women's group in June 1941, New York State Senator Frederic Coudert, Jr. threatened that "... if your dog had rabies you wouldn't clap him into jail after he had bitten a number of persons ... you'd put a bullet into his head, if you had that kind of iron in your blood. It is going to require brutal treatment to handle these teachers ..."[1] By the end of the year, the silk stocking district senator showed just how much iron he had in his blood.

Authorized in the spring 1940, a State Legislative Investigating Committee was established to look into the financing and administration of the state's public schools. By the end of its session in December, the Legislature expanded the committee's mandate to include an investigation of subversive activities in New York City's public education system. That part of the investigation was entrusted to a sub-committee headed by the iron-blooded Coudert.

On the eve of the Second World War, the largest purge of college teachers in the U.S. took place in New York City's municipal colleges, the future City University of New York, and continued on after war's end. At the City College alone, over 50 faculty and staff members lost their jobs in the short span of two years, from 1940 to 1942, at the hands of Coudert's legislative investigating committee, the Rapp-Coudert Committee. The target of the committee's ire was the New York Teachers Union, Local 45 of the American Federation of Teachers, along with the New York College Teachers Union, AFT Local 537. Certain that the union was Communist controlled, the committee set about to prove it and to rid the colleges and schools of suspected Party members. In the process, it invented the techniques that marked the McCarthy era.

Though seemingly marginal to the threat to disrupt production or to challenge the power of dominant elites, teachers had long been vulnerable to

---

[1] *New York Times*, June 3, 1941.

charges of indoctrination in the classroom and personal disloyalty. Marginal or not to concerns over industrial production or the threat of domestic violence, teachers do occupy a potentially critical position in the struggle for ideological hegemony. When they joined labor unions, or supported them, they were seen as all the more dangerous. To understand the significance of the New York purge, which began in the public colleges and spread to the public schools after the war, it is important to understand its context: the growth of a militant labor left in the 1930s, the role of the Communist Party in it, the practice of the left in these unions, and the emergence of a reactionary response to the perceived threat to the existing social order. The existing literature seldom provides this larger context.[2]

The opening salvo in the committee's investigation was its subpoena in January 1941 of the membership lists and all records of the New York Teachers Union and the New York College Teachers Union. Founded in 1916, the New York Teachers Union was one of the first locals of the American Federation of Teachers, established that same year. Its long-time leaders, Abraham Lefkowitz and Henry Linville, were Socialists. But in 1935 a coalition rank and file caucus took control of the union and Lefkowitz and Linville walked out, vowing to capture its AFT charter for their group of several hundred disaffected teachers, the Teachers Guild.

The Left in the Teachers Union

Were there Communists in the Teachers Union, as Coudert and others charged? There obviously were, and their presence and that of other militant leftists led to conflict with the Socialist old guard from at least the early 1930s on. Examining that conflict shows the militants' tactics and the bitter recriminations of the union leaders, and lets us understand how the sectarian attempt to purge the

---

[2]   David Caute, *The Great Fear: The Anti-Communist Purge Under Truman and Eisenhower* (New York: Simon and Schuster, 1959); Lawrence Chamberlain, *Loyalty and Legislative Action* (Ithaca, NY: Cornell University Press, 1951); Robert Iverson, *The Communists and the Schools* (New York, Harcourt Brace, 1959); Marjory Murphy, *Blackboard Unions: The AFT and the NEA, 1900–1980* (Ithaca, NY: Cornell University Press, 1990); Ellen Schrecker, *No Ivory Tower: McCarthyism and the Universities* (New York: Oxford University Press, 1986); Clarence Taylor, *Reds at the Blackboard: Communism, Civil Rights, and the New York City Teachers Union* (New York: Columba University Press, 2011); and Celia Lewis Zitron, *The New York City Teachers Union, 1916–1964: A Story of Educational and Social Commitment* (New York: Humanities Press, 1968).

local from the AFT foreshadowed the purge of the union teachers from the municipal colleges and public schools.

Evidence of a left presence in the union appeared in the mid-20s, when Scott Nearing, dismissed by the University of Pennsylvania for allegedly criticizing capitalism in his economic classes, was elected a TU delegate to the AFT Convention. Nearing, apparently already suspect, appealed to the union's Executive Committee to send Linville along with him in an apparent attempt at conciliation.[3] In a letter to the Committee he noted that Linville and other officers had written "... that I know little of the Union and imply that my election was part of an effort to capture the organization." Nearing's resignation as a delegate didn't stop Linville from publishing a derogatory letter in the *New York Times*, accusing him of radicalism.

By 1932 a Rank and File Committee had formed in the Teachers Union, not an uncommon Communist Party tactic in other AFL unions in this period.[4] And as the Party had also predicted, the committee was attacked by the old-guard Socialist leadership. A Rank and File broadsheet put out in June 1932 sardonically titled "Union Outlawry" (referring to allegations published under that title in the June issue of the *Union Teacher*), accused the leadership of refusing to permit its resolutions to be presented at the Union's annual luncheon in May, and of keeping the union from supporting the defense of the Scottsboro Boys or even discussing the case.[5] It also accused the anonymous authors of the "Union Outlawry" article in the union paper of lying.

In October 1932 the TU's leaders, acting as typical disaffected Socialists, tried to expel the left militants from the union. A Special Grievance Committee chaired by John Dewey was created to hear charges against the opposition groups and six individuals, including Alice Citron, Clara Rieber, Abraham Zitron, Joseph Leboit, Bertram D. Wolfe and Isadore Begun.[6] The committee included Charles Hendley, in place of an elected member who resigned in his favor, and who would later be elected president of TU Over 24 meetings, the committee heard 109 witnesses and produced a 721 page typed transcript. Dewey met with the accused to say that the committee's aim "was to try to understand the broader

---

[3]   Scott Nearing, letter to Henry Linville, May 19, 1925, in UFT Archive, box 13, folder 23.

[4]   "Work in the Old Unions," (fragment of mss report), n.d. (*c.*1929), in CPUSA Archives, reel 132, file 1831.

[5]   Rank and File Committee, "Union Outlawry," broadsheet, June 9, 1932, in UFT Archives, box 3, folder 38.

[6]   "Report of the Special Grievance Committee, to be submitted to the members for formal action at a special meeting of the Teachers Union ... April 28, 1933," in UFT Archives, box 1, folder 9.

phases of the situation in the Union ..." and considered itself "investigators and judges rather than prosecutors."

The trial report charged the opposition with divisiveness, citing a series of articles that appeared in the *Education Worker*, published by the Educational Workers League of New York and the Trade Union Unity League (TUUL), throughout 1932, beginning with this piece from the January issue:

> Some plucky teachers 'want to save the Union.' They will not let the old dame die. They want to rejuvenate it. Vain hope! Lefkowitz and his cronies carry her in their pockets. She will rot there unless they trade her to 59th Street (the Board of Education headquarters) for principalships and superintendencies. When this becomes quite clear the Educational Workers' League will grow even faster than it is now.[7]

From this the committee makes the astonishing conclusion that the EWL has teachers among its members!

In a minority report that they were prevented from presenting at the Board's October 27, 1932 meeting, Begun and three others spoke in their own defense. Lefkowitz, they said, had proposed expelling the entire Rank and File group that June, but by September asked that only the group's leadership, and all its candidates for office, be expelled, along with Bertram Wolfe, the Progressive candidate for vice president, and Scott Nearing. By the time of the union's membership meeting in October, only the above six were on the expulsion list.

The minority report blames Lefkowitz for his failed effort to change the rules on discipline beginning in 1931, then for trying to limit the number of membership meetings in a year, and finally for proposing to open union membership to supervisors while denying substitute teacher members the right to vote. The most damning charge is that Lefkowitz denounced the opposition members as Communists before a Board of Education committee, proclaiming that the Teachers Union would expel them. Then he brought formal charges against Begun and, in a hearing before Superintendent O'Shea testified against him and urged his firing. The minority report termed these "'Lusk-like' actions [as] against the very essence of unionism ..."[8]

When the "Report of the Special Grievance Committee" was sent to the accused in April 1933, it no longer recommended expulsion but rather lesser

---

[7] Ibid., p. 7.

[8] The reference is to the New York State Legislature's Lusk Committee in the early 1920s, which demanded loyalty oaths and other repressive measures of teachers.

discipline.[9] It labeled Begun "the acknowledged leader of the Rank and File Group," and found him guilty of having "trafficked with the secret dual union known as the Education Workers League." While the committee admitted having found no direct evidence of a relationship between the Rank and File group and the Education Workers League, it nevertheless convicted Begun of using tactics similar to those of the TUUL and of proposing to "ally" the union with the International Labor Defense (ILD), efforts that "indicate that his disruptive and dissident actions are not incidental ..." Begun and the others were guilty, the report continued, of trying "to embarrass the Union," in the eyes of the American Federation of Labor, by promoting such "controversial proposals" as support for freeing Tom Mooney or defending the Scottsboro Boys. Clara Rieber, in particular, was accused of sowing discord with the AFL by working with other AFL locals in support of unemployment insurance. Essentially, the committee was willing, even eager, to find Begun guilty by association, or even by resemblance.

At a special meeting on April 29, 1933, the TU's Executive Board put before the membership resolutions to withhold official recognition of the opposition groups and to prohibit TU officers from "complying in any official way with the requests or demands of any group describing itself as Rank and File or progressive ..."[10] The Board also proposed creating a Delegate Assembly.

Over 800 members attended the boisterous special meeting, which went on for 6 hours without recess.[11] Dewey addressed the meeting, proclaiming the investigation as "one of the best contributions to the examination of Communist strategy ..." Accused of trying to stifle democratic dissent, Dewey was reported as outraged: "Of course I believe in democracy!" Under the union's constitution, recommendations on suspension had to be approved by a two-thirds majority at membership meetings. A motion to suspend one of the accused failed by a vote of 451 for, 316 against, and a motion to dismiss charges against the other accused carried. The motion to create a Delegate Assembly carried as well.

In their machinations to quash opposition groups within the TU, Linville and Lefkowitz were acting on their own sectarian reasons for purging the

---

[9]   "Report of the Special Grievance Committee, relative to the charges against Miss Alice Citron, Miss Clara Rieber, Mr. Abraham Zitron, Mr. Joseph Leboit, Mr. Bertram D. Wolfe, and Mr. Isidore Begun, mailed to the defendants April 18, 1933," in UFT Archives, box 14, folder 9.

[10]   Resolutions and Amendments, Approved by the Executive Board of the Teachers Union and Presented to the Members for Consideration at the meeting of April 29, 1933," in UFT Archives, box 14, folder 9.

[11]   "Notes on the Trial Meeting, April 29, 1933," mimeod mss., in UFT Archives, box 14, folder 9.

294   *Little 'Red Scares'*

militants; they were also following the line of William Green, president of the AFL, who later warned affiliated locals in 1934 of "communistic groups" trying to "bore from within." "Communism is anti-American," he wrote, "and is committed to world revolution.[12] He called on AFL affiliates "to ferret out all communistic members, all communistic 'cells' ... [and every person and group] carrying on communistic propaganda." In Green's terminology, "communistic" described anyone or any group that took stands like those taken by the Party, for example supporting unemployment insurance.

As the old guard feared, or more probably hoped, the left opposition within the TU, now emboldened by the failure to suspend its members and by the creation of a Delegate Assembly, did arouse the ire of the AFL. In response to Green's letter on "communistic" activity, the Delegate Assembly resolved on January 3rd, 1935 to oppose "... any discrimination or disciplinary action against any worker because of his [*sic*] political opinions or activity ..." and condemned Green's letter as "Red-baiting." In her letter to Green reporting this resolution, union secretary Clara Naftolowitz described his call to "ferret out" the communistic as "a violation of Union democracy and Union principles," and reported that the resolution was adopted by a vote of 79 in favor, 58 against.

Green replied promptly on the 21st saying that her letter:

> ... leads me to the conclusion that your Local Union occupies a false position. In my judgment you are out of place in your affiliation with the American Federation of Labor. You properly belong to the Communist organization and to the communist movement. Communist philosophy is diametrically opposed to the philosophy of the American Federation of Labor. No one can subscribe to both. Evidently the majority of the members of your Local Union are willing to support a movement whose avowed purpose is the destruction of the American Federation of Labor.[13]

Following this exchange, the old guard TU officers asked the American Federation of Teachers to revoke Local 5's charter and issue a new one which would bar Communists, thus beginning a struggle to drive the TU out of the AFT that would culminate in 1941.

The struggle began in earnest after the AFT would not revoke Local 5's charter. The old guard walked out that September, taking about 200 members

---

[12]   William Green, "To the Officers and Members of All Organizations of Labor," open letter, September 11, 1934, in UFT Archives, box 10 folder 54.

[13]   Green to Naftolowitz, January 21, 1935, in UFT Archives, box 10, folder 54.

Shooting Rabid Dogs

with them to form the Teachers Guild.[14] In the meantime Linville recruited Selma Borchardt, a member of the Washington, D.C. AFT local and the AFT's Legislative Representative, to press Green for action. In response, Green got the AFL to authorize an investigation at its convention that summer. The investigating committee soon leveled charges not only against the T. U. but also against the AFT for allowing "locals that do not exist" and others that are "communistically controlled" to vote at its convention, thereby derailing the attempt to oust the alleged Communists from Local 5.

A new leadership, with Charles Hendley as president, took control of the TU after the split. Hendley, the unexpected member of Dewey's grievance committee, was a Socialist Party member.[15] Benjamin Mandel and Sidney Hook, expert witnesses on Communism for the Rapp–Coudert investigation, later claimed that Hendley was only a puppet, since there was no evidence he was a Communist. In fact, the union's record shows that Hendley was independent, trying to unite the warring factions. But he was also a long-time labor activist, swayed by some of the positions the Party took.

The union's Delegate Assembly decided in April 1936 to ask the AFL to delay its investigation and objected to the committee hearing testimony from Linville and Lefkowitz "since they are no longer in the labor movement."[16] In deciding on a strategy to deal with the AFL investigation, the delegates voted "... to fight the investigation on the ground that it is an aid to Red-baiting and reaction throughout the country, ... and that is a blow against the progressive bloc in the labor movement."

At the same time Borchardt was organizing the reaction. In an open letter to "Fellow Trade Unionists" she asked for support when the AFL investigating committee considers her allegation "That the New York local is trying hard to live up to Earl Browder's public claim 'that the Teachers' Union proves the practicality of our United Front.'"[17] Her goal was to force the AFT "... to remove from the organization such elements as are improperly functioning in it," in other words to purge the left.

In May 1936 the TU formally elected a new slate headed by Hendley as president, with a Prof. Keyes as V.P. for the college section, and a coalition of

---

[14] Henry Linville to Selma Borchardt, Mary Herrick, Stanton Smith, Florence Roof, May Darling and Frederick Ringdahl, September 16,1935, in UFT Archives, box 3, folder 39.

[15] Charles J. Hendley, at 3810 Fairfield Ave., New York is listed as a member of the Socialist Party since September 1932 in "Membership Recapitulation, Socialist Party, USA, Local New York", May 20, 1936, in Socialist Collection, Reel 14, file 35.

[16] Minutes, T.U. Delegate Assembly, April 23, 1936, in UFT Archives, box 13, folder 2.

[17] Selma Borchardt to unidentified "Fellow Trade Unionists," April 6, 1936, in UFT Archives, box 3, folder 38.

Communists, Socialists and Trotskyists including Dale Zysman, Layle Lane and Bella Dodd among others, and for the Executive Board Celia Lewis, Arnold Shukotoff, who would become one of the Rapp–Coudert victims at City College, and Isadore Begun and Clara Rieber as "hold-over members."[18] A week later candidates for delegates and alternates to the AFT Convention were nominated by caucus.[19] For the first time some of the activists at City College appear as nominees of the Rank and File caucus, including Morris Schappes and Arnold Shukotoff.

At the two largest colleges, Brooklyn and City, faculty and staff activists had formed Instructional Staff Associations by 1935. Reprisals against them came swiftly at both. In April 1936, Schappes, along with 12 others active in City's Instructional Staff Association whose members had affiliated with the TU, had just been notified that he would not be reappointed as tutor in English at City College, a post he had held since 1928.[20] Schappes, Shukotoff and nearly 50 others would lose their jobs at City College in 1941 in the Rapp–Coudert purge. But by June 1936, with widespread support from the labor movement, the Board of Higher Education reversed his non-reappointment. At Brooklyn, history tutor Henry Klein was let go for his union activism, and later pursued by the Rapp–Coudert Committee when he found a job teaching in the public schools.

The newly invigorated Teachers Union was living up to the allegations of its enemies by vigorously organizing all teachers regardless of rank, sending observers to the National Negro Congress, supporting students in a peace strike, fighting racism in Harlem schools, and organizing new members in its college section, as well as substitutes and unemployed teachers, and teachers in the WPA.[21] At the same time, Linville tried to arouse the conservatives in the AFT in advance of its convention by accusing the TU of including as members substitute, WPA and private school teachers and others who are not regular teachers and claiming that "Labor no longer pays any attention to Local 5 ..."[22]

---

[18]   Minutes, Executive Board, May 5, 1936 (revised copy, hand corrected, dated May 8), in UFT Archives, box 13, folder 4.

[19]   Minutes, Delegate Assembly, May 15, 1936, in UFT Archives, box 13, folder 2.

[20]   "Reappoint Schappes!" resolution of the Executive Board, April 25, 1936, in UFT Archives, box 13, folder 4; see also Stephen Leberstein, "Purging the Profs.: The Rapp Coudert Committee in New York," in Michael Brown et al. (eds), *New Studies in the Politics and Culture of U.S. Communism* (New York: MR Press, 1993), and Leberstein, "Morris U. Schappes at City College" *Jewish Currents*, September–October 2004, 22–6.

[21]   In January 1936 the T.U.'s college section reported its membership had grown from 36 in 1935 to 300. Minutes, Executive Board, January 3, 1926, in UFT Archives, box 13, folder 4.

[22]   Henry Linville to unidentified Dear Friends in the American Labor Movement, June 30, 1936, in UFT Archives, box 3, folder 38.

Shooting Rabid Dogs 297

A hallmark of the TU's position on the left of the labor movement was its anti-racist agenda and hence its involvement in Harlem and Central Brooklyn.[23] It worked for years to have racist texts removed from schools and to develop a "Negro" history curriculum.

One iconic emblem of this position was the publication of the poem "Bitter Fruit" in the January 1937 edition of *New York Teacher*, the union newspaper. Written by Abe Meeropol, a social studies teacher at DeWitt Clinton High School in the Bronx, and a member of the Teachers Union, the poem was written in response to reports of a lynching, and in support an anti-lynching bill stalled in Congress. Later set to music, the poem became Billie Holiday's signature song as "Strange Fruit." Meeropol may be best remembered as the adoptive father of Ethel and Julius Rosenberg's children, Michael and Robert, orphaned when their parents were executed in 1953.

Another example of the union's anti-racist campaign was the case of the October 1936 beating of a 14-year-old student in a Harlem school by its white principal.[24] The Robert Shelton case, in the eyes of the Harlem community and the TU leadership, demonstrated the tragedy of racial segregation in New York City's public schools. Shelton was responsible for bringing his six-year-old cousin Ollie Wyatt to school at 2, when his shift began, and for picking up his six-year-old sister Anna when hers ended; both were first graders. So overcrowded was the school that the first grade was taught in shifts.

On this October day, according to a report in support of charges filed against the principal, young Shelton had a hard time getting into the school building, and once inside is sent from one place to another by apparently hostile teachers until he is apprehended by principal Schoenchen. Locked in the principal's office, beaten, knocked to the floor and ordered to wash the blood from his face. Schoenchen then has the truant officer send him home. His mother sends him to Harlem Hospital for treatment. His father and witnesses file a complaint at the 151st Street Court, and have a warrant issued for Schoenchen to be tried on assault charges.[25]

The Shelton incident led to the formation of the Committee for Better Schools in Harlem, which the TU supported and joined. The Better Schools Committee attacked the condition of schools in Harlem, seeing the Shelton beating as

---

[23] Teachers Union, "Program-Harlem Committee," n.d. (*c.*1941), in Hendley Papers, box 7, f.ile 6.

[24] "Statement of Facts in the Case of the Brutal Beating of Robert Shelton by Principal Gustav Schoenchen of P.S. 5 ... " mss. In UFT Archives, box 5, folder 189.

[25] Poster issued by the Permanent Committee for Better Schools, "Mr. Schoenchen, principal of P.S. 5, did this to Robert Shelton, model student," in UFT Archives, box 5, folder 189.

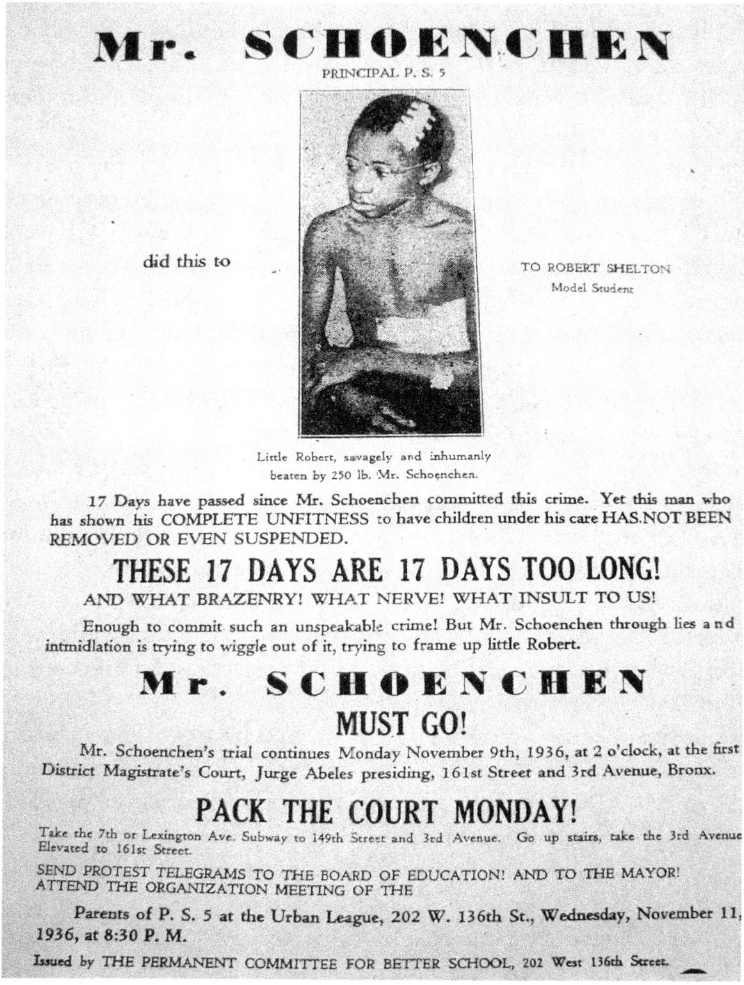

Figure 12.1   'Mr. Schoenchen, principal ...' poster. Courtesy of Tamiment
Library and Robert F. Wagner Labor Archives

an example of the "Savage corporal punishment of Negro school-children."[26]
Describing the dilapidated buildings and overcrowded classes, the Committee
called for a "Mass Trial of the Board of Education," which it accused of "wilfull [sic]
gross negligence of Harlem's school children." It "subpoenaed" the community to
act as jury at a trial on January 27th at the Abyssinian Baptist Church.

---

[26]   Committee for Better Schools in Harlem, "Re Gustav Schoenchen, principal P.S.
5, accused of beating Robert Shelton, 14 yrs. Old," open letter, January 15, 1937, in UFT
Archives, box 5, folder 189.

Shooting Rabid Dogs 299

When the union paper, *New York Teacher*, published an account of the incident, the Teachers Guild rallied to Schoenchen's defense, charging that the union "should have maintained a discreet silence."[27] Responding in a message to the City's school principals, TU president Hendley explained that "... [the union] took a stand on this case because it regarded it as an illustration of a situation and a condition which must be remedied but which will continue to be neglected unless public opinion is aroused." The union's anti-racism would soon become an issue for the Rapp–Coudert investigation.

In a shrill attack that resonated on the right in the period leading up to the AFL investigation, the Teachers Guild accused the union "with promoting race riots and class war and [it] thereby indicts many of the most prominent, intelligent and reliable citizens of the community." For his part, Schoenchen accused the union of "being dominated by reds and obedient to Communist discipline." The union pledged to continue its opposition to bad conditions in Harlem schools "even though some may accuse us of fomenting 'class war.'"

The incident showed the stakes in the attack on the labor left when Schoenchen wrote to "My Dear Colleagues" in late January claiming that he, not young Robert Shelton, was the victim in this case, a victim of character assassination:

> I am not referring especially to the two Negro papers in Harlem, which actually went so far as to urge physical violence, and incited to riot; *there may be some excuse for these people because, in their ignorance,* they were led astray and became the catapaw of the Communist strategy. But how can we excuse the Teachers Union ... who know so little about practical Americanism that they condemn without a hearing one of their own colleagues because he happens to be a supervisor and hence one of the 'bosses' in Communist ideology.[28]

Schoenchen concluded by praising the Teachers Guild for coming to his defense and for denouncing the Teachers Union as Communist.

Just how true was the Guild's characterization of the TU as Communist? In the election of TU officers in 1937, the political affiliation of its leaders appears to be a complicated coalition. For example, Hendley criticized the union's "fitful" policy changes over the last two years "in response to special interest and

---

[27]   To the Principals (Please post)," broadsheet signed Charles Hendley, president, n.d. (early 1937), in UFT Archives, box 5, folder 189.

[28]   Gustav Schoenchen, "My Dear Colleague," circular letter, January 27, 1937, in UFT Archives, box 5, folder 189.

expediency."[29] This is hardly the stance of someone in thrall of discipline to the Communist Party. He called instead for the formation of an independent slate and program for the coming election. On the same date as Hendley's letter, Ruth Schecter, announced the launching of the Independent Group: "We want the Independent Group to represent a substantial section of the Union membership – not simply comrades."[30] She concluded by saying that the new group would be a chance to increase Socialist influence in the union, noting that the Party's City Executive Committee had voted to run Hendley on this slate by 11 to 3.

Socialists still claimed Hendley as one of their own, however uneasily, when the Party's City Executive Committee endorsed him for TU president. But the Socialist Teachers League declared that it would be in the best interests of the Teachers Union and the Socialist Party if "Comrade Hendley ... should not again run for the presidency."[31] Although the union's leadership was in fact a coalition, the right-wing Socialists criticized Hendley for lacking party discipline, his willingness to appoint Communists to union posts, and for lending "the Union's influence to the building of a CP innocent organization known as, the Permanent Committee for Better Schools in Harlem." Neither Socialist nor Communist Party discipline seemed to be the rule.

Hendley handily won the election with 3,333 votes out of 3,411 returned.[32] The slate's candidates won overwhelmingly, and the Executive Board now included not only Isadore Begun but also Reinhold Niebuhr among the 20 Rank and File members, 5 Independents and one Progressive. Delegates elected to the AFT included a growing number of the City College militants, including Schappes, John Kenneth Ackley, Arnold Shukotoff, Seymour Copstein and David Goldway, all of whom would lose their jobs in the Rapp–Coudert purge.

None of this would matter to investigators who would charge that the TU was "communistically" controlled. Not all the elected officers of the union could be identified as Communists, and some were clearly either Socialists, Trotskyists or independents. On the face of it, the union was not "controlled" by the Party, although it did take some positions, especially on foreign policy issues, that left it open to the accusation.

Organizing college faculty members soon became a priority of the new leadership. Local Instructional Staff Associations active at Brooklyn and City Colleges soon joined the college section of the TU. Howard Selsam of Brooklyn

---

[29] Charles J. Hendley et al., "To Union Members," circular letter, April 19, 1937, in UFT Archives, box 13, folder 24.

[30] Ruth Schecter, "Comrades," April 19, 1937, in UFT Archives, box 13, folder 24.

[31] "Statement of the Socialist Teachers League," April 1937, UFT Archives, box 9, folder 32.

[32] Minutes, Executive Board, June 4, 1937, in UFT Archives, box 13, folder 5.

Figure 12.2 Local 537 members marching in the May Day Parade, Union Square, NYC, circa 1940. Courtesy of New York State Archives

College reported to the Executive Board in June 1937 that the NYU chapter had called for a separate college local, and that the college section would study the suggestion and report back in the fall.[33] He also suggested that the Negro history course that Max Yergan developed at City College be made available to all teachers at the other municipal colleges.

By that fall, the TU Executive Board agreed to ask the AFT to charter a separate college local, and to propose forming a joint board with representatives of the other teacher locals in New York.[34] Soon thereafter the AFT chartered the New York College Teachers Union, Local 537, and the TU then approved

---

[33] Ibid.
[34] Minutes, Executive Board, October 16, 1937, in UFT Archives, loc. cit.; photo of Local 537 in May Day parade in New York State Archives, Joint Legislative Committee on the State Education System, Investigation Files of the Rapp–Coudert Committee, Series L0260-09, folder 222.

302   *Little 'Red Scares'*

the creation of a joint board with representatives of Locals 5, 24, 453 (the WPA teachers) and 537.[35]

The College Teachers Union won a great victory shortly thereafter when the Board of Higher Education in June 1938 adopted what the union called its "democratization plan."[36] The plan granted tenure to virtually all ranks after three years satisfactory service and provided for faculty control of the curriculum and personnel decisions.

Trouble soon broke out at Brooklyn College, however, trouble which would contribute to the Rapp–Coudert purge. Henry Klein, a young history instructor and TU activist had been dismissed. The union chapter there campaigned for his reinstatement, and its tactics seem to have crystallized the left/right split in the faculty with charges that the TU had been taken over by the Communist Party, which did have a significant group there as well as at City College.[37] Bernard Grebanier, a union member who had belonged to the Party cell at Brooklyn, led the attack, asking the Dies Committee (the House Committee on Un-American Activities) to investigate Communist influence in the City's municipal colleges.[38]

Dies had little luck in 1938 when he sought cooperation from the chairman of the Board of Higher Education, Ordway Tead. When Dies asked his help in ridding the municipal colleges of "subversives," Tead declared that the political affiliations of the faculty and staff were none of the Board's business. "Our concern is with the scholarship and integrity of our faculties ... [and] differences of opinion and attitude among faculty members are a wholesome sign of vitality, and as this is reflected in the teaching, it supplies students with a useful cross-section of the divergence of views in the community at large."[39] Tead would later change his mind. Speaking at the AAUP annual meeting in St. Louis in 1948, he now said that the State had a legal right to bar members of the Communist Party from teaching in the public colleges.[40]

---

[35]   Minutes, Executive Board, February 25, 1938, in UFT Archives, box 5, folder 6.

[36]   In June 1938, the Board of Higher Education adopted a plan to "democratize" the colleges, providing for tenure after 3 years' satisfactory service, and giving faculty the right to elect department chairs, hire new colleagues, and decide personnel and curricular matters. "College Teachers Win Tenure," in *New York Times*, June 21, 1938; Morris Schappes, interview, September 20–21, 1981.

[37]   Minutes, Executive Board, May 21, 1937, in UFT Archives, box 13, folder 5.

[38]   I am indebted to Marvin Gettleman for sharing with me the notes of his interview with Grebanier.

[39]   *New York Times*, August 24, 1938.

[40]   Ordway Tead, "Faculty-Administration Relations," *AAUP Bulletin*, vol. 34, no. 1 (Spring 1948), 67.

The Rapp–Coudert Purge

That moment of tolerance was brief. The stage was now set for New York's infamous Rapp–Coudert Committee. While many voices were raised against the Teachers Union in particular and the labor left in general, they weren't an organized chorus. Disaffected business unionists, former Party members, right-wing Socialists and ideologues, the church, the Hearst press, professional witnesses and government agents, all found their moment in the short period between the Nazi-Soviet Non-Aggression Pact of August 1939 and U.S. entry into the Second World War.

A sign of how that trouble was brewing was Sidney Hook's address before the New York *Herald Tribune* Forum on Current Problems reprinted in the AAUP *Bulletin*.[41] Hook tried to distinguish between those who invoke the Bill of Rights to profess their beliefs and those who invoke it to conceal them. The latter are conspirators, he said, "totalitarians" who "represent a grave threat to the intellectual integrity of American education and culture." When exposed, the Stalinists attempt an "intellectual lynching" of their accusers. Claiming to have a list of "the names of the individuals, particularly the forty odd in 21 universities" who attacked his newly created Committee for Cultural Freedom, Hook, like McCarthy 15 years later in Wheeling, West Virginia, declined to provide it. But he stated that the way to meet the Communist threat was "not by governmental repression but by public exposure and criticism in the educational and cultural professions themselves." Not only was Hook already engaged in this guerilla warfare, but he would soon be actively collaborating with agents of the "governmental repression" he claimed to reject.

The incident that propelled the investigation onward with greater force was the bitter public acrimony surrounding Bertrand Russell's offer of a professorship at City College. Exercising their newly won rights to choose faculty, in February 1940 the City College Philosophy Department recruited Russell, then unhappily located at UCLA. The Hearst press began to attack Russell after he cancelled the column he had been writing. Hearst apparently didn't forgive him for what he regarded as a betrayal.[42] Unluckily for Russell, his old adversary William Manning was now the Episcopal bishop of New York, who regarded him as an unrepentant villain for his pacifism and unorthodox views on social and political

---

[41] Sidney Hook, "Academic Freedom and 'The Trojan Horse' in American Education," *AAUP Bulletin*, XV, no. 5 (December 1939), 550–53.

[42] Thom Weidlich, *Appointment Denied: The Inquisition of Bertrand Russell* (Amherst, NY: Prometheus Books, 2000); Stephen Leberstein, Review of Weidlich, *Appointment Denied in Academe: Bulletin of the American Association of University Professors*, vol. 87, no. 6 (September–October 2001), 82–7.

Figure 12.3 "Good Morning Dear Teacher ... ," in the Philadelphia *Inquirer*, March 23, 1940. Courtesy of the Philadelphia *Inquirer*

issues, especially those on sex and marriage. Manning rallied the religious right, including the Catholic archbishop of New York, Cardinal Spellman, in his campaign against Russell. While the Board of Higher Education backed the faculty and refused to rescind the offer, the opposition reached such a fever pitch that Mayor LaGuardia finally eliminated the budget line for Russell's position in the City budget.

For opportunist politicians, taxpayer groups, and those opposed to organized labor, the Russell case seemed to exemplify everything wrong with the municipal colleges and the Teachers Union. For them Russell became a caricature of a dodgy professor, promoting "free love," atheism and socialism behind the veil of academic freedom, as portrayed in the Philadelphia *Inquirer* cartoon. For Joseph Goldsmith of the Taxpayers Union, the Russell case showed the danger of a free college for the children of workers, so he urged that City College be shut down and that the City slash $10 million from the budget of the remaining municipal colleges[43] For anti-New Deal politicians, it was an opportunity to strike a blow against a militant union advocating broad social programs. And for the old guard of the Teachers Union who had been ousted from office, it was time to settle scores.

Religious conservatives had already begun to take aim at the TU in 1938, when a group of teachers founded the American Education Association which published a newsletter, the *Educational Signpost*. Headed by Milo McDonald, the principal of Bushwick High School in Brooklyn, the group joined the troops arrayed against Russell. It hoped the controversy would convince New York City voters to support a plan for vouchers so that public colleges could be closed.[44] A consistent advocate for religious instruction in public schools and for vouchers for higher education, *The Educational Signpost* explained its plan to defeat Communism by restoring "The superb Christian ideology and tradition and accomplishments upon which America was founded and from which our schools grew ... The only salvation for America and her schools lies in a crusade to make Christianity live in this country ... It is to this great task that the A.E.A. dedicates itself."[45] By 1939 the American Education Association included May Quinn, a schoolteacher accused of spewing racist and fascist statements in her classroom, and Gustav Schoenchen among its officers.[46] Little wonder, then, that teachers said they feared anti-Semitism in their schools and on their campuses.

After the March 1940 creation of a legislative committee to investigate the financing and administration of public education headed by Assemblyman Herbert Rapp, State Senator John J. Dunnigan, incensed that City College would try to hire the "godless advocate of free love," amended the Rapp bill to add a sub-committee to investigate subversion in the schools and colleges of New York City to be headed by State Senator Frederick Coudert. The Rapp–Coudert Committee emerged out of the maelstrom of the Russell affair and at a time when the strength of the Communist Party was sapped by the Comintern's sudden about-face in signing the Nazi–Soviet Non-Aggression Pact.

---

[43]   Cited in Lawrence Chamberlain, *Loyalty and Legislative Action* (Ithaca, NY: Cornell University Press, 1951), 162.

[44]   "Our Platform," *The Educational Signpost*, vol. I, no. 8 (Dec. 1938), Hendley Papers, box 5, folder 220.

[45]   "The New School Year," *The Educational Signpost*, vol. IV, no. 7 (October 1941), in Hendley Papers, Box 11, file 2.

[46]   *The Educational Signpost* (masthead), vol. II, no. 2 (February 1939), loc. cit.

306   *Little 'Red Scares'*

Coudert had already recruited staff headed by Paul Windels, former counsel to the Seabury Commission on municipal corruption and Mayor LaGuardia's corporation counsel, for his sub-committee, and they started work in the summer 1940. The Teachers Union was their main, and apparently only interest. Robert J. Morris, one of the committee's chief investigators, asked in August to meet with Linville, who readily agreed.[47] Morris asked for documents from the union files and then subpoenaed the materials of the Dewey Special Grievance Committee that met in 1932–33.

That October Morris and Windels met with Ben Mandel in a New York hotel room.[48] Pledging the investigators to secrecy, Mandel said that he had created a list of Communist teachers in the school system specifically for the Rapp–Coudert Committee. After explaining some of the Party's tactics, Mandel told Morris where to look for information and help: Lefkowitz in the Joint Committee of the Central Trades and Labor Council, Bernard Grebanier at Brooklyn College, and Sidney Hook at New York University, George Hartman and George Counts at Teachers College. He brought up the Schoenchen case "... as one that was particularly unsavory and typical of Party campaign." Finally, Mandel stressed the centrality of "force and violence" in Communist doctrine, and gave Morris a reading list of Lenin's works as an assignment.

The next week Morris traveled to Washington to see J.B. Matthews, the Dies Committee's chief investigator. Matthews agreed to be helpful, and then sent in Ben Mandel, his assistant, perhaps unaware that Mandel had already met him, to provide information and show him the Dies files. Morris was also sent to see Raymond Murphy, a State Department official, who "flatly and enthusiastically promised" information prior to the beginning of the Coudert hearings that December.

Sidney Hook, the Coudert Committee's public expert on the dangers of the Communist Party, appeared as a friendly witness at a private hearing on May 8, 1941.[49] In June Morris interviewed Hook further at his Brooklyn home.[50] Morris hoped Hook would produce "leads" for the committee, and recorded in his notes that "This proved profitable on two other occasions. Hook was very sympathetic and very laudatory in his estimation of the work of the

---

[47]   Robert J. Morris to Henry Linville, August 27, 1940; Linville to Morris, September 4, 1940; and other correspondence in UFT Archives, box 3, folder 18.

[48]   RJM (Robert J. Morris), "Meeting with Ben Mandel ..." (typed notes), October 21, 1940; RJM, "Memorandum of Trip to Washington," October 29, 1940, copies of documents in author's possession.

[49]   Sidney Hook testimony, May 8, 1941, transcript, copy in author's possession.

[50]   RJM, "Interview with Sidney Hook at his home ... June 17th (1941)," Rapp Coudert Files, box 3, file 95.

Committee." Morris wanted Hook to identify Party members, especially at Brooklyn College, and Hook volunteered that "The complaints of people who were members of the union indicated that Communism was rife within the union, and particularly in Brooklyn."

With apparent philosophic clarity, Hook further explained his method, "the behavior test," for identifying the Communists: "If you have been tasting cheeses, or tasting wines, for a long time you develop a sense of distinction that the ordinary person will not have." Hook began his wine-and-cheese tasting around 1932, he said, when the Rank and File group surfaced in the Teachers Union, a time when he claimed sympathy with the Party and asserted that Earl Browder even tried to recruit him. Asked what threat Communist teachers posed to schools, Hook replied:

> In any college where you have a group of people organized in a conspiratorial manner, who take their instructions from a foreign power – because the basic value and allegiance of the Communist power is oriented towards Russia, and that can be documented in a thousand details where you have such a group who publishes newspapers, organizes the students, aims to inculcate a point of view which is laid down by a foreign power, and then the very pre-suppositions of educational freedom are undermined ... the reliability of what is taught in class ... So that I think there can be no question but that if conspiratorial groups of that sort existed on the campus, it would make impossible the work of education of the university or college as such.

When asked why Communist teachers had been able to infiltrate the colleges so easily, Hook said that "... public opinion is in such a state that any man who comes out to attack the Communists has to be a pretty brave sort of fellow."

So, it was public opinion that had to be changed, and silencing leftist teachers was an important step toward that goal. In its first report to the Legislature, the Coudert Subcommittee stated that it had aimed to make the educational institutions themselves responsible for policing the "Communist Problem" in the municipal colleges.[51] The report attributed the spread of Communism among the faculty to the tolerant attitude of "... that amorphous section of the public referred to under the collective heading 'liberals' and 'intellectual'" which seemed to regard Communism as a legitimate form of political dissent.

The Committee went about its work deliberately, first subpoenaing the membership lists and all other records of the Teachers Union. The union sought

---

[51]   *Report of the Sub-Committee Relative to the Public Educational System of the City of New York*, New York State Legislative Documents, 165th Session, X (1942), no. 48:22–3; also see Leberstein, "Purging the Profs."

Figure 12.4   James Egleson, in Committee for Defense of Public Education, *Winter Soldiers: The Story of a Conspiracy Against the Schools* (1941)

an injunction to safeguard its records, but lost. Those activists in the union who could be identified as "communistic" by at least two witnesses were then called to a private hearing where they were confronted with the evidence, and asked to cooperate. Cooperation meant admission of Party membership or evidence that the suspect had left the Party, and that he name names. Usually the next day the newspapers carried the story of those who refused.

The committee held its first public hearing on December 2nd, 1940. The union's attorney, William J. Mulligan was present in an attempt to represent the accused at the hearing. In the private hearings that preceded the public hearing, those interrogated were refused the right to counsel, along with the right to

Shooting Rabid Dogs 309

see the evidence against them or to have a transcript of the hearing.[52] When Mulligan tried to present Coudert with a motion to allow him to cross-examine witnesses, Coudert refused to accept it. When Mulligan persisted, Coudert had the police forcibly remove him from the hearing room.[53]

Before the public hearing and continuing for some months afterward, the Committee pressed the Board of Higher Education to adopt policies compelling its faculty and staff members to testify before legislative investigating committees, and ultimately barring members of Communist or fascist parties from employment at the colleges.[54] Refusal to name names had now become cause for dismissal as an act of insubordination. By the time the hearings were suspended after the Nazi invasion of the Soviet Union in June, over 50 faculty and staff at City College had been dismissed or not reappointed, the single largest purge of academics in the U.S. Just as important, the committee had compiled a list containing the numbered names of 694 suspects and one un-numbered, many of whom would be pursued after the war when Robert Morris went to work as investigator for the McCarran Subcommittee on Internal Security.[55]

Typical of the entries was that for Celia Lewis, finally dismissed by the Board of Education years later, in 1950: "Married name Citron. Member of the Executive Committee of the TU, chairman of Democracy in the Schools Committee of the TU. Sponsored affiliation of League for Peace and Democracy and TU in January 1938. Mandel lists her as a Communist." Or Oscar Schaftel [*sic*]: "Bernard Reiss, of Hunter College, testified that he was the president of the Queens College Teachers Union chapter. Charles Halberg ... suspected him of leftist leanings. Believed by friend of Nelson Frank to be a Communist."

There seem not to have been enough informants at Brooklyn, Hunter or Queens Colleges in 1941 to bring charges against the professors that Grebanier, Hook and Mandel had identified. The McCarran Committee and other enforcers pursued them later, much as many of the schoolteachers identified by the Rapp–

---

[52]   A typical example was that of Alfred Kazin who taught in the summer session at City College from 1939 to 1941. When he refused to identify who had recruited him to join the T.U., Kazin responded: "I have been accused of being a member of the Communist Party. I never have been. I think it only fair to me and my reputation, whatever it may be, to see the people and certainly find out who is accusing me of that." His interrogator bluntly replied, "I am afraid that won't be possible." Hearing transcript, Alfred Kazin, February 1, 1941, in Rapp Coudert Files, box 16, file 533.

[53]   Transcript, Rapp Coudert Public Hearing, December 2, 1940, vol. I, pp. 5–7, in CCNY Archives.

[54]   Minutes, Board of Higher Education, November 1940 through April 1941.

[55]   "3rd and Very Incomplete Copy of List," in Rapp Coudert Files, box 8, file 380; my thanks to Ellen Schrecker for sharing with me her interview notes, Robert Morris, October 29, 1981.

Figure 12.5 Schappes teaching a class at the School for Democracy, where many of those dismissed from City and Brooklyn. Colleges taught in the mid-1940s. Courtesy of Tamiment Library and Robert F. Wagner Labor Archives[56]

Coudert Committee faced charges after the Second World War ended. At City College, only one of the accused, Morris Schappes, faced criminal charges.

Morris Schappes, the most prominent Communist on campus, had edited the *Teacher-Worker*, the Party's shop paper there. In a defense move he thought would protect him and others, Schappes decided to confess that he had been a Party member but had resigned in the late 1930s to pursue his Ph.D. at Columbia.[57] He also testified that during his time in the Party and as editor of City's shop paper, there were only three other Party members at the college, two who died in combat in the Lincoln Brigade in Spain, and the other who resigned to become a labor organizer.[58] There were no others to be named. The ploy was too transparent to work, and the politically ambitious Manhattan District

---

[56] "School for Democracy, Fall Term, September–December 1942," in Hendley Papers, box 17, file 5.

[57] Schappes interview, September 18, 1981.

[58] Hearing transcript, Morris Schappes, February 24, 1941, in Rapp Coudert Files, box 18, file 558.

Shooting Rabid Dogs 311

Attorney, Thomas Dewey, indicted Schappes on a felony charge of perjury.[59] Schappes was convicted and spent 13 months of hard time in prison before parole in 1945.

The Teachers Union along with other labor unions, civil liberties groups, and civic groups mounted a valiant defense against the Rapp–Coudert Committee, organized in the main by the Committee for Defense of Public Education. But the mechanisms of repression had been too well designed. Under pressure from the Rapp–Coudert Committee, the Board of Higher Education changed its bylaws so that teachers accused of subversion could be dismissed simply for insubordination if they refused to cooperate with the investigating committee by naming names. No unlawful act had to be proved, only that uncooperative teachers had been identified as Party members by two or more witnesses or as having associated with people thought to be members of the Party. When Lawrence Chamberlain, a friend of both Coudert and Windels, wrote about the dismissed teachers in the early 1950s, he concluded:

> No one can read through the verbatim [trial] testimony ... without being impressed with the generally superior character of the group ... There seems no doubt from evidence presented elsewhere that some of the group were Communists, but the impressive and inescapable fact is that the *only evidence presented by either side* points to: (1) outstanding scholarship, (2) superior teaching, (3)absence of indoctrination in the classroom.[60]

Chamberlain could hardly be accused of political sympathy for the accused. They were serious academics, mostly from working class immigrant backgrounds, who, like so many others of their generation, wanted to make the world they witnessed a better, more just one.

Many suspects identified by the Rapp–Coudert Committee but who survived the purge before the war were dismissed after the war under Section 903 of the City Charter (1936), which provided for summary dismissal without a hearing of any employee invoking the Fifth Amendment to avoid testifying about official conduct. That provision was stricken down by the Supreme Court in Slochower v. BHE in 1956, but not before many professors and teachers became its victims.[61] In 1949 the State enacted the Feinberg Law as an amendment to the Education Law, prohibiting members of the Communist

---

[59]   An interesting thought about the case is that of David Riesman, at the time a junior Assistant District Attorney assigned to Schappes's case. See his "The U-2 Affair: Aftermath and After Thoughts" in *Commonweal*, June 8, 1962, 273.

[60]   Chamberlain, op. cit., 125 (emphasis in original).

[61]   350 US 551 (1956).

312   *Little 'Red Scares'*

Party from employment in the schools and colleges and requiring an oath as a condition of employment. In 1967 the Supreme Court also struck down that law in Keyishian v. Board of Regents, again not before its use in dismissing other teachers and professors.[62]

Public opinion had already begun to change, and groups that might have been expected to join the defense of the accused shied away, notably the American Association of University Professors and the American Civil Liberties Union, which in 1939 voted to rid its board of Elizabeth Gurley Flynn because she was a Communist and so it was hardly in a position to protest the Red purge. While the AAUP did write to the Board of Higher Education and then to Mayor LaGuardia in support of Russell's appointment to City College, it did not oppose the Rapp–Coudert investigation of "subversion" at the municipal colleges.[63] At its April 1941 Council meeting, however, it did report that it was "... happy that the Board ... intends to safeguard scrupulously its action by observing procedural due process in the trial of the teachers suspended."[64]

At its convention in 1941, the AFT finally bowed to the pressure, enormously increased by the Rapp–Coudert investigation, to purge its ranks of the left. It revoked the charters of the New York locals, along with that of the Philadelphia local. Instead, the Teachers Guild which Linville and Lefkowitz had established when they walked out of the TU in 1935, got the New York charter as Local 2, which today is the United Federation of Teachers. The Teachers Union became CIO Local 555, part of the United Public Workers Union, and valiantly continued on until 1964.

The Long Arm of Repression

Soon after the war ended the effort to stifle dissenters in the schools continued. Some of the suspects were the very people identified earlier but who had survived those purges. Some of their former antagonists continued to pursue them.

Frederick Ewen at Brooklyn College, for example, was interrogated by the Rapp–Coudert Committee in 1941. In 1952 he was again summoned to testify, this time before the Senate Subcommittee on Internal Security (the McCarran Committee). Rather than face dismissal for refusing to name names, he resigned his position at Brooklyn College and claimed a small pension. Vera Shlackman and Oscar Shaftel of Queens College, named in 1941, likewise lost their jobs

---

[62] 385 US 589 (1967).

[63] "The Case of Bertrand Russell," *AAUP Bulletin*, XXVI, no. 3 (June 1940), 374–83.

[64] Council Record, *AAUP Bulletin*, XXVII, no. 5 (December 1941), 622–5.

for refusing to testify in the 1950s. Eight other City schoolteachers, among them Abraham Lederman, the president and Celia Zitron, the secretary of the Teachers Union were also fired in 1950. Repression of teachers active in the left-wing of the labor movement had a very long arm.

In 1953 the McCarran Committee claimed that it had "convincing evidence that the American school and college systems had been invaded to a dangerous degree by teachers bent on distorting education to Communist advantage." The committee's investigation was conducted by Robert J. Morris, the Rapp–Coudert's indefatigable investigator. The McCarran Committee claimed that it would take up where the Rapp–Coudert Committee left off.[65]

In tandem with Congressional investigations the New York City Board of Higher Education created a Special Committee in 1953 to conduct a "loyalty investigation" under cover of previous Board policies enacted during the Rapp–Coudert investigation and the Feinberg Law of 1949.[66] As Michael A. Castaldi, the committee's chair, explained, "We recognize the right of any faculty member to dissent or to be a non-conformist. Equally obvious must be the proposition that a dissenter or non-conformist has no license to indulge in acts of disloyalty." The committee reported in 1958 that 39 employees were dismissed, resigned or retired while under investigation. Another 18 were said to have left before they were questioned.[67] Virtually all of them had been active in the Teachers Union or the College Teachers Union.

At the Rapp–Coudert Committee's first public hearing in December 1940, then TU president Hendley stated that "It is not merely I or the Teachers Union with its 6,000 members who are being pilloried before this infamous Committee. It is the entire labor movement and all academic freedom in America."[68] The Teachers Union's progressive, inclusive unionism with its aim of combating racism was eclipsed by the early 1960s, replaced by Albert Shanker's United Federation of Teachers, the heir to the Teachers Guild. We can only wonder how differently the Ocean Hill-Brownsville conflict, pitting the United Federation of Teachers against a predominantly black community in the bitter NYC teachers' strike of 1968, would have been resolved had it not been for the death of the Teachers Union and the purge of progressive teachers and professors in New York's schools and colleges. While we can't know with any certainty, we do know that the stakes in eliminating the labor left and repressing dissent in the teaching

---

[65] *New York Times*, July 27, 1953.

[66] Michael A. Castaldi, "The Loyalty Investigation of Our Municipal Colleges," n.d. (1953), in Board of Higher Education Academic Case Records, box 2, file 18.

[67] Michael D. Solomon, Memorandum to CUNY General Counsel Mary Bass re "'903' and 'Feinberg Law' Terminated Staff Members," March 30, 1978, in possession of the author.

[68] Charles J. Hendley, Statement at Rapp Coudert Open Hearing, December 3, 1940.

ranks were momentous. The aims that Frederic Coudert and Paul Windels had set for their investigating committee seemed to have been achieved. Coudert had shot the rabid dogs.

Chapter 13

The History of the Smith Act and the Hatch Act: Anti-Communism and the Rise of the Conservative Coalition in Congress

Rebecca Hill

Watching and reading about the antics of the group now known as the "Tea Party" at President Obama's healthcare town halls in the summer of 2009 was for many the first encounter with the unlikely conflation of liberal social welfare policies, fascism, and communism. The bizarre ranting of TV personality, Glenn Beck, who so distorted the definition of national socialism that he warned church goers about the use of the term "social justice" and suggested that fascism originated with Woodrow Wilson, for example, led to a number of commentaries in the liberal and alternative press.[1] While Beck attacked Obama as a fascist/communist/dictator, grass-roots anti-health care reform activists claimed that Obama's proposed health care policies would force taxpayers to foot the bill for the healthcare of "illegal immigrants" and declared "keep your government hands off my Medicare!"[2] This odd combination of anti-immigrant

---

[1]   Paul Smith, "Glenn Beck is a Dangerous, Unhinged Moron," *The Corsair*, Pensacola State College, FL, *http://ecorsair.com/?p=4143*, date accessed, Oct. 8, 2011; Les Leopold, "Glenn Beck Auditions for Joe McCarthy's Job," Alternet, Feb. 25, 2010, *http://blogs.alternet. org/speakeasy/2010/02/25/glenn-beck-auditions-for-joe-mccarthys-job/*, date accessed, Oct. 8, 2011; David Neiwert, "Glenn Beck Claims Progressivism Leads to Nazis, Oh Really?" Crooks and Liars, Mar. 2, 2010, *http://crooksandliars.com/david-neiwert/glenn-beck-claims-progressivism-lead*, date accessed, Oct. 10, 2011; or this simple symbolic statement: *http:// www.prosebeforehos.com/political-ironing/08/24/barack-obama-the-nazi-socialist-communist-muslim/*, date accessed, Oct. 8, 2011.

[2]   Ellison Lodge, "Keep Your Government Hands off My Medicare: Healthcare Reform as an Interracial Wealth Transfer Program," VDARE, May 23, 2011. *http://www.vdare.com/ articles/keep-your-government-hands-off-my-medicare-healthcare-reform-as-an-interracial-wealth-trans, date accessed, Mar. 11, 2012.*

316 *Little 'Red Scares'*

zealotry and anti-communist free-market fundamentalism has appeared before in American politics.

While many aspects of the current right-wing attack on the specter of Keynesianism as the embodiment of socialism/fascism have to do with recent political trends, many of the central ideas of the contemporary neoliberal assault on the welfare state through association with both fascism and communism originated in the first reaction against Keynesianism in the 1930s. Although free-marketeers organized in the Liberty League failed to unseat Roosevelt in 1936, following the President's attempt to "pack" the Supreme Court in 1937, conservatives in Congress were able to create a bloc of Southern Democrats and rural Republicans and thwart many New Deal measures. Anti-communism played a critical role in that conservative coalition's electoral success, as the Dies Committee, created to investigate "subversive" and "Un-American" activities in the spring of 1938, functioned as a conservative campaign apparatus directed against New Deal candidates in the November elections. Reaching the peak of its power in the summer of 1939, the conservative coalition passed two major pieces of repressive legislation that would be used against the Communist Party of the United States (CPUSA) in the 1950s: The Hatch Act (1939) and the Smith Act (1940). The first law prohibited federal employees from belonging to organizations advocating the overthrow of the U.S. government by "force and violence" and the second law made it possible to deport immigrants for current or past membership in such organizations, as well as outlawing advocacy of the overthrow of the government by American citizens. Ostensibly, the laws were designed to be used against fascists, Nazis, and communists. Although liberal and left organizations actively opposed these laws, fear of fascism, or what historian Leo Ribuffo terms a "brown scare," also contributed to their passing. Historians disagree about the relative significance of anti-fascism and anti-communism to repression during the era. Ribuffo argues that the red scare was "muted" in contrast to the anti-fascist frenzy, but Robert Goldstein argues that anti-communism was more important, following M.J. Heale in referring to the period of 1938–40 as the "little red scare."[3] The evidence suggests that anti-communism was more important, partly because fascism and communism were often discussed as being synonymous, especially by conservatives. The conflation of communism and fascism as "collectivisms" against which Americanism is defined is one of the lasting impacts that the conservative Congress of the late 1930s has had on U.S. political discourse. While the little red scare may have been short in duration, its impact was long lasting in more concrete ways. The

---

[3] R. Goldstein, *American Blacklist: The Attorney General's List of Subversive Organizations* (Lawrence, 2008), p. 17; Leo Ribuffo, *The Old Christian Right: The Protestant Far Right from the Great Depression to the Cold War* (Philadelphia, 1983), p. 182.

Hatch Act is still being enforced and the Smith Act, while not enforced against domestic subversives, is still on the books. Both laws did more than simply outlaw the advocacy of revolution.

The Hatch Act was a Senate bill to prohibit the coercion of federal employees into political activity for any party and bans low-level federal employees from engaging in political organizing; it applied civil service rules to federal employees, most specifically to Works Progress Administration employees. The section which led to the creation of the Cold War federal employee loyalty program was added to the bill as an amendment during the House debate. The Smith Act made it illegal to advocate the overthrow of the government "by force and violence" and also prohibited the encouragement of "disaffection" in the military, expanded the reasons for deporting "aliens," implemented fingerprinting and documentation for all immigrants, and changed the process for hearings on exceptions for hardship cases. While the Smith Act wasn't passed until 1940, the most substantial debate on the bill occurred in the House just a week after the debate on the Hatch Act. So, the discussion of the two laws was almost simultaneous. Although many Congressional liberals, as well as newspapers, magazines, the Communist Party, and the ACLU opposed both laws, the President signed them. The Smith and Hatch acts constricted democracy in two ways. First, both laws drew boundaries around *who* could participate in the activities of citizenship by narrowing the political rights of specific groups (federal employees, immigrants) and second they defined *what* sorts of activity were legitimate by making the advocacy of revolution illegitimate for anyone.

Many historians have emphasized the way in which anti-fascism unwittingly contributed to Cold War repression because of liberal advocacy for the investigation of fascism during this period. The President's repressive use of the FBI against suspected fascists (and communists) is not debatable, nor is the fact that the left supported this surveillance. In one of its most self-defeating moves, the Communist Party chided the ACLU for defending Nazi free speech and insisted "Free speech does not mean democracy suicide," and demanded the repression of the German American Bund. The CP argument that the Bund was an "underground organization" that it was an agent of the German government, and that its "every meeting was an act of violence" was hardly different from the claims that conservatives were already making about the Communist Party.[4] However ironic the left's support for the repression of right-wing civil liberties may have been, the fact remains that conservative anti-communists, not liberal intellectuals or communist activists were the driving force behind the passage of repressive legislation. Samuel Dickstein may have been a loud voice arguing for

---

[4]   "Civil Liberties Doesn't Mean Democracy Suicide," *Daily Worker*, Apr. 4, 1939, p. 6.

318   *Little 'Red Scares'*

the repression of fascists, but he was not taken seriously by many in Congress. He was able to get the McCormack–Dickstein Committee to investigate fascism in 1934–35, and this committee did have an impact, but most of Dickstein's legislative efforts failed. It wasn't until the ascendancy of the conservative coalition in 1938 that really repressive legislation was passed. For the most part, as William Wiecek puts it, "small and impotent groupings of the far right proved a convenient cover for a suppressive crusade that was single-mindedly concerned with communists and the left."[5] Zechariah Chafee's account of events also argues against blaming anti-fascist fifth column hysteria for the passage of the Smith Act in 1940. He observed that the repressive tendency in the legislature was:

> by no means the result of the national defense program or German conquests or alarm about Trojan horses. Hearings on our first federal peace-time sedition law began in 1935, while the Rhineland was still neutralized; the bill was thoroughly debated and passed by the house in July 1939, a month before German troops entered Poland; the brief debates in June 1940 made not the slightest reference to France or fears of foreign attack.[6]

Chafee also noted the importance of conservative anti-immigrant lobbyists on the Congress, mentioning a "coalition of one hundred and fifteen 'patriotic' societies ... persistently advocating the suspension of all immigration for ten years, absolute prohibition of the admission of refugees, and the 'prompt deportation of all foreigners ... whose presence is inimical to the public interest'"[7] Specifically, the American Legion, Veterans of Foreign Wars, and the Patriotic Sons of America, who had much bigger numbers and greater political influence than the Communist Party, sent letters to Congress, testified to Congressional committees, and backed the leading anti-communist in the House, Martin Dies Jr., as well as the near-fascist senator from North Carolina, Robert Reynolds. As the conservative bloc in Congress attacked communists—or called the New Deal communist—it is not that surprising that those on the left responded with charges of fascism. Chafee himself commented that "I never realized how Nazis feel toward Jews until I read what congressmen say about radical aliens."

Leo Ribuffo has complained that the history of the 1930s anti-New Deal right has been left out of the spate of recent histories that locate the roots of the

---

[5]   William Wiecek, "The Legal Foundations of Domestic Anti-Communism," *The Supreme Court Review* 2001, pp. 375–434, pp. 399–400.

[6]   Zechariah Chafee, Jr., *Free Speech in the United States* (Cambridge, UK, 1941), p. 439.

[7]   Ibid., p. 444.

contemporary right in the Goldwater era.[8] One reason for this phenomenon is the focus on 1930s popular front hegemony and concentration on liberal anti-totalitarianism as the principle forerunner to Cold War politics. This focus minimizes the role that conservative anti-communism and powerful nativist organizations played, ignores the activities of Congress, and treats business reaction against the New Deal and the CIO as battles lost in the election of 1936. This story of the 1930s cannot explain the riot of 5,000 Texans against a small communist meeting held in San Antonio's City Hall in 1939 or the associated drive to recall Maury Maverick as mayor any more than it can explain the passage of the Hatch Act or the first passage of the Smith Act in 1939.[9] A careful reading of the Congressional debates during the late 1930s reveals that the laws were motivated by attacks on the Communist Party, and by an effort to attack the New Deal itself as communist. The German American Bund, which was criticized spectacularly in the media and repressed through F.B.I. surveillance and a variety of criminal charges, was nonetheless barely mentioned during the Congressional debates. The most frequent use of the term "fascism" in Congress was by liberals who opposed the passage of repressive legislation. This frequent comparison of enemies to fascists /or communists in the 1930s was part of what Samuel Walker refers to as the "contradictory" effect of the rise of dictatorships in Europe on civil liberties in the U.S. On the one hand it gave civil liberties activists a new point of contrast and a new argument for the importance of freedom. At the same time, the rise of fascism and communism produced enough fear of propaganda's impact in democratic societies to create enormous pressure for censorship.[10] Thus, the American Bar Association, the Justice Department, and the U.S. Congress all had Civil Liberties or Civil Rights committees in the 1930s. But, as Richard Steele argues, protecting civil liberties, for some extended to protecting vulnerable citizens from the influence of dangerous propaganda.[11]

---

[8]   Leo Ribuffo, "Twenty Suggestions for Studying the Right Now that Studying the Right is Trendy," *Historically Speaking* 12, no. 3 (2011), pp. 2–6.

[9]   "Maverick Encounters Free Speech Troubles," *New York Times*, Sept. 3, 1939, p. E10. The article lists the anti-CP protestors being led by the Catholic Church, the KKK, WWI veterans, the Texas Pioneers Association, a group of Baptist ministers, and 15 additional fraternal organizations.

[10]   Samuel Walker, *In Defense of American Liberties: A History of the ACLU*, 2nd edn (Carbondale, 1990), p. 115; see also Robert J. Goldstein, *Political Repression in Modern America 1870–1946* (Urbana, 2001), pp. 209–12.

[11]   Richard W. Steele, *Free Speech in the Good War* (New York, 1999); Frank Warren, *Noble Abstractions: American Liberal Intellectuals and World War II* (Columbus, 1999).

320   *Little 'Red Scares'*

It's sometimes difficult to separate anti-fascism and anti-communism. Liberal anti-fascists were often also opposed to communism, long before the Hitler–Stalin pact, although they were generally less sympathetic to fascist ideals. American newspapers first began making comparisons between Stalin and Hitler as political leaders between 1934 and 1935, Thomas R. Maddux found in his survey of American newspapers and magazines in the 1930s, with the comparison by both liberal and conservative papers of the 1934 Kirov purge in the USSR to Hitler's Night of the Long Knives the same year.[12] New York Congressman, Emmanuel Celler, who would be a leading anti-fascist spokesman and proponent of civil liberties in Congress, as well as Samuel Dickstein, who is frequently described as an anti-fascist zealot, were both also publicly hostile to communism, as was Jerrry Voorhis, the California New Dealer, formerly of EPIC, who authored the Foreign Agents Registration Act.[13] Harold Laswell, whose career is central to Brett Gary's story of anti-fascist liberalism, developed his first anti-propaganda project in collaboration with the Chicago red squad— and it was an investigation of Chicago communists.[14] The definition of fascism has been and continues to be notoriously imprecise, leading to easy conflations of fascism with other forms of anti-democratic or subversive "others," including those on the left.[15] For example, George Britt, in his 1940 book emphasizing the dangers of Nazi "fifth columnists" describes them as "sab-cats" using a term coined by the Industrial Workers of the World (IWW), which had been used against them during prosecutions of the group for criminal syndicalism.[16] Similarly, the Black Legion of Michigan was prosecuted under an anti-communist criminal syndicalism law following the legion's conspiracy to murder WPA worker Charles Poole in 1936. The prosecution did not rely on any anti-KKK statutes, even though the Black Legion was an offshoot of the KKK. In the Hollywood

---

[12]   Tomas R. Maddux, "Red Fascism, Brown Bolshevism: The American Image of Totalitarianism in the 1930s," *The Historian* 40, no. 1 (1977), pp. 85–103, pp. 89–90.

[13]   "Celler Attacks Stalin in Union Square; 'Heresy' Shocks Soapbox Crowd," *New York Times*, July 13, 1937, p. 1. J. Voorhis, *Confessions of a Congressman* (New York, 1947), pp. 56–8; for more examples of liberal anti-communism before the Cold War, see Frank Warren, *Noble Abstractions*.

[14]   Brett Gary, *The Nervous Liberals: Propaganda Anxieties from World War I to the Cold War* (New York, 1999), p. 79. Gary does not indicate Laswell's roots in anti-communist surveillance until the very end of a chapter in which he establishes him as being part of a generally liberal opinion-making elite that was concerned about the international threat of fascism.

[15]   On the difficulty of defining fascism see Roger Griffin, *The Nature of Fascism* (New York, 1993); R. Griffin, *Fascism* (New York, 1995); George Mosse, *The Fascist Revolution: Toward a General Theory of Fascism* (New York, 2000).

[16]   George Britt, *The Fifth Column is Here* (New York, 1940), p. 6.

representation of The *Black Legion* (1937), the murder was represented as populist revenge by workers against an immigrant hired as foreman, but most of the Black Legion's violent acts were against union organizers and many were done in collusion with both management and Detroit's police.[17]

The use of "fascist" and "communist" as labels for political opponents further confused the issue. Both the President and the conservatives in Congress increasingly used repressive tactics in their conflict with each other, muddying distinctions between different political ideologies as they traded in "anti-Americanisms." New Dealers and anti-New Dealers had become so polarized by 1938–41 that they both used the discourse of "un-Americanism" to describe their opponents as being part of a "fifth column." Harold Lavine observed the "hysteria" about the Fifth Column in 1940 and wrote that "New Dealers caught the Fifth Column marching in the ranks of the GOP. Republicans saw it slithering up the White House steps."[18] This exchange of insults represented a change in the way America defined democracy's "other."

The Use of Terms: From Anti-Monarchism to Anti-Anarchism to Anti-Communism and Anti-Fascism

In the pre-New Deal era, even the arch- anti- communist and American Legionnaire Hamilton Fish did not equate all radicals, but made clear distinctions when arguing for the creation of his anti-communist investigating committee in 1930. Fish reassured Congress that:

> I know of only one possible objection to this resolution and that is that the American people may get the idea that it is aimed at pacifists, socialists, radicals, free-thinkers or any other group of American citizens who have the right under the constitution to criticize and denounce our government in times of peace ... it is not the purpose of this resolution to interfere with any group except the communists in the United States and we propose to deport all the alien communists.[19]

Fish's attempt to distinguish communists from other radicals had disappeared by the end of the decade. By the late 1930s, totalitarianism defined the ideological threat to America and replaced the older republican discourse that saw American government threatened by the combination of monarchy and

---

[17]   On the Black Legion see Peter Amman, "Vigilante Fascism: The Black Legion as American Hybrid," *Comparative Studies in Society and History* 25, no. 3 (1983), pp. 490–524.

[18]   Harold Lavine, *The Fifth Column in America* (New York, 1940).

[19]   Hamilton Fish, *Congressional Record*, 9392 (May 22, 1930), pp. 71–2.

aristocracy from above and slavery/slavishness from below. New Dealers evoked that older republican perspective by referring to their opponents as "economic royalists" and "Tories," but increasingly, they defined business interests and conservatives as "fascists." At the same time, their opponents labeled the New Deal "communist." By the 1930s, theories about modern dictatorships characterized them as composed of demagoguery and mass hysteria or sinister unaccountable bureaucracy.[20] The argument linking mob rule and demagoguery had roots in classical political theory, but was adapted during the American Revolution to define citizens' direct action as different from disorderly slave revolt. With the rise of industrial capitalism and massive strikes, business and the state condemned the "anarchy" of the strikers and associated anarchic traits with recent immigrants who were steeped in "old world culture." To define legitimate labor action, the new progressive movement redefined "anarchy" as a danger coming from both above and below—on the one hand through unregulated and immoral business anarchy and on the other, the reaction to it: the mob revolt. For federal policing agencies, "communism" became a concern following the Russian revolution. During the Red Scare of 1919–20, communism was seen as very similar to anarchism, and the terms were used interchangeably throughout the 1920s. Anti-communist individualist anarchists worked to distinguish themselves from Leninism and were also the first critics in the U.S. of Italian fascism. Through the Sacco-Vanzetti Defense Committee (1920–27), they would play a significant role in shaping liberal opinion on both fascism and communism. Liberals involved in the Sacco-Vanzetti defense campaign came to define both anarchist individualism and their own liberalism against both communism and fascism. Several of the leaders of the liberal wing of Sacco and Vanzetti's defense became leading members of the liberal anti-communist organization, Americans for Democratic Action in the 1950s.[21] Anarchists were concerned with "bureaucracy" and the "castration" of individuals under the control in union organizations, while business leaders, from the beginning of labor reform legislation, argued against the closed-shop on the basis that it was a violation of individual worker rights to contract directly with employers.[22]

---

[20] For a more detailed discussion of theories of totalitarianism in the 1930s–1940s see Benjamin Alpers, *Dictators, Democracy and American Public Culture: Envisioning the Totalitarian Enemy 1920s–1950s* (Chapel Hill, 2003); Albert Gleason, *Totalitarianism: The Inner History of the Cold War* (New York, 1995).

[21] Rebecca N. Hill, *Men, Mobs and Law: Anti-Lynching and Labor Defense in U.S. Radical History* (Durham, 2010), pp. 69–208.

[22] On this use of individual rights discourse against unions see Christopher Tomlins, *The State and the Unions: Labor Relations, Law and the Organized Labor Movement in America*

The American left's analysis of fascism combined discourses rooted in the anti-lynching and labor defense campaigns the early twentieth century. Although labor defense was traditionally populist, pitting the people against the state, lynching and vigilante action against African-Americans and labor organizers demanded an analysis of power beyond the state. In the 1920s, socialists, communists, and liberals began developing a left analysis of mob terror, comparing lynching, extra-legal anti-union thuggery, and fascism. Their analysis of fascism differed from anti-mob theory by defining fascism as ruling-class terror that combined legal and extra-legal repression.[23] The phrase "legal lynching" used during the Sacco-Vanzetti campaign in the 1920s, and most famously in the Scottsboro defense in the 1930s, asserted that fascism was a combination of state and popular repression. This argument defined fascism as an extension of already existing capitalist techniques to divide and crush the working class through appeals to racism, xenophobia, or outright censorship and criminal prosecution. Thus, even as the film *The Black Legion* turned pro-management stooges into a working-class mob driven by *ressentiment*, it incorporated this left analysis by showing capitalists secretly manipulating workers through nativist appeals.[24] This left/liberal definition of fascism was quite different from the Congressional counter-subversive discourse, which defined both communism and fascism as diseases carried by foreigners. As conservatives pushed to drive out immigrants to stop fascism, liberals responded to them by arguing that fascism would be stopped by New Deal reforms that would prevent uninformed worker rebellions—whether they were described as communist or fascist. Understanding how both conservatives and liberals defined fascism and communism in the 1930s provides the context for the passage of the Smith and Hatch Acts in 1939–40.

Communism/Fascism as Atheistic

The first major critiques of both communism and fascism in Congress in the 1930s were religious. Hamilton Fish, leader of the decade's first anti-communist investigating committee, called attention to massacres of priests and church burnings in the USSR. Samuel Dickstein also drew attention to religious persecution in the USSR and urged the U.S. not to recognize the Soviet Union.[25]

1880–1960 (New York, 1985); and David Montgomery, *The Fall of the House of Labor: The Workplace, the State and American Labor Activism, 1865–1925* (New York, 1989).

[23] Again see Hill, *Men, Mobs and Law*, chs 3 and 5.

[24] *The Black Legion*, Warner Brothers, 1937.

[25] Samuel Dickstein, *Congressional Record*, 3474–3478 (Feb. 11, 1930); Hamilton Fish, *Congressional Record*, 4523–4528 (Feb. 28, 1930).

324   *Little 'Red Scares'*

Father Coughlin was probably the most important national figure to oppose communism on the basis of religion, and notably, he served as an expert witness on communism during the Fish hearings. Coughlin consistently attacked communism as a "godless" and "pagan" ideology.[26] By the mid-1930s, the Catholic Church reached an agreement with Franco during the Spanish Civil War in his war against-communism, and the Church's support of Franco played a significant role in shaping U.S. Catholic opinion.[27] While Catholics were focused on anti-communism, Jews and American communists were the first to protest Nazism, and by 1934, American Protestants on both the left and right also denounced Hitler's attempt to create a "German Christianity." When right-wing congressmen referred to what was wrong with fascism, they compared it to communism as an anti-religious, pagan ideology that had hurt the Church In its first report, the Dies Committee defined "Americanism" simply as the belief in God and in the Declaration of Independence.[28] Despite this characterization of fascism and Nazism as anti-religious, some of the most popular fascists in the U.S. during the 1930s were Christian activists. Coughlin is the best known example, but hard-right Protestants also supported European fascist regimes.

Communism/Fascism as Foreign Conspiracy or Network

Nativism suffused the string of investigations of "un-Americanism" that led to the proposal of numerous "anti-alien" bills in Congress, most of which failed until the passage of the Smith Act in 1940. Congressional committees investigating "un-American" fascists and communists drew from older anti-communist and anti-anarchist histories. Fish, whose hearings were dominated by representatives of "super patriotic organizations" thought communism could be cured by deporting "alien communists."[29] So did New Dealer Samuel Dickstein, who spoke avidly against recognition of the USSR in 1930 and did not avoid discourse long associated with right-wing nativism despite his own immigrant experience. Dickstein regularly harangued Congress about the Nazi threat and greatly exaggerated the international network of American Nazis and Fascists as well as the numbers of people involved in such groups.

His McCormack–Dickstein committee of 1934–35 helped shape the argument against both communism and fascism that would guide the Dies

---

[26]   Alan Brinkley, *Voices of Protest: Huey Long, Father Coughlin and the Great Depression*, pp. 95–6; Geoffrey Smith, *To Save a Nation*, (New York, 1973), p. 13.

[27]   Alpers, *Dictators*, 79; Smith, *To Save a Nation*, pp. 47–52, 103.

[28]   Ironically since the Declaration of Independence includes the "right of Revolution", or the right of the people to overthrow the government by force.

[29]   Goldstein, *Political Repression*, p. 201.

Committee as well as a host of anti-immigrant and anti-subversive laws proposed in Congress between 1935 and 1940. Although the McCormack committee focused primarily on fascist organizations, it also investigated and rejected communism, lumping both ideologies together on the basis that they were foreign. The committee's report denounced the overthrow of democratic regimes by "either Communism or Fascism" and emphasized the danger presented by immigrants promoting foreign ideologies.[30] This language contributed to a general anxiety about immigrants as carriers of foreign ideologies, a familiar trope from the anti-Russian deportations of the 1919 Red Scare and the anti-German campaigns of WWI. Arguments against the anti-Democratic "other" were put in nativist terms. For example, following the Black Legion's murder, Dickstein called for an investigation by Congress to determine whether the organization had any "international connections" or links to a "European subversive organization."[31] The committee report identified the Communist Party's connection to the Communist International (COMINTERN) led by the government of the USSR as particularly sinister. Rather than focusing on the activities of group members, the investigations suggested that the problem with these groups was that they were intrusions of alien governments into American political affairs. This kind of concern led to the use of the Post Office to intercept and destroy "foreign propaganda" following the passage of the Foreign Agents Registration Act (FARA).[32] Dickstein tried to suggest that the international communist model also applied to the German American Bund and other U.S. fascist organizations, which in reality were much more eclectic. Among the McCormack–Dickstein Committee's report's conclusions was a statement that "to the true and real American, communism, nazism and fascism are all equally dangerous, equally alien and all equally unacceptable to American institutions" [sic].[33] This argument for Americanism was echoed in the legislative agenda and anti-fascist/anti-communist campaigns of the American Legion, the largest grass-roots organization pushing anti-subversive legislation during the 1930s, which reduced its use of violence in favor of lobbying for laws to outlaw communism, establish loyalty oaths, and many other causes that the conservative coalition

---

[30] John William McCormack, Investigation of Nazi and Other Propaganda, House Report 153, Feb. 15, 1935, 74th Congress, 1st session (hereafter McCormack Committee Report).

[31] "House Member Urges Inquiry of Black Legion," *Washington Post*, May 27, 1936, p. XI.

[32] Gary, *Nervous Liberals*, pp. 158–9.

[33] Ibid., 23.

supported.[34] For this reason, and because immigrants were understood to have fewer constitutional protections, the majority of anti-subversive laws proposed between 1935 and 1940 targeted immigrants. Like Dickstein, Dies lambasted communism and fascism largely on the basis that they were "foreign ideologies."

During March and April of 1938 Dickstein continued to raise alarm about the German American Bund in America, stoking nativist fears by suggesting that members were Germans first and Americans only technically.[35] Given the Legion's and Dies' calls for immigrant restriction, it is worth considering whether for some, repression of communists and fascists was simply a means to deport immigrants. In Dies' case, and that of other conservative representatives and Senators particularly from the Southwest, nativism was a reason for opposition to the entire New Deal. Prior to Roosevelt's election, Hoover, at the behest of California conservatives had deported thousands of Mexicans in short order.[36] Before he became known as an anti-communist leader, Rep. Dies was a self-identified "restrictionist" and introduced numerous bills seeking to suspend immigration into the United States, maintaining that deporting all immigrants would end the Depression by freeing jobs for native-born workers. Dies explained his ideas in a radio address on the "Alien Menace" in 1935, during which he referred to the American Revolution as an individualist protest against "European collectivism," blamed immigration for the fall of the ancient Roman Empire, named it the primary cause of U.S. unemployment, claimed that immigrants were responsible for foreign collectivist doctrines importing fascism and communism into the U.S. In a conspiracist moment, Dies further identified the "high-powered and well-financed propaganda and activities of alien blocs" as the source of opposition that prevented restrictionist legislation from passing in the House.[37]

Dies and the American Legion were angry because the Roosevelt administration had rejected deportation as a solution to the Depression and liberalized immigration controls based on the recommendations of the Wickersham Commission, which advised immigration reform following the

---

[34] William Pencak, *For God and Country: The American Legion* (Boston, 1989), pp. 11, 208–77.

[35] 83 *Congressional Record*, 2725, 4064 (Mar. 2, 1938; Mar. 24, 1938).

[36] Jay Feldman, *Manufacturing Hysteria: A History of Scapegoating, Surveillance, and Secrecy in Modern America* (New York, 2011); Abraham Hoffman, *Unwanted: Mexican Americans in the Great Depression* (Tucson, 1974); Mae Ngai, *Impossible Subjects: Illegal Aliens and the Making of Modern America* (Princeton, 2004), pp. 71–90.

[37] Martin Dies, "The Alien Menace," radio address, in 79 *Congressional Record*, 10227–10232 (June 26, 1935).

mass deportations of the first great red scare.[38] Following Roosevelt's election, the number of deportations decreased by more than 50 percent as labor secretary, Francis Perkins halted numerous deportations that were initiated at the state level.[39] Dies Committee member, J. Parnell Thomas filed an attempt to impeach Perkins in January 1939 for not deporting immigrant labor leader, Harry Bridges, whom the American Legion had worked with California's Associated Farmers to deport since he led the general strike in San Francisco in 1934. Bridges became a symbol of "alien communism" and efforts to deport him were central to arguments for anti-subversive and anti-alien legislation in the late 1930s. In contrast, congressmen from urban districts representing second generation immigrant communities were supporters of reducing barriers to immigrants. Dickstein, the passionate anti-fascist had one foot in each camp. As Benjamin Alpers writes, most anti-fascists were also "deeply involved in building tolerance and reducing nativist sentiment"—but this was only true for liberal anti-fascists.[40] An example of the importance of the conservative coalition's anti-immigrant policies at the time was the failure of several bills designed to make it easier for refugees from fascist countries to enter the U.S. Between 1938 and 1939, a number of New Dealers attempted to change immigration quotas to allow Jewish refugees from fascism to enter, and conservative congressmen successfully organized to defeat all of them.[41]

Communists and liberals argued against immigration-restriction laws, with liberals explicitly working to disentangle "innocent" immigrants from charges of communism/fascism. Liberal anti-communists who opposed anti-immigrant laws denounced communism at the same time that they tried to associate both communism and fascism with native-born Americans and local causes instead of labeling immigrants as the "carriers" of these political views. They claimed that the answer to communism and fascism was not investigation but rather the end to unemployment which they considered the root of these movements in Europe. Emphasizing the universal possibilities for fascism, both liberals and communists identified ideological similarities between the regimes in Germany and Italy and the restrictionist congressmen who resembled in their beliefs and actions such native organizations as the KKK and the American Legion.[42] This approach was

---

[38] Ngai, *Impossible Subjects*, pp. 82–4.

[39] Reuben Oppenheimer, "Recent Developments in the Deportation Process," *Michigan Law Review* 36, no. 3 (1938), pp. 355–84, p. 357.

[40] Alpers, *Dictators*, p. 103.

[41] Sheldon Spear, "The United States and the Persecution of the Jews in Germany 1933–1939," *Jewish Social Studies* 30, no. 4 (1968), pp. 215–242.

[42] Read into the record by Rep. Sabath (Illinois) 84 *Congressional Record*, 1103–1106 (Feb. 3, 1939).

effective because it used the concept of fascism to define Americanism around civil liberties and anti-racism, but it could lead to problematic conclusions. First, instead of suggesting that Congressional investigations of political movements were inherently repressive, these critics suggested that such investigations would be acceptable if they were led by different (not fascist) people, targeted native as well as immigrant "subversives," were less public, and focused their counter-subversive energy on fascists instead of communists. Second, the attacks on right-wing political opponents as "fascists" adopted the slippery-slope rhetoric of Dies himself. The conflation of all anti-interventionist and anti-administration politics with fascism supported the use of federal surveillance against political enemies and, when applied to left opponents, mirrored Stalinist critiques of the left opposition as the secretly "fascist" allies of Germany.

Communism/Fascism as Bureaucratic, Collectivist Nightmare

Another element of the anti-communist discourse of the early 1930s was the argument that the welfare state was itself either communist or fascist. This notion, which would be the guiding force of what we now call neoliberalism and which has been charted through the activities of Frederick Von Hayek and the Mont Pèlerin Society, began with Herbert Hoover and the businessmen organized against the New Deal in the Liberty League.[43] William Randolph Hearst, the Liberty League and others warned Americans against the dangers of creeping socialism and tyranny that they identified in implicit in a number of major FDR initiatives in the 1930s.[44] This strategy of attack failed to hurt the New Deal in the mid-1930s, and the Liberty League itself was discredited, but the assault on the New Deal as tyranny did not disappear. The conflation of communism and fascism was important to the conservative fight against both the Court Packing Plan and especially the Executive Reorganization Plan in 1937, which conservative congressmen called the first step toward dictatorship. Judy Kutulas notes that ACLU leader Roger Baldwin opposed the Wagner Act as a "dangerous, fascist intrusion of the government into unions" and tried to convince the national ACLU board to oppose the new law that is now widely considered a major labor movement victory.[45]

---

[43]   David Harvey, *A Brief History of Neoliberalism* (New York, 2005); Kim Phillips-Fein, *Invisible Hands: The Businessmen's Crusade against the New Deal* (New York, 2009).

[44]   Goldstein, *Political Repression*, p. 215; Phillips-Fein, *Invisible Hands*, pp. 3–25 ; Ribuffo, "Twenty Suggestions," p. 3; Alpers, *Dictators*, p. 75.

[45]   Roger Baldwin quoted in Judy Kutulas, *The American Civil Liberties Union and the Making of Modern Liberalism 1930–1960* (Chapel Hill, 2006) pp. 25–6.

The Dies Committee, which was authorized at the end of May, 1938 with the support of some popular front organizations who believed that it would be like the 1934–35 McCormack–Dickstein committee and investigate fascist organizations, spent its first year attacking popular front groups, the CIO, and accusing various liberals and members of the New Deal administration of communist ties.[46] The committee's report defined totalitarian governments, whether communist or fascist, as "bureaucratic and paternalistic governments under a planned economy." Showing his antipathy to the New Deal by equating "planning" with tyranny, Dies declared that anyone supporting "political, economic or social regimentation based upon a planned economy is un-American."[47] This argument resurfaced during debate on reauthorizing the committee in February 1939, an effort led by the conservative coalition. Rep. Smith (Ohio) spoke in favor of the committee, which he said had served America by alerting it to the danger of communism. He argued that it had proven its case, remarking "there is no need to leave Washington to observe the present trend toward totalitarian government. The expansion of bureaucracy and regimentation of our citizens is well known to this body. Bureaucracy, fascism, nazism, communism are one and the same with slight variations."[48] Dies himself was the most direct in the argument of fascist and communist synthesis, claiming that Hitler's anti-communism was a "pretense" whose insincerity was revealed in the Hitler–Stalin pact, and that the German dictator had already adopted all the tactics of the communists.[49]

Communism/Fascism as the Tyranny of Reconstruction

By the mid-1930s, Congressional conservatives were increasingly alarmed about the activities of the Communist Party in the South. Communists had been organizing in the South since the late 1920s, and, with the Scottsboro campaign beginning in 1931, became nationally known as opponents of Jim Crow. Their work on that case, along with union efforts among sharecroppers, textile workers, coal miners, and unemployed activists won them enemies among Southern segregationists. To the extent that communist arguments about race influenced

---

[46]   The Dies Committee was also opposed by liberals in congress, most notably Maury Maverick of Texas. Popular Front groups whose support Dies claimed in his initial bid for the committee were the American League Against War and Fascism and the International Workers' Order. He spent much more time discussing (and reading into the record) letters of support from the American Legion and the Veterans of Foreign Wars.

[47]   Dies Report, I, p. 12.

[48]   Rep. Smith, 84 *Congressional Record*, 1113 (1939).

[49]   Martin Dies, Jr., *The Trojan Horse in America* (New York, 1940), p. 9.

the philosophy of the Congress of Industrial Organizations (CIO), they presented a national threat to white supremacy. Finally, at the outset of the Popular Front, the CPUSA joined the NAACP and other liberal organizations in supporting anti-lynching bills that were passed in the House and filibustered in the Senate during the 1930s.[50] Senator Richard B. Russell of Georgia delivered a speech in the Senate as part of one such filibuster in January of 1938 that indicated that a reaction against this organizing contributed to the association of the New Deal with communism, and to both with post-civil war Reconstruction. Attacking the anti-lynching bill, Russell declared that it was only one point in a four-point plan that was identical to the program of the Communist Party. Part two was to have federal "take-over of the election machinery of the South." Part three was to end to racial segregation on railroads and in public places, and part four was an effort to give the federal government control of all the marriage laws in the country in order to allow interracial marriages.[51] Senator Bilbo similarly attacked the anti-lynching bill as part of a communist plot to incite Blacks to revolution.[52] Liberal and left anti-fascists responded to this attack on communism and the New Deal from the South by comparing the Southern caste system to fascism, and by pointing to the Southern Democratic Party's ties to the Ku Klux Klan, which they deemed a fascist organization.[53]

Communism/Fascism as Subversive, Hateful, and Revolutionary

Both the Hatch and Smith Acts included a "criminal syndicalism" clause, prohibiting advocacy of the overthrow of the federal government. Attempts to ban revolutionary speech had begun with attempts to repress the speech of revolutionary anarchists, and by 1919, the communists were simply the new revolutionary villain. In the 1930s, opponents of Marxism borrowed from progressive anti-racist criticism of fascist "race-hatred" to condemn the notion of class warfare. The McCormack–Dickstein committee concluded among other things that the Communist Party sought to establish a government based

---

[50]   On the role of the Communist Party in the struggle against racial oppression in the 1930s see Robin D.G. Kelley, *Hammer and Hoe: Alabama Communists During the Great Depression* (Chapel Hill, 1990); Mark Naison, *Communists in Harlem during the Depression* (New York, 2004); Mark Solomon, *The Cry Was Unity: Communists and African-Americans 1917–1936* (Jackson, 1998).

[51]   83 *Congressional Record*, 1100–1102 (Jan. 24, 1938).

[52]   83 *Congressional Record*, 1548–1553 (Feb. 7, 1938).

[53]   For the long-term influence of communist anti-fascism on anti-racist discourse see my "Fosterites and Feminists: The Old Left and the Invention of AmeriKKKa," *New Left Review* 228 (1998), pp. 67–90.

on "class domination" to be achieved by fomenting "class hatred." Not only did communism not seek to reconcile the working and middle classes, the committee report argued, but it proclaimed that revolution was the only solution. The Dies Committee Report echoed the McCormack Report's focus on communist "class hatred," said that to hate one's neighbor because he "has more of the world's material goods" is just as bad as hating him because of his race or religion.[54]

Banning the advocacy of force and violence was a key element in both the Smith and the Hatch Acts, which lumped fascism and communism together as philosophies of hate. Here, the anti-subversive bloc in Congress sought to achieve what Palmer had failed to do in the 1920, pass a federal anti-sedition law. The Congress did this partly in reaction to the Supreme Court's increasing disinclination to ban revolutionary speech unless it reached the point of "clear and present danger."[55] Thus, the McCormack–Dickstein committee recommended that the government should ban the advocacy of revolution "without regard to the improbability of attainment and protect itself and its loyal citizens against such subversive attempts," rebuking the Supreme Court.[56]

While many historians have pointed out that the Silver Shirts and the German American Bund had little impact on American politics during the 1930s and that Dickstein's claims hugely overstated these groups' influence, the CPUSA did have a significant impact on American politics in the 1930s, largely through the leadership positions some communists held in CIO unions and broad "popular front" organizations including both communists and liberals. For this reason, communists were not only a concern for the conservative Congress, but for the President. Explaining why the President was more concerned with communists than fascists at the time of the Smith Act's passage in 1940, Attorney General Robert Jackson wrote, "Nazis never had an extensively organized espionage or sabotage ring in this country. Communists had planted their men in strategic positions in the labor movement."[57] It seems quite likely that the anti-subversive legislation was meant to curb labor militancy. The President's effort to crush labor action in the context of military preparedness was evident in the use of the Smith Act in an attempt to deport Harry Bridges, in the indictment of the

---

[54] Investigation of Un-American Activities and Propaganda, 76th Congress – 1st session, H. Rpt. 2 (Hereafter Dies Report 1), p. 10.

[55] The classic discussion of these decisions is Zechariah Chafee, *Freedom of Speech in the United States* (New York, 1941); for more recent discussions see William Wiecek, "The Legal Foundations of Domestic Anti-Communism," *The Supreme Court Review* 2001, pp. 375–434.

[56] McCormack–Dickstein Committee Report, p. 21.

[57] Robert Jackson, *That Man: An Insider's Portrait of Franklin D. Roosevelt*, edited and introduced by John Q. Barrett (New York, 2003), p. 73; on the same point see Richard Steele, *Free Speech in the Good War*, p. 88.

332   *Little 'Red Scares'*

Minneapolis Trotskyists in the summer of 1941, and in the President's wish, expressed in a cabinet meeting in early June 1940, to treat strikes in military-related manufacturing as "treason."[58]

Conservatives were more aggressively anti-labor. Until 1937, Representative Martin Dies was an unpopular man deemed "cynical" and a "demagogue" by his peers, but with his speech against the Flint sit-down strikes, in which he condemned the actions of "certain labor organizations" as a "lawless" seizure of property, and concluded that "without property rights there can be no rights of any kind," his prestige rose, and he became a leader in the fight to "expose" the CIO.[59] Leftist journalists Frank Rhylick and Allen Michie, authors of *Dixie Demaogues*, a classic text on Southern anti-New Deal activism in Congress, argued that Dies' antipathy for the CIO was motivated by the fact that he was he was the lawyer for the oil companies who were fighting a growing CIO effort based in Dies' own district, which encompassed the refinery districts of Beaumont and Port Arthur.[60] Similarly, the leading arguments for the Hatch Act began with attacks on the Workers' Alliance within the Works Progress Administration.

These five counter-subversive arguments were all in play during the passage of the Hatch and Smith Acts during the summers of 1939 and 1940.

The Story of the Hatch Act

As early as January, 1938, conservatives in Congress "began hearings on ways to revise or terminate the WPA."[61] Although they failed to cut the relief budget that year, or stop the WPA, they gathered steam to go after the WPA again by accusing the Roosevelt administration of using WPA workers as political pawns, and by claiming that the WPA was filled with communists, whom they said, led the Workers Alliance of America (WAA), a group that acted like a union for WPA workers, and which had successfully led to wage increases. Senator Carl Hatch of New Mexico first proposed his measure to ban the manipulation of WPA members by politicians as a rider on the appropriations bill in the summer of 1938. Supporters called the Hatch Bill an attack on political patronage, while its enemies said it was a "slander" on the New Deal and an attempt

---

[58]   On the President's wish to prosecute strikers as treason see Harold Ickes, *The Secret Diary of Harold L. Ickes*, v. 3 (New York, 1954), pp. 197–8, June 2, 1940.

[59]   Dies in 81 *Congressional Record*, 2637 (1937); Patterson, *Congressional Conservatism*, pp. 167–9.

[60]   Allan Michie and Frank Rhylick, Dixie Demagogues, (New York, 1939), pp. 62–3.

[61]   James T. Patterson, *Congressional Conservatism and the New Deal: the Growth of Conservative Coalition in Congress, 1933–1939*, (Lexington, 1967), p. 213.

The History of the Smith Act and the Hatch Act

to destroy the Democratic Party. In the same session, Congress passed an appropriations bill severely cutting the WPA's budget, reducing wages, cutting the number of workers in the WPA, banning the WPA from hiring "aliens" and denying relief to members of organizations who advocated the overthrow the government.[62] Before the debates on the Hatch Act began, Rep. Leland Ford of California proposed that the special committee investigating the WPA pursue an amendment to ban "subversives" from receiving relief.[63] That clause in the appropriations act immediately hurt the Workers' Alliance of America, as its leader, David Lasser (who was a socialist, not a communist) said that many employers interpreted it as specifically anti- WAA so that billboards at WPA worksites bore notices reading "If you are a member of the Workers' Alliance you can't work on this project."[64]

Before Hatch proposed his bill, three different committees, including the Dies Committee, had simultaneously investigated the WPA and its relationship to the Workers' Alliance. Melding arguments about dictatorship and chaos, the Dies Committee's report suggested that workers were coerced to belong to the WAA by communist leaders "in order to retain their jobs" and claimed that the organization was created by the Soviet Union based on the model of the St. Petersburg unemployed councils of 1905. The common use of the "Sit-down" tactic, Dies argued, was a key sign of their common origin.[65]

WPA employees were vulnerable because providing federal assistance to the unemployed was still such a novel idea in the 1930s. As Chad Alan Goldberg argues, the committee investigations used traditional republican arguments against the "unworthy poor" to define WPA workers in general as "anti-citizens whose civic inclusion and political participation threatened to pollute the Republic in various ways."[66] Goldberg argues that people hired by the projects were classified by opponents as "relief recipients" rather than as "rights-bearing workers," and were treated as if they should be grateful. At the same time, they were described as forming a dictatorial cabal, much as the Flint Sit-Down Strikers had. In the House. Representative Clifton Woodrum of Virginia warned that "no congressman would be able to win an election without acceding to their demands."[67] Conservative organizations at the local, state and national

---

[62]   James E. Sargent, "Woodrum's Economy Bloc: The Attack on Roosevelt's WPA 1937–1939," *The Virginia Magazine of History and Biography* 93, no. 2 (1985), pp. 175–207, p. 200.

[63]   84 *Congressional* Record, 5028–5029 (May 2, 1939).

[64]   Sargent, "Woodrum's Economy Bloc," p. 201, fn. 74.

[65]   Dies Committee Report, 1939, p. 31.

[66]   Chad Alan Goldberg, *Citizens and Paupers: Relief, Rights and Race from the Freedman's Bureau to Workfare*, (Chicago, 2007), pp. 133–4.

[67]   Sargent, "Woodrum's Economy Bloc."

334 *Little 'Red Scares'*

level attempted to pass legislation denying the vote to relief recipients, and while these measures lost, a sizable minority supported them.[68] Other attempts to curb the rights of WPA members included various mandatory fingerprinting policies proposed from municipal to the national level, all of which the ACLU tracked and opposed throughout 1938, on the grounds that these efforts were "fascistic" attempts at regimentation of the population.[69] Anti-immigrant sentiment also influenced the discussion of the WPA. Even some of those who supported the WPA jealously guarded "American" jobs. Particularly in Texas, California, and New York, state legislators and local activists called for a ban on immigrant benefits from the WPA. Even as "aliens" were deported in massive numbers in the early years of the Depression, cheap immigrant labor was still in demand, and major agricultural interests also-called for the denial of relief benefits for "aliens." According to Mae Ngai "the California Relief Administration and the Federal Works Progress Administration denied relief to 75,000 Mexicans in order to force them to work the harvests in Southern California."[70]

During the floor debate on the Hatch Act, all the proponents described the WPA workers as victims who needed protection from manipulating bosses. Attacks on the WPA as a vehicle of patronage being abused by Roosevelt were likely to have even broader appeal than attacks on it as infiltrated by communists. Polls found 90 percent of Americans opposed patronage and supported civil service reform, and some historians have argued that Roosevelt in fact did use the WPA for patronage, particularly during his effort to purge the Democratic Party of conservatives in 1938.[71]

Liberals and communists both opposed the Hatch Act and noted its connection to the campaign against the WAA and the WPA. Rep. Hook compared the prevention of WPA employees from political participation to the way that Hitler had depoliticized govt.[72] A number of articles in the *Daily Worker* urged members of unions and other organizations to oppose the "devilish" Hatch Act. Referring to its clause banning membership in subversive organizations as the "criminal syndicalism section" The CP called it typical anti-labor legislation.[73] The ACLU defended the right of workers in the WPA to organize and rebuked efforts to crush the Workers' Alliance, urging the President

---

[68] Goldberg, *Citizens and Paupers*, pp. 125–6.

[69] ACLU Records and Publications, Weekly Bulletins, Dec. 6, 1938, Mar. 18, 1939.

[70] Ngai, *Impossible Subjects*, p. 75.

[71] On poll, Goldberg, *Citizens and Paupers*, 134; on Maverick, Patterson, *Congressional Conservatism*, p. 175.

[72] Hook, 84 *Congressional Record*, 9609 (July 20, 1939).

[73] "A Devilish Piece of Legislation," *Daily Worker*, July 29, 1939; "CP Says Hatch Bill is Aimed at New Deal," ibid.

The History of the Smith Act and the Hatch Act 335

to veto the bill.[74] The American Federation of Labor passed a lengthy resolution opposing the Hatch Bill and other moves against the WAA and argued for the parity of wages in the WPA so as to preserve the wages of labor in general.[75]

Despite the opposition, Roosevelt nevertheless signed the Hatch Act. Along with his signature, the President added a comment that went to both houses, indicating his annoyance with the conservative bloc, which had attacked not only members of the WPA, but members of his cabinet. He said a worker could still "publicly answer attacks made on him or his work or the work of his superiors or on the work of his subordinates notwithstanding the fact that such attacks were made for political purposes or by newspapers or by individuals as part of a political campaign." He went on to note that the bill entirely excluded representatives of the legislative branch or their employees, and found it "Un-American" and "unfair" to suggest that executive branch employees could be subject to "misrepresentations, falsification, or vituperation" by employees of the House or the Senate, their friends, or candidates in political campaigns without any right to reply.[76]

Not only would the Hatch Act serve to reduce the influence of the Workers' Alliance, but it would lead to the creation of the Attorney General's List of Subversive Organizations (AGLOSO) in order to be enforced. As Robert Goldstein shows, this list was used to dramatically suppress the speech of federal employees in the Cold War.[77] This anti-subversive clause of the Hatch Act received little attention from mainstream newspapers at the time because it was slipped into the bill at the last minute and in the middle of the night, with very little debate. Rep. Nichols of Oklahoma proposed the anti-overthrow clause from the floor for the first time at around 10 p.m., describing communism and fascism as a "cankerous infection within the vitals of this government which is being nourished by those of foreign birth who advocate European 'isms' as a substitute for our form of government."[78] Despite Nichols' stated surprise that his proposal was not unanimously accepted, the amendment was voted down 94 to 92. The anti-overthrow clause appeared again, possibly as late as

---

[74]   ACLU *Records and Publications*, Weekly Bulletin: July 22, 1939, July 29, 1939.

[75]   Letter from William Green to Senator George W. Norris, July 13, 1939, and Report of Special Committee to the Conference and Representatives of National and International Unions on the WPA situation, George W. Norris Papers, Part 1, container 202, tray 43/6-7, Library of Congress, Washington DC.

[76]   "President Roosevelt's Message Explaining the Signing of the Hatch Bill," *New York Times*, Aug. 3, 1939, p. 2; Sen. George Norris had encouraged the president to sign the bill, claiming failure to do so would be the "biggest mistake of his political career." Richard Lowitt, *George W. Norris: The Triumph of a Progressive, 1933–1944* (Urbana, 1978), p. 273.

[77]   Goldstein, *American Blacklist*.

[78]   Nichols, 84 *Congressional Record*, 9635 (July 20, 1939).

336   *Little 'Red Scares'*

11:00 p.m., from reps. Hook and Kramer and passed without a vote count or a discussion. The following day, when the Senate received the bill again after passing the original version without debate, Hatch said that the House had not changed the bill from what the Senate had already passed, and called for Senate concurrence without giving the Senators time to read the amended bill.[79] The Hatch Act was interpreted by most newspapers as a form of protection for workers, rather than an effort to prevent federal employees from forming unions or organizing for political candidates. As the *New York Times* put it, the law was aimed at preventing government officials in supervisory positions from manipulating lower-level relief workers and others, or "bulldozing government servants and milking ... their pocketbooks for the benefit of the party."[80] It did not, as Democrats predicted, destroy the Democratic Party or kill the New Deal, but it would have a lasting impact on federal employees.

The Smith Act

The day before the Hatch Act was debated on the House floor, the Smith Bill went through its first substantive debate in the House. The Smith Act was a bit like Frankenstein. It was composed of various bills returned from the grave after being voted down multiple times in Congress between 1935 and 1938. By the time they hit the House floor in the summer of 1939 in what the ACLU called the "omnibus gag bill" the terms of debate were already established. If the Hatch Act was a creature of anti-labor action disguised in the cloak of civil service reform, the Smith Act (HR 5831), bundled an anti-syndicalism measure into an anti-immigrant bill. It was submitted to the House Judiciary Committee on March 20, 1939 as a:

> bill to make unlawful attempts to overthrow the government of the United States; to require licensing of civilian military associations; to make unlawful attempts to interfere with the discipline of the Army and Navy; to require registration and fingerprinting of aliens; to enlarge the jurisdiction of the United States circuit court of appeals in certain cases; and for other purposes.[81]

The most noxious portions of the bill to civil liberties and progressive organizations in 1939–40 were (1) the proposal to fingerprint all "aliens" (2)

---

[79]   84 *Congressional Record*, 9671–9674 (July 21, 1939).

[80]   "For Cleaner Politics," *New York Times*, Dec. 12, 1939, p. 26; similar wording appears in "Freer Elections," *New York Times*, July 22, 1939, p. 7.

[81]   84 *Congressional Record*, 3013 (Mar. 20, 1939).

the "sedition" or "criminal syndicalism" clause, (3) the expanded reasons for deporting immigrants, including clauses specifically aimed at labor organizer, Harry Bridges and (4) the clause making incitement to disloyalty in the armed services a crime. The first of the failed bills resurrected in the Smith Act were the Kramer Sedition Bill and the Tydings–McCormack Military Disaffection Bill, both of which came out of the McCormack–Dickstein committee. The Kramer Sedition Bill (HR 6427) introduced by Charles Kramer of California in March of 1935 would have punished with fines and imprisonment anyone "who knowingly or willfully advocate the overthrow of the government of the United States by force and violence" . The Tydings–McCormack Military Disaffection Bill H.R. would punish anyone encouraging people in the army or Navy to disobey or question U.S. laws, and was rightly seen as very similar to the Sedition Act of 1918. The "disaffection" bill was sponsored by the Secretary of the Navy, in response to "communist" propaganda being distributed in Navy shipyards.[82] Pushed primarily by patriotic (nativist) organizations, the military and the American Legion, both these bills inspired letter-writing campaigns in opposition by unions, liberal organizations, and Communist popular front groups such as the American League against War and Fascism, which voiced its opposition to both bills with a petition to Congress in 1936. Both acts were defeated in 1936 at the height of the Popular Front, and representatives Maverick and Kvale's report opposing the Disaffection bill in 1935 described it as "brash piece of Hitleristic Fascism"[83] in an example of how anti-fascist discourse could be used to define the repression of speech as a greater danger to "Americanism" than dangerous "subversive" speech itself.

The anti-immigrant elements of the Smith Bill were just as, if not more controversial than the sedition clauses. The bill's effort to expand deportable offenses in 1939 and to take away discretion over exemptions from the Secretary of Labor recalled earlier efforts along these lines that had begun in the very early 1930s. The biggest showdown on that issue in previous years had occurred over various competing immigration bills.[84] Before the Smith Bill was revised by the House and Senate judiciary committees, it contained even worse provisions, such as the Dempsey proposal, similar to an earlier proposal from the McCormack–

---

[82]   "Disaffection Bill Draws Opposition," *New York Times*, Aug. 11, 1935, p. E12.

[83]   "Congress and the Gag Laws," *New Republic*, Jan. 15, 1936, pp. 277–8; "Disaffection Bill Draws Opposition, "NYT, Aug. 11, 1935, E 12.

[84]   ACLU *Records and Publications*, Annual Report, 1936–1937, p. 25; ACLU *Records and Publication, International Juridical Association Bulletin*, June 1937; Reynolds on Reynolds Starnes Bill, 80 *Congressional Record*, 5791–5797 (Apr. 21, 1936).

338   *Little 'Red Scares'*

Dickstein Committee to deport immigrants who advocated "any change in the form of government."[85]

Opponents opposed not just the increased reasons for deportation, but also the registration provision in the Smith Bill, which called for mass fingerprinting, calling it "fascistic." Francis Perkins opposed fingerprinting of aliens throughout her term, and opposed the President on this point.[86] The ACLU opposed all such measures, writing in 1938 that fingerprinting one group would lead to the "regimentation of the entire population," a position that they continued to take throughout their opposition to the Smith Bill and to attempts to control government workers through similar "regimentation."[87] Despite their protests, however, not only Congressman Dies, but, according to a Gallup poll in January 1939, 87 percent of Americans supported requiring alien registration.[88]

The Smith Bill's first stop was at the House Judiciary Committee hearings in April, where officers of the Army and Navy testified in favor. These witnesses defined the subversive danger as communism, with a story of communist young ladies distributing propaganda to sailors. Even those testifying for the bill said it was a "composite of most of the anti-alien and anti-radical legislation offered in Congress in the last twenty years." Those who spoke against it represented the CIO and the American Civil Liberties Union.

While the judiciary committee discussed the bill, the House as whole debated the Hobbs "Concentration Camp" Bill (H.R. 5643), to resolve the problem the government faced when it tried to deport aliens whose countries had been obliterated by fascism or Soviet expansion during the war by detaining them indefinitely in camps. The Hobbs Bill passed in the House by 288 to 61, but was never reported out of committee in the Senate. During the same month, following the decision of the Labor Secretary to follow the Supreme Court and halt the deportation of Harry Bridges, Congressman Allen of Louisiana attempted to enable the deporting of Bridges by naming him directly. In May he introduced a bill to authorize the Deportation of Harry Renton

---

[85]   ACLU *Records and Publications*, Weekly Bulletin, Apr. 22, 1939; ACLU, "Should Congress Pass the Dickstein Bill to Terminate the Stay of Alien Propagandists?" *Congressional Digest*, Nov., 1935, p. 285; On the Dempsey Bill: ACLU *Records and Publications*, ACLU Radio June 1, 1939; "A Bill to Be Stopped Now," *Daily Worker*, Mar. 25, 1939, p. 6; *Daily Worker*, Mar. 29, 1939, p. 6.

[86]   Harvey Mansfield," Legislative Veto and the Deportation of Aliens," *Public Administration Review* 1, no. 3 (1941), pp. 281–286.

[87]   ACLU *Records and Publications*, Weekly Bulletin, May 28, 1938.

[88]   Michael Belknap, *Cold War Political Justice: The Smith Act, the Communist Party, and American Civil Liberties* (Westport, 1977, p. 21, fn. 37.

Bridges (HR 9766), which passed the House on June 13.[89] The bill was clearly unconstitutional because it identified an individual by name, and the Senate Judiciary Committee killed it on the advice of the Attorney General.[90] Also in the same month, Rep. McCormack tagged an amendment banning the advocacy of overthrow of the government by force and violence to a bill extending the punishment for espionage, and that bill passed by a vote of 357–17. After the judiciary committee removed the sedition prevision making it illegal for U.S. citizens to advocate the overthrow of the government, the Smith Bill arrived on the House floor on July 19, 1939.

That debate was spread over two days in July. The minority of congressmen who opposed the bill did so with intensity. John Coffee of Washington called it an imitation of Nazi Germany, because of its extreme nationalism and the implication that all "foreigners must ipso facto be aliens who are engaged in an effort to overthrow the government of the United States by force."[91] Describing the bill as just one of many attempts to "scapegoat" "helpless non-citizens" in the way Germany was scapegoating Jews, Coffee identified opposition to the bill from unions, fraternal organizations, and the ACLU, and read a list provided by the Emergency Conference on Civil Liberties that identified 35 different bills it opposed. His speech was met with such wild applause from the gallery that the House Speaker called for order.[92] The numerous letters congressmen received from CIO unions, as well as the conferences, meetings, and rallies organized by liberal and radical organizations in opposition to the "Smith Anti-Alien Bill" suggest considerable opposition to the bill.

The debate stopped on the 19th and resumed on the 29th, when the majority of discussion related to the provision in the bill meant to counteract the Supreme Court decision in the Strecker case. This decision had led to the cancelation of Harry Bridges' deportation order on the basis that it was unconstitutional to deport someone if he was no longer a member of an organization deemed subversive. The importance of the drive to deport Harry Bridges to the passage of the Smith Act cannot be overestimated.[93]

---

[89]   Steele, *Free Speech in the Good War*, pp. 101–102.

[90]   On the Bridges case see Steele, *Free Speech*, pp. 208–10; W.P.B and M.L.S., "Retroactivity and First Amendment Rights," *University of Pennsylvania Law Review* 100, no. 3 (1962), p. 400, n.33; C.P. Larrowe, "Did the Old Left Get Due Process? The Case of Harry Bridges," *California Law Review* 60, no.1 (1972), pp. 39–83; Ann Fagan Ginger, *Carol Weiss King.*

[91]   84 *Congressional Record*, 9534–9535.

[92]   84 *Congressional Record*, 9535–9536.

[93]   84 *Congressional Record*, 10449 (July 29, 1939).

340   *Little 'Red Scares'*

Almost every member of the House speaking against the bill also repudiated communism, but they argued that people should be forgiven for having made the mistake of joining the Communist Party if they left. Emmanuel Celler who had spoken against the Soviet Union in Union Square and had proposed a bill in 1937 that would grant asylum to refugees from the USSR, Nazi Germany and Fascist Italy, opposed the Smith bill despite his stated abhorrence of communism. He argued during the debates that the retroactive punishment of membership in the Communist Party could deport someone even if they were a communist for "five minutes" or "five days."[94] Rep. Martin of Colorado said the bill was like "Torquemada" and was enough "to make Thomas Jefferson turn over in his grave," because of this same provision, which he likened to creating an "unpardonable sin."[95] Despite opposition, the Bridges provision stayed in the bill after a close vote. Following the demise of the amendment to remove the Bridges provision, Howard Smith reentered his anti-subversion clause to the bill as an amendment. This clause would apply to non-citizens. Smith, argued in its favor:

> We have laws against aliens who advocated overthrow of this government by force, but do you know that there is nothing in the world to prevent a treasonable American citizen from doing so? He can advocate revolution, the overthrow of the government by force, anarchy, and everything else and there is nothing in the law to stop it.[96]

Rep. Hinshaw was the only conservative opposing the amended bill – because it applied to citizens (and not only immigrants). It "smacks of the laws of George III," he declared.[97] The amended version passed 79–32. Judging from the fate of the Hobbs bill, the Smith bill might have met the same fate and died in the Senate had it not been for the Hitler–Stalin Pact (August 1939) and the Fifth Column Scare that began in the spring of 1940 and continued as Hitler's army advanced across Europe until France fell in June. The Hitler–Stalin Pact ended the Popular Front and permanently disrupted the communist-Liberal alliance. Once the USSR was no longer among the allies, and as pressure for the U.S. to enter the war increased, communists and fascists appeared equally un-American.

---

[94]   84 *Congressional Record*, 9538–9539; (July 19, 1939) "Celler Attacks Stalin in Union Square; 'Heresy' Shocks Soapbox Crowd," *New York Times*, July 13, 1937, p. 1.

[95]   84 *Congressional Record*, 10446–10447 (July 29, 1939). Then, Martin, who argued that the Bill, which did not name Communist Party membership be amended to specifically name communism, Nazism and fascism as equally bad instead of just attacking communism.

[96]   Smith, 84 *Congressional Record*, 10451 (July 29, 1939).

[97]   Hinshaw, 84 *Congressional Record*, 10453 (July 29, 1939).

The History of the Smith Act and the Hatch Act   341

Within both the ACLU and the National Lawyers Guild, liberals closest to the Roosevelt administration worked to oust communists. Morris Ernst was the leader in the effort. A founding member of the National Lawyers Guild (NLG), he proposed that the Guild, in order to save its national reputation and ties to the administration, should make clear that it was for the Bill of Rights and "opposed to Communism, Fascism, and Nazism."[98] Because the group would not purge its communist members, a large group of liberal lawyers associated with the Roosevelt administration left shortly after their resolution failed.

Although he failed with the Lawyers Guild, Ernst was successful in leading the purge of the ACLU, where he joined with the socialist, Norman Thomas and ex-communist, Reinhold Neibuhr to form an anti-communist bloc on the national board. The ACLU's anti-communist faction finally succeeded after long efforts in early 1940 and passed a resolution banning communists and fascists from leadership positions, against opposition of Alexander Meikeljohn, Carey McWilliams, James Wechsler, Robert Lynd, Theodore Dreiser and I.F. Stone, who pointed out that it was really directed at communists in the organization and raised the question of Catholic support for fascism.[99] Following the changed policy, in May of 1940, the ACLU expelled Elizabeth Gurley Flynn, who as an IWW member and pioneer in American labor defense activism, had been a founding member of the organization.[100]

The ACLU debated communism in the midst of the "Fifth Column Scare," and their move shows a changing temper among liberals about communism during the Hitler–Stalin pact. The term "fifth column" began to appear in the mainstream American press in association with the fall of the loyalists in Spain, where the term originated with Franco's description of his allies inside Madrid who supported a foreign government. The use of the term "fifth column" to describe the Communist Party directly related to the Hitler–Stalin pact and the growing argument that anti-interventionists were de facto supporters of fascism. For example, in *The Fifth Column is Here*, George Britt claimed that fascists and communists were a fifth column "marching on parallel roads."[101] From May to July, 1940, the *New York Times* alone carried 470 different articles or editorials containing references to the "Fifth Column" in one context or another.[102] On

---

[98] Ann Fagan Ginger, *The National Lawyers' Guild from Roosevelt to Reagan* (Philadelphia, 1988), p. 31.

[99] Ibid., p. 132; ACLU papers etc.

[100] Kutulas, *The American Civil Liberties Union and the Making of Modern Liberalism 1930–1960*, p. 85; Walker, *In Defense of American Liberties*, pp. 132–133.

[101] Britt, *The Fifth Column is Here*, (New York, 1940), p. 94.

[102] Based on a search in *Proquest Historical New York Times Index* excluding duplicates, 185 stories referred to the "Fifth Column" in May, 193 appeared referring to it in June, and

342   *Little 'Red Scares'*

May 24th, members of both houses agitated for anti-alien legislation, with Sen. Reynolds attempting to amend the LaFolette Civil Liberties committee bill in order to allow employers to investigate "potential alien agitators."[103] Most dramatically, on May 27 President Roosevelt delivered a fireside chat warning of the dangers of the "Fifth Column" spies and saboteurs inside the United States.[104] On the same day, the Senate Judiciary Committee reintroduced the Smith Bill, which they had modified according to the recommendation of the Labor Department. Roosevelt had also moved the authority to suspend deportation proceedings out of the hands of the labor department and into the hands of the Justice Department, an expedient for his own security goals, and a compromise with anti-Perkins forces in Congress.[105] The new bill took out many of the more draconian anti-immigrant provisions, but retained Smith's anti-subversive clause. Little opposition to the bill was voiced in the Senate and there was no roll-call vote. After it passed in the Senate, the bill went back to the House, where it passed over the opposition of only four opponents, led by Vito Marcantonio, who declared that it was a march to fascism in "seven-league boots."

Emmanuel Celler had strongly opposed the Smith Act when it first was debated the previous year, but voted for and spoke on behalf of the amended version in 1940. As the voice of the "lesser evil" in Congress and dropped his opposition to the Smith Act's passage in the House with the comment:

> Candidly, I am informed that if we do not accept this bill, we will get one far worse. Any bill containing dreadful provisions against the alien would pass this House with no substantial opposition. In common parlance, it would go through "like a dose of salts." I am therefore endeavoring to be practical. In fear of a worse bill we must accept this bill.[106]

Given Roosevelt's involvement in the revision of the bill in the spring of 1940, it is not surprising that he signed it, or that his supporters in Congress voted to pass it.[107] The Smith Act achieved many things that he wanted. The bill was supported by the military, would allow him to deport the irksome Harry Bridges, who, as

---

92 stories appeared in July.

[103]   *New York Times*, May 25, 1940, p. 4.

[104]   Steele, *Free Speech in the Good War*, p. 69.

[105]   "Congress Moves to Control Aliens," *New York Times*, May 28, 1940, p. 9; Harvey S. Mansfield, "Legislative Veto and the Deportation of Aliens," *Public Administration Review* 1, no. 3 (1941), pp. 283; Ickes, *Secret Diary*.

[106]   Ibid., p. 446, quoting the *Congressional Record*, 86 (temporary) 13469 (June 22, 1940).

[107]   George W. Norris's silence during debates in the Senate is striking, given his dramatic speeches against "Fifth Column Hysteria" and his accusations that J. Edgar Hoover had

long as he opposed the war would be a threat to wartime industry. It retained executive discretion over deportation of aliens, implemented the registration by fingerprinting that he had been seeking against the objections of Perkins, and worked in tandem with the surveillance he was already pursuing of political enemies. As Michael Belknap put it, Roosevelt was also "angry" at communists for their turn against the New Deal.[108] So, the bill was passed, through a combination of the President's efforts to stifle political opposition and that very same opposition's effort to trim back the innovations of the New Deal. Zechariah Chafee lamented in his 1941 edition of *Free Speech in the United States* that the "comparative silence" and lack of opposition to "the most drastic restrictions on freedom of speech ever enacted in the United States during peace."[109] While that silence hung over in the Senate, editorials against the Smith Act appeared in numerous publications in June of 1940. Liberals continued to criticize Dies. In the *New Republic*, Wilson Whitman, while commenting on Dies' preference for attacking communists over fascists, did not suggest that anti-fascism itself was pure, but recalled Huey Long's comment that fascism would come to American "disguised as anti-fascism," lambasting Dies' "creed of class tolerance," support for the Texas poll tax, and ties to business leaders to differentiate the him from the populist Long.[110] Liberals counted on the Attorney General's office to enforce the new laws with discretion, and looked forward to Supreme Court challenge. Hays of the ACLU swore to "test it at the first opportunity."[111]

Impact of the Hatch Act and Smith Act

The Hatch Act and the Smith Act are still on the books, but it is the Hatch Act that is still enforced. The law is still primarily understood as part of the general history of civil service reform. In 1951, Milton Esman wrote in the *Yale Law Journal* in support of the Supreme Court's rulings validating the act that it meant that the federal government could not "crack the whip over federal

---

turned the FBI into an American Gestapo on May 31st following a raid of the Abraham Lincoln Brigade in Detroit. Norris, 85 Congressional Record 7259-7273 (May 31, 1940).

[108] Belknap, *Cold War Political Justice*, pp. 26–7; ACLU *Records and Publications*, reel 8 "Urge Veto Smith Bill," June 20, 1940; Mansfield, "The Legislative Veto, pp. 283–4.; Ickes, *Secret Diary*, 6/12/40, p. 197.

[109] Zechariah Chafee, *Free Speech in the United States*, pp. 441, 444.

[110] Wilson Whitman, "Blacklist in Action," *New Republic*, June 2, 1941, pp. 752–4.

[111] Steele, *Free Speech in the Good War*, p. 81.

344   *Little 'Red Scares'*

employees and force them to work for the party and its candidates."[112] The most
significant opposition to the Hatch Act has been against its banning of public
political activity, not its criminal syndicalism clause. The penalty for violation
of the Hatch Act is dismissal from government employment, and between its
passage in 1939 and 1950, before "McCarthyism" had officially begun, there
were 1665 complaints, and 172 removals of federal employees from office.[113]
The act, which was tested in a number of court cases was interpreted to allow
people to be members of political parties, but not to publicly be identified with
them, publish articles in political newspapers, distribute political literature or
otherwise be involved in public political activity.[114] Since its passage, the act has
been revised, once in 1978 following the revelations of the Nixon administration's
manipulation of the "loopholes", and again in 1993, to reduce the restrictions
on federal employees. By 2007, Congress was again conducting hearings on
the Hatch Act. These hearings revealed that the Bush Administration had used
it against federal employees who had engaged in union activity, supported
democratic candidates in elections, or circulated jokes mocking the President
through their email, while simultaneously violating its intent by mandating that
federal employees go to training sessions in preparation to back Republican
candidates in political campaigns.[115]

The Use of the Smith Act during World War II

Germany's invasion of the USSR and the Soviets' subsequent entry into the war
on the allied side significantly reduced the government's direct repression of the
CPUSA until the war's end. During the war, the Smith Act was reserved for
opponents of U.S. foreign policy. The example of Harry Bridges indicated just how
important U.S. foreign relations were to domestic anti-communist policy. After
the passage of the Smith Act, Richard Steele writes that J. Edgar Hoover wanted
to use Harry Bridges to establish the illegality of the CPUSA. Roosevelt was
eager to charge Bridges because of his role in egging on a wildcat strike in aviation
in 1941.[116] Once the Soviet Union entered the war, however, Bridges ceased to

---

[112] Esman, "The Hatch Act: A Reappraisal," *Yale Law Journal* 60, no. 986 (1951),
p. 994.

[113] Ibid., p. 989, fn. 8.

[114] Ibid., pp. 990–91.

[115] United States Senate Committee on Homeland Security and Governmental Affairs,
Subcommittee Oversight of Government Management, the Federal Workforce and the
District of Columbia, S. Hrg. 110–275, *The Perils of Politics in Government: A Review of the
Scope and Enforcement of the Hatch Act*, Oct. 18, 2007 (Washington, 2008).

[116] Steele, *Free Speech*, pp. 104–107.

advocate strikes and by the fall of 1941, he was deemed by at least some West Coast businessmen and political leaders to be making an "important contribution to labor peace," while the State Department wanted the Attorney General, Francis Biddle, to hold off on prosecuting communists because of the need to maintain Russia as an ally. Biddle did wait until 1942, when the pressure of Congressional anti-communists again mounted, and only then issued new deportation order[117]

While the Communist Party opposed the Smith Act as it was being debated in Congress the party supported its use against others once the Soviet Union joined the war. The first use of the Smith Act's anti-subversion clause against American citizens was the prosecution of Trotskyist labor organizers in Minneapolis. The CP supported this prosecution enthusiastically. The Trotskyists handled their own defense, but the ACLU did publicity for them and filed an *Amicus* brief in their favor. Ultimately, 18 were convicted under the "advocacy" clause in the Smith Act, as they were deemed "actually advocating revolution" rather than discussing it abstractly, and were sentenced to 1 year + 1 month in prison.[118] The liberal press supported the Trotskyists' rights, with the *Nation* commenting that the conviction was dangerous to liberty, indicating that the administration was not going to use the "Clear and Present Danger" standard.[119]

Despite their pro-war position, CPUSA's refusal to support opposition to the federal government during the war marked them as enemies of liberty, further alienating liberals and bolstering the "totalitarianism" argument in general. As the *New Republic* put it, after putting aside critiques of British imperialism and supporting the war effort, the CP was also "against anyone who stands in the way of these allied democracies, including John L. Lewis, the party's former hero."[120] The *Daily Worker* printed multiple attacks on Lewis's anti-war position, referring to him as an "international fascist." Carl Winter similarly described the Minnesota Trotskyists as "pro-Nazi agents of reaction," and now claimed that the Smith Act posed no danger to the Communist Party. The attacks on Lewis and the Trotskyists further destroyed Communists' credibility with liberals who had worked with them during the first Popular Front. It marked the CP not only as unprincipled, slavish in their devotion to the leadership of the USSR, and as hypocrites, but as disloyal to allies in the United States.

---

[117] Larrowe, "Did the Old Left Get Due Process?" p. 80; Steele, *Free Speech*, pp. 208–10, 228.

[118] Warren, *Noble Abstractions*, p. 113.

[119] "Civil Liberties in Minneapolis," *New Republic*, July 28, 1941; "The Issues at Minneapolis," *The Nation*, Dec. 31, 1941, p. 605; Walker, *In Defense of American Liberties*, p. 154.

[120] T.R.B., *New Republic*, Washington Notes "The Communists Reform their Lines," p. 436.

346   *Little 'Red Scares'*

While most American Nazi groups were crushed by federal executive action early in the thirties, those remaining, who were described as a rather insignificant group of "crackpots" were tried in 1944, on the charge of being in an international Nazi conspiracy in *U.S. v. McWilliams*. The McWilliams trial in 1944 was a disaster. Geoffrey Stone describes it as a "legal and public relations nightmare for the government," noting that not only the ACLU, but the *Washington Post* called it a "black mark" on American justice.[121] Indicating that what the ACLU had said about previously existing legislation making the Smith Act unnecessary was already true, most war era prosecutions related to fascism, such as William Dudley Pelley's conviction in 1942, were done under the 1917 espionage act.[122] Liberals opposed the prosecution on the basis of civil liberties, with the ACLU describing the case as a "monstrosity." It is worth noting that this prosecution, unlike the earlier attack on Trotskyists, failed. The Smith Act was thus used with success only against the left.

Communists continued to attack their opponents as "Fascists" during the McCarthy era, but with the shift from WWII to the Cold War, anti-fascism faded and anti-communism grew. The New Left used the concept of fascism to describe Keynesian economics—but from an entirely different perspective, one more similar to the libertarian socialist politics of Roger Baldwin and the old Wobblies, and now left critiques of fascism are largely concerned with authoritarian political leadership, ultra-right religious activism, and racism. Unlike the 1930s, left accusations of fascism are generally seen as markers of unacceptable left extremism.[123] The post-war attack on the left wasn't successful in stopping Keynesian policies, but the "slippery-slope" equations of communism, fascism and the welfare state by Martin Dies and Herbert Hoover never went away for the right. Now known as "neoliberals," they finally achieved political dominance in the 1980s.

---

[121] Stone, *Perilous Times*, p. 274.

[122] Steele, *Free Speech in the Good War*, p. 3; Stone, *Perilous Times*, pp. 264–9.

[123] Note for example the response to the lobbying group MOVEON's inclusion of a video contest ad comparing George W. Bush to Hitler in 2004.

Index

Abraham Lincoln Brigade 186, 283–4

Abrams v. US 16, 17

Alabama 53, 66

American Chamber of Commerce 135, 137, 141, 154, 156, 157, 158, 159, 161, 162

American Alliance for Labor and Democracy (AALD) 169–70, 172

American Association of University Professors 18, 302, 303, 312

American Civil Liberties Union (ACLU) 1, 7, 9, 11, 12, 13, 14, 15, 17, 18, 19, 58, 59, 62, 65, 77, 95, 107, 108, 118, 128, 250, 254, 256, 312
and Arthur Garfield Hays 12–13
and Communist Party 19–20
and Minneapolis Trotskyists 317, 328, 345
and opposition to Hatch Act 334, 336
and opposition to Smith 336, 338–9, 343–6
and ousting of Elizabeth Gurley Flynn 341–2
and US v. McWilliams 346

American Federation of Labor (AFL) 7, 12, 49, 57, 97, 117, 132, 165, 167–8, 169–74, 175, 178, 179, 183–6, 188–193, 243, 335

American Federation of Teachers 60, 109, 114, 117, 127, 132, 140, 152, 157

American Labor Party 62, 176–8, 180, 183

American League for Peace and Democracy 240, 257

American Legion 6, 8, 15, 48, 49, 51, 53–5, 58–60, 66–8, 108–9, 111–13, 114, 118, 119, 120, 121, 123, 130, 131, 200, 201, 203, 204, 205, 209, 245, 256, 266, 278, 279, 281, 318, 325–7, 337

American Plan 49, 135, 142, 166, 168

American Student Union 105, 126, 128, 245

American Trading Corporation (Amtorg) 82–3, 87

American Youth Congress 36, 182, 245

Americanism 263, 266, 267, 279

amnesty movements (for World War I political prisoners) 6, 7, 8, 10 *see also* Debs, Eugene V.

anarchists/anarchism 138, 140, 147, 150, 152, 156, 157, 324, 322, 330

anti-communism 51, 55, 56, 271, 285, 288
and anti-semitism 80
and business groups 98–101
and Catholics 49, 62, 63
and education 91–2
and gender 88–90
and immigration 80–81, 87–8
and race 81, 87–8, 90–91
and religion 75

anti-Semitism 80, 238, 239–40, 243

Associated Farmers, Inc. 55, 58, 61, 245–6

Association of Catholic Trade Unionists 62, 63

Atlanta 54, 57

Attorney General's List of Subversive Organizations 251, 335

Bachmann, Carl 81, 95, 97

Baldwin, Roger 1, 13, 15, 18, 20, 21, 58, 95, 328, 346

Beak, Ford 50, 51

348   *Little 'Red Scares'*

Begun, Isidore 291, 292, 293, 296, 300
Better American Federation 47, 55, 107–8
Biddle, Francis 41, 42, 248, 251, 252, 253, 345
Biggert, F. C. 145, 146
Birmingham, AL 94–5
Birmingham, Stephen 241–2, 25
black Americans 50, 53, 54, 57, 63
Black Legion 63, 320–21, 323, 325
Board of Economic Warfare 253–4
Bolshevism *see* Marxism
Borah, William 9, 10
Brady, Mildred 230, 231
Brady, Robert 230, 231
Brandeis, Louis 16, 17
break-ins (burglaries) *see* FBI
Brecht, Bertold 34, 36, 42
Bridges, Harry 28, 30, 34, 37, 57, 61, 155, 156, 189–90, 342–5, 258, 327, 331, 337–40, 342–5
Bridgman raid 14–15
Browder, Earl 62, 204, 208
"Brown" Scare 316–17
Buffalo 138, 141
bugging (wiretaps) *see* FBI
Burns, William 11–12

California 47, 48, 54, 55–7, 58, 61, 64, 65, 154, 155
Campbell, Persia 31, 4 317, 218, 221
Catholic Church 5, 49, 62, 63, 171, 186, 196, 200, 201, 202, 210, 215
Coughlin, Charles 63, 64, 203, 239, 324
Cellar, Emmanuel 318, 320, 340, 342, 343
Chafee, Zechariah 2, 15, 16, 17
Chaillaux, Homer 59, 60
Chamber of Commerce, US 114, 116, 117
Chicago 52, 60, 61, 141, 149
Chicago Defender 263, 264, 275, 276, 279
Chicago Tribune 239, 250
church groups 45, 53, 59, 62, 64 *see also* Catholic Church

Cincinnati 141, 142
civil liberties, social movements for 2, 10, 17, 20, 21 *see also* ACLU, amnesty
civil rights, social movements for 32–3, 34, 36, 39, 45, 64
Civil Service Commission (CSC) 228, 230, 231, 232, 233
clear and present danger doctrine 17, 331, 345
Cold War 45, 317, 319, 346, 335
colleges and universities 49, 51–2, 59–60, 67
Committee for Defense of Public Education 308, 311
Committee for Better Public Schools in Harlem, 297–8, 300
Committee on Cultural Freedom 117, 303
communism and communists 48, 56, 266, 267, 368, 69, 270 281, 282, 274, 276, 277, 278,1 279, 280 *see also* Communist Party of the United States, Marxism
Communist Party of the United States (CPUSA) 2, 11, 49, 50, 52, 53, 54, 57, 58, 62, 63, 65, 66, 67, 72, 135, 137, 149, 153, 55, 57, 158, 160, 161, 162, 170, 173, 175–7, 180, 185–6, 187, 188, 189, 190, 214, 219, 240–41, 242, 251, 252, 256–7, 258, 268, 269, 270, 272, 274, 275, 281, 284, 286,
and ACLU 19–20
and Bridgman arrests 11
and FBI surveillance 24, 26, 27–32, 33–4, 36–42
and Hatch Act 316, 317, 319, 334
and Nazi free speech 217
and popular front organizations 331
and Trotskyists 345
as alien threat 325
members banned by ACLU 340
membership outlawed 340

toleration when USSR entered World War II 344

company unions 137, 142, 148, 163

Congress of Industrial Organizations (CIO) 61, 62, 65, 137, 153, 168, 171–9, 182, 183, 196, 191, 193, 187, 214, 216, 218, 243, 258, 270, 277, 286, 287, 288, 319, 329, 331, 332, 338, 339

conscientious objectors 1, 5, 6, 7, 8, 9, 10, 16

consumer movement 246–7, 252

Consumers' National Federation 214, 215, 217–24, 227, 232, 233

Consumers' Union 215, 217, 220, 227, 229, 232, 233, 234

Coolidge, Calvin 9, 10, 14, 25

criminal syndicalism/anarchism laws 13, 14, 46, 47, 48, 49, 50, 52, 52, 54, 56, 62, 65, 66, 67, 68, 138, 150, 320, 330, 334, 337, 339, 344

Crisis, The 264, 284, 285

Count, George S. 109, 114, 117, 132

custodial detention program 31, 32

Daughters of the American Revolution 59, 89, 92, 97, 108–9, 111–13, 114

Daugherty, Harry 6, 7, 8, 10, 11, 12, 14, 25

Debs, Eugene 5, 6, 7, 16, 24

Democratic Party 330, 333, 334, 336

demonstrations, by hunger and unemployed 52, 53, 54

Dempsey Bill 337

Detroit 53, 63, 64, 195, 106–7, 149, 150, 211

Dewey, John 115, 116, 117, 132

Dewey, Thomas 251, 291, 293, 311

deportation policy 326–7, 338–40

Dickstein, Samuel 317–18, 319, 323–4, 325, 326, 331, 327

Dies, Martin/Dies Committee 121–2, 136, 155, 162, 179, 180, 199, 205, 206, 213, 218, 29, 220, 226, 228, 229, 230, 231, 235, 237–59, 286, 302, 306, 316, 329, 318, 332, 343
see also House Committee on Un-American Activities Committee
against planned economies 329,
"alien menace" speech 326
and consumer movement 246–7
and FBI 240, 242, 243–4, 247–59
and federal employees 250–57
and Franklin D. Roosevelt 239, 247–59
and police red squads 239, 242, 255–6
and WPA 333
attack on Flint sit-down strike 332–3
legacy of 237–8, 359
reauthorization 19, 39, 329
report of 324, 241
support for by popular front groups 329

Dilling, Elizabeth 105, 113–15, 120, 125, 128, 131

Dubinsky, David 175, 177

Edgerton, John 138 144, 147, 158, 160, 161

Educational Workers League of New York 292, 293

Eisler, Gerhart 36, 199

Eisenhower, Dwight 258–59

Elaine Massacre 266–7, 276

Elliott, Harriet 228, 229

Emerson, Thomas 31, 231, 232

Espionage Act (1917) 3, 4, 7, 8, 11, 24

Ezekiel, Lucille 225, 226

Ezekiel, Mordecai 216, 232

fascism 138, 154, 160, 162
American far right associated with 318, 327–8, 330, 346
anti-communist legislative associated with 319, 337, 341
anti-interventionism, associated with 342, 345
and Brown Scare 316–17

and fingerprinting 334, 338
conflated with Communism 315–16,
320, 322–5, 328–9, 331, 340, 341,
341–2
definition imprecise 320
definition by American left 323, 346
described as anti-fascism 343
FBI investigates 317
immigrants associated with 333, 336,
338
McCormack-Dickstein Committee
investigates 318
refugees from 327
fingerprinting
defined as fascism 334, 338
of immigrants 336
relief recipients 334
Federal Bureau of Investigation (FBI) 27,
68, 124, 131, 183–7, 188, 193,
205, 229, 230, 234, 235, 237–59
(passim), 265, 277, 283, 285, 286,
317, 319, 343
and appropriations and personnel 23
and Attorney General insight 25–7,
29–30, 33–5, 41–2
and break-ins 31, 34–6, 40–41, 242,
245
and bugging 30, 34
and civil rights movement 32–3, 34,
36, 39
and Cold War era 43–4
and COMPIC investigation 35–42
and COMRAP investigation 37, 39
and Dies Committee 240, 24, 243–4,
247–57
creation of 23
custodial detention program of 31, 32
expansion of powers 23, 44
General Intelligence Division 25
Hollywood investigations 39–42
intelligence investigations 28–34,
36–41

lawyers monitored 31
members of Congress investigated
24–5, 43
RACON investigation 32
Soviet agents 33, 36–9, 42
special records procedures 26–7, 35,
34–5
surveillance of communists 24, 26,
27–32, 33–34, 42–46
Teapot Dome 24–5
wiretapping 31, 33–4, 36
World War I era 24
World War II era 34–42
see also Hoover, J. Edgar
federal employee loyalty program 217, 231,
232 see also Attorney General's List
of Subversive Organizations
Federal Trade Commission 246–7
Feinberg Law 311, 313
fifth column 340–42
First Amendment 7, 10
Fish, Hamilton 53, 112, 119, 123, 133, 136,
179, 321, 323–4
Fish Committee 74–101
allegations of Naziism 72, 103
background 54–74, 81
character 73
conduct of hearings 75–7, 80–81, 84,
93, 94, 97
final report 102
response 71–2, 102–3
Flynn, Elizabeth Gurley 65, 312, 341
Foreign Agents Registration Act 320, 325
Foster, William 75, 85, 88, 141, 148, 149,
155, 174, 183–4
Franco, Francisco 201, 203, 324, 341
Frankfurter, Felix 248, 249
freedom of the press 3, 4, 5
Frey, John 170, 180, 243, 255

Gastonia Strike 50, 51, 150, 151, 152, 190,
271

Georgia 54, 57, 59, 67
German-American Bund 62, 317, 319, 325–6, 331
Gilmore, Glenda 271, 272
Goldstein, Robert Justin 316, 333
Gompers, Samuel 7, 140, 169, 170, 172, 183–4
Goretarian, Bertrand 302, 306, 309
Green, William 97, 204, 165, 170, 171, 172, 180
Gulag, investigations into 83–5

Hadley, Edwin 113–14
Hall, Helen 221, 223, 233
Hall, Otto 272, 273
Harding, Warren 1, 2, 3, 4, 5, 6, 7, 9, 10, 11, 12, 14, 20, 21
Hatch Act 191, 251, 316–17, 331–6, 343–4 *see also* federal employees loyalty program
Hatch, Carl 332–3, 336
Hayek, Friedrich 79, 328
Haymarket bombing 138, 156
Haywood, Harry 218, 282
Hays, Arthur Garfield 12–13
Hays, Will 4, 5
Hearst, William Randolph/Hearst Press 58, 59, 60, 106, 114–16, 120, 130, 133, 197, 217, 218, 220, 246–7, 256, 328
Henderson, Leon 216, 226, 228, 230, 231, 232, 251–2
Hendley, Charles 291, 295, 299–300, 313
Herndon, Angelo 54, 274–5
Hewitt, Nelson 115, 124
Highlander School 278–9, 284, 287
Hiss, Alger 43, 238, 239, 252
Hitchman Coal and Coke v. Mitchel 168, 190
Hitler, Adolph 196, 320, 324, 329, 334, 340
Holmes, Oliver Wendell 16, 17

Hollywood 39–42
Hollywood Ten/Blacklist 195, 237, 238
Hook, Sidney 59, 60, 295, 303, 306–7, 309
Hoover, Herbert 12, 27, 252, 326, 328, 346
Hoover, J. Edgar 15, 25, 26–7, 28–42, 68, 96, 136, 159, 162, 183–7, 205, 206, 210, 240, 244, 245, 248–59, 264, 285, 286, 341, 344 *see also* Federal Bureau of Investigation
House Judiciary Committee 336, 337, 338
House Committee to Investigate Un-American Activities 43, 62, 64, 65, 121–2, 177–88, 193, 237, 238, 246, 258, 259, 285, 286 *see also* Dies Committee, Fish Committee, McCormick-Dickstein Committee
Hudson, Hosea, 26, 269
Hynes, William 47, 54, 55

Ickes, Harold 240, 247–8, 249, 253, 254
immigrants 49, 51, 63, 66, 68, 318, 326 *see also* nativism
Imperial Valley, CA 54, 55, 58, 59
International Labor Defense 208, 243, 272, 274, 281
International Ladies Garment Workers Union 175, 180, 245
International Longshore and Warehousemen Unions 243–4
International Workers Order 36, 65, 241
Industrial Workers of the World (IWW) 7, 8, 9, 12, 13, 46, 140, 142, 155, 167, 172, 174–5, 178, 184, 186, 190, 320, 341

Jackson, Robert 33, 68, 244, 248, 256–7, 331
Jefferson, Thomas 144, 160
Johnston, Eric 161, 162
Joint Anti-Fascist Refugee Committee 36, 198, 199, 200
Jung, Harry 118, 120

352   *Little 'Red Scares'*

Justice Department 6, 7, 10, 11, 12, 14, 15, 47, 68, 319, 237–59 (passim), 265, 285, 342

Kelley, Robin 268, 269, 285
Kenyon, Dorothy 232, 242
Kerr, John 254–55
Keyserling, Leon 21, 233
Keyserling, Mary 215, 228, 232, 233
King, Carol 31, 36
Klein, Henry 296, 302
Knights of Columbus 202, 203, 204
Knowles, Harper 245–6
Korstad, Robert 266, 286
Kramer, Charles 336–7
Ku Klux Klan 8, 15, 19, 20, 21, 48, 49, 51, 53, 54, 57, 63, 65, 94–5, 108, 131, 188, 190, 273, 276, 329, 327, 330

Labor organizations 3, 7, 12, 13, 24, 25, 29–32, 34, 36, 39–40, 49, 50, 51–7, 58, 61–3, 65, 155, 170, 176, 276, 313 *see also* specific unions
Labor Department 244, 249
LaFollette, Robert 24, 167
LaGuardia, Fiorello 304, 306, 312
Lasswell, Harold 18, 320
League of Struggle for Negro Rights 270, 281
League of Women Shoppers (LWS) 213, 214, 217, 219, 220, 222, 224–9, 231, 232, 233
Lefkowitz, Abraham 290, 292, 293, 306, 312
Lenin, Vladimir 144, 147
Lewis, John L 28–31, 34, 97, 99, 178, 345
Liberty League 316, 328
Lincoln, Abraham 144, 160
little "HUACs" and legislative investigations 17, 56, 62, 63, 64, 65, 118–24, 204
Lloyd, Henry D. 232, 233

loyalty oaths 48, 59, 60, 61, 67, 108, 111, 112, 113, 118–19, 123–9, 133
Lyons, John 89, 96

Mandel, Benjamin 177, 180, 256, 295, 306, 309
Mann, Heinrich 34, 42
Mann, Thomas 34, 42
Massachusetts 50, 52, 52, 60, 62, 63, 204
Marcantonio, Vito 32, 342
Marx, Karl 13, 145, 146, 157, 162
Marxism 142, 143, 144, 145, 146, 147, 161, 167, 172–3, 176, 264, 265, 267
Mathews, J. B. 21, 205, 218, 220, 225, 226, 233, 240, 243, 244, 246–7, 256, 258, 306
Mattei, Albert 252, 258
Maverick, Maury 319, 329, 337
McCarthy, Joseph/McCarthyism 43, 45–6, 69, 237, 238, 240, 258, 259
McCormick-Dickstein Committee 318, 314–25, 329, 330–31, 338
McGrew, Louis 89, 94
McKinley, William 138, 156
McNaboe, John 60, 120–21
McWilliams 69, 341
Medical Bureau to Aid Spanish Democracy 197, 204, 205
Menshivism 73, 186
Messenger 32, 264
Mexican workers 54, 55, 153, 154
Michigan 53, 60, 61, 63, 66
Military Intelligence Division 47, 186–7, 188, 205
Milwaukee 195, 206–7
Minneapolis 56, 61, 154, 155
Minnesota 46, 56, 62
mob violence 1, 3, 7, 15, 21, 46, 54, 55, 57, 58, 59, 67, 68, 141
Morris, Robert 306, 309, 313
Montgomery, Viola 273, 274
Murphy, Frank 63–4, 209–10, 249

Nation, the 32, 345
National Association for the Advancement
  of Colored People (NAACP) 32,
  34, 54, 264, 268, 270, 330
National Association of Consumers 224,
  227, 273
National Association of Manufacturers
  (NAM) 61, 116–17, 130, 135, 137,
  139, 140, 142, 143, 145, 147, 149,
  150, 152, 153, 154, 157, 158, 159,
  162, 166, 220, 247
National Civic Federation 94, 171
National Defense Advisory Council 215,
  228
National Education Association 106, 108,
  114, 132
National Founders Association 138, 139,
  145
National Guard 47, 50, 56, 57, 68, 159, 204
National Labor Relations Board/Act 58,
  182, 213, 216, 217, 220, 222, 328
National Lawyers Guild 31, 341
National Maritime Union 176, 182
National Metal Trades Association 135,
  138, 141, 141, 149, 154
National Negro Congress 282, 284, 296
National Student League 114, 128
National Textile Workers Union 50, 150
nativism 315–16, 322–8, 334, 317–18,
  336–9, 342 *see also* immigrants
Nearing, Scott 292, 292
Nelson, John 88, 102
Nelson, Steve 37–8, 64
Neoliberalism 316, 328
New Deal 182, 270, 286, 287
  anti-communist supporters of 320, 324
  critics called fascist 321
  critics called Tories and royalists 322
  described as Communist or subversive
    237–59 (passim), 318–19, 322,
    328–30
  immigration policy 326–7, 336

solution to communism or fascism 323
  Target of Hatch Act 332, 334
New Leader 180, 181, 191
New Republic 343, 245
New York City 52, 53, 60, 67
New York state 47, 48, 60, 62, 66, 67
New York Times 48, 245, 275, 336, 341
New York World-Telegram 242–3
Nichols, Louis 34, 252, 258
Nixon, Richard 43, 181, 246, 237, 238, 239,
  252
Nomsi, George 335, 342–3
Norns, Frank 210, 211
North American Committee to Aid
  Spanish Democracy 197, 304
North Carolina 50, 57, 65

Office of Naval Intelligence 186–97
Office of Price Administration 215–16,
  217, 220, 228, 229, 230, 231–4,
  251–2
O'Hare, Kate Richard 8, 9
Ohio, 50, 56, 66
Oklahoma 66–7
Olson, Culbert 64, 65
O'Neal, James 181–2
One-Hundred Percent Americanism 49, 52
Open-shop movement 140, 43, 146, 147,
  152

Padgett, Pau 206–7
Palin, Sarah 237, 238
Palmer, A. Mitchell/Palmer Raids 2, 3, 10,
  11, 24, 46, 136, 166, 183, 210, 331
Parry, David 139, 140, 146
patriotic societies 45, 49, 57, 59, 51, 68,
  108–9, 111–18 *see also* individual
  groups (American Legion, etc.)
Pegler, Westbrook 242, 245, 202
Pennsylvania 49, 61
Perkins, Francis 244, 327, 338, 343
Peterson, Esther 215, 234

Philadelphia 47, 65
Picator, Eric 36, 4
Piedmont 159, 150
Pinchot, Cornelia 223, 224
Pittsburgh 66, 141, 149, 162
Plant, Thomas 155, 156, 157
police 94–5
popular front 52, 63, 65, 110, 133, 196,
    201, 329–31, 337, 340, 345
Post Office 1, 3, 4, 5, 242
Progressive Education Association 109–10,
    114, 132

racism 151, 160
Randolph, A. Philip 81, 264, 282, 284, 385
Rank and File Committee 291, 292, 293,
    300, 307
Rapp-Coudert Committee 67, 121–22,
    127, 129, 132
Rayburn, Sam 247, 253
red squads 47, 49, 52, 68, 242, 243
Red Summer (1919) 264, 266, 267
Republican Party 61, 64, 180
Reserve Officer Training Corps 109, 111
    112, 128, 291–311 (passim)
Reuther, Walter 31, 176, 179
Ribuffo, Leo 316, 318
Roosevelt, Eleanor 291, 245, 247, 250
Roosevelt, Franklin D. 45, 56, 58, 59, 60,
    61, 62, 67, 68, 205, 206, 211, 219,
    221, 228, 242–5
  and Dies Committee 239, 247–59
  and FBI 28–29, 33
  attempt to purge Democrats 334
  fireside chats 342
  opposition to 316, 326–7, 332–4
  reasons for supporting Smith Act 331,
    332, 342–44
  signing statement on Hatch Act 335
Rosenberg, Ethel and Julius 43, 297
Rossi, Angelo 56–7
Rubin, Jacob 146, 147, 161

Russell, Bertrand 303–4
Russell, Charles 173, 180
Russia 136, 136, 142, 413, 144, 145, 146,
    147, 148, 151, 152, 156, 161, 162
Russian Revolution 136, 140, 142, 143,
    144, 146, 152

Sacco-Vanzetti Case 52, 63, 322
San Francisco 56, 57, 59, 155, 156, 157
San Joaquin Valley CA 55, 58
Scarlet Empire 139, 144, 146
Schlink, Fredd 246–7
schools 48, 49, 60, 67 *see also* colleges and
    universities
Scottsboro case 53, 272, 273, 374, 279, 323,
    329
Senate Subcommittee on Internal Security
    43, 309, 312, 313
Seattle 141, 156
Sedition Laws *see* criminal syndicalism laws,
    Smith Act, Espionage Act (1917)
Shafarman, Eugene 208, 208
Shappes, Morris 296, 300, 310–11
Shukotoff, Arnold 296, 300
Smith Act 67, 159, 191, 211, 239, 316–18,
    330, 331, 332, 336–42, 342–6
Smith, Gerald 230, 248
Smith, Howard 136, 159, 329, 340, 342
Social Democratic Federation 172–4,
    175–7, 178, 180, 181, 186, 191–3
Social Democratic League 171–72, 180,
    193
Socialist Party 53, 66, 141, 167, 171–4,
    176, 178, 180
Sokolsky, George 220, 240, 247
South, the 52, 53, 57, 53 *see also* specific
    state and cities
Southern States Industrial Council 135,
    137, 158, 159, 160
Southern Tenant Farmers Union 278, 287
Soviet Union 320, 323, 324, 325, 333, 340,
    344–5

and FBI surveillance 33, 36–39, 42
anti-religious campaigns 75
allegations of "economic warfare" 78–9, 83, 87, 99–100
Commissariat of Foreign Affairs 87
covert action in US 82
denunciation by Fish Committee 102–3
Gulag 83–5
Spanish Civil War 63, 110, 121, 196–211 (passim), 234, 257
Stalin, Joseph 161, 196, 320, 329
State Department 237, 242, 250, 254
Steele, Richard 319, 344
Steele, Walter 97, 243
Stone, Harlan 14–15, 25–7, 184
Strecker v. Kessler 244, 339
strikes 4–7, 50–51, 54–8, 59, 61, 63–4, 190
1919 strike wave 137, 140, 142, 155, 156 *see also* specific strikes (Gastonia, etc)
Sugar, Maurice 31, 281, 282
Sullivan, Edward 239–40, 244
Supreme Court 46, 47, 168, 170, 190, 238, 245, 248–9, 316, 328, 331, 338, 343 *see also* specific cases
syndicalism 172–3, 174–5

teachers guild 295, 299, 312, 313
textile strikes 150, 151, 153
Thomas, J. Parnell 43, 243–4, 250, 327
Trade Union Educational League 170, 174, 175, 183, 184
Trade Union Unity League 292, 293
Transoceanic News Service 255–6
Trotskyistsm 322, 345–6

unemployed councils 52, 276, 279, 289
unions *see* labor unions and individual groups
Union of Soviet Socialist Republics *see* Soviet Union

United Automobile Workers 31, 34, 176, 177, 178–9, 185–6, 255
United Mine Workers, 13, 170, 177, 184, 185, 188–9

veterans' groups 45, 48, 49, 41, 61, 68 *see also* patriotic groups and specific organizations
Veterans of Foreign Wars 4–8, 318
Victory, James 281, 282
vigilantism *see* mob violence
Voorhis, Jerry 181, 246–67, 249, 250, 257–8, 320
Vultee strike 255–6

Wagner Act *see* National Labor Relations Board/Act
Waldman, Louis 169, 178, 180, 181
Wallace, Henry 277, 253–4
Walsh, Edmund 78, 86, 88
Ware, Caroline 21, 224, 226, 228, 229, 230, 232, 234, 235
Waterfront Employers' Union 155, 156
Weigel, Helene 34, 42
West, the 51, 53 *see also* individual cities and states
West Virginia 66, 142
Whalen, Grover/Whalen documents 92, 93–4, 102
Whitley, Rhea 240, 243
Wickenden, Elizabeth 226, 232
Wiggins, Ella May 151, 272
Williams, Frances 224, 228
Wilson, Edmund 85, 100–101
Wilson, Woodrow 1, 2, 6, 15
Windels, Paul 306, 311, 314
wiretapping *see* FBI
Wolfe, Bertram 291, 292
Workers Alliance of America 249, 332–5
Works Progress Administration 317, 320, 332–5

World War I 1, 2, 4, 7, 10, 17, 20, 46, 47, 67, 68, 99, 140, 146, 262, 263, 265, 266, 267

World War II 45, 62, 63, 65, 67, 68, 138, 160–63, 284

Young Communist League 110, 121, 206, 208, 243, 269

Zapp, Manfred 255–6

Zubilin, Vassili 37–8

CPSIA information can be obtained
at www.ICGtesting.com
Printed in the USA
BVHW04*0804101018
529215BV00009B/123/P